Sheetfed Offset Press Operating

by
Lloyd P. DeJidas
and
Thomas M. Destree

GATF*Press*
PITTSBURGH

Library of Congress Catalog Card Number: 94-76299
International Standard Book Number: 0-88362-171-1

Printed in the United States of America

Order No. 1530
Second Edition, Reprinted 1998

Printed on Williamsburg Offset, 60lb., Smooth Finish

GATF*Press*
Graphic Arts Technical Foundation
200 Deer Run Road
Sewickley, PA 15143-2600
Phone: 412/741-6860
Fax: 412/741-2311
Email: info@gatf.org
Internet: http://www.gatf.org

Contents

Foreword

The Graphic Arts Technical Foundation is pleased to introduce the second edition of *Sheetfed Offset Press Operating*. All of the chapters have been updated and expanded. Information on waterless offset lithography, and a chapter on safety as it applies to sheetfed offset press operation have also been added.

The concepts presented in this book are applicable to most sheetfed presses. However, actual press adjustments must be made following the press manufacturer's recommendations.

The authors of this edition are Thomas M. Destree, GATF editor in chief, and Lloyd P. DeJidas, business manager of GATF's Graphic Services and Facilities Group. They were assisted in this endeavor by Charles J. Lucas, senior graphic designer, and Deborah L. Stevenson, assistant editor.

I would like to acknowledge and thank the following technical reviewers, comprised of outside consultants and GATF staff, for their suggestions:

Richard Grim, Ph.D., California University of Pennsylvania
Frank J. Gualtieri, GATF
Frederick W. Higgins, GATF
John Hughes, Böttcher America Corp.
Gary A. Jones, GATF
Brian S. May, GATF
Dillon R. Mooney, GATF
Raymond J. Prince, GATF
Kenneth E. Rizzo, GATF
Murray I. Suthons, GATF

Frank S. Benevento
Business Manager, Technical Information Group

1 Introduction to Offset Lithographic Presses

Offset lithography, a planographic printing process, requires an image carrier in the form of a plate on which photochemically produced image and nonimage areas are receptive to ink and water, respectively. In addition, the image on the plate must be right-reading; i.e., it is oriented the same way that the printed image will be.

The basic principle of lithography

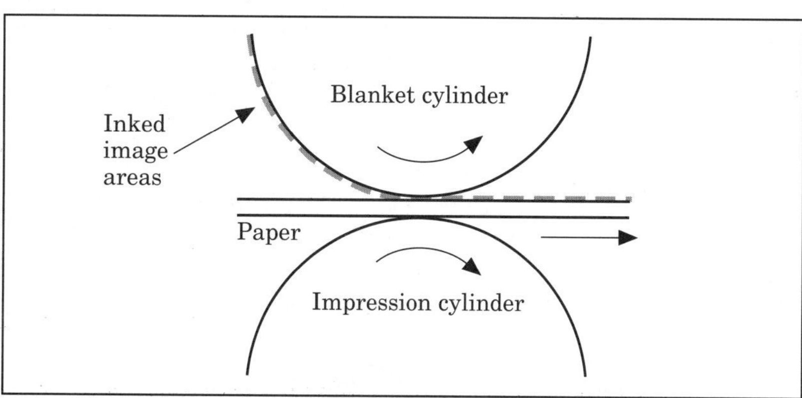

Following are the basic steps involved in printing by offset lithography:

1. Plate with photochemically produced image and non-image areas is mounted on a cylinder.
2. Plate is dampened with a mixture of chemical concentrates in a water-based solution, which adheres to the nonimage areas of the plate.
3. Plate surface is contacted by inked rollers, which apply ink only to the image area of a properly dampened printing plate.
4. Right-reading inked image on the printing plate is transferred under pressure to a rubber-like blanket, on which it becomes reversed (wrong-reading).

5. Inked image on the blanket is transferred under pressure to a sheet of paper or other printing substrate, producing an impression of the inked image on the paper.

An **offset lithographic press** is a mechanical device that dampens and inks the printing plate and transfers the inked image to the blanket and then to the printing substrate. A **sheetfed offset lithographic press** is a printing press that feeds and prints on individual sheets of paper (or other substrate) using the offset lithographic printing method; the operation of such a press is the focal point of this book. A **web,** or **webfed, offset lithographic press** is a press that prints on a continuous web, or ribbon, of paper fed from a roll and threaded through the press. A modern sheetfed press reaches speeds of 10,000–12,000 impressions per hour (i.p.h.) or higher, whereas a web press reaches speeds three or four times greater. Both types of presses are increasingly being controlled from remote consoles, from which the operator can adjust inking, dampening, and circumferential and lateral register; control ink density; and monitor dot gain.

Waterless lithography. Waterless lithography is a planographic printing process that does not require the use of a water-based dampening solution. The process uses an ordinary offset press equipped with temperature-controlled inking systems. It requires special inks and presensitized negative- or positive-working waterless plates.

In order to use the waterless plate, a press must have a temperature control system to maintain a temperature at which printing is satisfactory. Two types of press temperature control systems exist: an **ink oscillator (vibrator) cooling system** and a **plate cylinder cooling system.** The ink oscillator cooling system is said to be the more effective of the two. It pumps a chilled or *heated* water solution through hollow oscillator rollers on the press. Presses outfitted with the special provisions are on the market. Some are equipped with dampeners to give the printer the option of printing dry or wet. Printers can also choose to have their conventional lithographic offset presses retrofitted to use the waterless plate technology.

Wraparound printing. Sometimes called **dry offset** or **letterset,** the wraparound printing method uses a rotary letterpress (relief) plate on an offset press. Because the image is in relief, this method does not require the use of a dampening system. Wraparound printing is a popular way to apply water-based and UV coatings using a sheetfed lithographic press.

A rotary relief plate is commonly 0.030 in. (0.76 mm) thick with a relief of 0.020 in. (0.51 mm). Because this plate is considerably thicker than a conventional lithographic printing plate, the undercut of the plate cylinder must be extra deep. An undercut of about 0.035 in. (0.89 mm) is common. Printers using these plates must special-order their presses with deep undercuts.

Plates are available in a variety of materials such as copper, zinc, magnesium, and photopolymer. Each plate material offers length of run and image fidelity advantages.

The rollers of the inking system must be set to just touch the top of the relief image on the plate. Plate-to-blanket pressures must be set very lightly.

Sheetfed Press

A sheetfed press consists of a feeder, one or more printing units, transfer devices to move the paper through the press, a delivery, and various auxiliary devices (such as a control console).

The printing unit of a sheetfed offset lithographic press generally consists of three primary cylinders and systems for dampening and inking the plate:

- **Plate cylinder,** a cylinder that carries the **printing plate,** a flexible image carrier with ink-receptive image areas and, when moistened with a water-based solution, ink-repellent nonimage areas
- **Blanket cylinder,** a cylinder that carries the **offset blanket,** a fabric coated with synthetic rubber that transfers the image from the printing plate to the substrate
- **Impression cylinder,** a cylinder running in contact with the blanket cylinder that transports the paper or other substrate
- **Dampening system,** a series of rollers that dampen the printing plate with a water-based dampening solution that contains additives such as acid, gum arabic, and isopropyl alcohol or other wetting agents
- **Inking system,** a series of rollers that apply a metered film of ink to a printing plate

Other major press components. In addition to one or more printing units, a press also includes the following:

- **Feeder,** which lifts and forwards the sheets of paper or other substrate from a pile to the first printing unit
- **Transfer devices** (often auxiliary cylinders with sheet grippers), which facilitate sheet transport through the press
- **Delivery,** which receives and stacks the printed sheet

A single-color sheetfed press

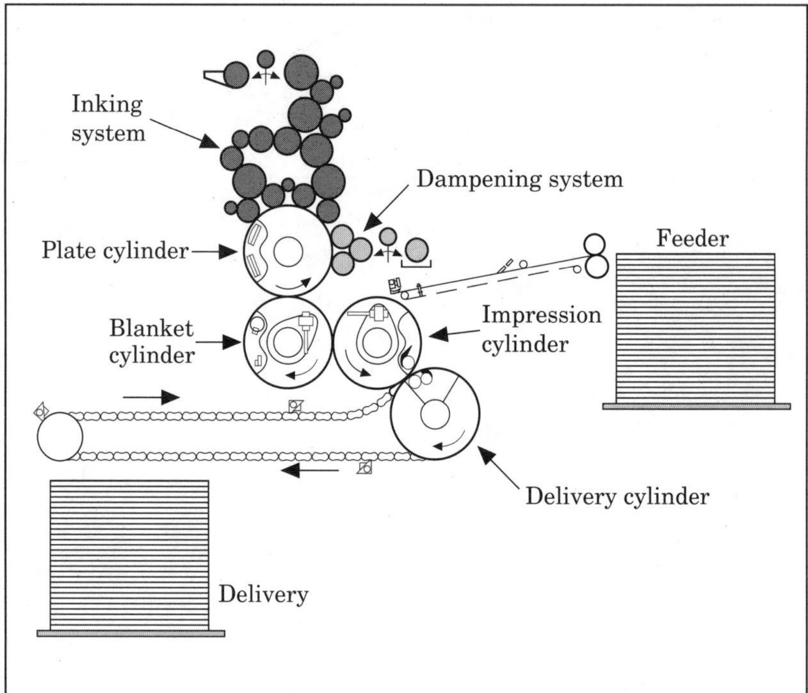

Press Configurations

A variety of sheetfed printing presses are available. These presses can best be classified according to their offset press cylinder configurations (arrangements), although the placement of the feeder and delivery are also important considerations in the design of a press. For sheetfed lithographic printing, the printing unit cylinders are arranged in three basic ways:

- The single-color sheetfed press, in which there is one set of printing cylinders arranged to print only one color on one side of each sheet as it passes through the press
- The multicolor sheetfed press, in which more than one color is printed on one side of a sheet during a single pass through the press because there is more than one printing unit
- The perfecting sheetfed press, in which sheets are printed on both sides during one pass through the press

Single-Color Press

A press consisting of a single printing unit, with its integral inking and dampening systems, a feeder, a sheet transfer system, and a delivery is called a **single-color press.** Normally, it can print only a single color in any one pass through the press. On some presses, the inking system can be modified—split—with ink fountain and ink roller dividers so that two or more colors can be printed at one time. On these presses, the same printing plate is used, and the colors are widely separated.

Single-color sheetfed press
Courtesy Omnitrade Industrial Co.

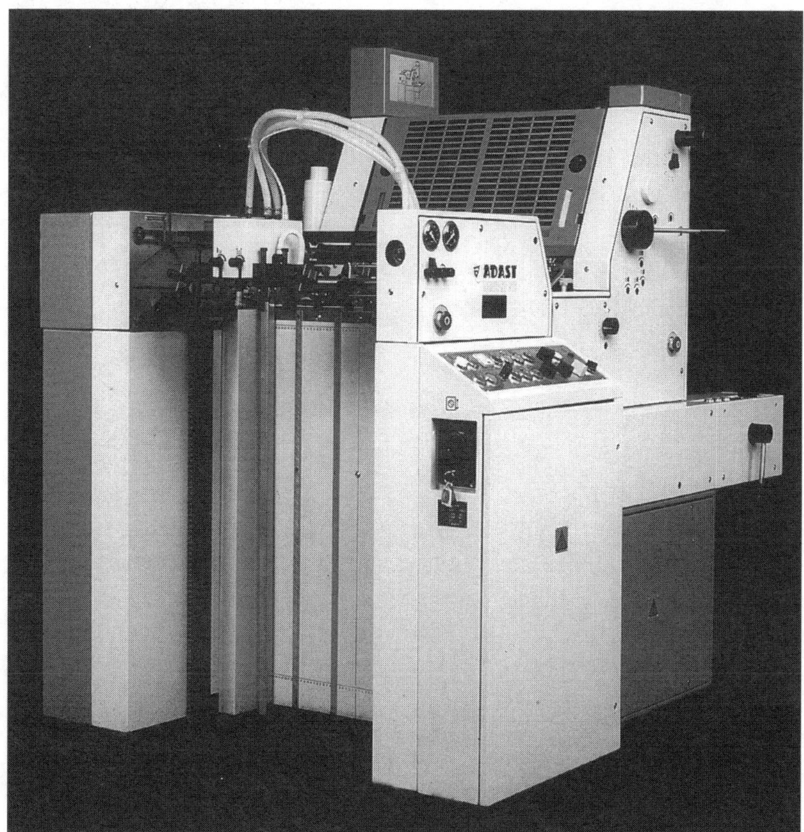

A single-color press can also be used for true **multicolor printing,** the printing of two or more colors, often one over another. Multicolor printing on a single-color press requires that the sheet be fed through the press as many times as there are colors to be printed. After each printing, the just-used plate is removed and the inking system is thoroughly cleaned. A new plate is mounted on the plate cylinder, and the inking system is filled with the next color. After the just-printed ink dries, the sheet of paper is run through the press again and printed with this new color. (Multicolor printing on a single-color press is dependent upon **dry trapping**—the ability of a dry, printed ink film to accept a wet ink film over it. The wet ink dries by oxidation polymerization.)

The printing unit of the single-color sheetfed press is sometimes described as an "open unit." The plate cylinder, blanket cylinder, and impression cylinder are usually arranged in a near right-angle relationship. This arrangement is common for three reasons:

- To reduce the overall height of the press
- To make it easier to feed the paper into the impression cylinder grippers
- To make it possible, by movement of only the blanket cylinder, to throw all three cylinders out of contact with each other.

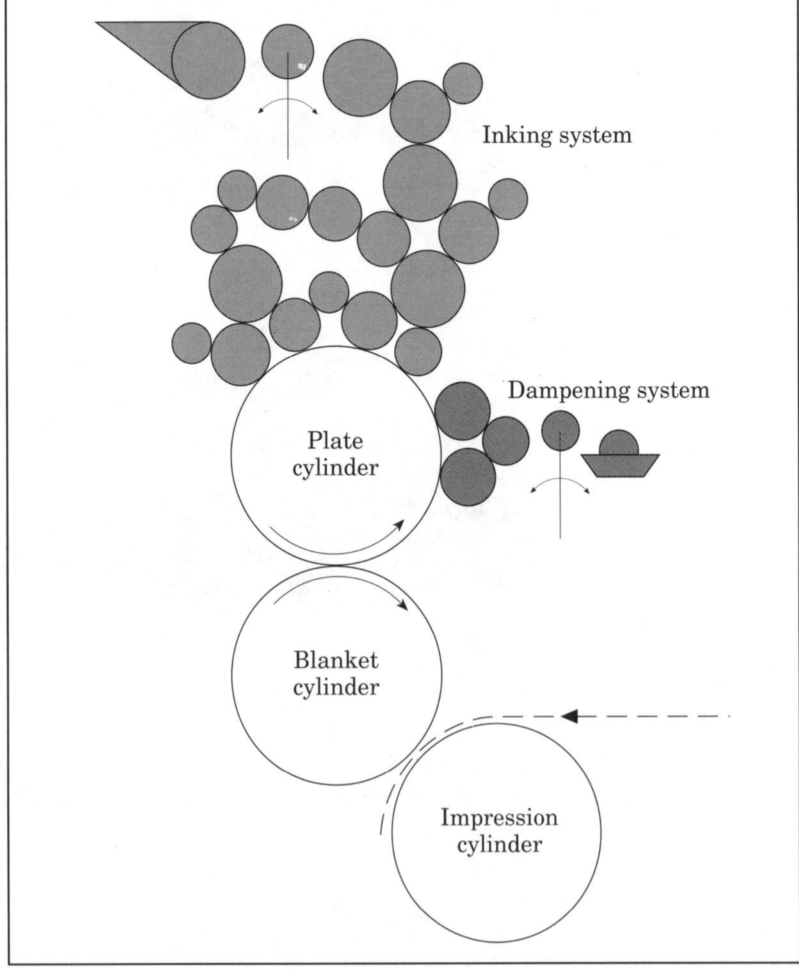

The most common arrangement of the plate, blanket, and impression cylinders for single-color printing

Exceptions exist to this nearly right-angle (L-shaped) arrangement of cylinders. With one type of metal decorating press, the cylinders are stacked directly above each other so that the rigid metal sheets can pass through the printing nip (the line of contact between the blanket and impression cylinders) without being bent around the impression cylinder. Another exception is a press that has a single, oversized cylinder that is used as both the plate and impression cylinder. Yet another exception is a press that has a single oversized cylinder functioning as the impression cylinder for two printing units.

Multicolor Press

A press consisting of several printing units (each with its own inking and dampening system), a feeder, a sheet transfer system, and a delivery is called a **multicolor,** or **multiunit, press.** A multicolor press can have two, four, five, six, or more printing units, and two or more colors are printed in a single pass through the printing press. High-quality printing on a multicolor press depends on **wet trapping,** which is the ability of a wet, printed ink film to accept another wet ink film printed over it.

A typical four-color (four-unit) sheetfed press

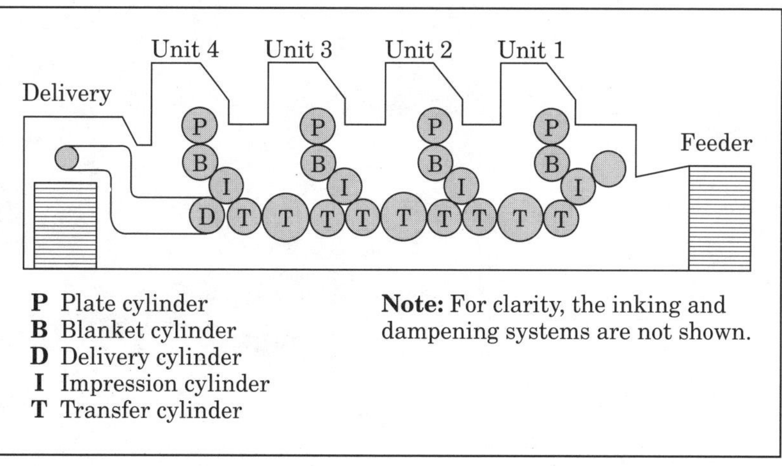

In the larger press sizes, the printing units are almost identical and are arranged in tandem. With some of the other two- and four-color presses, one printing unit may be higher than the other to obtain better accessibility.

When placed in tandem, the open-unit type of single-color sheetfed press becomes a multicolor press, capable of printing a different color on each unit. One or more transfer cylinders are placed between units to transport the sheet from one

Six-color sheetfed press
Courtesy Heidelberg USA, Inc.

printing unit to the next. Some presses have three transfer cylinders between units, while other presses have a single, double-size transfer cylinder. An odd number of transfer cylinders is needed between units so that the side of the sheet to be printed faces away from the impression cylinder.

In another multicolor sheetfed press design, sometimes called the "semiopen design," a single impression cylinder serves two pairs of plate and blanket cylinders. The printed sheet is held by the common impression cylinder and successively brought into contact with each blanket. A press consisting of two semiopen units would then be capable of printing four colors on one side of the press sheet in a single pass.

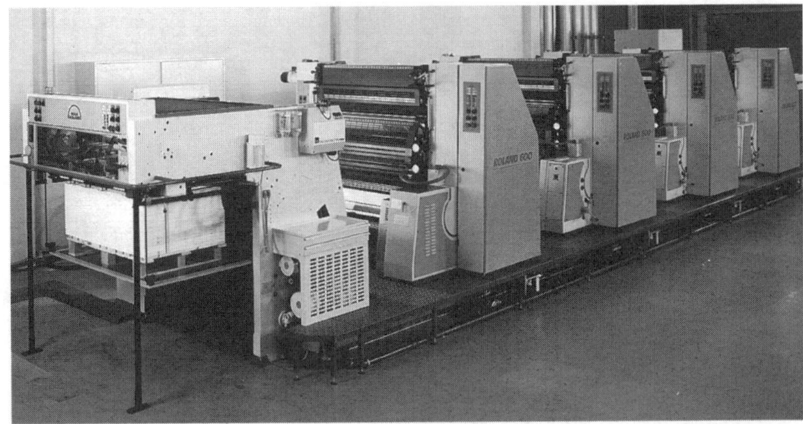

Eight-color sheetfed semiopen press
Courtesy MAN Roland Inc., Sheetfed Press Division

Perfecting Press

Most sheetfed presses can print on only one side of the sheet in a single pass. For the other side to be printed, the entire paper pile must be turned over and the paper run through the press a second time. There is, however, a type of sheetfed press that can print on both sides of the sheet in a single pass. The printing of at least one color on both sides of a sheet in a single pass through a press is called **perfecting;** any press that can do so is called a **perfecting press,** or **perfector.**

The most common sheetfed perfecting press is called a **convertible perfector.** Special reversing cylinders tumble

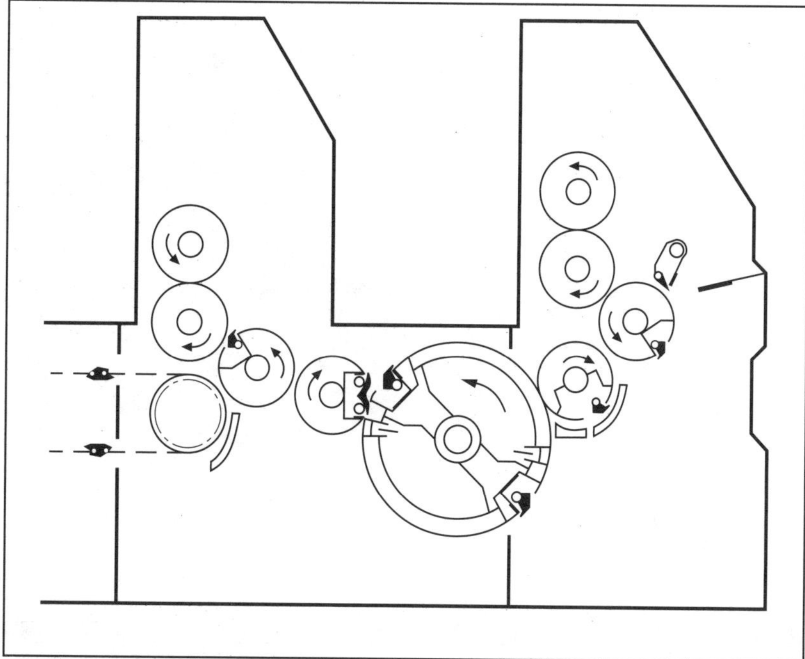

A two-color convertible perfector
Courtesy MAN Roland Inc., Sheetfed Press Division

the paper end for end between printing units so that the other side of the sheet is printed by the second unit. This type of press usually has the capability, by adjusting the reversing cylinder, to print either two colors on one side of the sheet or one color on each side in a single pass through the press. (Other color combinations are also possible.)

A two-color convertible perfecting press
Courtesy Komori America Corp.

With another type of sheetfed perfecting press that is used infrequently, the blankets from two printing units are in contact, with the paper passing between the two blankets. This type of press is called a **blanket-to-blanket press,** because the two blankets are in contact. No impression cylinder is

Sheetfed perfecting press
Courtesy Western Paper Co. Import Group—Ryobi

A four-color sheetfed perfecting press
Courtesy Shinohara Tech USA

needed; each blanket acts as the impression cylinder for the other. (Most web offset presses print blanket-to-blanket.)

Proofing

A **proof press** is a printing machine used for making a **proof,** a trial print from a plate, film negative, or film positive to verify correctness and quality. It usually has most of the elements of a production machine, but not the automatic features for sustained production.

The most commonly used proofing presses have a flat bed for holding the plate and paper and a rollable blanket cylinder. The blanket cylinder rolls over both, picking up the image from the inked plate and laying it down on the paper.

In the older types, the plate was dampened and rolled up (inked) by hand. The blanket cylinder rolled on bearers and gear racks. The cylinder was necessarily heavy in order to apply sufficient pressure, and on larger presses, it took two people to roll one. Later, this cylinder was put in a carriage that enabled additional pressure to be put on it, and a gear reduction crank made it easier to roll. Next, the carriage became power-driven. Still later, automatic dampening and inking systems were installed.

Proof presses are used less and less. Some proofing is done using a press similar to the one used for production, or even the same one. Most proofing is done photomechanically using light-sensitive papers (principally to proof single-color printing), colored films, or photopolymers. This procedure is called **off-press proofing.** Two basic types of proofs are used for multicolor or process-color proofing:

- **Single-sheet proof,** where the printing colors are built up on a base through lamination, exposure to a halftone negative or positive from a set of color separation films, and toning or other processing
- **Overlay,** or **multiple-sheet, proof,** where pigmented or dyed sheets of plastic are exposed to a halftone negative or positive and then registered to each other and taped or pin-registered to a base

Another method of producing a color proof, called **direct digital color proofing** (DDCP), does not require the use of a film intermediate (a halftone negative or positive). Instead, in this proofing method, digital information is used to directly image the color proofing material. Various technologies are used to image the color proofing material.

Small Offset Press

Generally, any press smaller than 11×17 in. (279×432 mm) without bearers (hardened metal rings attached to the ends of the cylinder or to the cylinder's journal) is called a **small offset press** or, more often, a **duplicator.** Duplicators started out as office machines using the offset principle. They are extremely simple, but they have developed into efficient offset presses that fill many printing needs. Many are being used for multicolor work.

The gap between "duplicators" and the more heavily built offset presses is being filled by some new presses. These have the simplicity of the duplicator plus many of the quality features of the larger presses.

Total Copy Center

Total copy centers have become very popular in the past few years. Such systems are capable of printing both sides of a sheet of paper in a single pass through the press. The copy is automatically fed into the system, a photo-direct plate is exposed, and the programmed number of impressions is made. After the count is reached, the plate is ejected, the blanket is washed, and the next plate is automatically mounted and wetted with fountain solution while the previously printed copies are being collated.

In addition to total copy centers that print using the offset lithographic principle, total copy centers that use a variety of nonimpact printing technologies (such as electrophotography and ink jet printing) to produce the image have started to offer competition. However, the speed, image resolution, and color capabilities of these systems are generally limited when compared to those of conventional printing processes, although remarkable advances in image quality have been made in the past decade.

Electronic Printing

While the traditional printing processes are focusing on higher-quality color, a significant share of the single-color market is being taken away from the presses and being reproduced through electronic high-speed, **intelligent copier/printer** (IC/P) technologies, such as the Xerox DocuTech and the Kodak Lionheart.

When the first photocopiers were introduced to the market in the late 1950s, the quality was only acceptable for the most basic copying needs. Today's IC/Ps can produce high-quality single-color copies in formats of up to 11×17 in. (279×432 mm), rivaling that of offset. Makeready time is virtually nothing for such jobs. Turnaround time can be a few hours or less.

Many printers are beginning to realize the potential that IC/Ps offer and are using them for short-run, single-color jobs, thereby freeing their high-quality offset presses to run higher value-added multicolor jobs. The single-color, 300-dpi (or higher) print quality is acceptable to most customers for many applications. Thus, it is expected that high-speed IC/Ps and traditional presses will be compatible processes in the future instead of competing against one another.

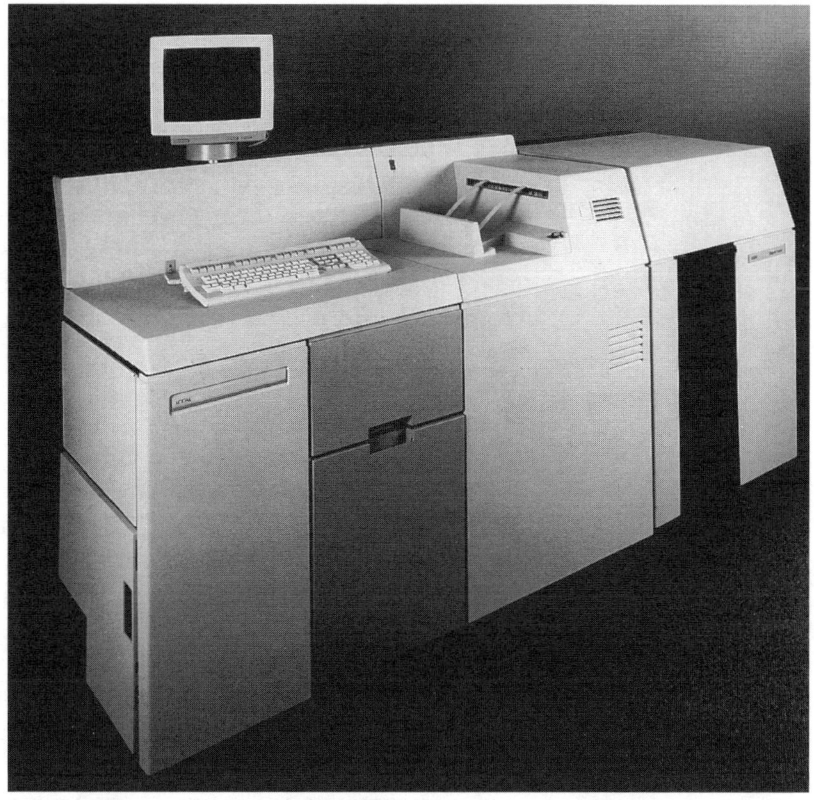

Kodak Lionheart
Courtesy Eastman Kodak Co.

One IC/P on the market, the Xerox DocuTech, is a hybrid between a high-speed copier and a laser printer. The 600-dpi machine is able to scan, manipulate, store, and print paper originals, as well as read electronic files from a disk or a

DocuTech Production Publisher
Courtesy Xerox Corporation

local area network. The various parts of the system are designed to operate concurrently. For example, the print engine can run at 135 pages per minute while a job is being scanned in at 23 pages per minute and the operator manipulates images from the user interface. The machine also has bindery capabilities. An in-line finisher, which comes standard with the DocuTech, contains a two-head stitcher, an adhesive-tape binder, and a stacker. An optional finishing attachment, the Signature Booklet Maker, takes finished signatures and produces saddle-stitched, folded, and trimmed booklets.

Evolving Press Technologies

Several new reproduction technologies are receiving considerable attention for short-run color printing.

The Heidelberg GTO-DI, for example, uses direct imaging technology invented by Presstek. The GTO-DI printing press is a combination of the Heidelberg four-color GTO 14×19-in. (356×483-mm) press and the Presstek direct imaging technology. The system allows for direct imaging of the plates on the press from a computer front end. The plate cylinders on the GTO has been refitted with imaging heads, which receive imaging instructions simultaneously. The press accepts digital data (including PostScript files) from a variety of electronic prepress systems, including those based on Macintoshes or PCs. Users are able to select Heidelberg GTO-DI directly from their printer chooser menu on their computers.

In recent demonstrations, total makeready time was under 15 minutes for a four-color, half-image-sized piece. The plate imaging segment of the makeready took an impressive 7.5 minutes. The plates are imaged in registration, thereby reducing makeready spoilage to as few as 25 pull sheets. Makeready in a true production setting would certainly take more time, perhaps 30 to 45 minutes.

The original Presstek system included a spark-discharge plate-imaging process and a proprietary plate that did not require photochemistry. The plate had three layers: a silicone surface, an aluminum ground plane, and a 7-mil polyester base. The imaging head, consisting of an array of sixteen tungsten-needle electrodes, generated sparks that removed the silicone surface and the aluminum ground plane in the image areas. The exposed polyester base attracts ink, while the silicone surface repels ink, thereby making it a waterless system. The resolution of this imaging technology is 1,016 dots per inch (dpi).

Heidelberg GTO-DI that uses the Presstek direct-to-plate imaging technology
Courtesy Presstek, Inc.

In 1993, Presstek released a new plate system, called PEARL, which replaces the original spark-discharge system. PEARL uses an array of sixteen infrared laser diodes, rather than a spark, to remove the silicone surface. The imaging resolution can be changed at the start of the pressrun to one of four resolutions: 1,016, 1,270, 2,032 or 2,540 dpi. Each laser diode is connected to an optical fiber, which carries the light to an array of lenses spaced across the width of the plate cylinder. The plate used with PEARL is still a three-layer sandwich. The bottom layer is either 6-mil polyester or metal. The middle layer is now an infrared-absorbent material. The top layer is still silicone, but the silicone has been reformulated for strength and durability.

The ElectroPress, from AM Graphics, is another new technology. The first commercially successful nonimpact-press hybrid, the ElectroPress is a 300-ft./min. (1.5-m/sec) webfed nonimpact printer that looks like a press. It has two 300-dpi LED print engines, which can print in two colors on one side of the paper or one color on each side using a liquid toner. Residual solvents in the toner are burned off in a hot-air dryer with a catalytic converter. The ElectroPress allows a 20-in. (508-mm) print width and repeat lengths up to 27 in. (686 mm).

Each impression produced on the press can be different from the preceding one; or a specified number of the same page can be printed, and, upon signal from the computer, a different page can be printed. Markets for this product include printed material in which information is constantly changing, such as direct mail, business forms, check printing, and bar coding.

Other emerging printing technologies that have the potential to impact the short-run color market include the DCP-1 digital color web press from Xeikon and the E-Print 1000 digital color sheetfed press from Indigo. The DCP-1 uses dry toner and allows each page to be customized. It has eight printing units, four for each side of the paper. The print engine images organic photoconductor (OPC) drums by using arrays of light-emitting diodes (LEDs). After the drum is imaged, toner is applied to the drum, transferred to the paper, and permanently fixed to the paper using a heat-fusing system.

The E-Print 1000 uses liquid ink and a sheetfed press. The press can print up to six colors at 800 dpi on an 11×17-in. (279×432-mm) sheet. A laser driven by a raster image processor (RIP) images a reusable electrophotographic plate. ElectroInk, a special ink developed by Indigo, is applied to the image areas of the plate. The inked plate image is transferred to a blanket and then transferred from the blanket to the paper. The press can print on one or both sides of the sheets of paper.

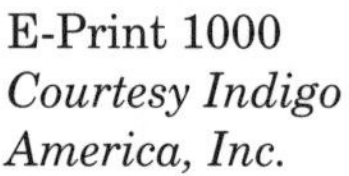

E-Print 1000
Courtesy Indigo America, Inc.

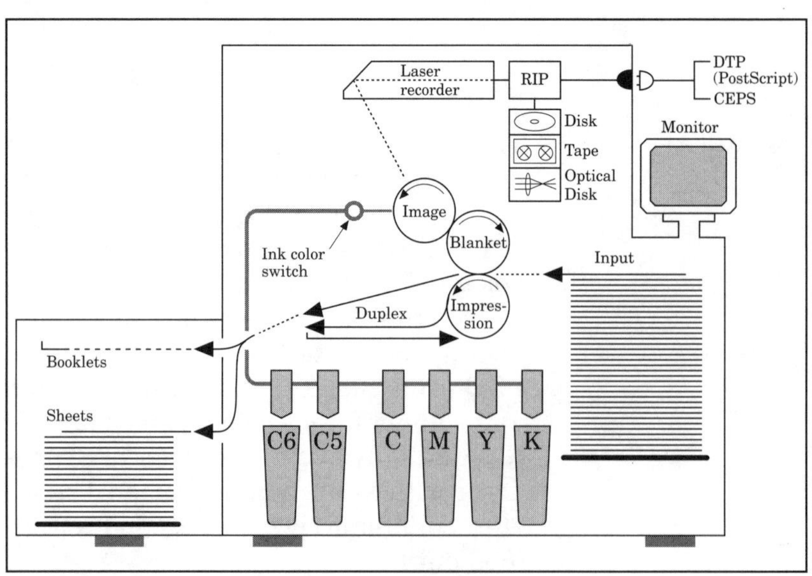

2 The Printing Unit

The printing unit is the section of the offset lithographic press where the plate is inked, and the inked image is transferred to a blanket and subsequently applied to a substrate, usually paper. On a single-color offset press, printing is accomplished by a three-cylinder unit, consisting of a **plate cylinder, blanket cylinder,** and **impression cylinder;** the arrangement of which does not matter as long as the proper ones touch. The cylinders must be brought together under pressure in order to transfer the ink; they must be released to stop printing. The line of contact between cylinders is called the **nip.** The contact pressure is roughly 200 lb./sq.in. (1,380 kilopascals). On a multicolor press, printing is accomplished by a number of three-cylinder units with auxiliary sheet-transport cylinders between them.

Plate Cylinder

The **plate cylinder,** which is usually the uppermost cylinder of the three, carries the printing plate. Since the plate is frequently changed, this cylinder has to be easily accessible.

The plate cylinder has four primary functions:

- To hold the lithographic printing plate tightly in position
- To hold the plate while the dampening rollers are contacting it and wetting the nonimage area
- To hold the plate while the inking rollers are contacting it and applying ink to the image area
- To help transfer the inked image to the blanket

The plate cylinder consists of a metal body ground to close tolerances in diameter. On sheetfed presses, it is not a complete cylinder but has a depressed gap (about 20% of the circumference) running across the cylinder to accommodate the plate clamping bars. The gap also permits the inking system to recover before the next press sheet is printed, and

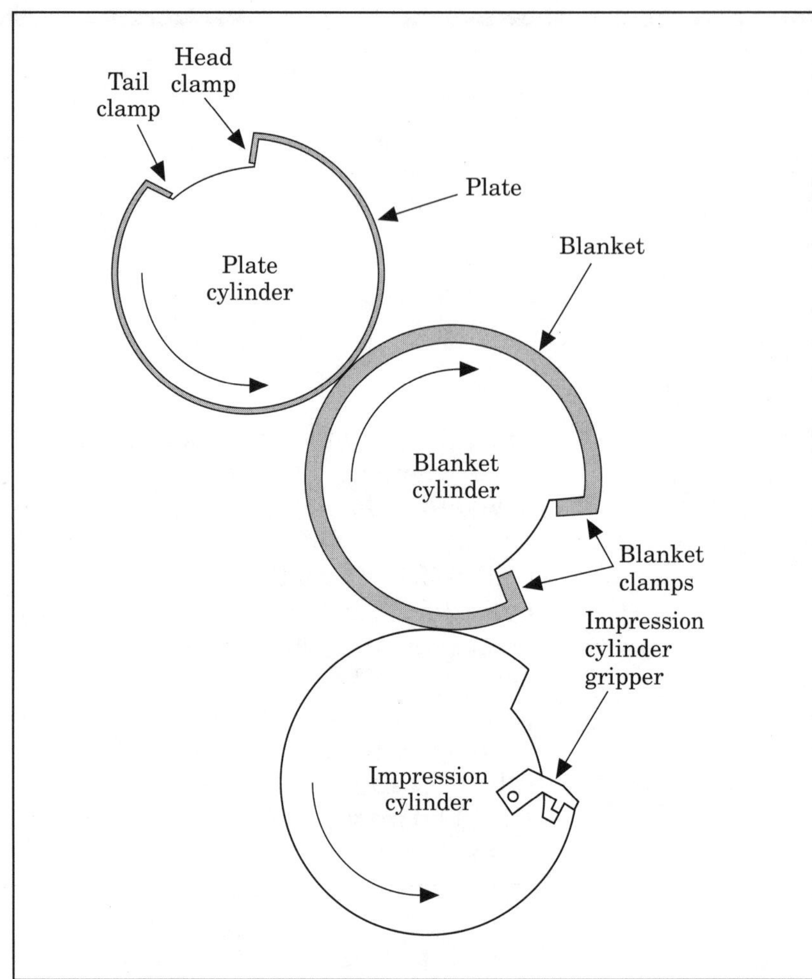

The three cylinders that comprise a printing unit

compensates for the feeding of sheets individually instead of as a stream: each sheet is stopped on the feedboard and moved laterally, but the cylinders continue to rotate, reducing the amount of cylinder surface that can be used for printing.

At each end of the plate cylinder is a **bearer,** which is a hardened metal ring attached to the cylinder body or journal. On many presses, the bearers of the plate cylinder run in contact with the bearers of the blanket cylinder during printing. The diameter of the bearer is the effective diameter of the cylinder and is the same as the pitch diameter (i.e., the working diameter) of the gear attached to the journal. The plate cylinder is driven by this gear, which is, in turn, driven by a similar gear on the blanket cylinder. The cylinder gears may be spur (on older presses) or helical (on newer presses). A **spur gear** has teeth cut straight across it, and a **helical**

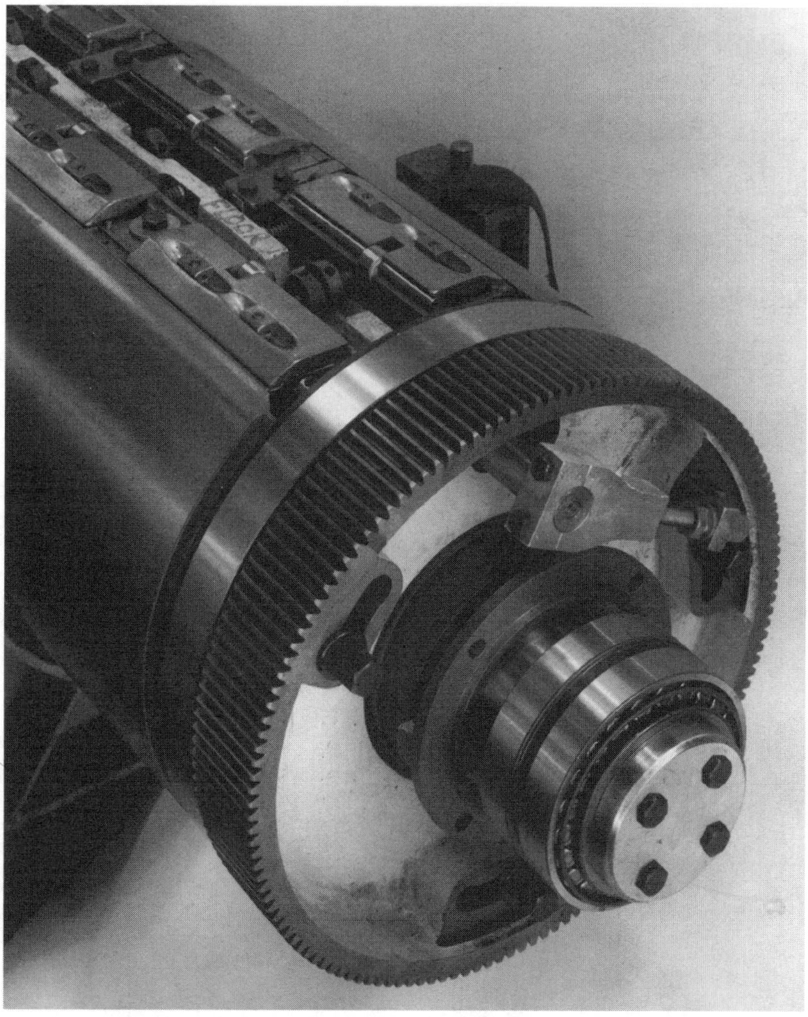

Gear end of a plate cylinder from an older sheetfed press

Notice the spur gear and how it is attached to the plate cylinder

gear has teeth cut at an angle. A spur gear used as a plate cylinder gear nearly always has a **backlash gear,** a thin second gear bolted to it to reduce **play** (free or unimpeded movement) between gears. Presses that print with the plate and blanket cylinder bearers out of contact always have helical gears to reduce gear play and provide a smooth drive.

The plate cylinder gear has several slotted holes. It is bolted directly to the cylinder body just beside the bearer or, more commonly, to a flange on the cylinder journal outside the press frame. (By being located outside the press frame, the gear remains cleaner and better lubricated.) Loosening of the bolts allows the cylinder to be moved forward or backward in relation to the lead or gripper edge. This movement is desirable in order to adjust the front margin of the sheet

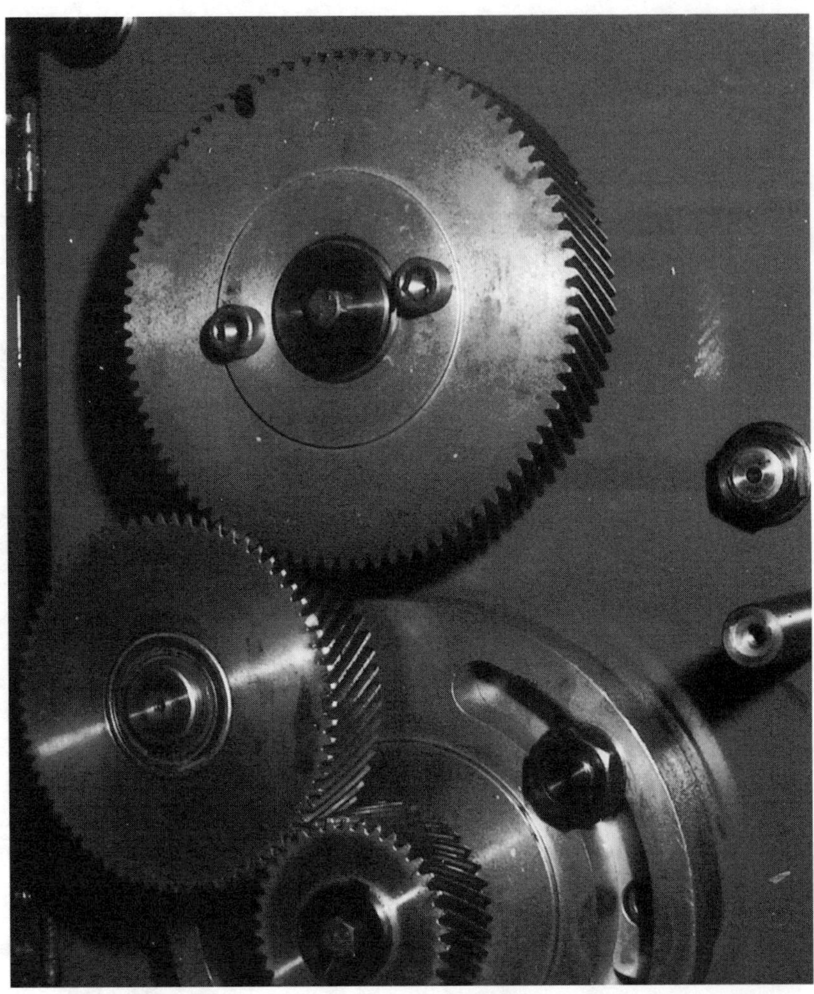

Helical gears

or change the position of the plate. Most multicolor presses have a register mechanism that makes lateral or circumferential register moves from a remote control console or the unit while the press is running.

The body of the plate cylinder is smaller in diameter than the bearers. The difference between the radius of the body surface and that of the bearers is called the **undercut.** The undercut provides space for the plate and its **packing**—paper or other material that is placed between the plate and cylinder to raise the plate's surface to printing height or to adjust cylinder circumference to obtain proper print length. The amount of undercut is usually stamped on a metal plate mounted on the press. These stamped values can be used to establish basic packing amounts for the cylinders in the absence of a press operator's manual.

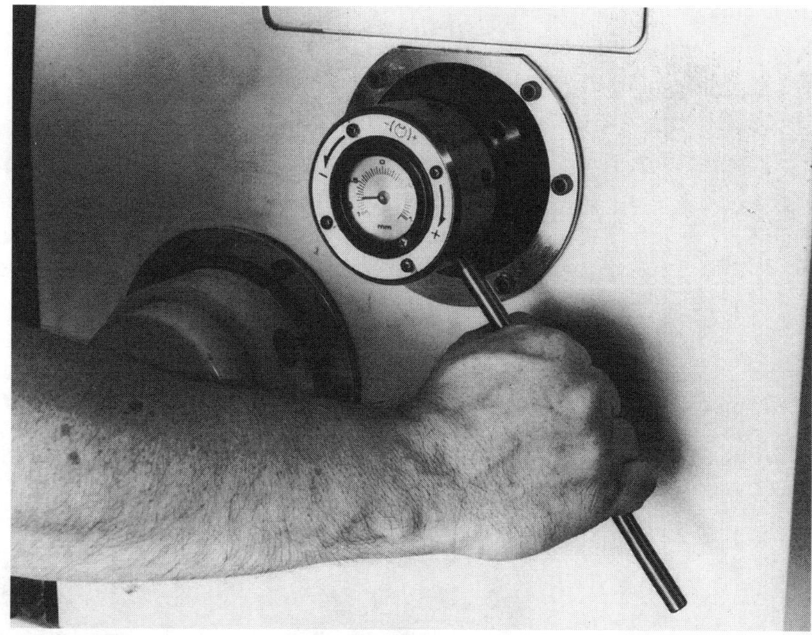

A press operator making a minor circumferential register move (±0.04 in. or ±1 mm) on a Komori sheetfed press

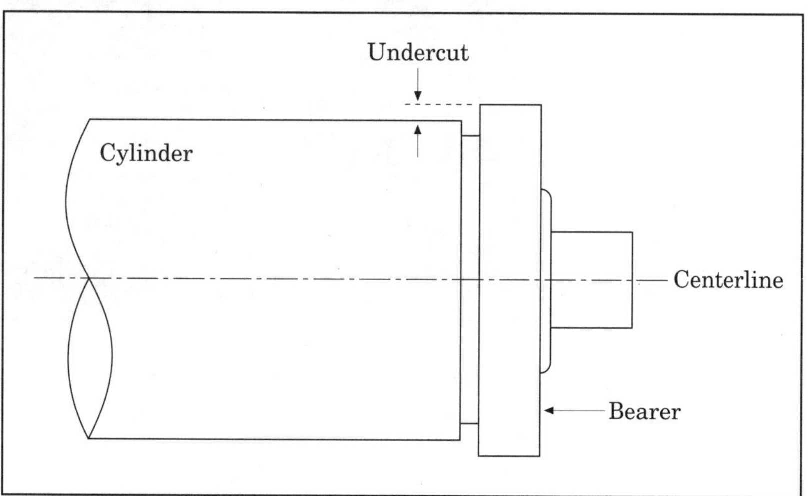

Cylinder undercut

On some plate cylinders, a **start-of-print line,** a horizontal line that indicates the limit of the printing area, is engraved in the gutters about an inch behind the cylinder's leading edge. From that line toward the leading edge of the cylinder, the radius of the cylinder is progressively reduced to form a slight ramp. This ramp allows the inking and dampening rollers to mount the plate smoothly when the press is running at higher speeds. When the plate is in position on the cylinder, all image areas should be behind the start-of-print line.

A **plate clamp** is a device designed to first grip the edge of the plate and then pull it tight against the cylinder body. Plate clamps have widely varied designs, but they all do the same thing. Some clamps are quick-release; a simple twist of a cam actuates the grip. Others are segmented and operate independently. All clamps have provisions for moving the plate circumferentially and laterally in order to position the print on the paper. The plate clamps on some new presses can also be moved from a remote control console to tilt the plate on the cylinders.

Press operator adjusting a quick-release plate clamp

Increasingly, plate cylinders or plate clamps are equipped with register pins. The pins on the plate cylinder correspond with holes that are punched in the printing plate. Such a plate-positioning system reduces the amount of cylinder adjustments necessary to properly position the printing image.

Blanket Cylinder

The **blanket cylinder** carries the printing blanket and has two primary functions:

- To carry the offset rubber blanket into contact with the inked image on the plate cylinder
- To transfer, or offset, the ink film image to the paper (or other substrate) carried by the impression cylinder

It is very similar to the plate cylinder because it has a gap, gutters, bearers, a gear, and bearings. However, it does not

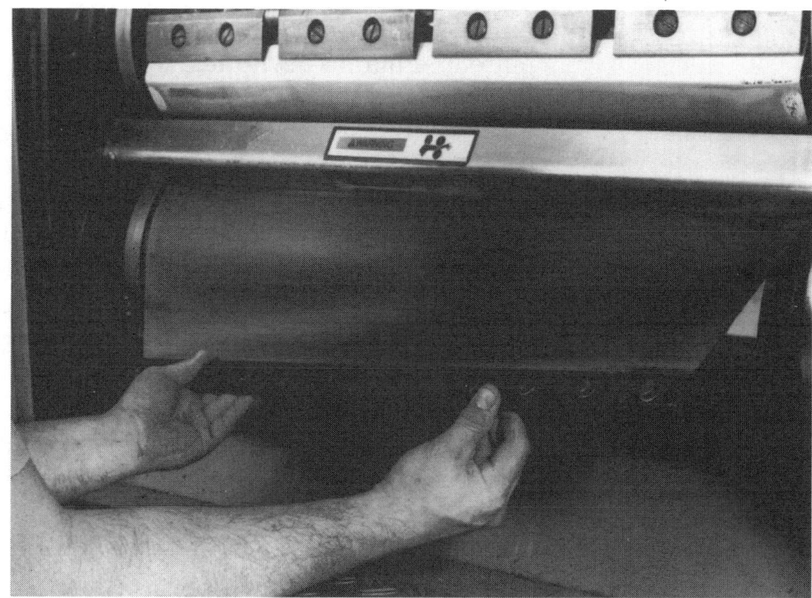

A blanket, attached to blanket bars, being mounted on a press

have clamps like a plate cylinder does. Instead, it has one or two reels for holding and stretching the blanket tight. With some presses, the blanket ends are attached to bars, which, in turn, are mounted to reels.

The reels rotate to tighten the blanket against the cylinder. The rotating mechanism is either a worm gear or a ratchet-and-pawl device. Premounted bars are an option on most presses.

The position of the blanket cylinder in relation to the other cylinders must be adjustable for two reasons: to bring it in and out of contact with them, and to compensate for variations in substrate and packing thicknesses. When contact between the cylinders is broken, the blanket cylinder is backed away from the other two cylinders, but the distance is not great because the gears on the cylinders must remain in mesh. However, the distance is sufficient to permit plates to be mounted and washed without getting the blanket dirty, and to allow the blanket to be washed or changed without any solvent getting on the plate. It also allows the press to idle without transferring the image on the plate to the blanket. Eccentric bushings permit this movement of cylinders.

The distance between the blanket cylinder and the impression cylinder must also be adjustable to accommodate different thicknesses of substrate and blanket packing. This distance is adjusted by another pair of eccentric bushings. Adjusting the position of the blanket cylinder relative to the impression cylinder does not affect the relationship between plate and blanket cylinders.

On single-color presses, the blanket cylinder gear is generally the driving gear for both of the other cylinders. It is driven by the drive train from the main motor. The blanket cylinder gear is attached to the cylinder in much the same way as the plate cylinder gear. It is adjustable, but only for press timing purposes. The press operator never adjusts the position of this gear.

The body of the cylinder is undercut to accommodate the blanket and packing. The blanket cylinder does not have a ramp like the plate cylinder does; its radius is constant from leading to trailing edges. With some presses, particularly those that print with the plate and blanket cylinder bearers out of contact, the undercut is deeper to accommodate two blankets plus packing. Presses sold in the United States usually have a single undercut, while those sold in Europe could have a double undercut.

Impression Cylinder

The **impression cylinder** carries the paper into the printing unit. Contact pressure from the blanket cylinder transfers the print to the paper. The impression cylinder also has a gear and gap. The gap accommodates the gripper shaft on which the gripper fingers that hold the sheet during printing are mounted. The grippers hold the unprinted paper in register as the cylinder turns and presses it against the inked image on the blanket cylinder.

The body of the impression cylinder is not undercut. It is approximately the diameter of the bearers of the other two cylinders. The impression cylinder bearers are, in fact, undercut and are used only as paralleling devices when setting up the press.

Two basic mechanical designs are used to vary the clearance between the blanket and impression cylinders to accommodate different thicknesses of stock. In the first design, the impression cylinder is mounted on a set of eccentric bushings. A shift of the eccentric bushings by an impression lever moves the impression cylinder toward or away from the blanket cylinder. The second method uses two sets of eccentric bushings, but these are on the blanket cylinder. The inner set adjusts the blanket-to-plate bearer pressure and actuates automatic on-and-off printing contact. The outer set moves the blanket cylinder only in relation to the impression cylinder.

Transfer Cylinder

After printing, the impression cylinder transfers the paper to a cylinder that moves the paper between printing units or carries it to the delivery. The paper-transport cylinders between printing units are **transfer cylinders**. An odd number of transfer cylinders are placed between printing units.

A transfer cylinder may be covered with a variety of materials to avoid marking the wet ink. One of these is a frictionless, ink-repellent coating applied to a base material that is then adhered to the existing transfer cylinder. The cylinder is then covered with a loose-fitting, ink-repellent cloth net that moves freely between printed sheet and transfer cylinder. This rub-free movement reduces marking, and the ink-repellent surfaces reduce the chance of ink redepositing onto the press sheet.

As a stopgap measure, some press operators apply adhesive-backed ⅛- or ¼-in. (3- or 6-mm) foam insulation to the portions of the transfer cylinder that correspond to nonimage areas of

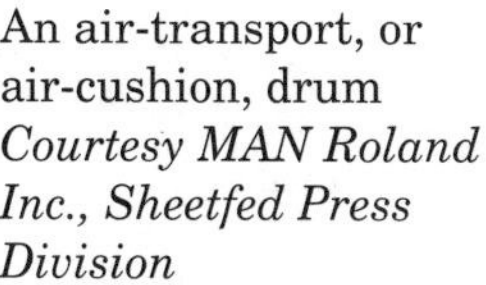

An air-transport, or air-cushion, drum
Courtesy MAN Roland Inc., Sheetfed Press Division

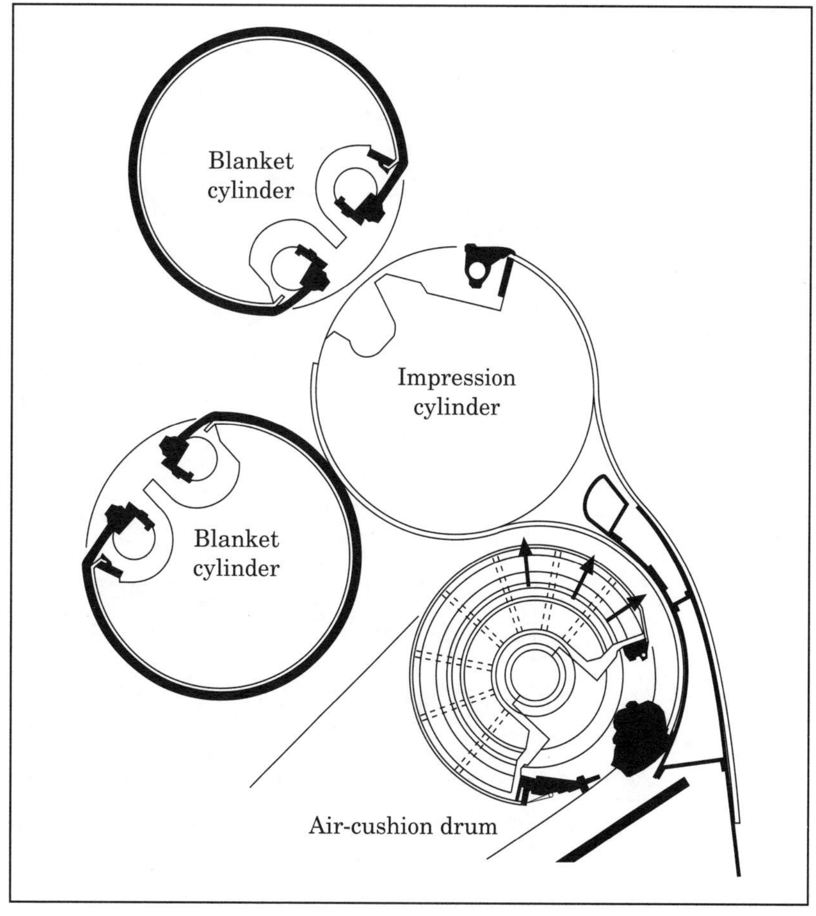

Sheet turning in three phases on a MAN Roland convertible perfector
Courtesy MAN Roland, Inc., Sheetfed Press Division

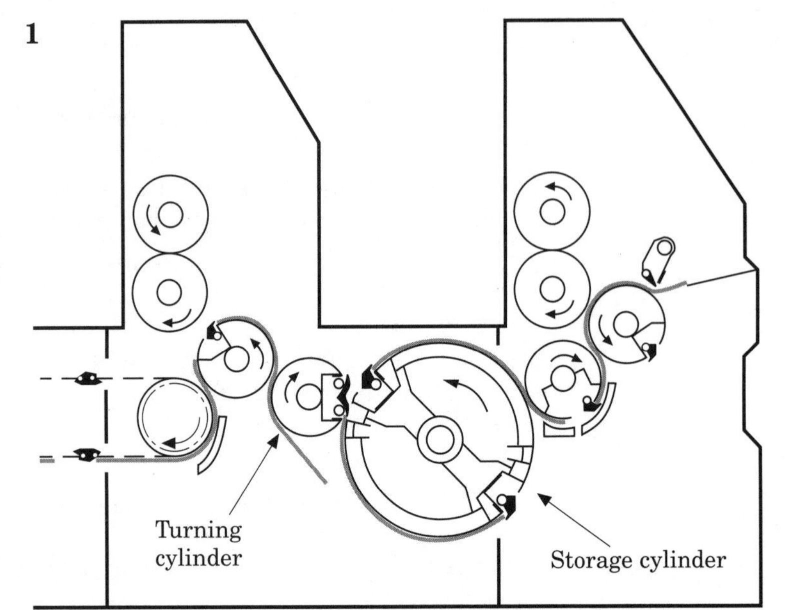

Two straight-forward sheets are on the large-diameter (storage) cylinder. The tail edge of the lower sheet is taken by the grippers of the turning cylinder; at the same time, the grippers of the storage cylinder open.

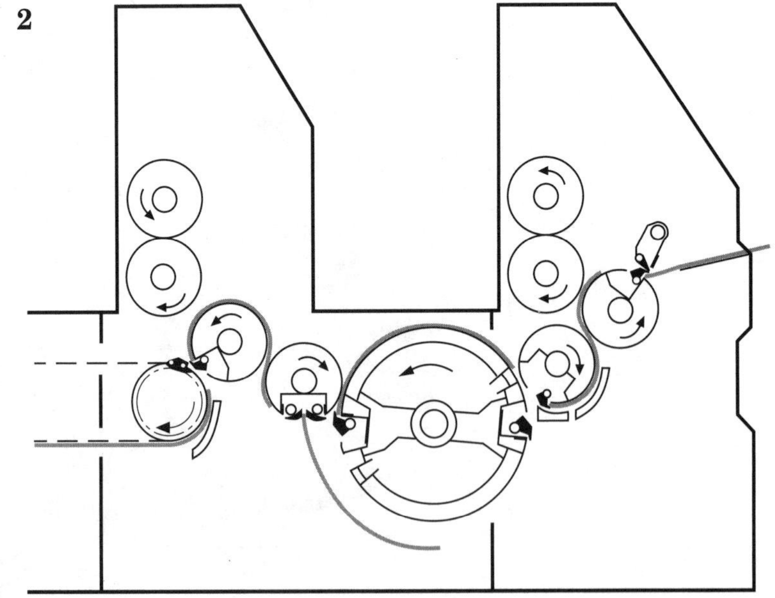

The sheet is held by the grippers of the turning cylinder. The tail edge of the sheet becomes the leading edge.

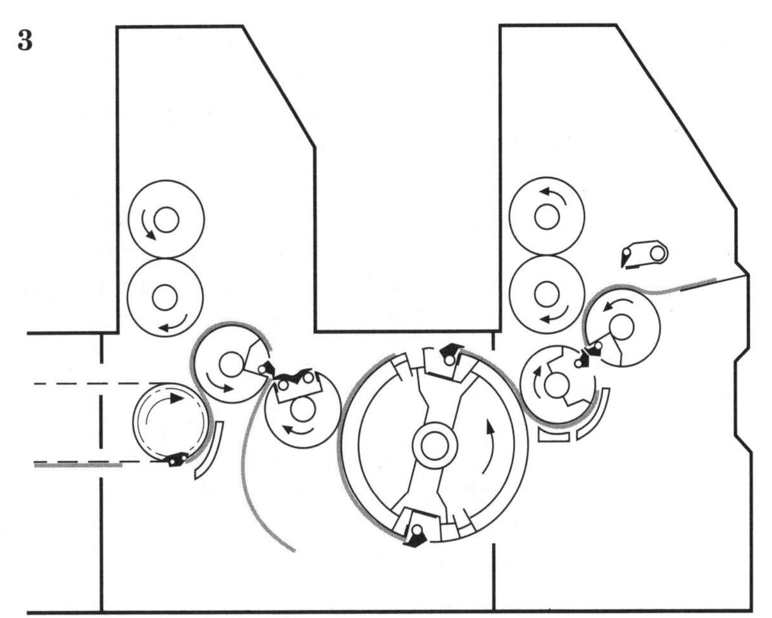

The sheet is transferred to the impression cylinder grippers in the second unit for perfecting.

Sheet travel on a MAN Roland convertible perfector set for single-side printing
Courtesy MAN Roland, Inc., Sheetfed Press Division

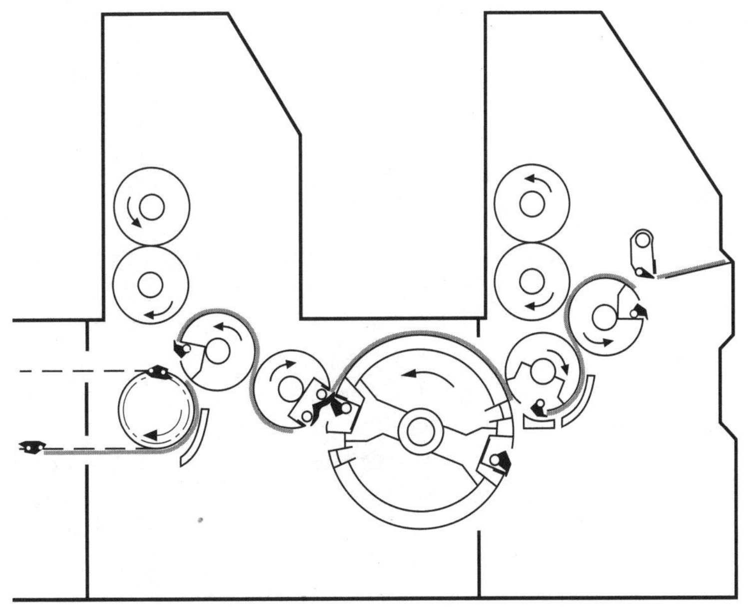

In single-side printing, the leading edge of the sheet travels directly from the storage cylinder to the turning cylinder, which now acts as an intermediate transfer cylinder.

the press sheet. The foam supports the image areas above the cylinder surface, preventing marking. The foam insulation must be replaced for each new job.

Some presses come equipped with an **air-transport,** or **air-cushion, drum** instead of the typical transfer cylinder. An air-cushion drum is a device that supports the sheet on a cushion of air to lessen the chance that ink will smear on the press sheet. One air-cushion drum, for example, has a ribbed aluminum core covered with an air-permeable jacket. Air flows through this jacket, cushioning the printed sheet above the drum's surface.

In one type of perfecting press, three transfer cylinders are used between printing units: a conventional transfer cylinder, which is positioned immediately after the previous printing unit's impression cylinder, a large-diameter storage cylinder that can hold two press sheets, and a turning cylinder with two sets of grippers. On the storage cylinder, the tail, or trailing edge, of a press sheet is taken by the grippers of the turning cylinder. At the same time, the grippers of the storage cylinder open. During this transfer from one cylinder to the other, the tail edge of the sheet becomes the leading edge, and the just-printed side of the sheet is placed against the impression cylinder of the next printing unit. In single-sided printing, the three cylinders act as conventional transfer cylinders—that is, the lead edge of the sheet is transferred to the next cylinder.

Delivery Cylinder

Although technically a transfer cylinder, the cylinder after the last printing unit is called the **delivery cylinder.** It powers the chain delivery and coordinates the transfer of the printed sheet from the last impression cylinder to the delivery gripper bars attached to the two delivery chains.

The most common delivery cylinder consists of a shaft on which a series of disks, or **skeleton wheels,** are mounted. The wheels can be moved laterally to support the wet sheet in nonprinted areas. If they are not positioned properly, the press sheet can become marked with ink.

An alternative system called Super Blue manufactured by Printing Research, Inc. replaces the skeleton wheels with a solid delivery cylinder that is first coated with a frictionless, ink-repellent material and then covered with a loose-fitting, ink-repellent cloth netting that moves freely between printed sheet and delivery cylinder, reducing or eliminating the tendency to mark.

"Mark-less" Super Blue system for preventing marking of wet ink

Transfer and delivery cylinders that contact the wet side of a sheet are coated with a frictionless, ink-repellent substance and covered with a loose-fitting, ink-repellent cloth net.

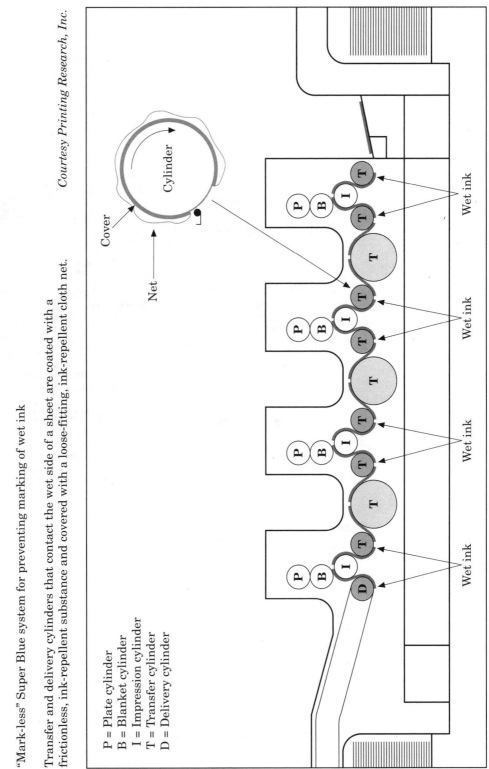

Courtesy Printing Research, Inc.

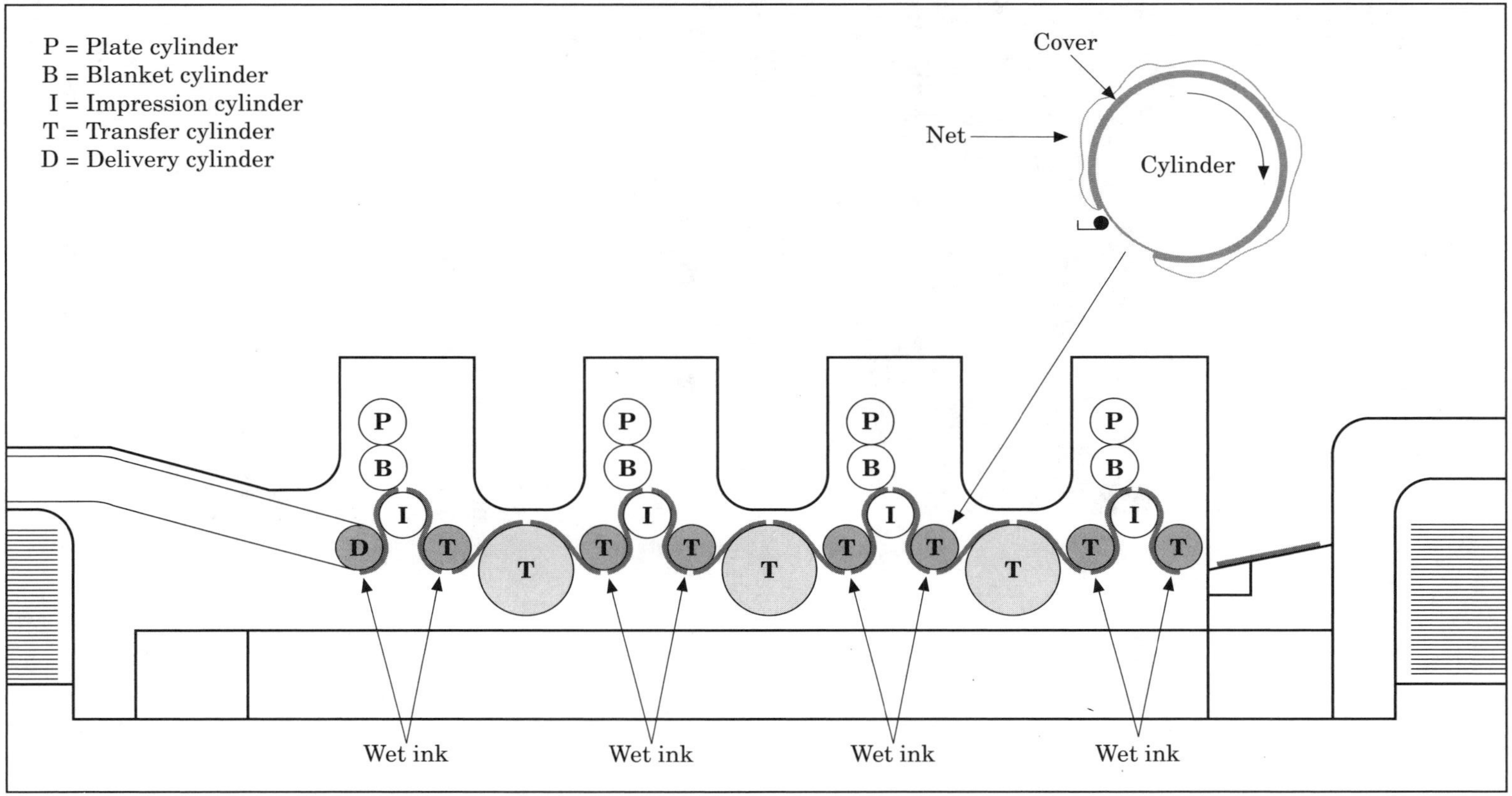

Another alternative is the BacVac system from Printing Research, Inc. In this system, the sheet on the unprinted side is drawn against the contour of the BacVac by vacuum and a series of rollers holding the sheet away from the rotating skeleton wheels to eliminate marking, and to provide sufficient sheet support. The BacVac is adequate for most printing and coating situations. However, it can not be used during perfecting, because the wet ink surface against the vacuum rollers will cause severe smearing.

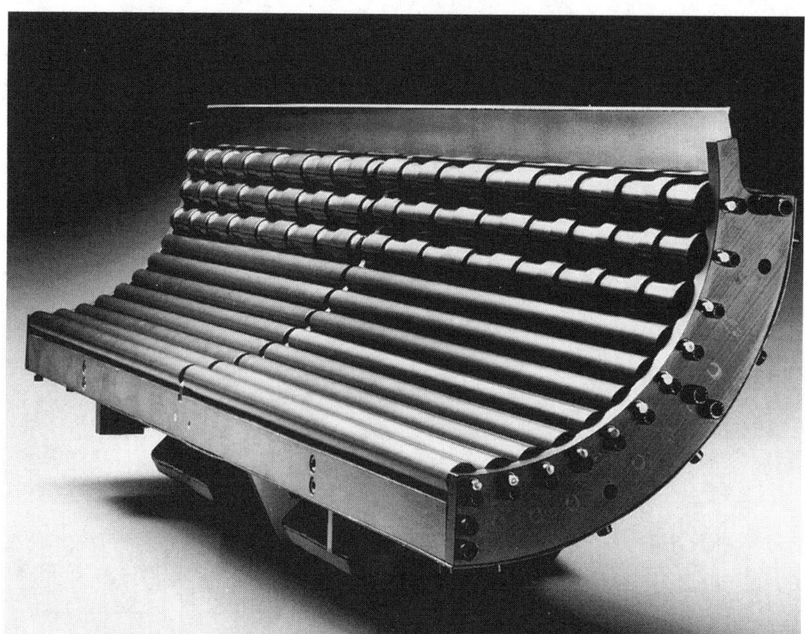

BacVac
Courtesy Printing Research, Inc.

Cylinder Setting

Setting the cylinders is a part of preventive maintenance, not a part of makeready. The procedures for setting the cylinders on a bearer-contact and non-bearer-contact press are discussed.

Cylinder Setting on a Bearer Contact Press

Bearer pressure is an important part of cylinder setting on a **bearer-contact press,** a press that runs with the bearers of the plate and blanket cylinders in contact. The bearers perform several functions:

- They act as an alignment device. When bearers touch at both ends, the blanket cylinder and plate cylinder are in perfect alignment.
- They protect against excessive gear wear. When the bearers are touching, the gears mesh perfectly. The pitch lines of the two cylinder gears are running together just as they

were designed to do, and it is impossible to jam the gears together beyond the pitch line and cause excessive wear. When the pressure is off and the press is idling, the bearers are apart and the teeth are not fully meshed. However, at this time the press is not under load, and there is little strain on the gears.

- They act as a reference point for measuring the actual height of the plate or blanket when packed. The bearers represent the effective diameter of the cylinder, and if necessary, the cylinder undercut can be determined from them.
- They help to smoothly transfer power from one cylinder to another. Since all running gears have clearance between the teeth and are subject to wear, a smooth flow of power between gears is impossible. Properly set bearers roll together smoothly and overcome run-out between the driving gear and the driven gear. If the bearers are not in firm contact, gear streaks sometimes appear.

To make bearers really effective, it is necessary that they be forced together under pressure by the bearings. This is called **preloading.** Just the weight of the upper cylinder forcing the bearers together is not enough. The pressure between bearers must be greater than the pressure between plate and blanket to prevent gear streaks.

In many printing plants, setting bearer pressure is considered a factory service technician's work. However, press operators can check bearer pressure with the following steps:

1. Make sure the plate and blanket are packed to their correct working height.
2. Lift the blanket and increase the packing slightly with a thin sheet—about 0.003 in. (0.07 mm). Refit and tension the blanket.
3. With both blanket and plate cylinder bearers absolutely clean and dry, apply thin thumbprints of ink at several spots around both blanket cylinder bearers. The ink used must not be fast-drying. If necessary, the ink can be thinned (reduced) slightly with machine oil.
4. Isolate the sheet detectors, start the press, and turn on the impression. After two or three press revolutions, release the pressures and stop the press.
5. Look for the transfer of the thumbprints to the plate cylinder bearers. If there is no transfer, the cylinders must be adjusted. If there is a light impression only in

the gap, the cylinders must be adjusted slightly. If there is a good, even impression in the gap and around the bearers on the gear and operator's sides of the press, no adjustment is needed. Release the pressures during adjustments, and reapply pressures to check the transfer.

6. Remove the extra sheet from the blanket and engage the sheet detectors.

Thumbprints that have transferred from the blanket cylinder bearer *(bottom)* to the plate cylinder bearer *(top)*

Cylinder Setting on a Non-Bearer-Contact Press

Setting the cylinders of presses that run without bearer contact is relatively straightforward. The setting mechanisms to adjust cylinder positions are similar to those on other presses.

The procedure for setting the cylinders of non-bearer-contact presses is as follows:

1. Slightly overpack the blanket, especially on older printing presses.
2. Pack the plate correctly and adjust the blanket-cylinder-to-impression-cylinder pressure to apply approximately 0.004-in. (0.1-mm) squeeze to the impression cylinder without paper.
3. Refer to the operator's manual to determine how much gap is necessary between the bearers for normal packing heights.
4. Select feeler gauges of the same thickness, single pieces if possible. A **feeler gauge** is a thin strip of steel ground to precise thickness and marked accordingly.

5. With the bearers absolutely clean and dry, isolate the sheet detectors and roll the press into pressure.
6. Stop the press with the blanket in contact with both the plate and impression cylinders.
7. Shut off the power to the press.
8. Insert the feeler gauges between the bearers of plate and blanket cylinders. If the cylinders are set correctly, the feelers will be snug between the bearers. They should be just movable with a strong pull and should retain a new position after being moved from side to side. Gradual adjustment to achieve this setting should be done with the cylinders off pressure, and tested with the pressures reapplied.
9. When satisfactory settings are found, remove the extra packing, engage the sheet detectors, and reset the blanket and impression pressure to normal.

On some European presses, the distance between plate and blanket cylinders can be altered by moving the plate cylinder, which is mounted in eccentric bushings. After adjustment, the inking rollers may have to be reset to the plate.

Paralleling Blanket Cylinder to Impression Cylinder

The procedure described for setting the plate/blanket cylinder relationship of a non-bearer-contact press can be applied to the blanket/impression cylinder relationship by adjusting the appropriate controls.

In all cases, the press manufacturer's instructions must be followed to ensure long press life. Procedures given by manufacturers for adjusting cylinders and bearer pressures must be clearly understood and executed, even if they differ from those presented here.

Maintenance

The upkeep of the printing unit, particularly lubrication, requires strict attention. On many presses, considerable lubrication is done automatically. Oil reservoir levels in these automatic oiling systems must be maintained. Other presses are manually oiled or greased and require regular servicing. The lubrication of the printing unit is usually simple and therefore is often overlooked. The bearings of the blanket-tightening reel, as well as the pawls or worm gears, need lubrication. The gripper shaft bearings and the cam follower should be lubricated. The moving parts of the plate clamp must be kept clean and lubricated with a good grade of clinging-type lubricant. Manufacturer's specifications should provide the necessary information concerning lubricants.

The labeling of grease fittings to ensure that the proper lubricant is used

Cylinder gears that do not run in oil baths must also be lubricated with a grade of grease recommended by the manufacturer. Before new grease is added, the gear teeth should be cleaned down to the bottom of each tooth to remove any particles of ink, paper, lint, or gum that have accumulated.

The linkages and levers that throw pressure on and off must be clean and well oiled. Oil holes and threads of adjustment screws must be kept clean. Eccentric bushings should be lubricated thoroughly. At every oil hole or grease fitting, excess oil or grease should be removed with a rag. Any damaged grease fitting should be replaced to ensure proper lubrication.

Bearers should always be clean and dry. Materials such as gum and ink get on the bearers. If left there, they gradually start to damage the bearers when they are in contact.

Many presses have cylinders that are chromium-plated or skinned with stainless steel to avoid rusting. When cylinders do rust, the rusted areas can develop into high spots causing extra pressure. The cylinders should be kept clean. Any rust should be removed with nonabrasive scouring pads, and the area coated with a thin film of oil. Never use files, razor blades, or coarse abrasives to clean the cylinders.

Presses equipped with infrared (IR) or ultraviolet (UV) dryers require special heat-resistant lubricants because of the heat buildup caused by the dryers. Normal lubricants would break down in such applications.

Caution: Lubricating and cleaning must be done only when the press is stopped. Excess oil should be wiped from the press to prevent it from running onto the floor, where it will be hazardous. Absorbent socks, designed to control hazardous materials, can be placed in the oil drip pans to absorb waste oil. Socks should be replaced once a month, or as necessary. If they are left in the oil pan long after they are capable of absorbing waste oil, they can pose hazards.

Preventive maintenance. The primary objective of a preventive maintenance program is to keep equipment in top operating condition and to prevent breakdowns. GATF's Technical Services Report 7230, *Sheetfed-Press Preventive Maintenance,* discusses the subject of preventive maintenance and includes a series of maintenance checklists, which are reproduced on pages 35–39. In developing the report, GATF reviewed maintenance programs in hundreds of plants and studied service manuals provided by many press manufacturers. Five time-related preventive maintenance checklists and a malfunction report were then developed.

(Text continues on page 40.)

Daily maintenance checklist

DAILY

Daily Maintenance Checklist

Press No. ______

- ☐ Review malfunction report for the last 24 hours.
- ☐ Oil daily lubrication points.
- ☐ Grease dampener roller bearings.
- ☐ Check oil level in **all** gear boxes, machine drives, and central lubricators.
- ☐ Clean and desensitize all chrome rollers in dampening systems.
- ☐ Clean plate and blanket bearers.
- ☐ Clean electronic detector eyes.
- ☐ Check cleanliness of dampener covers.
- ☐ Check condition of blankets.
- ☐ Check condition of plates.
- ☐ Check level of dampening solution in reservoirs.
- ☐ Measure pH and conductivity of dampening solution.
- ☐ Measure alcohol percentage, if alcohol is used.
- ☐ Measure plate-to-blanket squeeze.
- ☐ Clean sponges and pails. Refill pails.
- ☐ Pick up wastepaper.
- ☐ Dispose of empty containers.
- ☐ Clean up oil and ink spills.
- ☐ Return all tools to proper locations.

End of Shift

- ☐ Empty and clean ink fountains.
- ☐ Clean ink roller train.
- ☐ Clean impression cylinder.
- ☐ Check malfunction report.
- ☐ Stripe ink form roller.

WEEKLY

Weekly Maintenance Checklist for Month of ____________, 19___
Press No. ______

Person performing maintenance must initial each operation on date performed.

Operation	Date	Date	Date	Date
1. Drain and flush all dampening systems and recirculators.				
2. Inspect all covered dampener rollers.				
3. Inspect all ink and dampening form rollers and check form roller settings.				
4. Wash all plate cylinders and impression cylinders with solvent and wipe down with lightly oiled rag.				
5. Blow off entire press (dry) and wipe down with clean rags.				
6. Clean all filters in feeder, delivery, decurler, and vacuum cleaner systems.				
7. Wipe down and wax feedboard. Check feeder valves. Replace suckers if worn. Inspect feeder tapes for wear, and replace worn tapes. Clean glazed tapes.				
8. Blow off delivery bars and wipe off spray powder. Clean and check all suction wheels.				
9. Brush spray powder off unit and check tube gap.				
10. Wash all open feeder and delivery gears.				
11. Oil and grease all weekly lubrication points.				
12. Lightly oil all feeder tape conveyor rollers that are not automatically lubricated. Oil blanket lockup reels.				
13. Grease infeeds and all grippers in impression cylinder, transfer cylinders, and delivery gripper bars.				
14. Lubricate delivery chains.				
15. Lubricate ink fountain rollers.				
16. Lubricate ink and dampening systems.				
17. Grease and oil feeder heads and all side guide and front guide mechanisms.				
18. General cleanup. Pick up all trash around press and on platforms. Sweep floors and platforms, wipe up all oil, and clean up ink spills. Clean and dry drip pan. Empty rag cans and trash cans.				
19. Clean shelves; return chemicals, tools, and ink to proper location for use. Clean washup trays, buckets, and sponges and return to proper location for use.				
20. Fill washup bottles and solvent containers. Refill grease guns and oil cans.				
21. Check supply of spare blankets and covered dampening rollers.				
22. Update information on Malfunction Report.				

500-HOUR Part 1

500-Hour Maintenance Checklist, Performed ____________, 19___
Press No. ______

Operation	Performed by	Remarks and Additional Repairs Required
1. Check durometer and condition of all ink and water rollers. Replace all damaged rollers and remove glaze from hardened rollers. Clean roller ends and check journals for wear before installing.		
2. Clean press side frames and roller sockets while rollers are out of press and apply light film of oil.		
3. Reset all ink and dampening system rollers.		
4. Check oil level in all self-oscillating ink and dampening oscillators.		
5. Remove all ink fountain blades, inspect for wear and damage, and replace with new or reconditioned blades where necessary. Clean all keys, lubricate key screws, and parallel blade.		
6. Clean and inspect all washup blades.		
7. Clean all cylinder bearers and check for proper bearer pressures. Reparallel cylinder and reset bearer pressures.		
8. Clean ink, rust, gum, etc., from the body of all plate, blanket, and impression cylinders and apply a light film of oil.		
9. Clean cylinder gaps and cylinder ends. Clean plate clamps and reset.		
10. Spray-clean all pickup, impression, transfer, and delivery grippers. Clean gripper pads and check settings. Reset as necessary. Replace badly worn gripper pads. Check for broken compression springs and replace as necessary.		
11. Clean all oil pump filters. Clean regulating valves on all suction and air blast pumps.		
12. Vacuum dust from all electric motors and wipe clean. Clean dust filters on electrical controllers and press control consoles.		
13. Remove powder from antisetoff spray unit; blow out powder and air lines; clean nozzles. Clean etched roller, set tube gaps, and check tubes for brightness. Clean or replace tubes as necessary.		
14. Clean feeder pickup, forwarder, and side guide mechanisms; lubricate side guide positioning shaft.		

(Checklist continues on next page.)

500-HOUR Part 2

500-Hour Maintenance Checklist, Performed ____________, 19___
Press No. ______

Operation	Performed by	Remarks and Additional Repairs Required
15. Check sensitivity of sheet detector; clean and lubricate.		
16. Clean and lubricate jogger mechanisms.		
17. Clean and inspect hoist mechanisms.		
18. Grease and oil all 500-hr. (red) lubrication points.		
19. Clean and lightly grease all exposed springs and spring rods.		
20. Clean and lubricate all exposed gears on cylinder ends and elsewhere.		
21. Spray-clean and lubricate delivery chains. Check chain tension.		
22. Complete all repairs on malfunction list since last major maintenance period.		

SEMIANNUAL

Semiannual Maintenance Checklist, Performed ___________, 19___
Press No. ______

Every third 500-hour maintenance and in addition to that maintenance.

Operation	Performed by	Remarks and Additional Repairs Required
1. Drain oil in feeder and delivery pumps and refill. Inspect for wear and repair as necessary.		
2. Remove feeder separator pistons and air valves. Clean, lubricate, and reinstall.		
3. Clean and lubricate feeder clutch; clean and repack feeder universal joints.		
4. Check oil levels in **all** gear boxes. Add or replace as needed.		
5. Inspect brakes and brushes on all press drive motors. Clean interior of all electrical controllers, drive cabinets, and press control consoles.		

ANNUAL

Annual Maintenance Checklist, Performed __________, 19___
Press No. ______

Every sixth 500-hour maintenance and in addition to that maintenance.

Operation	Performed by	Remarks and Additional Repairs Required
1. Inspect press by a qualified service technician (might be the manufacturer's technician) for overall wear.		
2. Drain all press oil reservoirs, clean filters and pumps, and refill.		
3. Drain and refill all gear boxes in main drive.		

MALFUNCTION REPORT

Press No. ______

Keep this form at press at all times.
Write down all repairs and special maintenance required.

Date	Operator	Problem, or Work Required

Cylinder Low Spots

Cylinder low spots are more common than may be imagined. Even newer presses can have this fault as the result of flawed metal in the cylinders. A wad of paper, a rag, a screw, or even the bent up corner of a sheet of cardboard passing through the cylinders can cause a depressed area. The damaged area can be larger than supposed; e.g., a small setscrew makes a visible dent in both impression and blanket cylinders, but it also makes a depression larger than the dent that cannot be visually detected.

The following procedures can be used to find low spots in the blanket cylinder:

1. Pack the plate and blanket cylinders normally. Put an old plate on the plate cylinder.
2. Ink up the dry plate completely.
3. Print a solid to 20 press sheets.
4. Decrease the impression pressure by 0.002 in. (0.05 mm) and print another 20 sheets. Repeat this step until no ink is transferred to the paper.

If a low spot appears anywhere on the press sheet, wash and reverse the blanket end for end. If the low spot comes in a different place, the blanket is the cause. If the spot is in the same place on the press sheet, one of the printing cylinders has a low spot or is misaligned. Therefore, a factory service technician should be contacted.

3 The Inking System

The **inking system,** or **inker,** of the sheetfed press has four basic functions: (1) to move the ink from the ink fountain to the plate, (2) to break down the thick charge of ink into a thin, uniform film around the rollers, (3) to work the ink into printing condition, and (4) to remove image repeats on the form from previous printing cycles.

Typical inking system

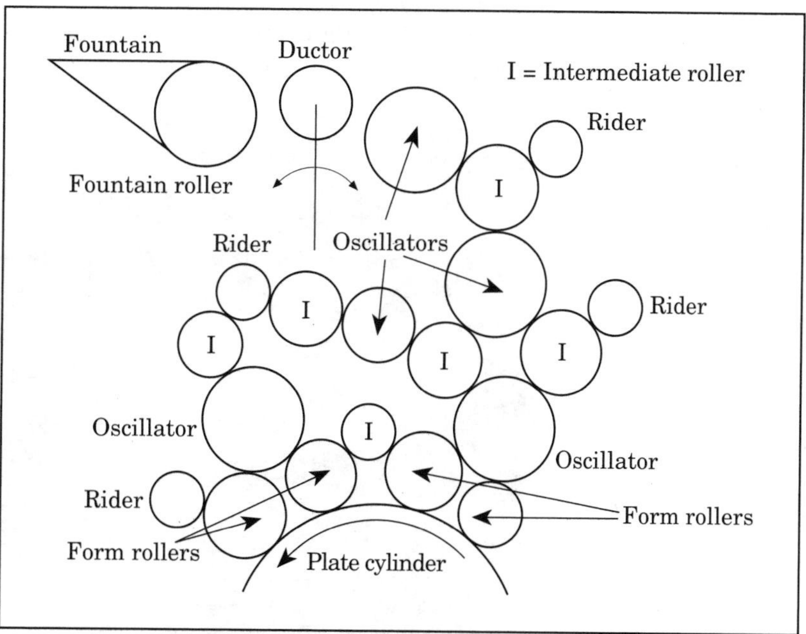

The inking system of most large sheetfed presses usually has at least ten rollers and consists of the following parts:

- **Ink fountain**—a pan that contains the ink supply
- **Ductor** or **ductor roller**—a transfer roller that alternately contacts the ink fountain roller and the first roller of the inking system, often an oscillator

- **Oscillators,** or **vibrators**—gear- or chain-driven rollers that not only rotate but oscillate from side to side, distributing and smoothing out the ink film and erasing image patterns from the form roller
- **Intermediate rollers**—friction- or gravity-driven (i.e., surface-driven) rollers between the ductor and form roller that transfer and condition the ink; often called **distributors** if they contact two rollers and **riders** if they contact a single roller, such as an oscillator
- **Form rollers**—a series of three to four rollers, usually of differing diameters, that contact the printing plate and transfer ink to it

The series of rollers excluding the ink fountain and fountain roller is often referred to as the **roller train.** The roller train is comprised of a series of alternating hard and soft rollers. The hard rollers are usually steel covered with copper, ebonite, or nylon. The resilient rollers (ductor, intermediate, and form rollers) are often made of a synthetic rubber such as PVC (polyvinyl chloride), Buna-N (a copolymer of butadiene and acrylonitrile), or polyurethane. These substances are applied to a steel shaft.

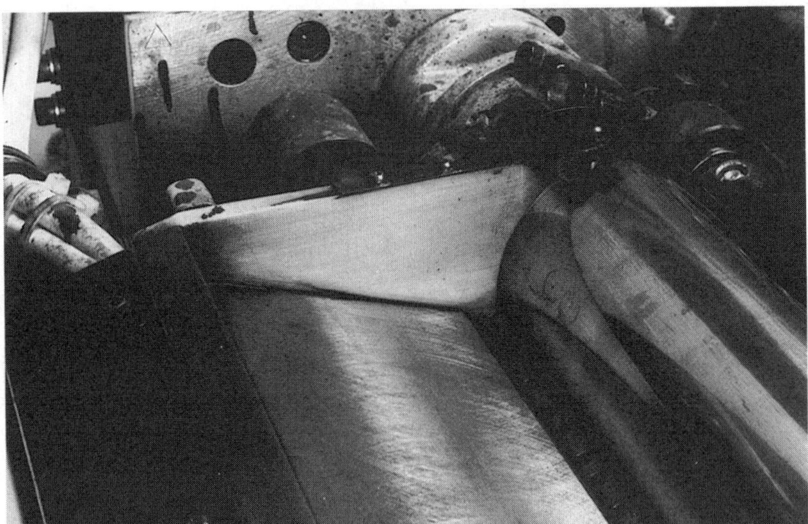

Portion of the ink fountain, showing the fountain cheeks, the blade, and the fountain roller

Ink fountain. The ink fountain, the trough that holds the ink supply, is formed by the **fountain roller,** which is a metal roller that turns either intermittently or continuously, a **fountain blade,** which can be a spring steel plate, steel segments, or plastic approaching the fountain roller at an angle, and two **fountain cheeks,** which are vertical metal pieces that contact the fountain roller edges and the fountain blade edges to form an ink-tight trough. One press manufacturer has replaced the fountain blade with a disposable sheet of polyester that is held in contact with the fountain roller by a series of small cylinders lying parallel to it. Each cylinder has bearers at the ends. The space between bearers, about 1¼ in. (32 mm), is undercut and eccentric. As the cylinder rotates, more or less ink can pass to the fountain roller because the undercut of the eccentric roller increases or decreases. This produces controllable bands of ink on the fountain roller, which are blended by the oscillators. Each cylinder is adjusted by an individual motor controlled from the press console, which has an illuminated display showing the fountain profile.

As the fountain roller turns, the majority of the ink in the fountain is held back by the fountain blade, which is set very close to the fountain roller. The distance between the blade and the roller is adjusted by means of **fountain keys,** a series of thumb screws (ink fountain keys). On presses equipped with control consoles, the keys are motor-driven screws or cams behind the blade. Adjustment of the fountain keys varies the ink feed across the press according to the demands of the plate.

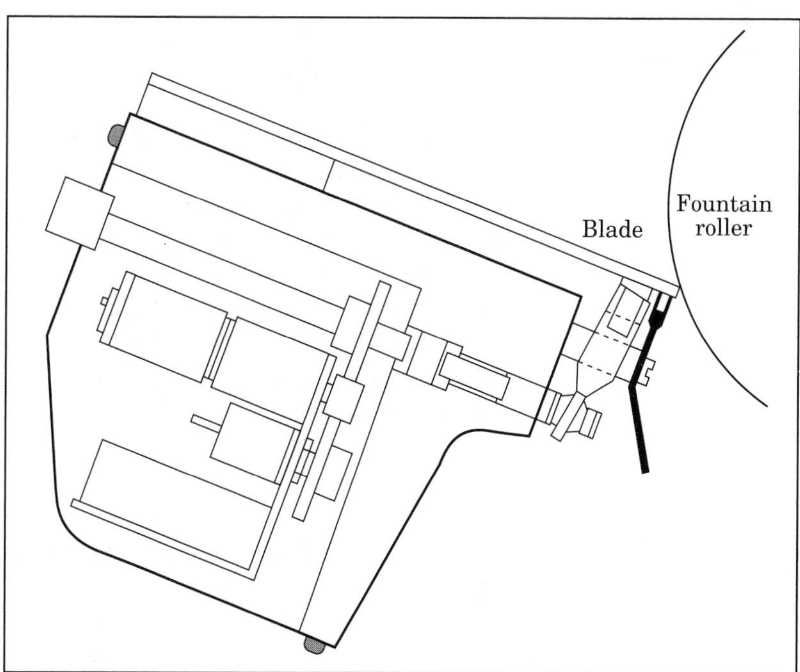

Single ink key for a remotely controlled ink fountain with a continuous blade

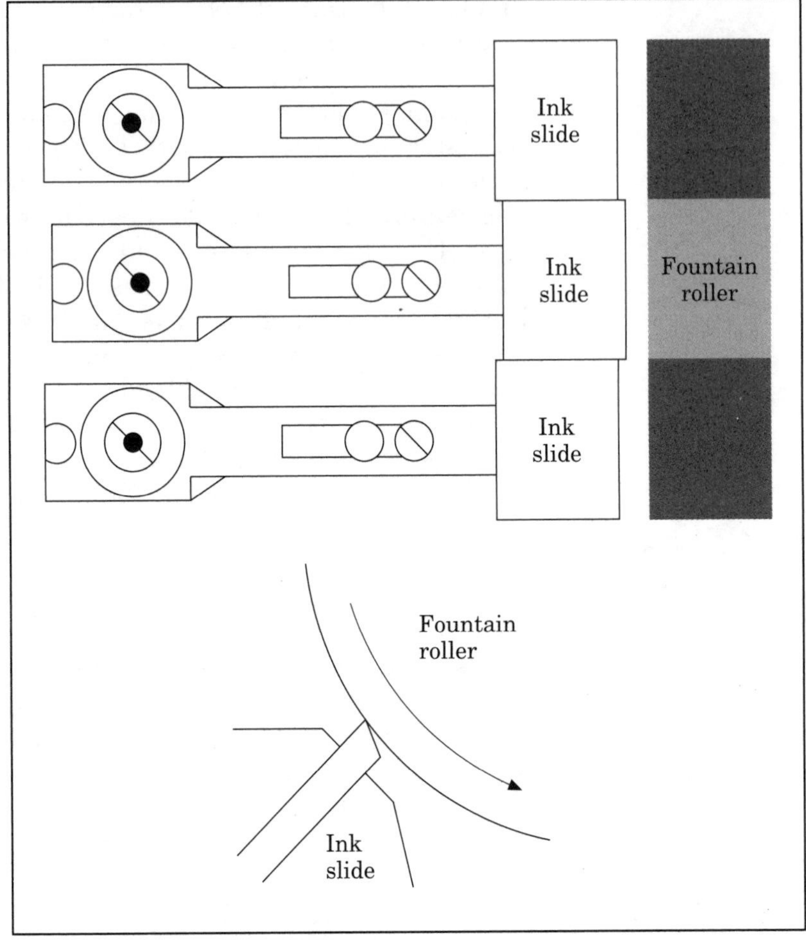

Ink slide for a sheetfed press
Courtesy MAN Roland Inc., Sheetfed Press Division

The overall adjustment of ink feed is controlled in one of two ways. **Dwell**—the length of time that the ductor roller contacts the fountain roller—can be varied with a dwell cam mechanism. If the fountain roller is the type that turns intermittently, the degree of rotation can be adjusted with a ratchet mechanism that varies the number of teeth exposed to the pawl. If the fountain roller turns continuously, the press operator controls the speed of the turning fountain roller to increase or decrease the amount of ink that is feed through the system. The faster the pan roller turns, the more surface area of the ductor roller that is covered with ink.

Ductor roller. The ductor roller, the first roller of the ink distribution system, feeds a metered amount of ink from the fountain to the full inking system by alternately contacting the ink fountain roller and the first oscillator. Depending on

Inking fountain on a Heidelberg Speedmaster press

the design of the system, the ductor roller contacts the fountain roller once or, more usually, every other or every fourth revolution of the plate cylinder (this varies by press design). Ductor timing is related to the reversal of the oscillator, which is operator-adjustable on some presses. A properly timed ductor roller contacts the oscillator when the form rollers are in the plate gap or the trailing edge of the plate.

Press operator adjusting ratchet mechanism

Ductor shock, the vibration sent through the inking system when the ductor first contacts the oscillator, does not interfere with print quality as long as the form rollers are over the plate cylinder gap when the initial contact is made.

When the ductor roller makes contact with the intermittently rotating ink fountain roller and then again with the rapidly moving oscillator, slippage or skidding may occur, causing an uneven ink flow. Some presses are equipped with a braking device to control this skid; other manufacturers make the ductor very light in weight to decrease its momentum and tendency to skid.

Oscillators. The heavy ink film carried by the ductor roller is fed onto an oscillator and is then worked down into a smooth film by the rest of the rollers in the inking system.

An inking system has several oscillators, which are also called **drums,** or **vibrators.** They are usually made of steel tubing covered with copper, ebonite, nylon, or some other oil-receptive material that is resistant to roller stripping caused by dampening solution chemicals. The oscillators move laterally, or from side to side. They change side-to-side direction at least once for every revolution of the plate cylinder, which helps control inking by smoothing out the ink film and reducing banding. Oscillators are driven by gears or chains, which indirectly power all other rollers by surface contact. The surface speed of the oscillators is the same as that of the plate when the plate is packed to manufacturer's specifications.

When the ink fountain keys are set to feed varying amounts of ink across the plate, it is desirable to adjust the amount of roller oscillation. Too much oscillation will even out the ink to be fed to the plate and can cause starvation in the solids, and too little oscillation can cause overinking. The press operator should adjust the amount of roller oscillation accordingly.

Under normal plate demand, however, using just about the maximum amount of oscillation is commonly desirable, especially for the oscillators contacting the form rollers. The oscillators must supply the form rollers with a uniform charge of ink for each revolution over the plate to minimize ghosting.

Distributors. The distributors are resilient rollers that carry the ink supply from one oscillator to the next through the inking system. The nap on these rollers works the ink and water in the inking system into a uniform emulsion. Distributors are friction-driven by surface contact with the oscillators and rotate at the same speed as the plate cylinder.

Riders. Riders, which are driven by surface contact with the adjacent oscillator, are hard rollers that generally make contact to only a single roller and do not transfer ink. They help to condition the ink by increasing the ink path, and they collect debris such as paper fiber and dried ink. Riders have the smallest diameter of any type of roller in the inking system, which causes them to rotate at the highest number of revolutions per minute (RPM).

Form rollers. Most large presses have three to four resilient form rollers that transfer ink to the printing plate. These rollers usually are of different diameters to lessen mechanical ghosting problems.

Some presses have an **oscillating form roller,** which is a roller substituted for a form roller to reduce ghosting. This form roller oscillates (moves laterally, or side to side) at a rate different than the adjacent oscillator to smooth the ink film. The oscillation of the form roller can be turned on or off by the press operator.

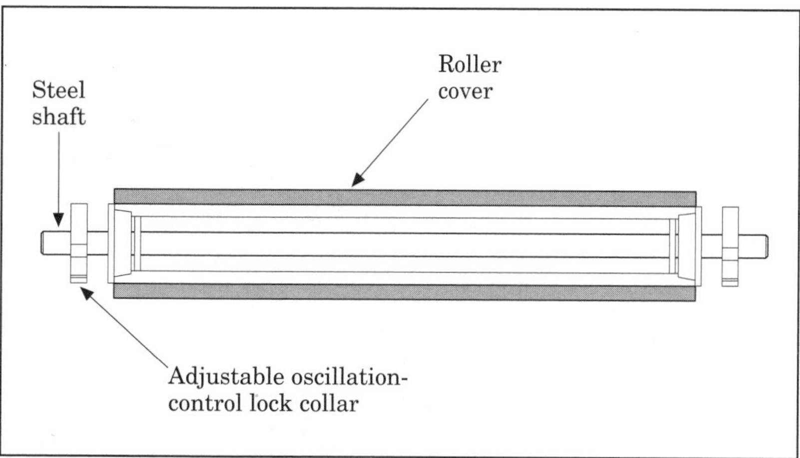

An oscillating form roller

An oscillating ink form roller, the Ghost ContRoller™ *Courtesy AirSystems, Inc.*

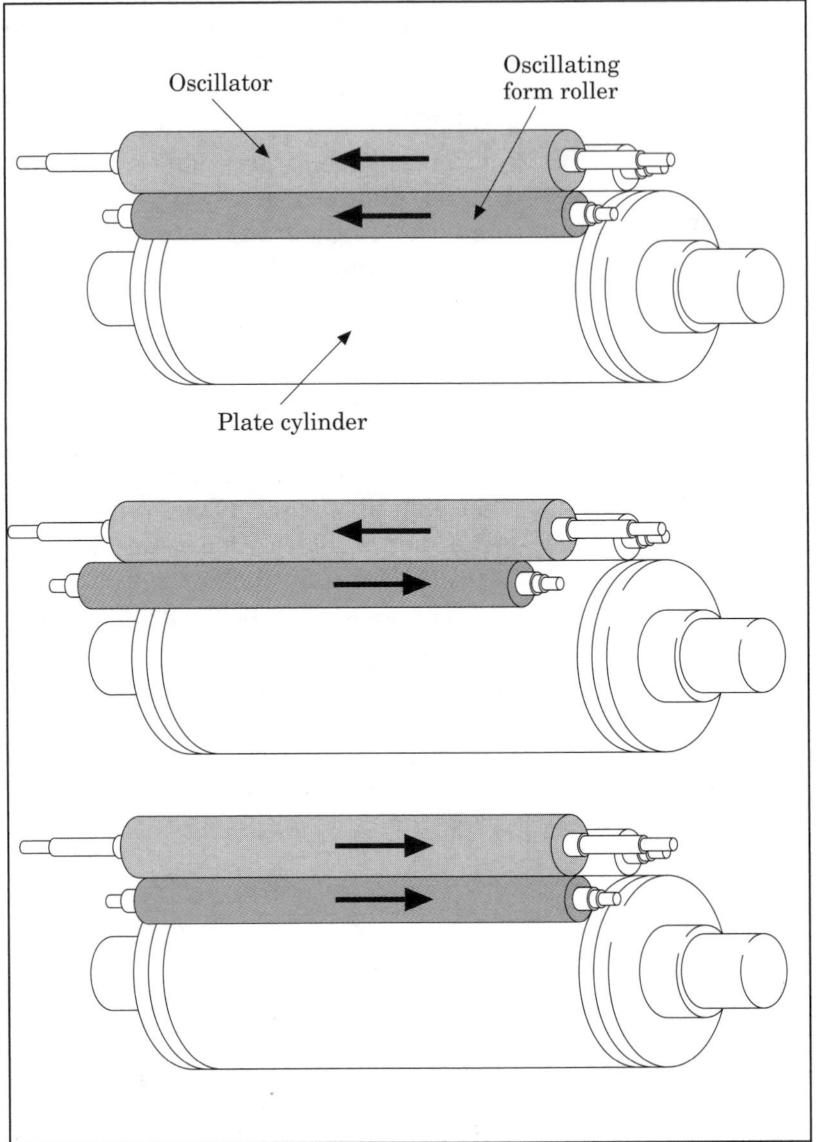

An inking system equipped with an oscillating ink form roller, which reduces ghosting when substituted for the first form roller
Courtesy MAN Roland Inc., Sheetfed Press Division

The form rollers are lifted automatically from the plate when the press is idling or when a sheet is missed, or they can be thrown off manually when necessary. At the same time, ink feed from the ink fountain ceases because the ductor roller does not contact the fountain roller. When printing is to resume, the rollers are brought back into contact with the plate either automatically or manually, and ink feed is resumed. If the throw-off mechanism is clogged with ink, rust, or dirt, the form rollers will not return to their original setting when they are lowered to the plate.

Inking systems for waterless lithography. Waterless lithography requires a printing press that is equipped with a temperature control system. Two types of press temperature control systems are used: an ink oscillator cooling system and a plate cylinder cooling system. With the ink oscillator cooling system, a standard inking system is used with the exception that chilled or *heated* water solution flows through hollow vibrator rollers on the press. These temperature control systems allow the press operator to maintain ink temperature within a narrow range of only a couple of degrees.

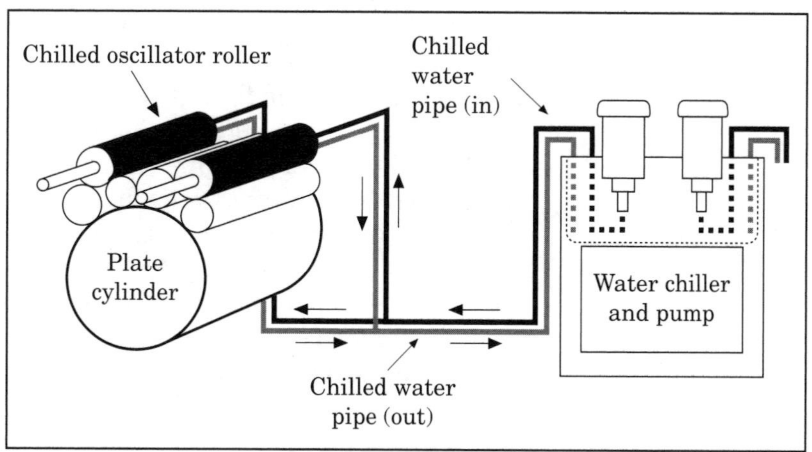

The ink roller cooling system used in conjunction with the Toray Waterless Plate *Courtesy Toray Marketing & Sales (America), Inc.*

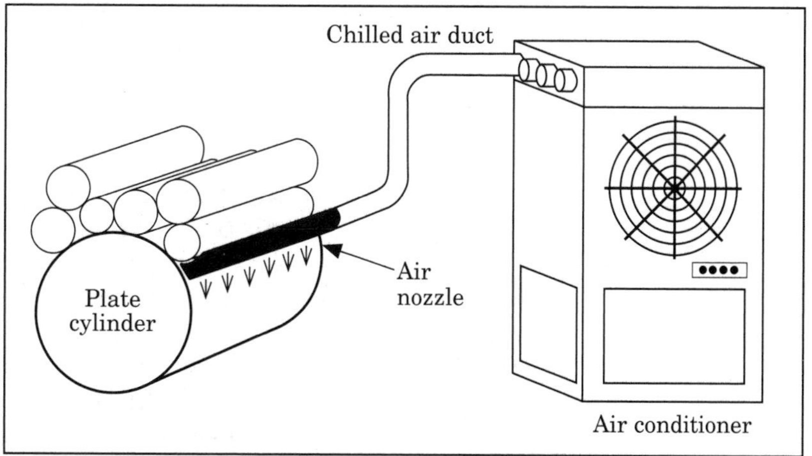

The plate cylinder cooling system used in conjunction with the Toray Waterless Plate *Courtesy Toray Marketing & Sales (America), Inc.*

It is not unusual for each of the inks on the press to perform best at a slightly different temperature. For example, a black ink might operate best at, say, 72–74°F (22.2–23.3°C), while a cyan might operate best at, say, 68–70°F (20–21.1°C). Therefore, the temperature of each inking system on the press is independently controlled by using a zone control unit that blends hot and cold water to the proper temperature for the ink being used. In addition, infrared sensors monitor the temperature of each printing unit, providing immediate feedback to maintain the proper temperature level.

Inking system weaknesses. One weakness of the inking system is that the form rollers become slightly overloaded with ink during the interval when the cylinder gap passes them. During this interval they make one complete revolution. Ink continues to be fed to them but there is no plate to receive it. This slight overload is discharged on their first revolution over the plate and is sometimes noticeable as a rise in ink density on the first several inches (centimeters) of the sheet that suddenly ends in a streak. To partially compensate for this roll-out, the ink form rollers are varied slightly in diameter, which tapers the streak to an acceptable level.

Another weakness is the loss of controlled ink displacement when the press idles. As long as the press is running and printing, the fountain settings deliver a controlled amount of ink to each area of the plate. When a press idles for a few minutes, the oscillators tend to even out the supply of ink across the rollers. When the press starts up again, the areas of heavy demand on the plate are slightly starved and the light-demand areas get too much. This problem continues for only a few sheets, but it does cause variations. In high-quality work, these sheets are often removed from the delivery and discarded.

Ink Film Thickness

The thickness of the ink film on the rollers is a very important consideration in printing. Typical ink film thickness on a lithographic press is 0.2–0.4 mils (0.0002–0.0004 in., or 0.005–0.010 mm), depending on the ink color and printing sequence. The press operator should control the amount of ink being carried by the inking system for more precise control of ink density and color and to avoid problems related to excessively thick or thin ink films.

Common problems resulting from an excessively thin film of ink are low color strength and color saturation, low gloss, incomplete coverage of paper, picking, and hickeys. Also, ink/water balance is difficult to achieve.

Common problems resulting from an excessively thick film of ink are increased ink consumption, ink setoff, drying problems, slight degradation of light colors, graininess of print due to irregular dot gain, excessive emulsification of ink, and low contrast in the shadows due to dot gain.

Print contrast is a means of determining optimum inking levels during the pressrun. Print contrast is calculated from a solid ink patch and a 75% tint patch, according to the following formula:

$$\text{Print contrast} = \frac{D_S - D_{75}}{D_S} \times 100$$

where D_S is the density of a solid (including paper) and D_{75} is the density of a 75% tint (including paper). Some densitometers perform print contrast calculations automatically.

During the pressrun, the press operator should adjust inking levels until the maximum print contrast level is obtained, because the higher the print contrast, the greater the number of tones that can be distinguished between the 75% tint level and solid ink density. As the press operator increases ink density by increasing ink feed, the print contrast will increase until a point is reached where further increases in density will cause lower print contrast values. This is due to the excessive ink film thickness needed to raise density beyond this point. This causes dot gain to rise at an accelerated rate, and thus, print contrast decreases. The aimpoints for maximum print contrast are best based on shop standards. The average print contrasts reported by E. I. du Pont de Nemours & Co., Inc., in the North American Commercial Print Survey are reasonable starting aimpoints for process control. They are as follows:

Yellow	37
Magenta	41
Cyan	39
Black	43

Setting Rollers

In the inking system, few things are more important than setting the form rollers correctly. Roller streaks and many other problems can often be traced to poorly set rollers, so carefully follow the manufacturer's instructions for setting them.

Several problems result from setting the form rollers too heavy to the plate. For example, the form rollers may bounce at the cylinder gap and cause a roller streak. Excessive pressure may also cause severe plate wear and roller wear.

Excessive roller pressure may contribute to ink slurring or dot gain. If the pressure between the form rollers and the plate is greater than the pressure between the form rollers and the oscillators, the form rollers may skid and cause streaking. Excessive pressure between the form rollers and oscillators can cause the form rollers to bow. Excessive pressure anywhere in the inking system generates heat, which can cause the rubber compound to break down.

When rollers are being set, it is the resilient rollers that are adjusted, not the hard rollers. Following are several general recommendations to follow when setting rollers:

- Back off all adjustments completely before setting any rollers in the inking system. (Perhaps, the greatest single error in roller setting is not backing off roller adjustments prior to setting rollers. This can result in bowed rollers; the stripe on the plate will be wide in the middle and narrow on the ends.)
- Always set a roller by moving it forward into contact with the plate or other roller.
- Never set a roller by backing it away from the plate or contacting roller.
- Back off all adjustments completely before inserting new rollers into the inking system.

Setting Form Roller to Oscillator

A form roller is usually mounted in brackets that pivot around the shaft of the oscillator that it contacts. The pivoting bracket permits the form roller to be set to the plate without disturbing the form-roller-to-oscillator setting. The bracket also permits the raising and lowering of the form roller without affecting any roller setting.

The form roller is always adjusted to the oscillator before being adjusted to the plate. Usually changes in the setting of the form roller to the plate will not affect the setting of the form roller to the oscillator. However, large changes in the setting of the form roller to the oscillator may affect the setting of the form roller to the plate on many printing presses, depending on the design of the adjustment mechanism.

The accepted method of setting the form rollers to the oscillators is called the **strip method.** A set of thin packing paper or plastic strips are inserted between the form roller and the oscillator, and the strips are pulled out, providing a "feel" that can be used to judge if the rollers are properly set. Paper strips are used to set the form rollers when no ink is on the rollers, and plastic strips are used when the rollers

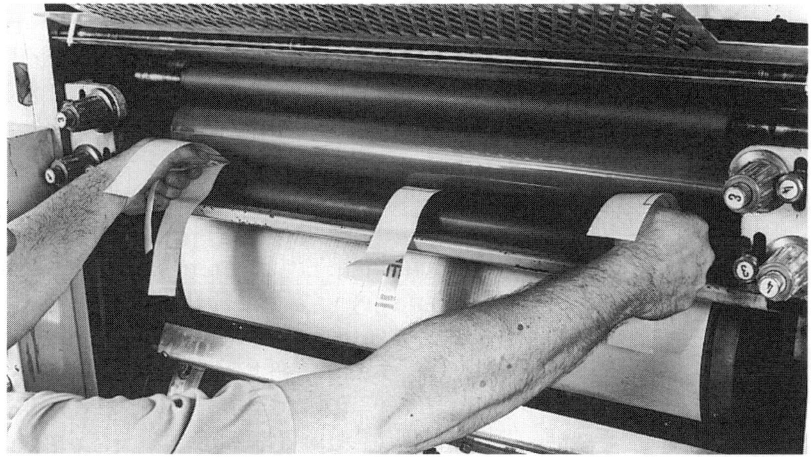

Press operator using strips of paper to set the form roller to the oscillator

are already inked. The strip method, however, is usually performed when no ink is on the rollers.

The strip method of roller setting provides a measurement of the following factors: pressure between the two rollers being set, width of the nip between them, roller hardness, stiffness vs. flow, glaze condition of roller surface, existence of an excessively hard roller surface, and the uniformity of the setting.

It is not advisable to use single strips of paper to test for contact, because friction from the surface of the rollers will affect the "feel." The use of a sandwich of three strips of paper is a better method. The smoother paper helps eliminate the effect of friction on the "feel" of the pulled strip, allowing for a more accurate pressure reading. The outer strips should be about twice the width of the center strip, which is the one that is pulled to set the roller. (For clarity, this method of setting rollers will be referred to as the "three-strip sandwich method.")

An even better alternative to using single strips of paper is to make a sandwich of just two strips of paper. In this method, a single outside strip that is twice as long and wide as the inner strip is folded in half lengthwise. The narrower inner strip is placed inside it, and this sandwich is then fed closed-end first between the two rollers being set. This method is preferred to the previous method if the rollers being set are already inked. The closed end of the outer strip prevents the inner strip from contacting the ink on a roller, which can affect the "feel" when the inner strip is pulled. The closed end of the outer strip also prevents the inner strip from becoming trapped between rollers if it is pushed in too far. (For clarity, this method of setting rollers will be referred to as the "folded-strip sandwich method.")

Setting rollers using the sandwich methods. Following is a typical procedure to set a form roller to the adjacent oscillator using either the three-strip sandwich method or the folded-strip sandwich method:

1. Locate the adjustments and determine which way to turn them for inward and outward movement. The operator's manual usually contains this information and sometimes illustrates the settings. The adjacent machine guard may also have this information. **Note:** Back off all adjustments relating to the form roller.
2. Assemble the tools needed to make adjustments.
3. If you are using the **three-strip method,** cut nine strips of 0.004-in. (0.1-mm) packing paper, three about 12×1 in. (300×25 mm) and the other six about 12×2 in. (300×50 mm). If you are using the **folded-strip method,** cut six strips of 0.004-in. (0.1-mm) packing paper, three about 12×1 in. (300×25 mm) and the other three about 24×2 in. (600×50 mm). **Note:** Do not use 0.002-in. (0.05-mm) packing paper, because it tears too easily.
4. If you are using the **three-strip method,** assemble the strips into three sandwiches: each 12×1-in. strip is placed between two 12×2-in. strips. If you are using the **folded-strip method,** assemble the strips into three sandwiches: fold each of the 24×2-in. strips in half lengthwise, and insert a 12×1-in. strip inside it.
5. Insert a sandwich near each end of the form roller and in the middle of the roller. Jog the strips into the oscillator and form roller nip. If the strips are fed in too far, they will become trapped between several rollers in the inking system, resulting in excessive drag (resistance).
6. Adjust the distance between the form roller and the oscillator until the strips are gripped firmly and evenly. Remember that adjusting one side of the press affects the setting on the other side.
7. Using only one hand, pull the inner (center) strip from the sandwich on one side of the press. The inner strip should pull out easily; it should not have to be "started." With the same hand, pull the inner strip from the sandwich in the center of the press, and finally pull the inner strip from the remaining sandwich at the other side of

the press. **Note:** Make sure to pull the inner strip straight from the point of contact, not at an angle.

8. Determine if the amount of resistance (drag) is the same from one side of the press to the other. There is no description of the right drag; one must develop the feel through experience.
9. If drag is unequal, move the form roller toward the oscillator on the side offering the least resistance. Reinsert the paper sandwiches, and retest the pressure.

Use of a roller-setting gauge. Since there is no way to describe the right drag, a **roller-setting gauge,** a device that shows the amount of pressure exerted by pulling the strip, can be used to fine-tune the pressures. A widely used procedure is to initially set the rollers using a sandwich of three strips of paper and then to fine-tune the setting using a sandwich of two strips of paper and a roller-setting gauge.

Setting Form Roller to Plate

To set the form roller to the plate, follow the same procedure described above, but position the form roller over the plate. Form rollers should be set slightly heavier to the oscillator than to the plate so that they are driven by the oscillators rather than by the plate.

Final checking of settings can be done using the **picture,** or **ink stripe, method,** which is an inked impression of the roller setting:

1. Ink up the rollers.
2. Pack the plate to printing height, gum it, dry it, and move it under the form roller to be tested.
3. Carefully lower the rollers to the plate, making an ink transfer.
4. Lift the rollers and turn the cylinder until the printed stripes are visible.

The manufacturers of newer presses usually provide recommendations regarding the appropriate width of the stripes. The required width of the stripe should be stated in the operator's manual. If not, a rough rule of thumb is to allow 1⁄16 in. (1.6 mm) of stripe for every 1 in. (25.4 mm) of diameter. For example, a 4-in. (101.6-mm) diameter roller should produce a stripe on the plate about 1⁄4 in. (6.3 mm) wide. The "feel" resulting from the strip pull should be referenced to the stripe width as a means of solving roller-setting problems later.

The stripe should be as even as possible in width throughout its length. If the stripe is uneven, the press operator should make the necessary adjustments. Depending upon the age and condition of the form rollers, width may vary. A stripe that is fat at the ends may mean that the roller ends are swollen. A stripe that is fat in the middle may indicate shrunken roller ends or, more likely, excessive form-roller-to-oscillator settings. In circumstances where the inking system has deteriorated, a compromise setting will have to be made.

Roller stripes

Ink band swollen at ends: Setting roller too tightly against the oscillator causes rubber to break loose from the roller shaft. This allows solvent to swell rubber at the roller ends. Grind rollers or replace.

Too heavy at one end, too light at the other end: Uneven setting. Reset rollers to obtain uniform band.

Heavy in the center, light at the ends: Roller bowed or worn at ends. Caused by form roller being set too tightly against the oscillator. Correct by resetting rollers. Regrind or replace rollers if it is no longer possible to obtain the desired setting.

Light areas in ink band: Indicates improper grinding or manufacture of roller. Regrind or replace.

Ideal setting: Uniform, parallel bands.

The settings between form roller and oscillator can be rechecked at this time:

1. Run the press for several seconds with the form rollers off the plate.
2. Stop and allow the press to stand for about 15–20 sec. Then inch the press, just moving the cylinders 2–3 in. (50–75 mm).

Stripes on the plate from the form roller

Notice the unevenness of the stripes, indicating that both form rollers must be adjusted.

Press operator checking the width of a stripe on the plate using a roller stripe gauge

An impression of the form roller at rest against the oscillator will be seen on the oscillator roller. This impression should be inspected with the same criteria as a stripe to the plate, i.e., even and about the same width. The stripe on the oscillator should be slightly wider than the stripe on the plate to ensure that the form roller is set slightly harder to the oscillator and to ensure that the form roller is being driven by the oscillator rather than by the plate. If the form roller is not in contact with the plate, the form roller will produce a stripe on the oscillator without any influence of the plate. However, if the form roller is in contact with the plate, a bowed stripe on the plate will produce a stripe on the oscillator that is narrow in the middle and wide at the ends.

The picture, or stripe, test for roller settings can be repeated for all form rollers by removing the distributor rollers for clear viewing of the inner ink form rollers.

Many press operators repeat the strip method of roller setting as a final check of roller setting after performing the stripe test.

Many press operators also gauge the form-roller-to-plate setting by the degree of bounce that they can see or feel at the roller ends when the rollers cross the plate cylinder gap while the press is printing. It is risky to rely solely on this method even with a great deal of experience and a thorough knowledge of the machine's behavior. Some of the things that can affect the bounce are roller durometer; shock transmitted from the other side of the roller; play and wear in roller brackets, bearings, and linkages; and the presence or absence of a plate cylinder lead-on ramp. In short, it is better to set the form rollers as directed and use bounce as a gauge for testing accuracy or mechanical deterioration in the system.

In addition to bounce, **endplay,** the undesirable lateral movement due to poor fit between roller shaft and roller bracket, should be monitored. Endplay occurs as the oscillators change direction, usually as the plate cylinder gap passes beneath the rollers. As they change direction, the oscillators will move the form rollers sideways if there is play between the roller shaft and bearing or bracket. A very slight amount of endplay is acceptable. However, if the movement is more than about 1⁄64 in. (roughly 0.4 mm), it should be reduced; otherwise it will increase as the assembly wears, and in severe cases can cause slurring, excessive plate wear, and roller streaking. Some presses have a mechanical adjustment to reduce the amount of endplay. If no adjustment is available, shims can be used, but follow the directions in the press operator's manual for the proper procedure. The endplay must never be reduced so much as to strain the assembly or cause rapid wear, roller drag, or roller hangup that prevents the roller from being lowered properly.

Excessive endplay can also be caused by bearing-related problems. If the entire roller body moves, the cause is probably due to poor fit between the bearing and the journal. If the bearing is locked in place and the journal moves back and forth in the bearing, the roller should be removed from the press because the bearing is indexing, which can damage the roller shaft.

Mechanical action that occurs at the roller nip. Perhaps even more important than roller durometer (which is discussed later in this chapter) is the mechanical action that occurs at the nip (transfer point) between a resilient roller (e.g., form roller) and a metal roller (e.g., oscillator). At the nip between a resilient roller and a metal roller, the surface of the resilient roller is no longer convex (i.e., cylindrical). The portion of the roller in contact with the metal roller is, in fact, concave because of the pressure exerted on it by the metal roller. In addition, the surface of the resilient roller bulges out on both sides of the nip. The convex surface and the bulges all have different radii. This is helpful to the press operator because a number of radii changes are needed to properly separate and move the ink by shearing it into an ever-thinner ink film at each stripe through the inking system.

Having the proper stripe (shear) width is very important when it comes to feeding ink through the inking system. The work ratio must not be excessive. The higher the work ratio, the harder it is to move ink and water. A high work ratio creates a dam at the nip—the reason that ink or water has to be overfed.

Work ratio

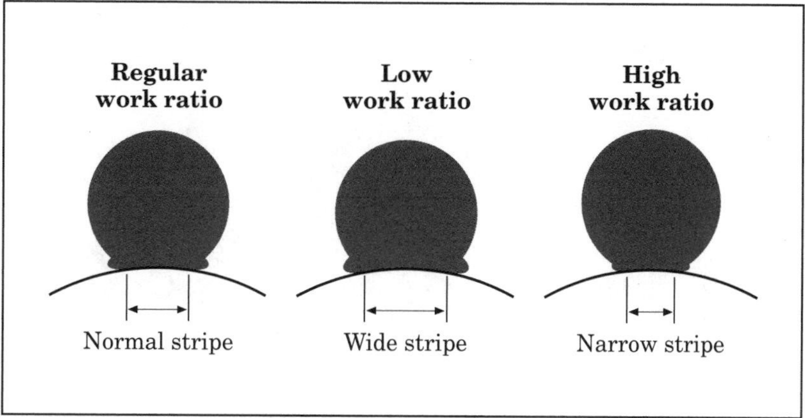

The work ratio is the pressure (in pounds/sq.in.) divided by the width of the stripe:

$$\text{Work Ratio} = \frac{\text{Pressure}}{\text{Width}}$$

The pressure is determined by dividing the load (in pounds) on each journal by the area occupied by the stripe (i.e, the width of the stripe multiplied by the length of the roller).

$$\text{Pressure} = \frac{\text{Total Load}}{\text{Width} \times \text{Length}}$$

Determining the work ration on a resilient roller

Here is a sample problem to help clarify the concept of work ratio. If the load on each journal is 12 lb. (5.44 kg), the width of the strip is 0.156 in. (4 mm), and the length of the roller is 40 in. (1,016 mm), what is the work ratio?

$$\text{Pressure} = \frac{\text{Total Load}}{\text{Width} \times \text{Length}} = \frac{2 \times 12}{0.156 \times 40} = 3.84 \text{ lb./sq.in.}$$

$$\text{Work Ratio} = \frac{\text{Pressure}}{\text{Width}} = \frac{3.84}{0.156} = 24.6$$

In this example, the work ratio would be 24.6.

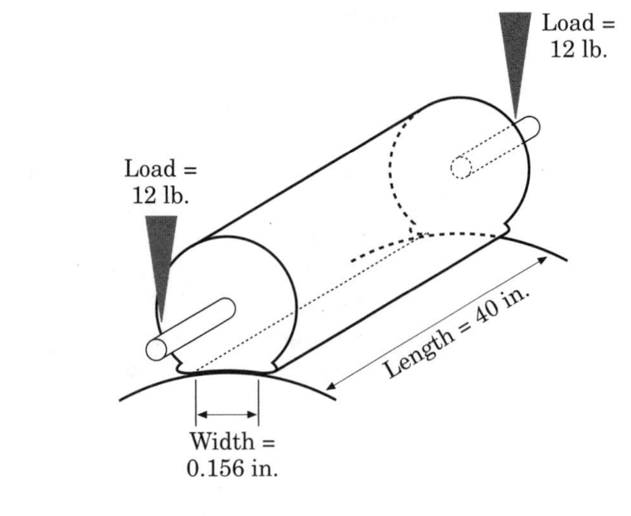

Setting the Ductor Roller

Since the resilient ductor roller carries the entire flow of ink from the fountain, it must be carefully checked for surface uniformity and proper parallelism. On most presses, the ink ductor roller must also be set in respect to both the ink fountain roller and the receiving oscillator. On a few presses, this roller is only adjusted in one direction—either to the ink fountain roller or the receiving oscillator. Its movement is controlled by springs or cams. Use the following procedure to set the ductor roller:

1. Make sure that the ink system is clean.
2. Manually engage the ink feed mechanism.
3. Inch the press until the ductor roller has fully completed its stroke to the roller against which it is to be set—either the fountain roller or the receiving oscillator.

4. Locate the adjustments and determine which way to turn them. The operator's manual usually contains this information and sometimes illustrates the settings.
5. Assemble the tools needed to make adjustments.
6. If you are using the **three-strip method** of roller setting, cut nine strips of 0.004-in. (0.1-mm) packing paper, three about 12×1 in. (300×25 mm) and the other six about 12×2 in. (300×50 mm). If you are using the **folded-strip method,** cut six strips of 0.004-in. (0.1-mm) packing paper, three about 12×1 in. (300×25 mm) and the other three about 24×2 in. (600×50 mm).
7. If you are using the **three-strip method,** assemble the strips into three sandwiches: each 12×1-in. strip is placed between two 12×2-in. strips. If you are using the **folded-strip method,** assemble the strips into three sandwiches: fold each of the 24×2-in. strips in half lengthwise, and insert a 12×1-in. strip inside it.
8. Insert a sandwich near each end of the ductor roller and in the middle of the ductor roller. Jog the strips into the nip between the ductor roller and the fountain roller or receiving oscillator.
9. Adjust the distance between the ductor roller and the fountain roller or receiving oscillator until the strips are gripped firmly and evenly. Remember that adjusting one side of the press will affect the setting on the other side. Make sure that the spring-controlled setting in the reverse direction still results in proper ducting.
10. Using only one hand, pull the inner (center) strip from the sandwich on one side of the press. The inner strip should pull out easily; it should not have to be "started." With the same hand, pull the inner strip from the sandwich in the center of the press, and finally pull the inner strip from the remaining sandwich at the other side of the press. **Note:** Make sure to pull the inner strip straight from the point of contact, not at an angle.
11. Determine if the amount of resistance (drag) is the same from one side of the press to the other. If drag is unequal, make the necessary adjustments. Reinsert the paper sandwiches, and retest the pressure.
12. Inch the press until the ductor roller completes its stroke in the opposite direction to ensure proper functioning.
13. Fine-tune pressures by using a sandwich of two strips of paper and a roller-setting gauge, instead of a sandwich of three strips of paper.

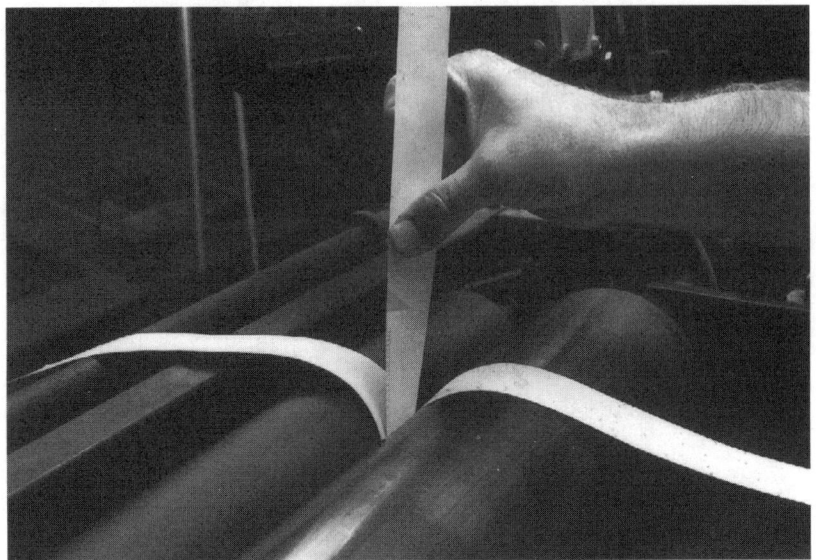

Press operator using the sandwich method to set the ductor roller to the fountain roller

As a final means of checking the setting of the ductor roller, ink up the press, make an inked impression of the ductor against either the fountain roller or the receiving oscillator, and check the resulting ink stripe for evenness.

Operation

The mechanical operation of the inking system is relatively straightforward. Most of the skill required lies in the setting of the rollers and the fountain.

On most presses, the automatic raising or lowering of the form rollers and the engaging or disengaging of ink feed can be manually overridden. This allows the plate to be rolled up without applying pressure.

The amount of roller oscillation can be adjusted on some presses, though in normal commercial printing this adjustment would be related to a specific problem.

The setting of the ink fountain is dictated by the demands of the plate. However, there are some basic fountain setting considerations. Care should be taken when changing the blade from a relaxed position (e.g., after removing, cleaning, and replacing the blade or fountain keys for maintenance following instructions in the press operator's manual or after a job with particularly heavy ink coverage) to a running position. The blade should be reset gradually, starting at the center of the fountain and moving to the outside edges. This method allows the blade to rise gradually on all the keys and avoids the distortion that would occur if setting started at one end and moved to the other.

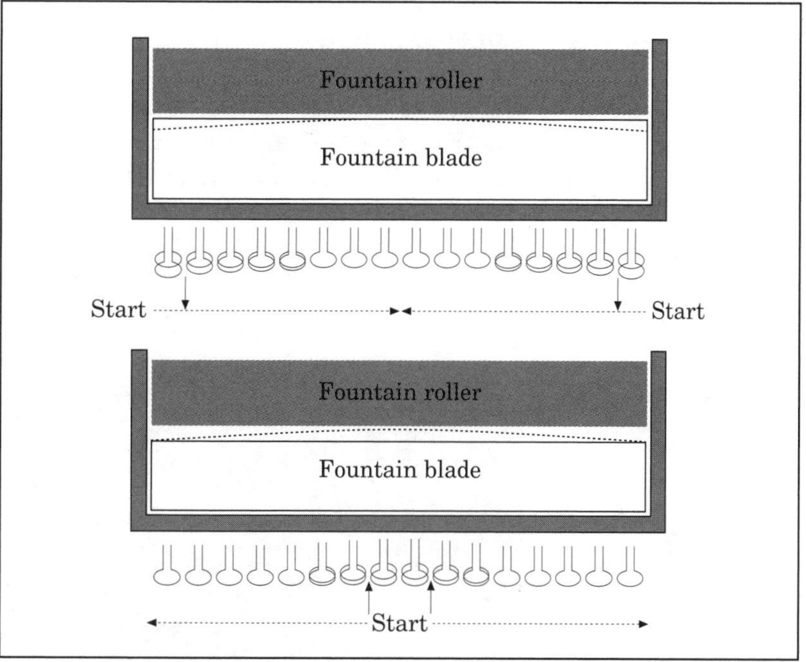

Setting the fountain blade of the inking system

To open fountain keys, start at the ends and work toward the center. To close fountain keys, start at the center and work toward the ends.

As previously mentioned, the amount of ink running through the press is controlled in two ways. Across the press (laterally), it is controlled by the fountain keys; this setting reflects plate demands. The overall ink feed may be increased or decreased by varying the distance that the fountain roller rotates (sweeps) before being contacted by the ductor or by varying the length of time that the ductor roller contacts (dwells) against the fountain roller. During press makeready, it is necessary to establish a basic fountain setting from which the running setting can be fine-tuned. The accuracy of this basic setting depends heavily on the press operator's experience. The important point is the overall ink feed. In general terms, it is desirable to have a long sweep of ink feed to the ductor roller with a corresponding thin film of ink on the fountain roller. This relationship allows sensitive response to slight adjustments of both fountain key and ink feed. For example, if there were twenty points of adjustment on the ink feed and the form to be printed was of moderate coverage, it would be advisable to set the ink feed at ten to twelve points and adjust the fountain keys to correspond with this sweep.

During that portion of the makeready devoted to establishing color on the run, the sweep should be kept as constant as possible, with the fountain keys used to establish color. When a job is being printed, subtle increases or decreases of color can be achieved by raising or lowering the ink feed by one point. If the fountain sweep is set at four points instead of ten, a decrease of one point theoretically reduces the ink feed by 25%, which means that fine control of color on the press has been lost. In short, avoid extremes in one setting by increasing or decreasing the other.

Press operator adjusting inking levels across a press sheet by using the controls provided by a remote control press console

Inking System Problems

Originally, inking systems were driven by the cylinder drive gears. When the gears became worn and noisy, they contributed to gear streaks. Any jarring, bumping, or interruption of the smooth inking of the plate is apt to cause a streak. To reduce this possibility, ink drives are now made independent of cylinder driving gears.

Roller Streaks

Most roller streaks are caused by glazed rollers or by rollers that are set too close to the plate or too far from the oscillators. A roller that bumps noticeably at the gap is set too hard.

In some cases, the form rollers bow so much in the center (because of excessive pressure to the oscillator) or are so out-of-round that they will not touch the plate without a bump. Excessive total indicated runout (TIR) verifies the existence of an out-of-round form roller.

Glazed Rollers

Several serious problems can originate from glazed rollers. **Glaze** is a combination of embedded ink pigment, dried ink vehicle, gum from the fountain solution, paper coating, and paper dust that accumulates on the surface of a resilient roller, such as a form roller. It is generally a result of the

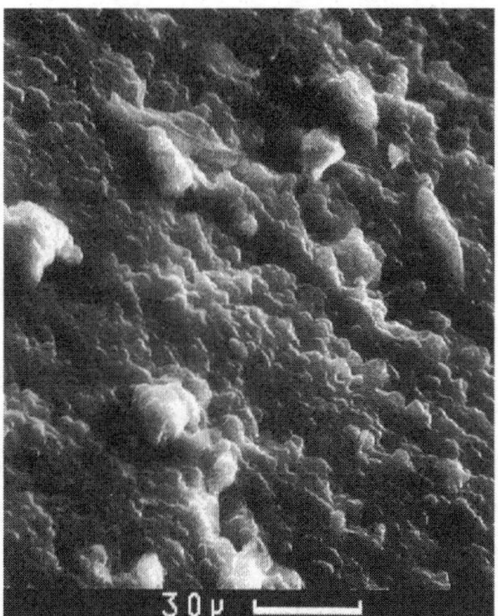

Photomicrographs of the surface of a new roller *(left)* and a glazed roller *(right)* *Courtesy Böttcher America Corp.*

unavoidable effects of press chemistry compounded by poor cleaning. Glazing seriously reduces the efficiency of the inking system. Glazed rollers cannot adequately transfer ink from the oscillator or intermediate rollers. This inability to feed ink properly increases starvation problems such as ghosting, roll-out (where there is a distinct drop in ink density as the rollers complete their first revolution over the plate), and drop-off (where there is a gradual loss of density from gripper to back edge of the sheet). A glazed inking roller actually moves water easier than it moves ink.

If the press has any tendency to streak, streaking will definitely show up with glazed rollers because they lack traction against both the printing plate and oscillator. Skidding also occurs; it not only slurs the print but wears the plate as well.

How glazing occurs. The surface of a new roller is composed, not of pores, but of mountain-like protrusions, due to the rubber stretching and snapping off at various lengths around the edge of the grinding wheel. These protrusions, which have a velvet-like feel, function in a manner similar to the bristles of a paint brush. As long as the bristles of the paint brush remain flexible, they are able to provide even paint coverage. The same holds true with the protrusions on the surface of the roller. As long as they remain flexible, they are able to transfer an even, consistent layer of ink to the printing plate. The protrusions also help to work a uniform emulsion of water and ink down through the inking system.

The mountain-like protrusions of a new roller are typically about 500 microns (0.02 in., 0.5 mm) long, which is about five times the depth of the ink film on the plate. However, as the roller receives use, ink pigment, dried ink vehicle, paper coating, paper dust, and dried gum from the fountain will become embedded in the spaces between the protrusions, forming glaze. Consequently, as the thickness of the glaze increases, the protrusions will become less flexible, and printing problems will become noticeable if the glaze is not removed periodically.

Cleaning glazed rollers. When rollers are only slightly glazed, their condition can be improved by scrubbing them with roller-compatible solvent, hot water, and a commercial paste cleaner and using a blanket and roller pad. Deglazing should reduce the hardness of the roller by about 3–4 durometer units. If the hardness does not decrease, the roller should be reground or replaced. Regrinding should be performed by a roller manufacturer according to press specifications.

Improper cleaning of the rollers results from poor roller settings, a worn washup blade, or inadequate solvents. If the rollers are not contacting each other properly, dissolved inks will not transfer properly up the roller system to the washup blade. A worn washup blade should not be used. The moderate cost of replacing these blades can be lost many times over in long washup times, increased glaze and roller deterioration, and the eventual scoring of or damage to the adjacent oscillator due to the use of excessive blade pressure.

A frequent cause of glazing is an improperly formulated solvent. As a cost-saving measure, a general purpose industrial solvent may be used and may appear to do the job properly. However, the removal of ink from the system is not enough. There are several other substances that must be removed from the rollers, e.g., paper coating, ink additive compounds, and emulsified fountain solution components, especially gum. These are often left behind by common solvents, and they contribute to glaze. Washup solutions that are specially formulated for lithographic rollers are recommended. Several of these are two-step solutions; the first should be a water-miscible solvent. The extra cost of these solutions is quickly recovered in faster washup times, the use of less solvent, and easier color changes. If low-grade solvents are used, a good detergent-type glaze-removing solvent should be applied to the rollers once or twice a week.

Along with the proper solvents, the washup technique is important:

1. Gum and dry the plate to protect it against stray drips.
2. Turn the press on and run it at medium speed, usually about 6,000–7,000 i.p.h. on newer presses.
3. Thoroughly wet the rollers away from the washup blade with solvent to soften the ink.
4. Allow the press to idle for a couple of minutes, and then gently engage the washup blade to the oscillator roller, increasing pressure until contact is achieved.
5. Add solvent to one side of the ink system at a time, being careful not to allow the washup blade on the other side to become too dry. In this way, roller skidding, drips, and excessive buildup of ink at roller ends are avoided.
6. Apply solvent with a squirt bottle to various points of the roller system away from the washup blade. To avoid waste and drips, do not apply more solvent than can be held at the nips of the rollers.
7. Continue applying solvent periodically until the fluid running into the drip tray appears clear, and the rollers are clean. **Note:** Never run a finger or a rag across the edge of the washup blade while it is working.
8. Apply a water-miscible solution to the rollers as a final flushing of the rollers.
9. When the rollers are satisfactorily clean, release the washup blade while the press is still operating. Occasionally, if the washup blade is released on the run, a buildup of ink behind the blade will run back into the rollers, meaning that they have to be washed again.
10. To evaluate the thoroughness of the washup, stop the press, put the safety on, and then rub cheesecloth across the rollers. Any residue remaining on the rollers will be easily seen on the cheesecloth.

Fountain Blade Problems

The ink fountain blade can also cause problems. The blade must be removed and cleaned occasionally. Dried ink accumulates on the underside of the blade, preventing the ink fountain keys from touching the blade.

When the blade gets wavy or worn, color control becomes very difficult and the fountain responds inaccurately. Blades become wavy when fountain keys are screwed in too tightly. The blade's edge wears unevenly and becomes scalloped, which is particularly evident at the extreme corners. Sometimes, the fountain roller becomes scored.

It is not necessary to jam the keys up hard to stop the flow of ink at a given point. They need only be tightened until a thin film of ink is on the fountain roller. Do not squeeze the ends of the duct, where there is no printing, until the duct roller is clean. Such a practice causes the blade to wear or the fountain to leak at the corners.

Sometimes the keys are too tight to start with, or they become tight through lack of maintenance.

Roller Problems

The ductor roller is often overlooked as a source of trouble. In some ways this is the most important roller in the inking system because it is the first roller to carry ink.

If the ductor roller has a low spot in it, or if it is out of round or out of adjustment, uniform inking is impossible. This roller must be free turning (to a certain point), carefully adjusted, and true in every respect.

When uneven printing occurs and nothing else seems to correct it, the rollers in the inking system should be checked using the "picture" method.

On older presses that use steel oscillators, **roller stripping** is a common problem. It occurs when the rollers lose their affinity for ink and fail to carry it. Roller stripping is caused by the desensitizing agents in the dampening solution—the gum-acid combination primarily—that help the nonimage areas to refuse to take ink. If stripping occurs, the gum and acid content of the dampening solution should be reduced. Roller curing and the calcium carbonate in alkaline paper has also been known to cause stripping. Washing up the rollers and applying copperizing solution helps temporarily. If practical, it would be advisable to have the roller electroplated with copper.

A roller that is stripping

The surface of metal rollers on most new presses have a "Rilsan" (nylon 11) plastic coating that helps to reduce roller stripping.

Maintenance

Mechanically, the inking system gives very little trouble if properly maintained. It must be lubricated properly to prevent excessive wear in bearings and linkages. The oscillation mechanisms work particularly hard and, therefore, should be lubricated and examined for wear frequently. All inker drive components that are not pressure-lubricated should be cleaned and lubricated regularly.

Roller Removal and Replacement

When rollers are removed from the press, their ends should never be "thumped" on the floor. Such a practice could bend the roller shaft or cause the ends of the roller shaft to flare out, preventing the easy removal of bearings or damaging the bearings. When installing new bearings with an interference fit, the bearings should be pressed onto the roller shaft with an arbor press, making sure that pressure is only applied to the inner ring with the interference fit. Rollers should be placed on a vertical rack when removed from the press and stored for a long period.

Even if the best washup solutions are being used, the rollers should be removed once in a while to remove ink cuffs

An ink cuff at the end of a roller

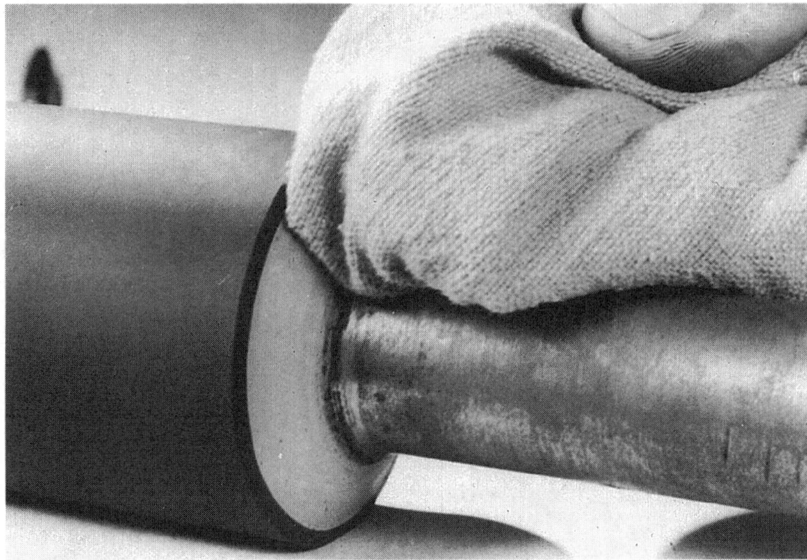
The ends of a roller being cleaned to prevent the buildup of dried ink

(a buildup of ink at roller ends), to inspect for replacement, to lubricate or replace bearings, etc.

The rollers in the inking system should be replaced as a unit for greatest color consistency. The performance of a set of rollers will be no better than the performance of the roller in the worst condition.

New rollers should be inspected upon receipt. Items to check are the roller's trueness, its durometer, its diameter (because roller diameter must be very precise), its length, and the quality of its surface. When measuring a roller's durometer, remember to use the weight with the durometer gauge; otherwise, the reading will be 5–8 points too high. A cast roller sometimes has an imperfect surface due to the casting process. A roller having any defect should be returned to the manufacturer.

Ideally, the rollers used in the inking system should be perfectly round. Total indicated runout is used to determine any variation from perfect roundness. **Total indicated runout** (TIR) is a measure of the difference in the lengths of the radius from the centerline of a roller to its surface. Roller manufacturers often use a laser to measure TIR, and only those rollers that are within accepted tolerances are shipped to customers. The standard manufacturing tolerance for TIR is 0.005 in. (0.127 mm). If an old roller becomes out-of-round (e.g., if it has a TIR significantly greater than 0.005 in.), it should be replaced or reground by the roller manufacturer. The stripe method of roller setting provides a good indication of roller roundness. After the roller is adjusted so that the inked stripe is even along the length of the roller, three or more ink stripes are made to check for roller roundness. The press operator compares the widths of the stripes. If the stripe widths are unequal, the roller is out-of-round.

Roller Bearings

Some bearings must have an **interference fit,** which means that the inside of the bearing race is smaller than the diameter of the roller's **journal.** Interference fit is typically 0.0005 in. (0.013 mm). The press operator should never use emery cloth on the journals except to remove burrs on the very end of the journal. Only a few rubs with emory cloth will remove the interference fit of 0.0005 in. If the diameter of the shaft is too large, the balls will not turn freely. If the shaft is 0.001 in. (0.025 mm) too small, the bearing race will rotate 360° on the journal for each 1,000 revolutions of the roller.

Bearings that require an interference fit should never be reused. They can only be removed by pulling on the seals and twisting the rows that carry the balls. For any bearing to be reused, it must be pulled against the race with the interference fit. This is never possible on printing rollers with either shafts or housings. The best tool for removing bearings is the arbor press, but some form of bearing puller is often used in the field.

Needle bearings can be reused because they slide off the race, which itself is in interference fit to the working journal. Bearings that are slip-fit and anchored to the shaft by allen screws, or some other tightening device, can be reused because they can be loosened before being removed from the working journals.

New bearings should always be mounted on a journal using an arbor press; they should never be pounded onto the journal. When mounting bearings, make sure that pressure is applied only to the ring with the interference fit.

Roller Storage

Spare rollers should be stored properly. The surface of a roller is sensitive to light and hardens due to the oxidation caused by the light. Ideally, rollers should be stored in a cool, dark area, standing on end in racks, and away from sources of heat and from electric motors.

Many manufacturers supply new rollers with a special paper wrapper. When resilient rollers are stored, they should be covered with this paper wrapper, in order to minimize oxidation that may occur in storage.

Ideally, rollers should be stored vertically. If stored for long periods of time, vertically stored rollers should be turned end for end periodically.

There is a danger in storing rollers on racks horizontally for long periods. Longer rollers, particularly, can become **eccentric,** or out-of-round, because the roller's composition covering flows downward. No adjustments can permit an eccentric roller to perform efficiently on press. If the rollers must be stored horizontally, each one should be given a quarter turn periodically, at least once a month.

Roller Hardness

Roller hardening is caused by several factors. **Glaze** is the most common cause, but such things as fluorescent light, sunlight, heat, and solvents that draw plasticizers from the roller compound also cause roller hardening and shrinking.

The instrument that measures the hardness of roller compounds is an ASTM **type-A durometer.** Specifically, the durometer measures the compound's resistance to a spring-loaded probe in units indicated on a dial or scale. On a scale of 0–100, 100 indicates an inflexible surface such as cast iron. (The term "durometer" also refers to the readings taken with the instrument.) According to a note in the ASTM standard for measuring durometer, "better reproducibility may be obtained using either a mass centered on the axis of the indentor." The recommended mass for a Type A durometer used by press operators is 1 kg; the weight fits in the hole at the top of the durometer.

The hardness specifications of a newly manufactured form roller varies considerably—depending on where the roller will be used and on how the roller was made. For example, a form roller has a slightly lower durometer reading than an ink distributing roller. Typically, a roller's durometer increases 10–15 points during its useful lifetime; this increase is due almost entirely to the buildup of glaze on the roller's surface. Beyond these hardnesses, the roller becomes less and less efficient, and it contributes increasingly to ghosting and roll-out problems—primarily due to the glaze that is present. The durometer of the roller can often be reduced by deglazing the roller. A roller can be deglazed by scrubbing it with roller-compatible solvent, hot water, and a commercial deglazing paste cleaner. If deglazing does not solve the printing problems, the roller manufacturer should be consulted.

Up to 25% of the weight of the rubber covering of a roller is plasticizer. Since plasticizer is a solvent in the ink vehicle,

Press operator screwing the 1-kg weight into the top of the durometer *Courtesy Pacific Transducer Corp.*

some of the plasticizer in the roller will be lost with each pound of ink used. In addition, plasticizer is driven off by the heat generated as the roller rotates and flexes on the printing press. As a result, the roller diameter will decrease slightly and the roller will become harder.

Using a durometer properly. Durometer use in the pressroom has several limitations. First, the durometer was designed to be used in a laboratory, not in the pressroom. Second, the ASTM standard (ASTM D-2240) specifies that the surface of the specimen being measured "shall be flat and parallel over a sufficient area to permit the presser foot to contact the specimen over an area having a radius of at least 6 mm (0.25 in.) from the indentor point. A suitable hardness determination cannot be made on a rounded, uneven, or rough surface." The ASTM standard also says to "place the specimen on a hard, horizontal surface" and to "hold the durometer in a vertical position with the point of the indentor at least 12 mm (0.5 in.) from any edge of the specimen."

However, this method is inappropriate for rollers: rollers should never be placed on a flat surface; they have no edges in the circumferential direction; and only a few rollers can be measured on press with the durometer held vertically.

The instrument manufacturer Pacific Transducer Corp. recommends the following procedure for measuring roller hardness:

1. Place the durometer against the roller at approximately a 10:00 position.
2. Slowly rotate the durometer through the vertical position until about a 2:00 position.
3. Take the durometer reading from the "lazy hand" of the durometer, which stays fixed at the highest reading obtained until the instrument is reset. The reading should be greatest when the instrument is vertical.

This method offers good repeatability, which is essential for comparing readings of roller hardness.

If the roller cannot be accessed easily on press, remove it and place it in a V-notched rack before taking any readings.

Recognizing the constraints of a working pressroom, it may not always be feasible to remove rollers to check their hardness. This does not mean that durometers should not be used; rather, the same operator using the same instrument and the same method can obtain valuable comparative readings that can reveal changes in hardness.

A supplemental test. Only when a roller is new is the durometer reading a true measure of the hardness of the roller surface. Once a roller is used on the press, it becomes glazed; at that point, the durometer is effectively measuring the hardness of the glaze, which covers the surface of the roller. The durometer reading will increase over time, not because the rubber is hardening but because the layer of glaze is becoming thicker. Therefore, in addition to measuring a roller's durometer, the press operator should also perform a finger drag test to determine if the nap moves; i.e., does the roller still have a velvety feel when the press operator moves a finger across the surface of the roller. If the nap still moves, the roller should print with uniformity. If the nap no longer moves due to a buildup of glaze, the roller should be removed and deglazed. The safe button must be engaged for this test.

The finger drag test and the durometer should be used together because they both give the press operator useful information about the roller's condition.

System Cleanliness

General cleanliness of the inking system is important. (Inking system washup is discussed in Chapter 12, "Makeready.") Ink cuffs should not be allowed to build up on the roller ends to the point where they break off during the pressrun, causing hickeys. Small-diameter rollers known as **pipe,** or **knife, rollers,** help to keep the ink system clean by picking up ink skin particles, lint, etc. They should be removed and cleaned periodically.

Many presses have drip trays located underneath the ink fountain. These should be periodically removed and cleaned. Any "stalactites"—hardened ink underneath the fountain that can break off and fall into the system—should also be removed.

When rollers are removed for replacement or deglazing, the rods that connect the inker side frames should be cleaned. Roller bearings should be checked for wear or dryness. At this time, it is a good idea to clean the roller-supporting sockets and setting mechanisms with a paintbrush and solvent, and to check for freeness of operation. When you clean the sockets and setting mechanisms, keep solvent out of the bearings.

Many ink fountains have a blade assembly that can be removed easily for cleaning and replaced to the same setting as before. An adjustment for the forward positioning of the blade is also provided. If it is necessary to adjust the blade to the fountain roller, all the keys must be fully backed away from the blade. The blade should be adjusted according to manufacturer's instructions.

Fountain keys should turn smoothly and easily. If they do not, they may be damaged, insufficiently lubricated, or clogged with dry ink. Simple one-piece keys can be placed in a can of solvent and soaked, while the threads in the fountain frame are cleaned according to the press manufacturer's directions.

Some inking systems have modular fountain keys. These modular keys are complex assemblies and are best left to a mechanic for servicing. These modular keys must be replaced in the press in precisely the same position from which they were withdrawn.

Ink Agitators

A common auxiliary device attached to many inking systems is the ink agitator. Inks of certain body characteristics tend to back away from the fountain roller, which means that the press operator has to stir the ink every few minutes. An **ink agitator** is a revolving, motorized cone-shaped device that runs on a track from one end of the ink fountain to the other keeping the ink soft and flowing. It also reduces the formation of a skin on the ink in the fountain, helping to reduce hickeys. Additionally, it helps control color variation by keeping the ink conditioned.

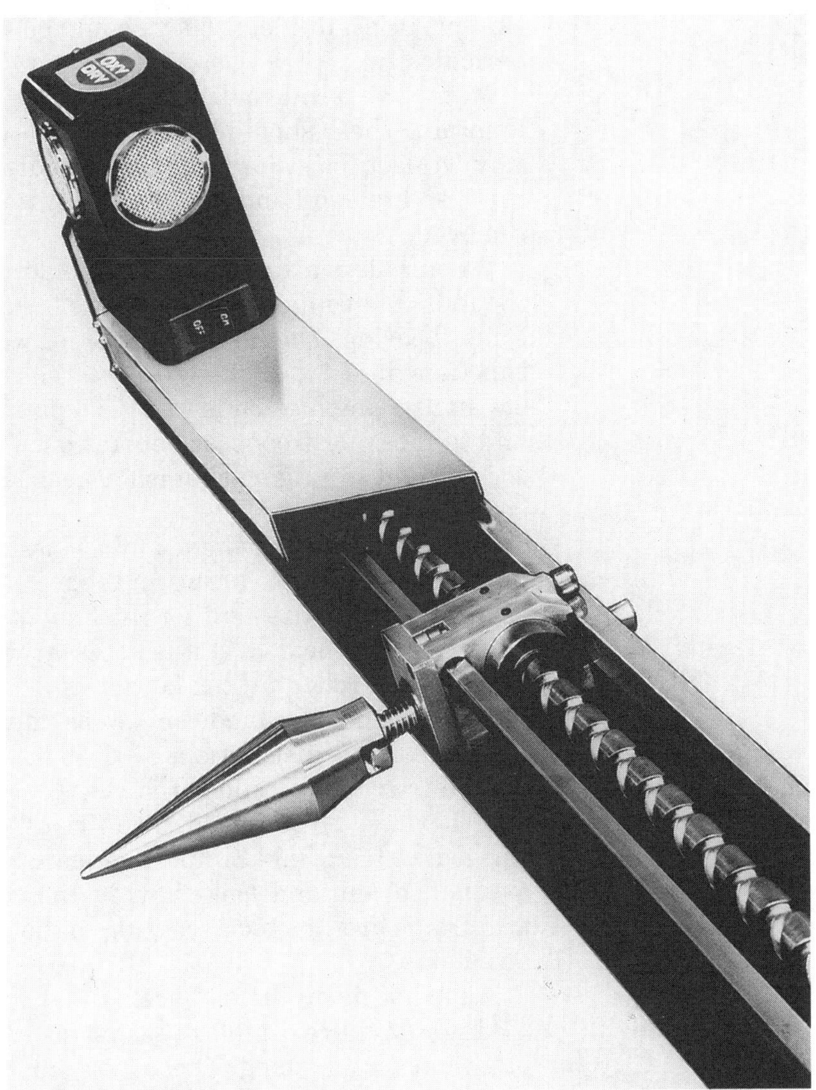

Conical ink agitator
Courtesy Oxy-Dry Corporation

Conical ink agitator

Fountain Splitters

Using a special color to highlight an image, such as a headline, is referred to as **spot-color printing.** Sometimes, two spot colors may be widely separated on a press sheet, such as blue printing on the far left side of the sheet and red printing on the far right side. In such a case, it may be possible to print both inks with a single ink fountain by using **fountain splitters.**

A fountain splitter is a vertical metal block that is inserted into the ink fountain and placed against the fountain roller. It serves the same function as the fountain cheeks—creating an ink-tight trough by contacting the fountain roller and the fountain blade. For split fountain work, a pair of fountain splitters are placed about 4 in. (101.6 mm) apart. They prevent any ink from working its way into the part of the ink fountain between them. When two colors of ink are printed using the same inking system, the lateral movement of the oscillators is reduced as much as possible. This lessens the chance that the two colors of ink will mix together as they work their way through the inking system to the form rollers. The splitters should be wider than the oscillation stroke.

Fountain splitters in an ink fountain

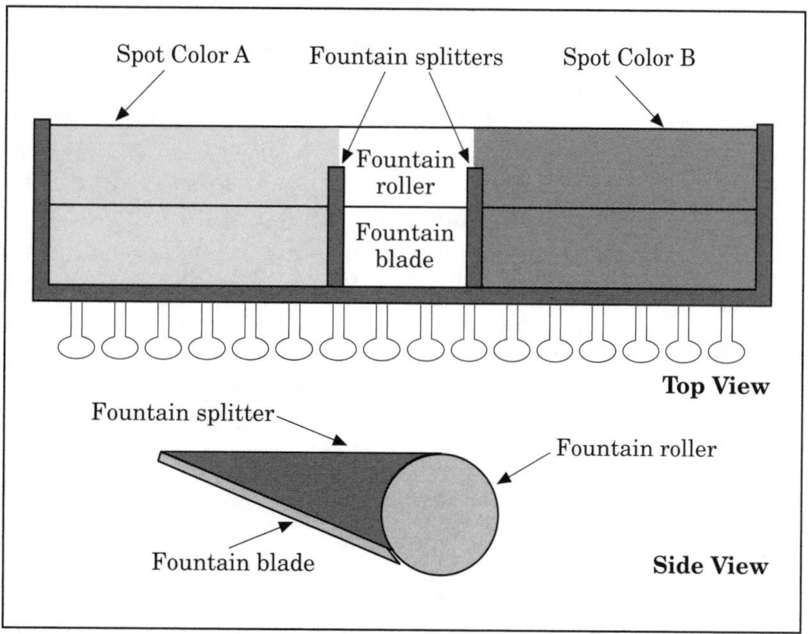

Hickey-Picking Rollers

A **hickey** is a print defect that often appears as a void of ink or as a small, sharply defined solid area surrounded by a white halo. Hickeys are caused by solid particles that stick to the plate or blanket, e.g., ink skin, a chip of roller composition, a particle of antisetoff spray powder, cutter dust, paper fibers, or paper coating. The specific cause can sometimes be determined by removing the contaminant from the inking roller, plate, or blanket with a piece of clear adhesive tape. The tape is placed on a flat surface and cut in half, permitting particle identification.

The best solution to a hickey problem is to remove the cause of the problem. However, even in the cleanest pressroom, hickeys will still appear. Mechanical devices can be used to lessen the hickey problem. For example, a special "hickey-picking" roller can be added to the inking system to help remove hickeys from the plate during printing. There are several models available, all working on a similar principle. The surface of the roller appears to be fuzzy, due to the embedding of synthetic fibers, which may be plastics, elastomers, etc. This roller picks off the hickey as it appears or hides the white ring by filling it in with ink. Its efficiency depends on periodic maintenance. Depending on the type, maintenance may include removal from the press and cleaning following the manufacturer's instructions.

Due to the fibrous nature of the hickey-picking roller's surface, it is best to install this roller as the first form roller over the plate. If that space is occupied by a combination dampening/inking form roller, the hickey-picking roller should be placed in the second or third contacting position. If it is installed in the fourth or last position over the plate, mottling could appear in solids and dense tones. Wherever the roller is installed, its settings to both the oscillator and plate should be somewhat lighter than if it were a conventional roller. In addition, the nap of the fibers depends on the position of the roller in the inking system. If the hickey-picking roller is in the first ink form roller position (the one closest to the dampening system) the roller can have coarse-nap fibers. The farther back the hickey-picking roller is, the finer napped the roller should be, so that roller patterns do not show.

Fountain Height Monitors

Available as an auxiliary device on some presses, particularly those used for folding carton work, a **fountain height monitor,** or **ink leveler,** is an ultrasonic sensing device that checks the height of ink moving over the agitator. It signals a pneumatic ink pump to pump ink into the fountain when a certain level is reached. Ink levelers eliminate manual ink replenishment and reduce the waste caused by color varia-

Ink leveler
Courtesy Baldwin Graphic Products

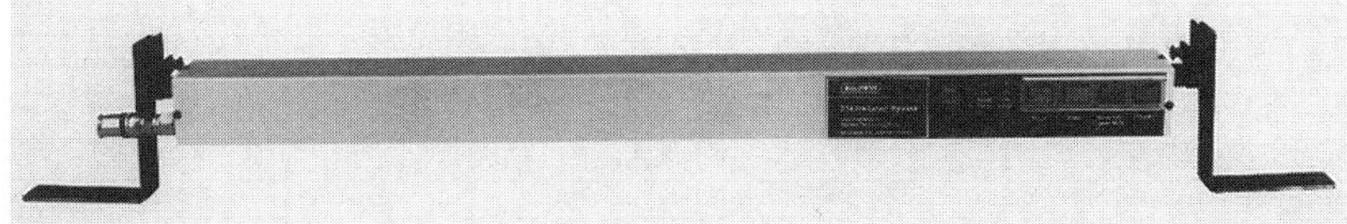

tions and print density inconsistencies. Some of them are constructed so that they can be easily moved to another printing unit if the color sequence is changed.

Air Curtin

An Air Curtin™ is an auxiliary device used with some press inking systems to remove excess moisture from the inking system. An air bar directs streams of low-pressure air against a strategically located roller to evaporate the excess water.

Air Curtin™, available from AirSystems, Inc.

Notice that the Air Curtin has been installed to remove excessive moisture on the down side of the inking system.

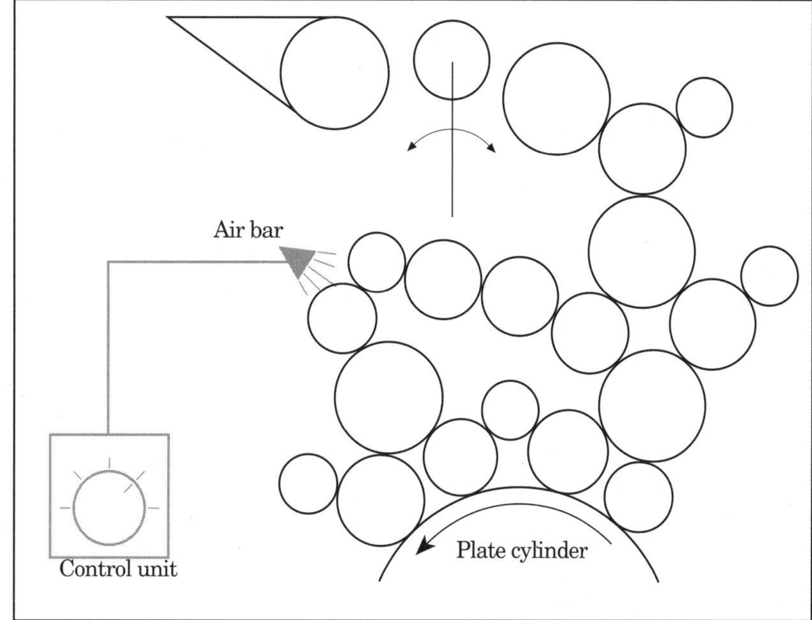

4 Dampening

The dampening system on a lithographic sheetfed press applies a water-based **dampening,** or **fountain, solution** to the printing plate before it is inked. Dampening solution keeps the nonimage areas of a plate moistened so that they will not accept ink. It is applied to the entire plate. However, the desensitized nonimage areas of the plate, which are made that way by adsorbing a thin film of gum arabic to them during platemaking, are *hydrophilic,* or water loving, while the image areas are *hydrophobic,* or water repellent. Water by itself can, in fact, be used to dampen the plate. Some sheetfed printers may opt to use it alone on a short run. However, the desensitized film wears off gradually as a plate continues to run on the press. The chemicals in the dampening solution replenish the desensitized film.

Ink, plate, press speed, paper, temperature, and relative humidity are the principal factors that influence the need for various dampening solutions. Dampening solution is applied to the printing plate in a number of ways, most of which are discussed later in this chapter.

Dampening Solution

Dampening solution is a water-based mixture specially formulated to dampen lithographic printing plates before they are contacted by the inking rollers. In concentrated form, it is commonly referred to as *fountain concentrate, fountain etch,* or just *etch.* Most fountain concentrates today contain synthetic desensitizers. Very few manufacturers still use natural Sudanese gum arabic because of its cost. The term dampening solution is used for the diluted etch.

Composition of a Dampening Solution

Dampening solution composition varies for a number of reasons. A metallic or fluorescent ink, for example, may require an alkaline dampening solution. Most dampening solutions, however, are acidic with a pH of 4.0–5.5 being typical. The dampening system itself also influences the composition of the dampening solution. For example, some dampening systems require the use of a percentage of alcohol (or alcohol substitute) due to the method of applying the solution to the printing plate. Sometimes, in a conventional dampening system, the use of such an *additive* improves print quality although its presence in the dampening solution may not be essential.

In general, a dampening solution will consist of the following ingredients:

- **Water,** with minimal impurities.
- **Acid** or **base,** depending to a large extent on the ink being used. Acids used include phosphoric acid, acid phosphate compounds, citric acid, or lactic acid.
- **Gum,** either natural (gum arabic) or synthetic, to **desensitize** nonimage areas, i.e., to make them prefer water instead of ink.
- **Corrosion inhibitors,** to prevent the dampening solution from reacting with the plate. Magnesium nitrate is sometimes used; it also acts as a scratch desensitizer and **buffer**—a substance capable of neutralizing acids and bases in solutions and thereby maintaining the acidity or alkalinity level of the solution.
- **Wetting agents,** such as isopropanol or an alcohol substitute, which decrease the surface tension of water and water-based solutions.
- **Drying stimulator,** a substance—e.g., cobalt chloride—that complements the drier in the ink. Drying stimulator is an additive that is used only if ink is not drying fast enough. Typical concentrations are 1–2 oz. of stimulator per gallon (8–16 mL per liter) of dampening solution.
- **Fungicide,** to prevent the formation of mildew and the growth of fungus and bacteria in the dampening system.
- **Antifoaming agent,** to prevent the buildup of foam. Foam can interfere with the even distribution of dampening solution on the dampening rollers.

Suppliers of dampening solutions provide a premixed (usually proprietary) one-step concentrate that contains all of the additives, except for the water and the alcohol or alcohol substitute, although some also include the alcohol substitute. Printers dilute the one-step concentrate with water, adjust its pH and conductivity (the ability, or power, to transmit or conduct an electrical charge) to acceptable levels, and then add the alcohol if needed. The manufacturer of the dampening system will indicate whether alcohol is necessary for the successful operation of the dampening system. Under closely controlled conditions, it is possible to operate dampening systems with no isopropyl alcohol using either a one-step solution or a two-step system of etch and alcohol substitute, but many printers prefer to use 2–5% isopropyl alcohol and use the alcohol substitute as an extender.

One-step dampening solution concentrates already contain a natural or synthetic gum. Two-step concentrates require the addition of gum. This extra step is an inconvenience, but it permits the press operator to control the gum/acid ratio. The supplier of the concentrate usually indicates the amount of gum to be added. The addition of 0.5–1.0 oz. of gum per gallon of dampening solution (4–8 mL per liter) is common.

Water. Local water conditions affect the dampening solution. **Hard water** requires a stronger acid than does **soft water.** Water is described as hard or soft in relationship to the total concentration of calcium and magnesium ions it contains. Hard water may require conditioning. Ion-exchange systems can be used to soften or demineralize the water.

Approximate water hardness can be determined by multiplying the total dissolved solids (TDS) in parts per million (ppm) by 1.5 to get the conductivity in micromhos per centimeter (μmhos/cm). *Conductivity,* as defined earlier, is the ability, or power, to transmit, or conduct, an electrical charge. It is determined by the number of ions present as a result of minerals or TDS in the water. The higher the concentration of ions, the higher the conductivity and usually the harder the water. Water with a hardness greater than 220 ppm (or conductivity greater than 330 μmhos/cm) is considered very hard. If it has a conductivity higher than about 300, purification is usually recommended. Very soft waters (those with very low conductivity) are not known to cause problems with lithographic dampening solutions. Local water authorities can provide the hardness figure for the water in their area.

Although the hardness of raw water is sufficient to change the pH of dampening solution by one to three units, the consistency of the raw water hardness is more important than the actual hardness. Manufacturers can prepare dampening solution concentrates to work with raw water of any hardness, but they can not accommodate water that varies in hardness. Some printers mix purified water with raw water to produce process water of constant and known hardness.

Sometimes, it is desirable to have nearly pure water—water with most of the dissolved solids removed. Three ways to accomplish this are distillation, deionization or demineralization, and reverse osmosis. Distillation and reverse osmosis are the two methods discussed in the following paragraphs.

Distillation can be performed by boiling ordinary tap water in a water still. The condensate from industrial boilers also yields distilled water. The steam that rises from the boiling water is almost free of the mineral and organic matter that is present in tap water. This steam is fed through condenser coils where it is cooled and converted back into a liquid called distilled water.

One might assume that distilled water would be free of all mineral matter because the mineral matter is not volatile. A small amount of mineral matter, however, is carried over in small droplets in the steam, and a tiny amount of the container, metal or glass, dissolves in the water. If the water initially contained about 200 ppm of dissolved solids, the distilled water will often contain 10 to 20 ppm, a level that is suitable for most applications. If even purer water is required, the distilled water can be distilled again and sometimes a third time. Energy costs are high for this process except when steam from an industrial boiler is available.

Reverse osmosis can remove most of the dissolved solids at a cost less than that of producing distilled water. Reverse osmosis not only removes most of the positive and negative ions in the initial water but also removes un-ionized dissolved solids (such as sugar), suspended matter, and even bacteria. Sometimes the resulting water is referred to as "RO water."

To understand this process, it is necessary first to understand osmosis. When two aqueous solutions of different concentrations are separated by a semipermeable membrane, water passes through the membrane from the weaker solution to the stronger solution. Reverse osmosis is the opposite of osmosis. Applying pressure to the more concentrated solution forces water through the semipermeable membrane into the more dilute solution. The membrane allows water to pass through, but only a small amount of materials dissolved in the water pass through. For water purification, the "more concentrated solution" is the initial

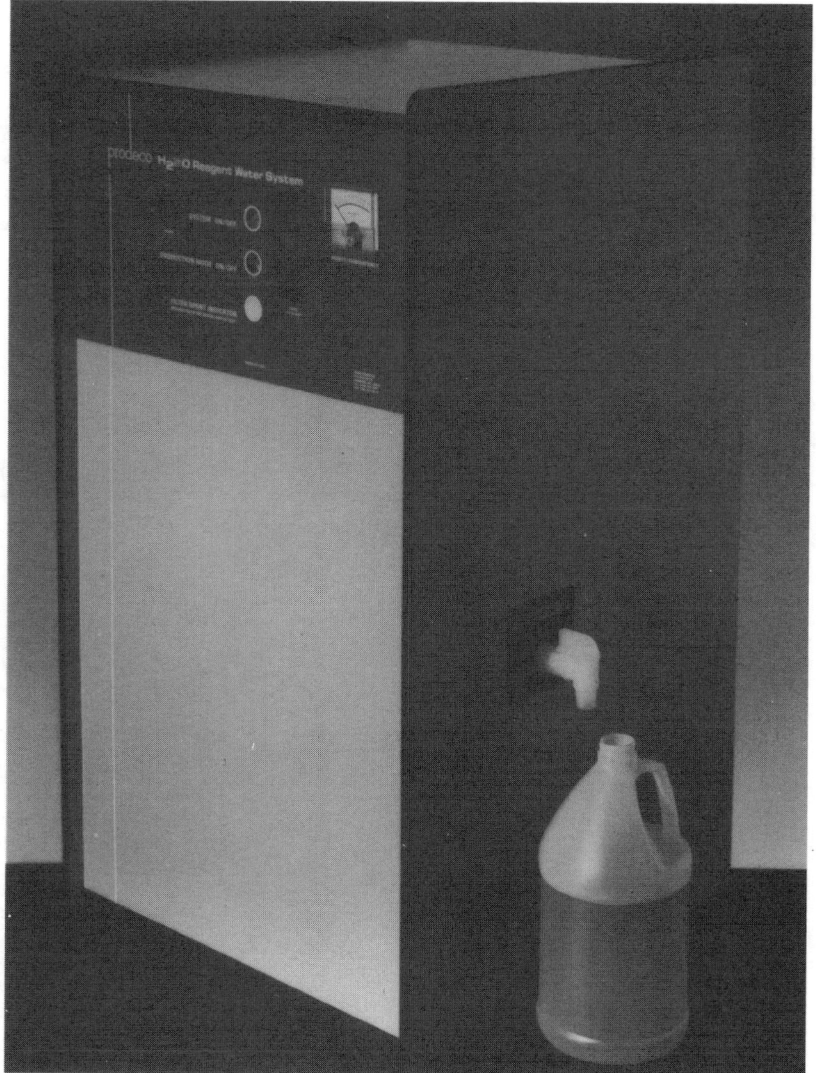

The mid-size H_2lithO water refining system for pressrooms
Courtesy Prodeco

tap water. The liquid that is forced through the membrane is water that contains only a very small amount of dissolved solids. Some positive or negative ions are held back better than others. Approximately 90% to 95% of dissolved solids are held back with an applied pressure of 50 lb./sq. in. (35 g/m^2 or 3.4 atmospheres). As the pressure is increased above 50 lb./sq. in., the purity of the water increases since more dissolved solids are rejected by the membrane.

The membrane is such a good filter that water containing suspended matter must first be passed through a regular filter, in order to prevent clogging the semipermeable membrane. With a hard-scale-forming water supply, it may be necessary to pretreat the water using a water softener or deionization unit.

The only energy required with reverse osmosis is that needed to produce the necessary pressure. Because it is a continuous process, storage capacity is required for the treated water, and another pump is often needed to pump the stored water to its place of use. The semipermeable membranes must be replaced about every two years.

Obtaining a reasonable amount of purified water requires a large semipermeable membrane area. One company uses special cellulose acetate tubing for the membrane, wrapping it into a spiral.

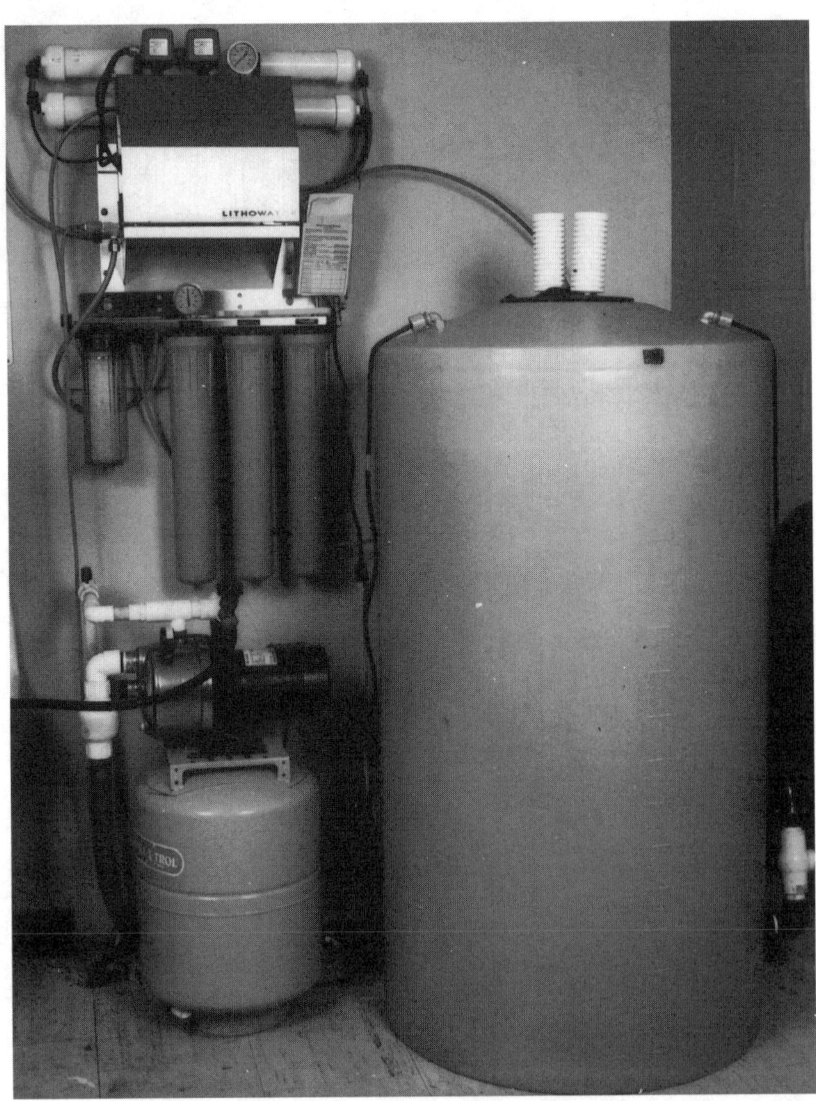

LithoWater™ system
Courtesy Procam Controls, Inc.

Since the TDS removed by reverse osmosis at any given pressure are a matter of percentage, the quality of the purified water depends on the amount of dissolved solids in the initial water supply (and the applied pressure). If the water is not high in TDS initially, the effluent from a reverse osmosis unit is purer. For example, a water supply in one particular town contains 1,440 ppm of dissolved solids; reverse osmosis reduces this to 228. In another town, water containing 1,150 ppm is reduced to 71.

Surface tension. Fast plate wetting and the ability to form thin water films are two critical requirements for lithographic dampening solution. These characteristics are largely determined by the surface tension of the solution. Surface tension can be compared to a thin elastic field stretched over a liquid's surface.

Pure water has a surface tension of 72 dynes/cm. In dampening solution, an alcohol concentration of 10–25% reduces the surface tension down to 35–45 dynes/cm, enabling the solution to spread over the plate rapidly in a thin continuous film. In alcohol-free dampening solutions, surface tension is reduced by additives called **surfactants.**

Surfactants, or surface-active agents, are organic chemicals that tend to concentrate at interfaces because of their polar molecular structures. When functioning properly, they travel to the interfaces between the dampening solution and both air and the ink on the image areas of the plate. At high press speeds, interfaces are used and reformed rapidly. Surfactants must diffuse quickly to replenish the new interfaces. The amount of surfactants in the dampening solution must be precisely controlled during the pressrun. Too much surfactant can contribute to excessive ink emulsification.

Alcohol

When discussing dampening systems, the word "alcohol" means 98% pure isopropyl alcohol (isopropanol, or IPA). The amount of isopropyl alcohol required in the dampening solution depends on the type of dampening system and condition of the press and is typically 10–25% by volume, although some newer systems require only about 5%. Including alcohol in the dampening solution became popular for several reasons:

- **Easier control of the press.** Alcohol allows the press operator more time to devote to other aspects of quality control. Ink/water balance can be attained more rapidly, and quality signatures can be produced more quickly at startup.

- **Reduction of the surface tension of water.** Alcohol is a wetting agent. By reducing the surface tension of the water, the alcohol helps the water to wet the dampener form roller evenly, requiring less dampening solution. A thinner film of solution will keep the nonimage areas of the plate clean. Alcohol also helps to properly spread water over the ink on rubber or bareback form rollers that apply both ink and dampening solution to the plate.

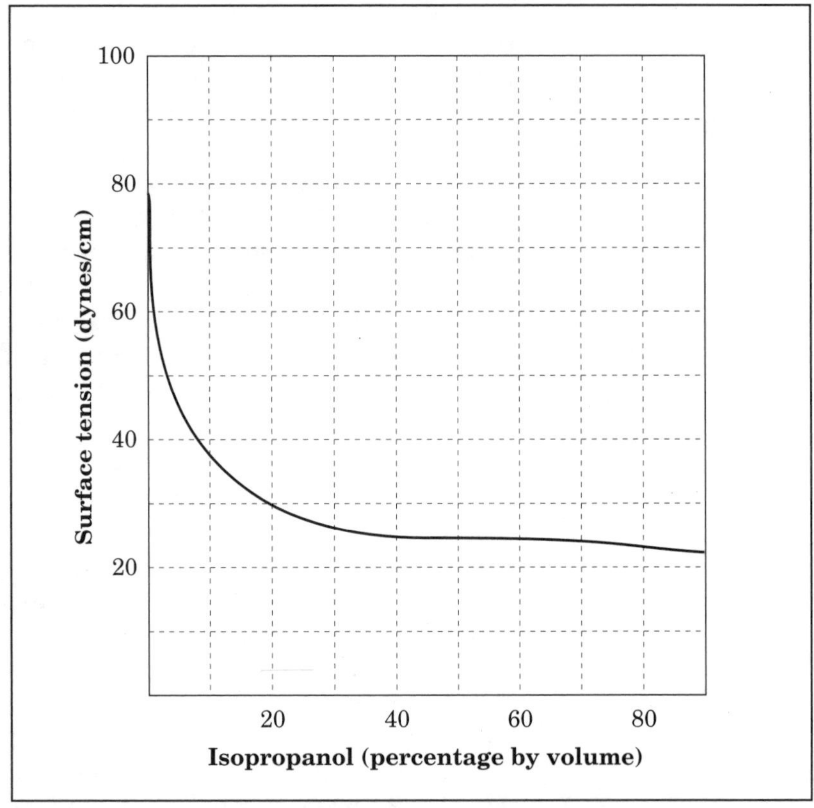

The effect of isopropanol on the surface tension of water

- **Increased viscosity of dampening solution.** The use of alcohol increases the viscosity of the dampening solution, which allows a thicker layer of dampening solution to be applied to the ink and to the nonimage area and improves the performance of the ink, paper, and printing plates.
- **Rapid evaporation.** Less dampening solution is carried to the blanket due to the rapid evaporation of alcohol. Consequently, less moisture is transferred to the printing paper, and ink drying is faster.

Hydrometer readings at various alcohol percentages and solution temperatures, using a hydrometer calibrated for 60°F

Percent Alcohol in Solution	Solution Temperature 50°F 10.0°C	60°F 15.6°C	68°F 20.0°C	75°F 23.9°C	80°F 26.7°C
0%	0.9997	0.9991	0.9982	0.9973	0.9966
15	0.9809	0.9808	0.9802	0.9795	0.9793
20	0.9765	0.9769	0.9757	0.9745	0.9737
25	0.9723	0.9710	0.9703	0.9688	0.9671
35	0.9598	0.9570	0.9552	0.9532	0.9518

- **Reduction in contamination of system components.** The use of alcohol reduces the tendency of ink to emulsify. It also minimizes **snowflaking,** the tiny, white, unprinted specks that appear in type and solids. Snowflaking occurs when water becomes **emulsified** (dispersed) in the ink. IPA readily evaporates from the ink train; therefore, no traces of alcohol are left to contaminate the ink, plate, or blanket.
- **Reduction of time and materials.** With alcohol in the dampening system, quality printing is achieved sooner after startup. This saves paper, ink, and time. In addition, since less dampening solution is needed on the printing plate, less ink is required, resulting in decreased consumption of dampening solution and ink.

The use of alcohol in dampening systems is not as common as it once was because regulations of the United States Environmental Protection Agency (USEPA), the Occupational Safety and Health Administration (OSHA), and state air pollution control agencies, as well as the 1990 Clean Air Act Amendments, demand specific, scheduled reductions in the release of volatile organic compounds (VOCs) from lithographic printing processes. Isopropyl alcohol, ink oil, and cleaning solvents are sources of VOCs. VOCs contribute to air pollution by reacting with nitrogen oxides in the presence of sunlight to form ozone, a component of smog.

Several state and local air pollution agencies have set limits on the permissible amount of IPA in dampening solution. USEPA is currently working on a Control Techniques Guideline (CTG) for offset lithography, and an Alternative Control Technology Guideline (ACTG) that are to be used by the states in establishing IPA limits. For more information, contact GATF's Office of Environmental Information.

In addition to being a volatile organic compound, alcohol has other disadvantages:

- **Expense.** Alcohol is more expensive than alcohol substitutes and conventional dampening solutions.
- **Toxicity.** Alcohol is highly toxic if ingested.
- **Flammability.** Alcohol is flammable and must be stored in approved, fireproof containers.
- **Irritability.** Alcohol fumes can be an irritant, especially in pressrooms without adequate ventilation.

Alcohol Substitutes

In recent years, numerous alcohol substitutes have been introduced. Alcohol substitutes generally do not have any of the disadvantages of isopropyl alcohol, but using an alcohol substitute is more complicated.

Substitutes differ from IPA in several key properties, including how they affect viscosity, surface tension, pH, and conductivity of the dampening solution. Dampening solutions require much lower concentrations of alcohol substitutes (about 3–5% by volume) than of alcohol.

Several kinds of substitutes are being offered to the industry. They are composed of one or more chemicals from the glycol and glycol ether families and can be combined with ethylene glycol.

Some alcohol substitutes are intended to completely replace IPA in dampening solution, while others are formulated to be combined with IPA, thus reducing the total volume of IPA used.

Following are the principal benefits of alcohol substitutes:

- Less volatile than alcohol, reducing VOC emissions and the amount of substitute needed to replenish the dampening solution over the course of a day
- Used in lower concentrations (5% or less) than alcohol
- Brighter and higher-gloss printing, because less ink and less water is needed for acceptable color, producing sharper dots and reducing dot gain
- Some are odorless

Following are some problems that have been encountered with some alcohol substitutes:

- Increased paper debris on the blanket
- Buildup of dampening solution on the blanket
- Incapable of being mixed directly with concentrated gum and etch
- Increased drying time in some cases

- Occasional roller stripping
- Difficulty in running with nonabsorptive substrates, such as plastic papers

In contrast to alcohol, many substitutes have little or no effect on dampening solution viscosity. Thus, omitting IPA (and adding an alcohol substitute) results in a dampening solution with significantly lower viscosity.

Because of the decrease in viscosity with substitutes, less dampening solution is metered by the squeeze rolls used in the majority of continuous-flow dampening systems. The immediate effect is that the dampener speed must be turned up, which leads many press operators to conclude erroneously that they must use more water to print with a substitute. To partially offset the loss in viscosity produced by eliminating alcohol, the dampening solution can be cooled (in much the same way that other fluids, such as automobile engine oil, become thicker when cooled).

Storage and Handling of Alcohol and Alcohol Substitutes

Many chemicals and materials used in the printing industry can cause fires or explosions. Other chemicals are toxic and can harm the handler through skin contact or inhalation. Isopropanol is both flammable and toxic.

The biggest safety risk with stored isopropyl alcohol is flammability. Pure IPA has an extremely low flash point—53°F (11.7°C)—and must be handled with extreme caution. (Its flammability *is* greatly reduced when mixed in dampening solution.) IPA can also act as an irritant when present in the form of vapors in the air. OSHA has set maximum exposure limits of 400 parts per million (ppm) over an eight-hour time-weighted average or 500 ppm for fifteen minutes.

Fire prevention practices are essential when handling flammable materials like isopropanol. Isopropanol must be kept in fireproof cabinets or rooms and stored in clearly labeled, approved safety containers; all sources of ignition should be removed from this area. The flame-arresting screen in the spout of these containers should be left in place. Bulk storage of flammable liquids is regulated by specific U.S. Occupational Safety and Health Administration (OSHA) standards. If possible these liquids should be stored in buildings other than the printing plant. Only immediately required quantities (limits are set by OSHA standards) should be brought into work areas. A practical rule of thumb is to keep no more than a day's needs in the work area.

The storage area must be away from any exits or escape routes; it must be well-ventilated, cool, clean, and orderly; and it must allow for grounding of the bulk containers. Smoking is prohibited in the areas where flammable liquids are stored, handled, or used.

All bulk containers should be bonded and grounded to prevent static electricity sparks. **Bonding** is the elimination of a difference in electrical potential between objects, while **grounding** is the elimination of a difference in electrical potential between an object and the ground.

Hazardous chemicals must be stored in properly labeled containers using the Hazardous Materials Identification System (HMIS). In addition, all users of chemicals in the plant must be familiar with the Material Safety Data Sheet and first-aid procedures for each chemical. Protective gloves, goggles, and aprons must be used when handling hazardous chemicals.

Since the flash points of substitutes are greater than 100°F (37.8°C), flammability is not a major concern. Any adverse health effects of substitutes are dependent on the exact chemical composition of the material. Ethylene glycol and glycol ethers are generally recognized as safe when used properly and with adequate ventilation and personal protection. OSHA's permissible exposure limits for one glycol ether used as a substitute or extender (known in the printing industry as butyl Cellosolve©) is 25 ppm over an eight-hour time-weighted average. However, the National Institute of Occupation Safety and Health (NIOSH) recommends limits of 5 ppm for butyl Cellosolve© and butyl Cellosolve© acetate based on their study. (Note: These exposure limits are subject to change; contact OSHA or NIOSH for current limits.)

Dampening Solution pH

For a dampening solution to perform effectively, its acidity or alkalinity must be controlled not only during the initial mixing of the solution but also during the pressrun. If the proper level of acidity or alkalinity is maintained, quality printing should be easier to produce.

Acidic solutions. A dampening solution that has an incorrect acid level or a dampening solution in which the acid level changes excessively during a pressrun can cause several serious printing problems. Among these are slow drying or nondrying ink, plate scumming, plate blinding, and roller stripping.

The gum arabic film protecting the nonimage areas of the plate is slightly acidic; however, it requires additional acid to adhere properly. Gum arabic used in most of these solutions will not effectively desensitize plates if the pH is above 5.0. The acidic compounds added to the dampening solution enable the gum arabic to cling to the plate's nonimage areas.

Insufficient acid in the dampening solution lessens the gum's ability to adhere to the plate. Eventually, ink starts to replace the gum in nonimage areas, causing **plate scumming,** the pickup of ink in nonimage areas of the plate. Scumming can be caused by excessive acid if it attacks the plate metal and the protective coating. This type of scumming appears darker and more uneven than scumming due to insufficient acid.

Excessive acid also causes **plate blinding,** the loss of ink receptivity in the image area. The extra acid attacks the plate in the image areas, causing the image to deteriorate.

Another problem associated with excessive acid in the dampening solution is **roller stripping,** the failure of ink to adhere to the inking rollers. Stripping that occurs at the beginning of a pressrun is usually caused by glazed roller surfaces, and stripping that occurs during a pressrun is probably caused by an excessively acidic dampening solution.

Poor drying or nondrying of ink can be caused by excessive acidity. Drying problems can arise independently of scumming, blinding, and stripping problems and become obvious only after the completion of the pressrun. Excess acid reacts with the cobalt drier in the ink, rendering it practically useless as a drying stimulator.

Alkaline, or base, solutions. Most dampening solutions are slightly acidic. Some dampening solutions, however, are alkaline, particularly those for offset newspaper presses. These alkaline solutions do not contain a desensitizing gum and are made more basic by adding sodium carbonate or sodium silicate. An alkaline dampening solution sometimes contains a **sequestering agent,** a substance that prevents the calcium and magnesium compounds in the solution from precipitating, and a **wetting agent,** which lowers the surface tension of the water in the dampening solution.

pH measurement. pH—the potential of hydrogen—is a measure of a solution's acidity or alkalinity. The pH scale runs from 0 to 14.0.

If the pH of a solution is 7, it is neutral; it is neither acidic nor alkaline. A solution with a pH of 5 is slightly acid; a pH of 3 is considerably more acidic. The lower the pH reading, the more acidic a solution is. The opposite is true as the pH rises above 7. Thus, a solution with a pH of 8 is slightly alkaline, while one with a pH of 10 is considerably more alkaline, or basic.

A pH scale

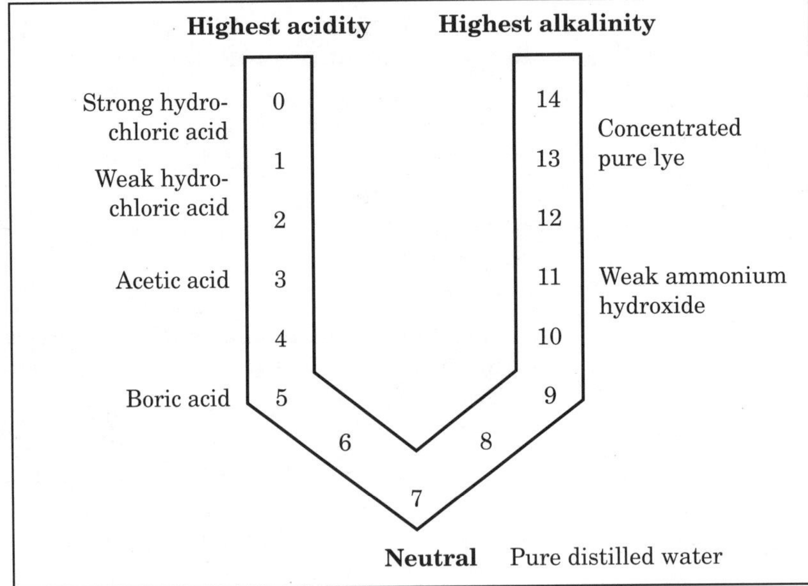

As a general rule, an acidic dampening solution should have a pH of 4.0–5.5.

Three general methods are used to measure the pH of a solution. One colorimetric method of pH measurement depends on the color change of indicator dyes added to the solution. Each indicator changes color over a range of about two pH units. To determine the approximate pH of the solution, three dyes are used: one to determine the maximum pH, one to determine the minimum pH, and the last one to determine the approximate midpoint between the maximum and minimum pH levels.

Another colorimetric method of pH measurement depends on the color change of dye-impregnated papers. The widely used litmus paper strips permit quick reading but not pinpoint accuracy. Short-range pH testing papers have an effective range over a shorter portion of the pH scale and, consequently, are accurate to within 0.3–0.5 pH of the actual pH value.

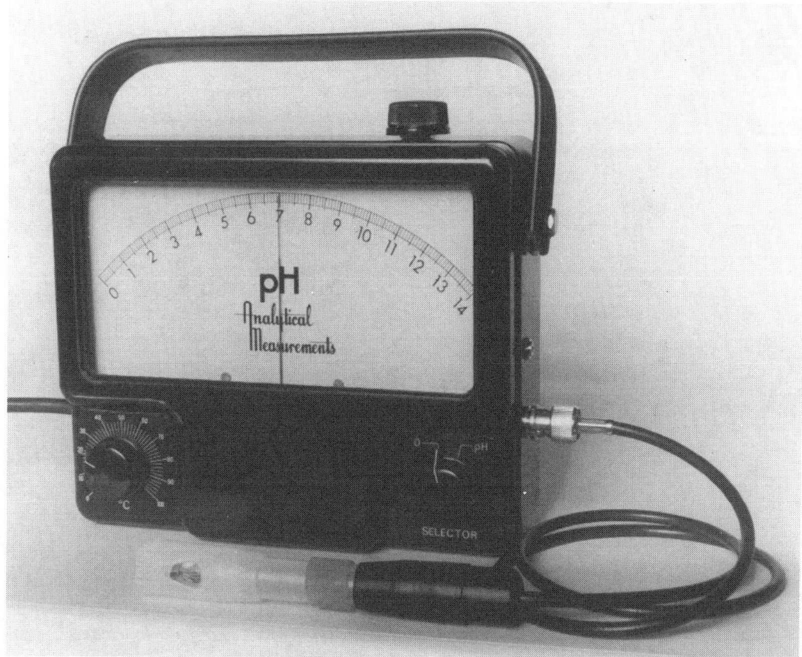

Model 707 pH meter
Courtesy Analytical Measurements, Inc.

The most accurate method of measuring pH uses electronically operated meters. Although more expensive than indicator dyes and pH papers, some pH meters are accurate to within 0.01–0.05 pH.

Additional information on the use of indicator dyes, pH papers, and pH meters can be obtained from manufacturers or suppliers of these products.

Conductivity of a Dampening Solution

Conductivity is a measure of the capacity of a material to conduct electricity. Pure water is a very poor conductor of electricity. As materials dissolve or go into a solution, they form ions and the water becomes conductive. The conductivity of water increases directly with increases in the amount of dissolved matter (ions). Low (partially) ionizable materials such as alcohol and gum arabic are poor electrical conductors and usually lower conductivity of dampening solutions.

Pure water approaches a conductivity of 0 micromhos. Typical tap water might have a conductivity of 200 micromhos or more. As the amount of dissolved matter increases, the conductivity increases directly in a straight line. Thus, conductivity is commonly used as a measure of water purity. Soft water has a conductivity of 0–225 micromhos, and hard water has a conductivity greater than 450 micromhos. The relationship between water hardness and conductivity varies

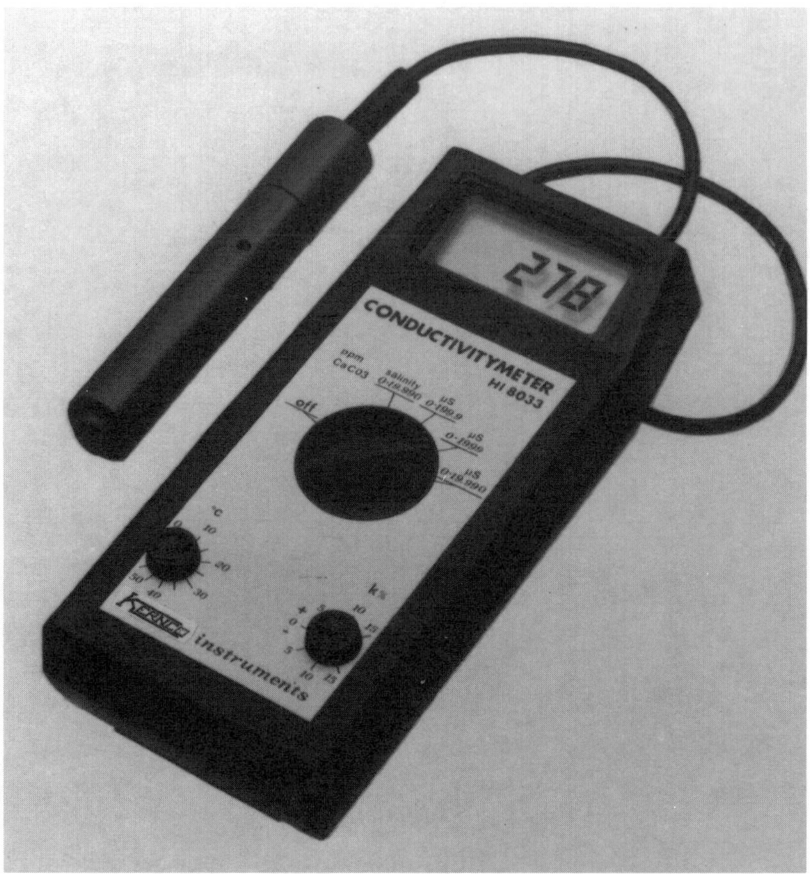

Conductivity meter
Courtesy Kernco Instruments Co., Inc.

somewhat, depending upon the specific minerals and compounds in the water.

If the water quality varies in conductivity and pH, the printer will not be able to control the dampening solution.

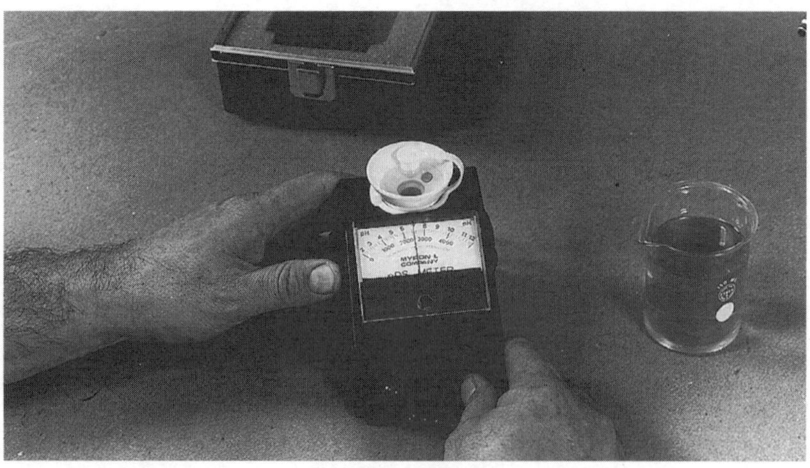

Myron L meter being used to measure the conductivity and pH of a sample of dampening solution

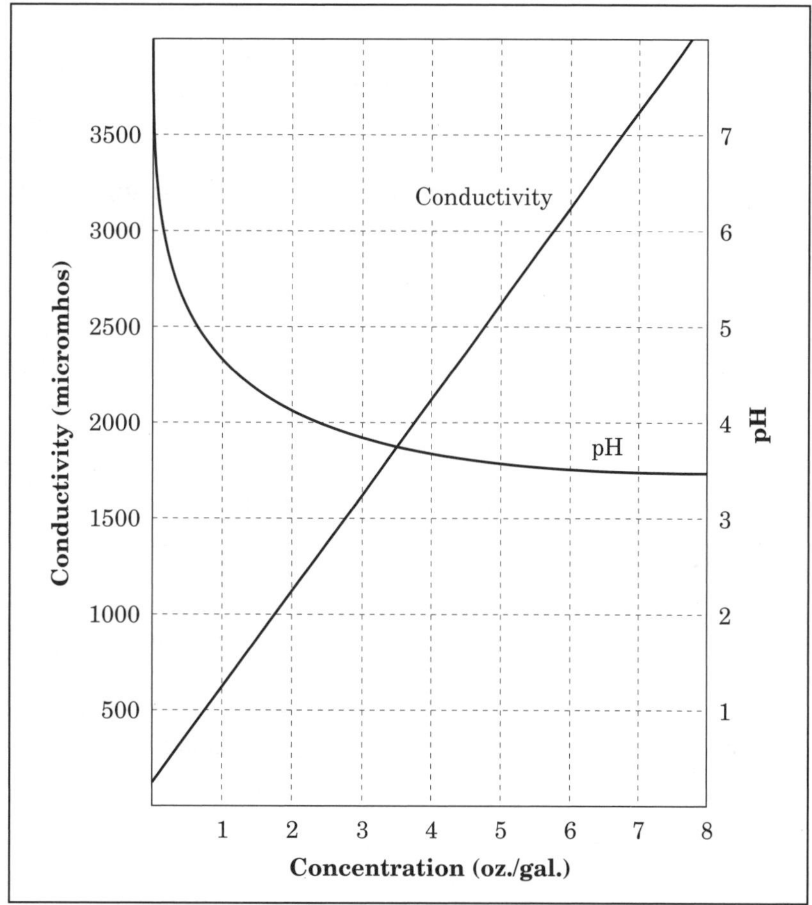

Graph of concentration vs. pH and conductivity for a hypothetical combination of dampening solution concentrate and water

If the conductivity of the incoming water varies less than ±50 micromhos, consistent dampening solution can be mixed. Day-to-day fluctuations of 200 micromhos indicate that some type of water treatment equipment may be needed to keep incoming water constant. Water treatments include reverse osmosis, deionization, filtration, or distillation.

If the conductivity of different amounts of dampening solution concentrates in water is known, it is easy to measure the strength of a solution by measuring its conductivity. The following procedure can be used to develop a graph that plots conductivity and pH against concentration:

1. Measure the conductivity and pH of the water normally used to make the dampening solution. Place water in a clean 1-gal. (3.8-L) bottle.
2. Add 1 oz. (29.6 mL) of fountain solution concentrate. Remeasure both conductivity and pH. Record these values.

3. Add another ounce (2 oz. total) of fountain solution concentrate and remeasure both conductivity and pH. Repeat this process until the amount of fountain solution concentrate added exceeds the manufacturer's recommendations.
4. Plot these values on a graph that has concentration (oz./gal. or mL/L) on the horizontal axis and conductivity and pH on the vertical axis.

A similar graph can be developed if alcohol or an alcohol substitute is also used in the dampening solution. Pure alcohol has little effect on pH but does lower conductivity. Most substitutes in the proper amounts have little effect on pH or conductivity.

New graphs must be made whenever the water or dampening solution concentrate changes. If the conductivity of the dampening solution is known, the amount of either dampening solution concentrate or alcohol can be read directly from the graph. Depending on the alcohol substitute, the graph may not prove helpful in determining its concentration.

The most important factor in preparing dampening solution is to make sure that it is the proper concentration. Most acidic dampening solutions are buffered so that, as the amount of concentration increases, the pH drops initially but then levels off, while the solution's conductivity increases in a straight line. Thus, conductivity is better than pH for determining the amount of concentrate in the dampening solution. However, the pH must still be measured, because it must be between 4.0–5.5 for good printing.

With neutral dampening solutions and neutral water, the pH of the solution is constant, regardless of concentration. Therefore, conductivity must be used to measure the concentration of neutral or slightly alkaline dampening solutions.

Any unusual conductivity readings justify rechecking the conductivity of the water and the dampening solution concentrate. It is normal for the conductivity to increase during the pressrun because materials from the ink and paper contaminate the dampening solution. Therefore, conductivity measurements should be made before the dampening solution is used on the press.

Conventional Dampening Systems

Dampening systems used for sheetfed offset lithography are classified into two categories: the intermittent-flow (ductor, or conventional) and continuous-flow. The intermittent-flow system is discussed first.

The intermittent-flow dampening system, usually referred to as a **conventional dampening system,** consists of the following:

- **Water pan,** or **fountain,** which holds the dampening solution to be fed to the plate
- **Fountain pan roller,** which rotates in the fountain and carries dampening solution on its metal surface
- **Ductor roller,** which intermittently contacts the fountain roller and an oscillator roller, transferring the dampening solution
- **Oscillator roller,** which oscillates from side to side to even out dampening across the press
- **Form roller,** which transfers dampening solution from the oscillator roller to the printing plate

The design of a conventional dampening system resembles that of an inking system. A supply of dampening solution is held in a fountain. A chrome-plated or treated aluminum fountain roller rotates in the fountain. As the roller turns, it draws a film of dampening solution onto its surface. On some presses, this roller is covered with cloth to increase its solution-holding capacity. It is usually driven by its own motor, separate from the main press drive, or by a variable-speed drive off the press. The fountain roller is operated through gear reduction, because if it is operated at press speed it would sling solution all over the press area. All other rollers in the conventional dampening system are operated at the surface speed of the plate.

A ductor roller is a roller that alternately contacts the fountain pan roller and the oscillator roller. It transfers dampening solution from the fountain pan roller to the surface of the oscillator. The ductor roller is made of a plasticized-rubber compound and is always covered, often with a molleton fabric, to increase its solution-holding capacity.

The oscillator roller, chrome-plated or treated aluminum and power-driven, has a dual purpose: it drives the dampening form rollers by direct surface contact and its lateral oscillation equalizes water feed across the press. The rotational surface speed of the oscillator is the same as that of the plate when the plate is packed to manufacturer's specifications. There is no setting adjustment on this roller; it is permanently fixed in the dampener unit frame.

The form rollers apply dampening solution directly to the plate. Most presses have two form rollers. Form rollers are

A conventional dampening system that uses covered form and ductor rollers

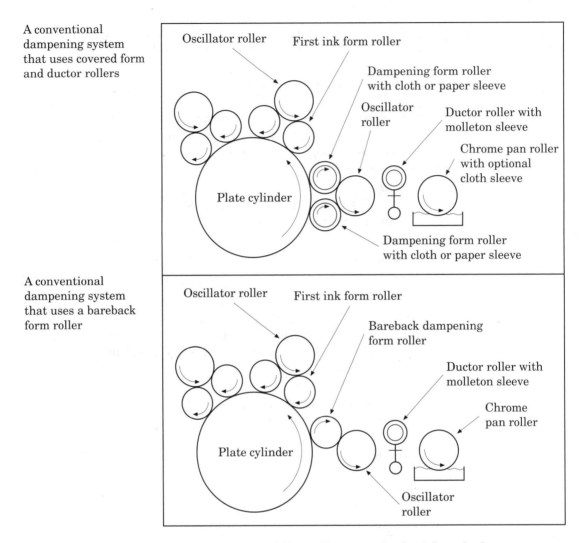

A conventional dampening system that uses a bareback form roller

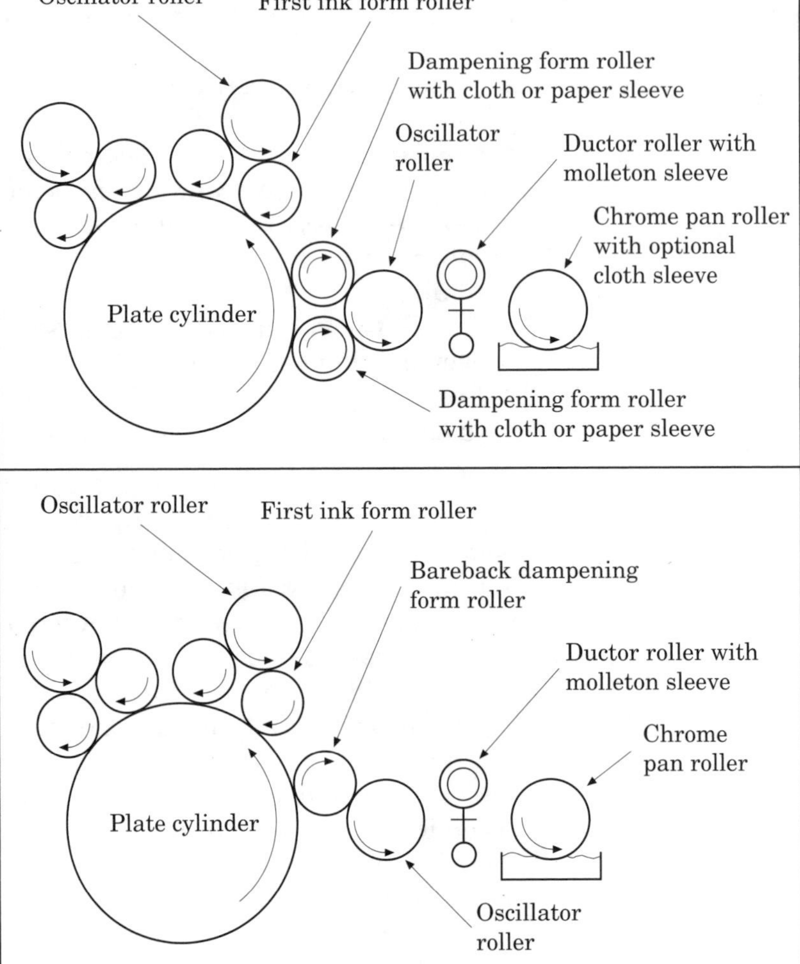

contact-driven rubber rollers, covered with a cloth or paper sleeve or run bareback. They contact both the oscillator and the plate.

The conventional dampening system is an intermittent-feed system. Dampening solution does not move continuously from the fountain pan to the plate. The amount of solution in the dampening system is lowest just before the ductor contacts the oscillator. Dampening solution surges through the system when the ductor makes contact. These surges make it difficult to control the conventional dampening system, and the problem is more serious here than in the inking system because the dampening system has very few rollers. Because the problem is inherent in the design, the press operator must learn how to control it.

Roller Covers

Cloth and paper dampener covers help to provide more continuous dampening by increasing the solution-carrying and solution-storing capacity of the rollers. The covered rollers act like sponges, absorbing excess water (becoming reservoirs) and giving it up when the supply becomes low. The dampening flow to the plate varies less, and less total solution is delivered. The advantages of increased volume capacity are better control and minimum dampening solution delivered to the plate.

An assortment of dampener covers *Courtesy Jomac, Incorporated*

In order to further enhance the carrying capacity, the operator sometimes puts a double cover on the roller, with the undercover made of cotton or flannel.

The problem with large-capacity dampening systems is that they respond slowly to changes. If the press operator wants to increase the amount of dampening, the speed of the fountain roller is increased. On the other hand, if the operator wants to cut back on the level of dampening, it is necessary to turn the dampening supply off and let the press reduce the amount of dampening solution in the system. In both cases, skill is required on the part of the operator to make the change without producing waste.

Cloth (usually a fabric called molleton) is a widely used material for covering dampening form rollers. It is woven as a sleeve, slipped over the roller, and tied at the roller ends. Molleton has a relatively long nap and is good for storing water. However, it releases lint when new and rapidly becomes greasy. In addition, depending on how dirty or greasy the cover gets, its thickness can vary; this changes the effective radius of the roller, which, in effect, changes the roller setting, making it difficult to maintain a uniform film of dampening solution unless the dampener rollers are reset.

A variety of dampening sleeve products
Courtesy REL Graphic Systems and Marketing Corp.

Because of the shortcomings of cloth covers, paper covers were developed. The paper used is a special vegetable parchment, available originally as strips for winding around the roller, and presently as tubular sleeves. Probably the greatest advantage of paper covers is that when they get dirty (as all covers inevitably will) they are easier to clean or replace than cloth. Paper covers are also less grease-absorbent. Because of their limited water-storage capacity, they require a skilled operator to maintain balance.

Another dampener covering material that has proven successful consists of a randomly laid blend of 50% rayon fiber and 50% fusible fiber that serves as a binder to hold the rayon fibers in place. Loosely held rayon fibers permit the construction of a seamless sleeve. Rayon is hydrophilic and easily accepts water, but it does not hold excessive amounts that might cause flooding. When immersed in water, the sleeve shrinks tightly onto the roller. With a smoother surface than molleton, rayon sleeve material responds more quickly to press adjustments.

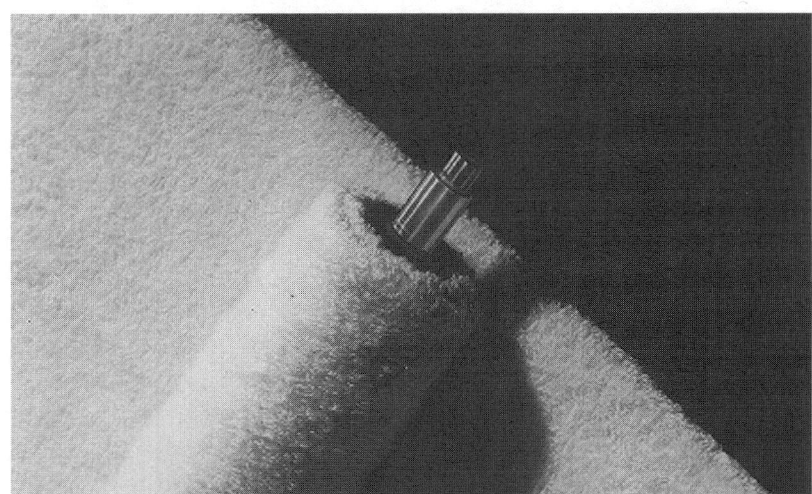

Shrink-type dampener cover
Courtesy Jomac, Incorporated

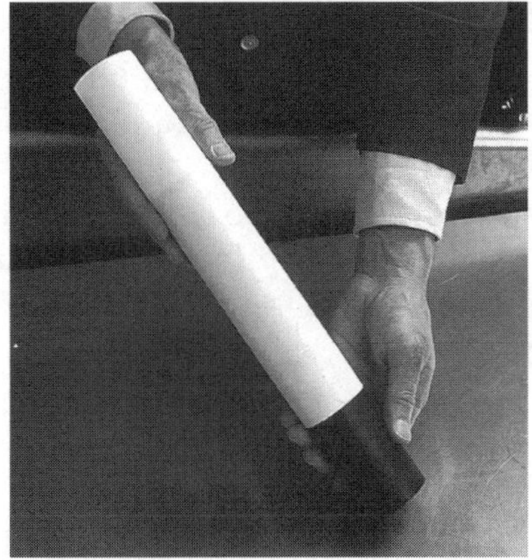

Press operator installing a dampening sleeve on a roller *(left)* and using warm water to shrink the sleeve *(right)*
Courtesy 3M

Adjustments to a Conventional Dampening System

Setting accurate pressure between the various dampening rollers is critical. The form roller's contact with both oscillator and plate is adjustable. Contact between form rollers and oscillator must be just enough to transfer dampening solution and maintain the driving action, and no more. If the contact is too weak, dampening solution will not transfer properly and the power-driven oscillator may fail to drive the form rollers at full speed. On the other hand, too much contact pressure will also fail to transfer dampening solution. Instead, the solution will be wrung out of the covers. Plastic feelers or mechanical gauges should be used to determine the proper adjustment.

In most cases, the pressure between the dampening form roller and the plate should be less than that between the form roller and the oscillator. A tight setting can "squeegee" dampening solution off the plate and increase plate wear. The ideal setting exerts just enough pressure to smoothly transfer an adequate amount of dampening solution to the plate.

As in the inking system, the oscillator is the reference point used in setting the rollers. It must be parallel to the fountain roller and to the plate cylinder. Alignment should be checked periodically as part of long-term maintenance. If the oscillator is not parallel, only a press mechanic should reset it; such settings are extremely critical.

The pressure between the form roller and oscillator is set with smooth strips of 0.002-in. (0.05-mm) plastic. Sandwiches of three strips are placed between the form roller and the oscillator. A sandwich is put about 3 in. (76 mm) from each end, and another one or two are placed near the middle. The middle strip, about 1 in. (25 mm) wide, is pulled to gauge or judge the roller pressure. The outer two strips, each about 2 in. (50 mm) wide, help to remove the effect of friction on the tension. If roller covers are clean and soft and the oscillator is clean, the middle strip should pull out with a resistance of about 0.5 lb. (0.2 kg).

A properly set, concentric roller with a soft cover should not "bump" at the plate cylinder gap. Running the press fully engaged with the dampening system on helps to show the action of the roller at the gap.

Most dampening systems have a disengaging device to back the form roller away from the plate during gumming and other operations. If the system is in good mechanical order, the form rollers may be backed away from the plate and brought back into contact repeatedly with no change in setting. On some systems, the form rollers may even be removed and replaced without the settings being changed. Many systems are designed so that dampening feed can be stopped while the form rollers stay in contact with the plate. Stopping the ductor or fountain roller stops dampening feed; this ability can be helpful to the press operator in some situations.

The ductor can be set using the following procedure:

1. Inch the press until the ductor is at maximum pressure against the oscillator.
2. Insert a single plastic strip at three points between the two rollers.
3. Test for drag.

4. Inch the press until the ductor touches the fountain pan roller.
5. Again, insert a plastic strip at three positions between the two rollers. Equal drag indicates correct setting and alignment. Readjust the ductor, if necessary, according to instructions in the press operator's manual.

Metering Dampening on a Conventional System

All dampening systems meter, or control, the dampening solution fed to the plate. With a conventional system, metering is done in two, sometimes three, ways. One way is to control the rotation of the fountain pan roller. The fountain pan roller can be adjusted for faster or slower rotation. On some presses, fountain roller rotation is controlled through a ratchet or clutch arrangement similar to that found on the inking system fountain roller.

A second method of metering dampening solution is to adjust the length of time the ductor dwells against the fountain roller. When the fountain roller rotates at high speed and the ductor dwells against it for a comparatively long time, dampening solution is put on the entire surface of the ductor. On the other hand, when the fountain roller turns slowly and the ductor dwells for a short time only, a narrow band of water is deposited on the ductor. These are, of course, extreme settings. The important thing is that the flow of water to the plate be as continuous and uniform as possible.

Press operator adjusting a water stop
Courtesy Baldwin Dampening Systems

A third means of metering dampening feed involves the use of special tabs, squeegees, or rollers. The devices, called **water stops,** are set against the surface of the fountain roller. The pressure exerted by the water stops controls the

Using water stops to control water feed

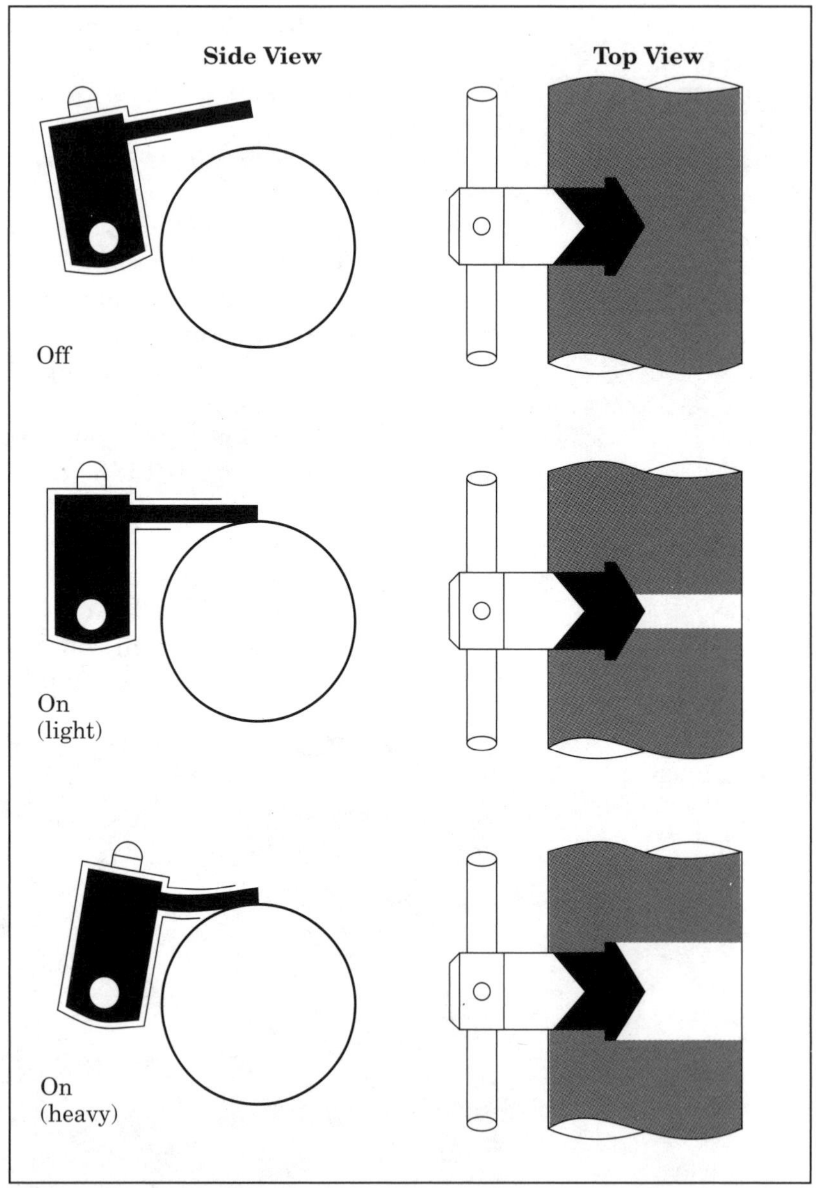

flow of dampening solution across the rollers and is equivalent to adjusting the blade in the ink fountain. Water stops are commonly used to reduce the amount of solution reaching heavily inked areas of the printing plate.

Bareback Dampeners

Some press operators change the conventional dampening system by running the dampeners **bareback,** i.e., without cloth or paper covers. A system with bareback rollers is more sensitive (responds more rapidly) to changes in the rate of rotation of the fountain roller or to changes in the length of time that the ductor dwells against the fountain roller.

Wetting agent is usually added to the fountain solution to help bareback dampeners run efficiently. Alcohol reduces the surface tension of water, in effect making it “wetter.” The reduced surface tension helps the uncovered rubber roller in picking up solution and wetting the plate.

Continuous-Flow Dampening Systems

The other major category of dampening systems for sheetfed offset presses is the continuous-flow dampening system. It is divided into two basic categories: plate-feed and inker-feed. In inker-feed systems, the dampening solution is fed indirectly through the inking system; in plate-feed systems, it is fed directly to the plate. Some continuous-flow dampening systems combine plate-feed and inker-feed features. The trend in the industry is toward plate-feed systems.

Continuous-flow systems eliminate some of the dampening control problems associated with conventional systems because the dampening solution is no longer supplied intermittently. A very important advantage of these systems is their rapid response to changes in fountain settings. This fast response is largely due to the absence of storage capacity in the system because the form rollers are not covered.

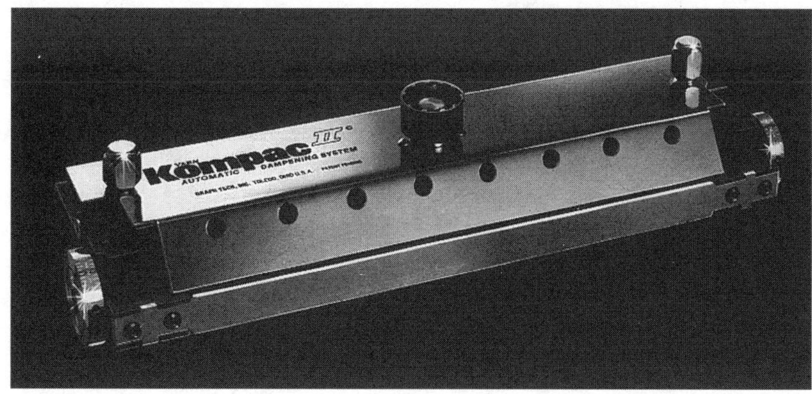

Varn Kompac II automatic dampening system for small offset presses
Courtesy Varn Products Co.

Inker-Feed System

An inker-feed, or integrated, system is quite different from conventional and plate-feed systems. It uses the first inking form roller as a combination inking/dampening form roller. Another feature is the absence of a ductor roller.

Two configurations of the Dahlgren inker-feed dampening system

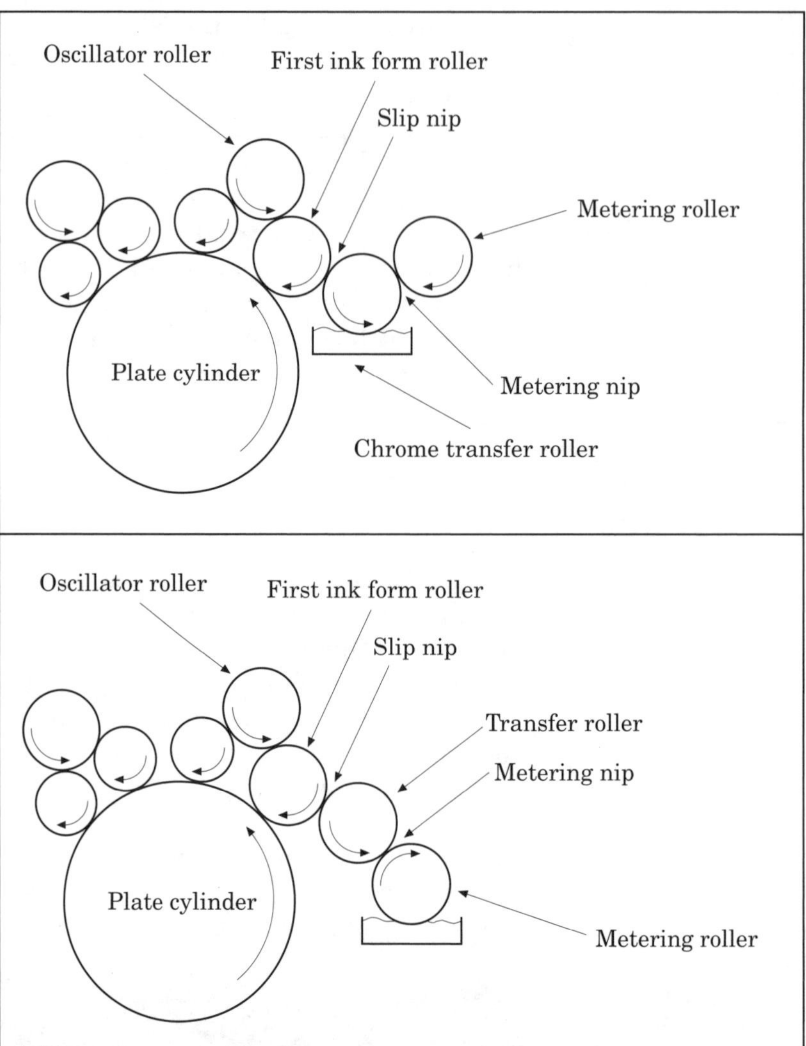

An inker-feed dampening system often consists of two rollers that deliver dampening solution to an ink form roller. One is a chrome-plated steel roller, and the other is a soft roller that meters (controls) the thickness of the dampening solution film on the hard roller. The line of contact between the two rollers is called the **metering nip.** Depending on the particular press requirements, either roller could be the fountain roller. They are driven independently of the press, and their surface speed is not the same as that of the plate. The hard roller rubs against the first ink form roller, which transfers the dampening solution directly to the plate. Dampening solution supply is controlled indirectly through speed control of the two rollers and the adjustable squeeze between them.

An important consideration of an inker-feed dampening system is that the dampening solution film must lay smoothly on top of the already inked form roller. The wetting properties of either alcohol (5–10% by volume) or a satisfactory substitute assist in the formation of an even film of dampening solution.

Setting the rollers on an inker-feed system is different from setting the rollers on a conventional system. The inking form roller is set heavier to the plate because it is considerably softer and larger in diameter than those in a conventional system. Follow manufacturer's specifications for the stripe width that the inking form roller should leave on the plate when the picture method of roller setting is used.

Plate-Feed Systems

In addition to inker-feed dampening systems, there are several plate-feed, or segregated, continuous-flow systems. Unlike an inker-feed system, which uses the first ink form roller for dampening, these systems all have separate dampening form rollers. As with the inker-feed system, each has a metering nip formed between a soft metering roller and a hard chrome roller. Because these two rollers are driven independently of the press, there is also a slip nip. Usually, the roller farthest from the plate can be skewed to modulate the water feed across the press. These systems have either a metering roller or a water pan roller.

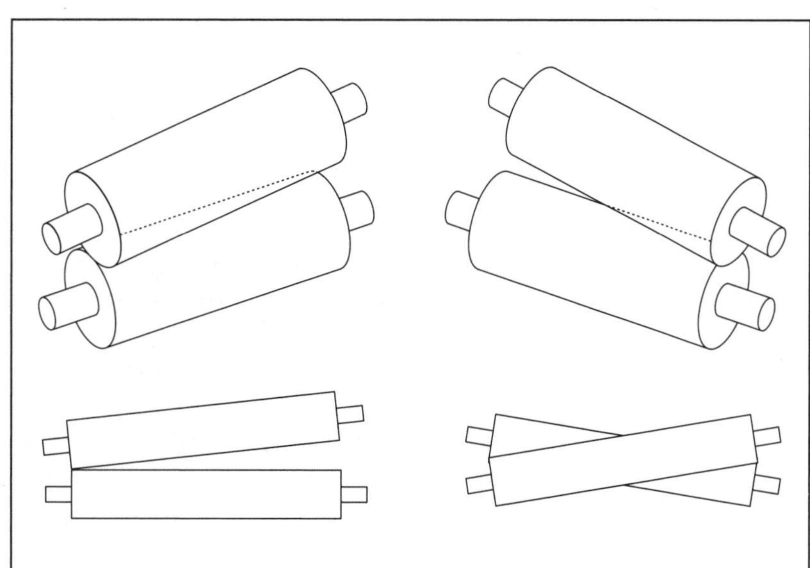

Adjustments at the metering nip on a Roland-Matic dampening system: rollers skewed to get more dampening at the end *(left)* and rollers angled to either reduce dampening at the center or increase dampening at both ends *(right)*

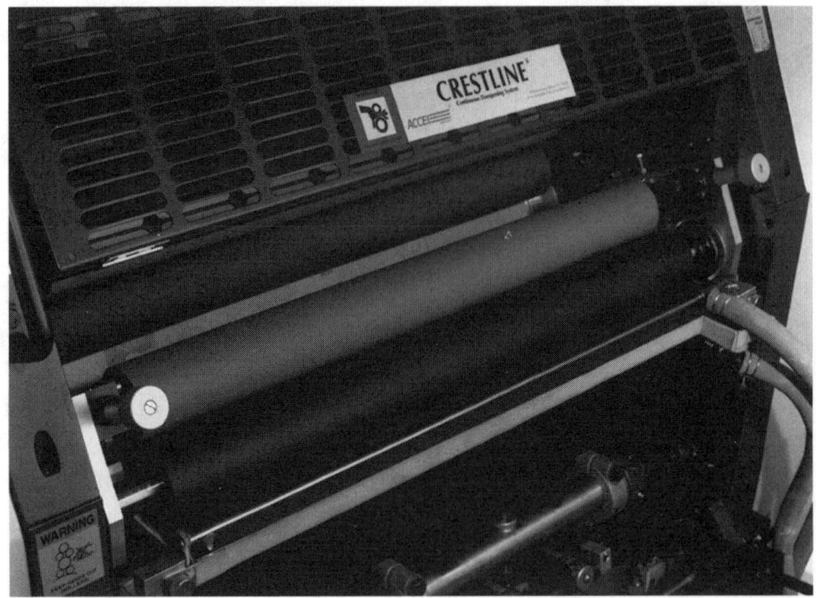

Crestline® Altra Series plate-feed dampening system
Courtesy Accel Graphic Systems, Inc.

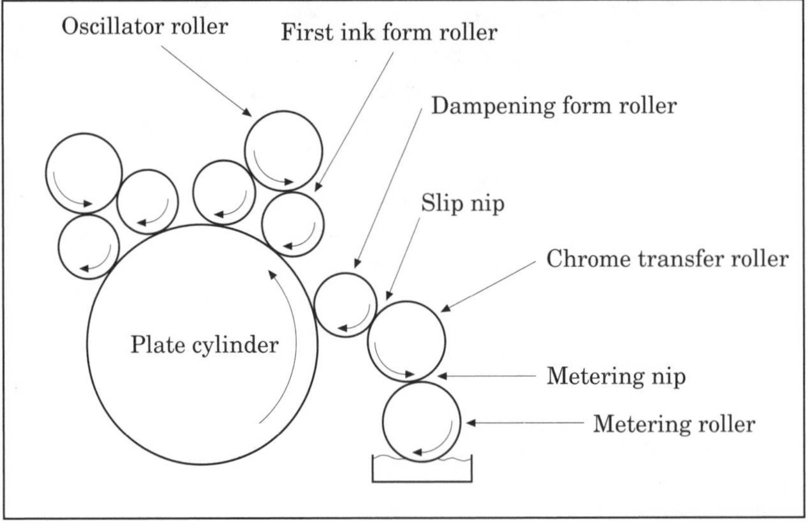

Epic Litho/Dampener plate-feed continuous-flow dampening system

Most plate-feed continuous-flow systems also require the use of a wetting agent or surfactant (e.g., alcohol or an alcohol substitute) in the dampening solution.

Combination Continuous-Flow Systems

A combination continuous-flow dampening system incorporates features of both inker-feed and plate-feed systems. In a combination system, an oscillating or vibrating bridge roller contacts both the dampener form roller and the first ink form roller.

Heidelberg Alcolor continuous-flow combination dampening system

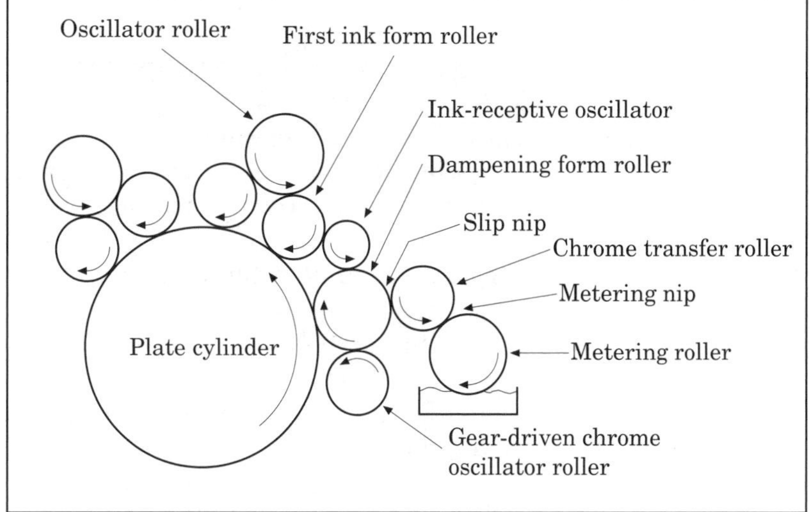

The Epic Delta system, for example, consists of an oscillating bridge roller and a form roller that is driven at a slower surface speed than the plate. The differential speed results in a scrubbing action on the plate, giving the system a hickey-elimination feature. The bridge roller can be used either as a rider or as a connection between the dampening form roller and the inking system.

Epic Delta continuous-flow combination dampening system, which has a dampening form roller driven at a slower speed than the plate

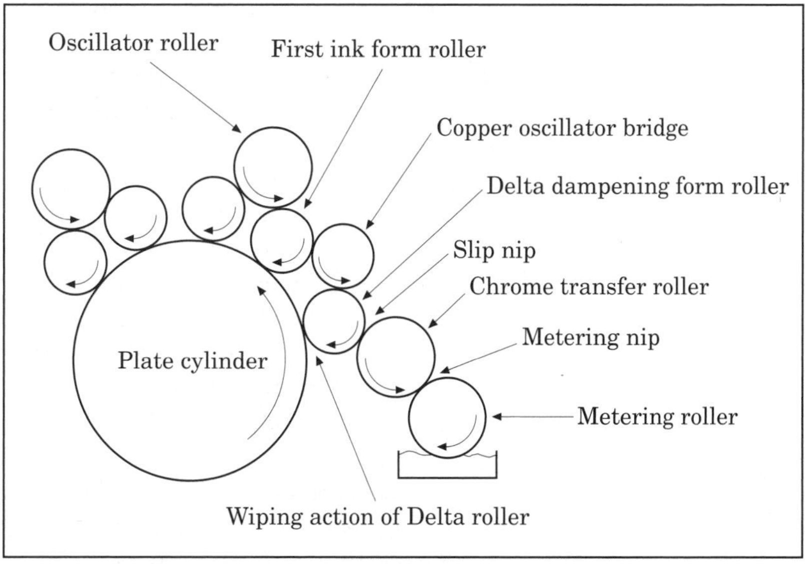

Another combination system has rollers that cannot be skewed to control dampening distribution. With this system, an airflow pattern (with water stops and an air bar) is used

to achieve (as well as possible) an even distribution across and around the plate cylinder. At startup, the dampening form roller is contacting the plate ("on impression"), the ink form rollers are "off impression," and the bridge roller is in place, feeding dampening solution to the inking system. As a result of the bridge roller carrying dampening solution to the inking system, ink/water balance is quickly achieved.

Critical Metering Nip

All continuous-flow dampening systems have a metering nip (formed by a chrome transfer or pan roller and a resilient roller) that distributes the dampening solution into a thin, even film. The two rollers are geared to each other and run at almost the same surface speed. The thickness of the metered dampening film at the nip *exit* is dependent on the hardness of the resilient roller, the pressure exerted between rollers (determined by roller settings), and the viscosity of the dampening solution. An increase in the viscosity of the dampening solution results in a thicker metered film, and vice versa.

Reverse Slip Nip

With most continuous-flow systems, one of the rollers at the metering nip rotates clockwise and the other rotates counterclockwise. As a result, the surfaces of the two rollers are traveling in the same direction at the point of contact.

However, with several dampening systems, both rollers rotate in the same direction (both clockwise or counterclockwise). Consequently, at the point of contact, the two rollers are rotating in opposite directions, producing a **reverse slip nip.** The objective of this system is to reduce the interaction between dampening solution being fed to the plate and the solution returning from it.

A reverse slip nip produces a wiping action that is intended to prevent the flow of dampening solution through the nip. Theoretically, all of the metered dampening solution is carried to the printing plate, and all of the return solution is carried to the fountain pan.

Dampening systems incorporating a reverse slip nip can operate with a relatively low alcohol concentration—e.g., 5–10%—or none at all. In addition, response to changes in dampening feed rate is quickened due to the elimination of interaction between the metered film and the return solution. The elimination of interaction also results in a linear relationship between the speed of the metering rollers and the feed rate.

Refrigeration

Refrigerating the dampening solution has three principal advantages: a reduction in hot-weather scumming, the maintenance of a constant operating temperature, and reduction of alcohol evaporation.

Hot-weather scumming. Although metal plates and improved inks eliminated many printing problems associated with hot weather, hot-weather scumming was not one of them. **Hot-weather scumming** is the tendency of ink to print in nonimage areas when the dampening feed rate is too low. Hot-weather scumming is more properly referred to as **tinting,** the bleeding of ink pigment particles into the dampening solution, which increases as the temperature increases. This problem can be eliminated by controlling the temperature of the solution.

Constant operating temperature. Refrigeration of the dampening solution helps maintain a constant feed rate of dampening solution to the plate, independent of the temperature of other parts of the press or the surrounding air. A constant feed rate helps to maintain consistent print quality and reduce waste.

Maintaining the fountain pan temperature at 50–55°F (10–13°C) helps to keep the ink roller temperature from rising too high due to roller friction on high-speed presses.

Temperature affects viscosity of the dampening solution. This relationship is particularly noticeable at the metering nip. Variations in temperature results in variations in the metered film thickness, which affects the level and consistency of print quality.

Reduction in evaporation of alcohol. Refrigeration permits the cooling of the dampening solution to temperatures below, say, 50–55°F (10–13°C) instead of the typical operating temperature of 68°F (20°C). Reduced operating temperatures are particularly important with dampening systems that use alcohol. The lower operating temperature reduces the amount of alcohol that evaporates from the dampening solution. As a result, alcohol consumption can be reduced as much as 50%, and less alcohol will be in the pressroom atmosphere.

Although cooling the dampening solution is thought to improve print quality, several possible problems could be introduced:

- The formation of condensation in the fountain pan, which could drip onto the paper causing paper deformation. The fountain pans on new presses are insulated on the outside.
- An increase in the tack of printing inks, resulting in **picking**—the delamination, splitting, or tearing of the paper surface due to an ink film's resistance to being split between blanket and paper.

Printing Using Alcohol Substitutes

Many different alcohol substitutes on the market have been tested extensively at GATF. The key to successfully running most substitutes is the durometer and nip relationship of the dampening system rollers. Primary consideration must be given to the metering roller, which requires a somewhat lower durometer than when running alcohol. Normally, metering rollers are supplied with a durometer of 25–30 and sometimes will further harden after being run on press. It is recommended that the durometer (durometer A) of the metering roller be reduced to 18–22 when running alcohol substitutes. Softer rollers tend to be more water-receptive. Their softness increases the nip between the metering roller and the chrome roller without increasing the pressure.

Some of the problems encountered when using metering rollers of normal hardness include rollers becoming sensitive to ink, as well as water banding, or "ridging," on the chrome roller and metering roller, which results in print streaking. The increased nip created by the softer metering roller tends to smooth out the water film thickness on the chrome roller.

Another necessary deviation from normal conditions when running alcohol substitutes is reducing the nip between the chrome roller and the dampening form roller. Normally, when running alcohol, this nip is between 5⁄16–3⁄8 in. (8–10 mm), depending upon the diameter of the rollers. However, when running alcohol substitutes, this nip may have to be reduced to as little as 1⁄8–3⁄16 in. (3–5 mm) to regain the thinned water film created by the increased nip between the metering and chrome rollers, and to induce slippage between the chrome and the form roller. Under normal conditions, the form roller is driven by the oscillator. If there is not enough slippage, the form roller tends to drive the chrome roller.

On one of the typical alcohol dampening systems, the metering and chrome rollers are gear-driven by the dampening system motor, and the form roller is driven by the press. If the form roller begins to drive the chrome roller, roller speed increases. As the dampening system rollers accelerate beyond normal conditions, water tends to build up at the roller ends, causing splashing or spraying. Excessive roller speed also creates undue stress on the dampening system motor, which is a common cause of circuit breaks and motor failures. Ideally, the dampening system should be able to run at the same speed (or slightly faster) with an alcohol substitute than with alcohol.

The skew of the metering roller is another consideration. Some alcohol substitutes work best with the metering roller skewed, while others require parallel positioning of the metering roller to the chrome roller. This reduces pressure in the center of the roller. The metering roller usually must be skewed when the form is running too wet in the middle and dry at the ends. The roller should be set parallel to the chrome roller if the middle of the form is not receiving enough water. The optimum angle of the skew should be determined by experimenting, as it may vary depending upon the particular alcohol substitute being used.

A good indication of ink/water balance is the scum line that forms on the bend of the lead edge of the plate. After the press has stabilized, stop the run and evaluate the scum line. This is best done at delivery load changes. Perfect ink/water balance yields a thin even scum line across the width of the plate. If the plate is too dry in an area, the scum line widens, and if it is too wet in an area, the scum line disappears.

Another crucial adjustment is the speed of the metering roller. Higher dampening roller speeds are needed to meter substitute-based dampening solutions (which can lead to slinging and an insufficient control margin at high speeds).

Problems Due to Alcohol Substitutes

Following are some problems that may occur when using alcohol substitutes in the dampening solution:

Metering roller sensitivity. Alcohol substitutes sometimes cause the metering roller to become sensitive to ink. The ink is first picked up by the chrome roller and then distributed to the metering roller. A solution to this is to etch the chrome roller. A 1:32 etch of 1 oz. (29.6 mL) phosphoric acid to 32 oz. (947.2 mL) gum usually restores the water-receptiveness of the chrome roller. Water-receptivity of the metering roller is maintained by applying gum or a coating.

Banding due to hard metering roller. Banding can occur when using an alcohol substitute with a metering roller of normal durometer (25–30). The water banding on the roller results in very fine light and dark streaks around the cylinders and on the print. The solution is to use softer metering rollers.

Some manufacturers offer metering rollers with a slightly grained surface. The grained surface allows more water to be carried through the nip, and the softer covering provides the operator with a wider setting latitude for improved dampening control.

Maintaining proper dampening solution concentration. Since the water in the dampening solution evaporates but most alcohol substitutes do not, the substitute concentration can increase significantly with time. For some substitute solutions, this causes significant problems with ink/water balance, ink lay, and even coating adhesion. Since substitute concentration cannot be easily determined, the system must be drained at least once a week.

Overcooling the dampening solution. Overcooling the dampening solution makes the ink very tacky and can lead to picking and piling problems. The best temperature setting for the refrigeration unit for dampening solution is 50–55°F (10–13°C), although it is normal for the temperature to increase slightly in the fountain pan.

Roller stripping. Roller stripping sometimes occurs when the inking system is not thoroughly cleaned between uses of different alcohol substitutes. When stripping occurs, the common procedure of copperizing the inking rollers could be employed for older presses. If the problem occurs on presses equipped with nylon- or Teflon-covered oscillator rollers, flushing the ink rollers with warm water (after the ink has been removed with solvent) may correct the problem.

Flooding during press trip-off. If the feeder trips when running alcohol substitutes, it is a good idea to shut off the dampening system to prevent flooding. Flooding could be enhanced by the reduced nip between the chrome roller and form roller required for many of the alcohol substitutes. As a standard operating procedure, it is a good idea to shut off the dampening system if the press must idle for more than a minute and a half or two minutes to keep the inking system from loading up with dampening solution.

Foaming. When foaming occurs in the dampening solution pan, foam buildup tends to hit the edge of the metering roller which, in turn, causes splashing onto the press sheets. Antifoaming agents can be used with alcohol substitutes that cause foaming difficulties. Also, some manufacturers of press recirculators offer foam-free systems, which are mechanically engineered to eliminate foaming.

Plugging. Plugging of halftone shadows or small reverse type sometimes results if there is too little alcohol substitute. In other words, the water is "not being made wet enough."

Deposit on metering roller. Some dampening solutions tend to cause a deposit of white material (salts) to build up on the metering roller. These white deposits can become sensitive and take on ink. The buildup usually occurs when the press stands idle overnight. To overcome this, the metering roller should be backed away from the chrome roller and washed with the proper cleaning solutions to clean and desensitize the metering roller.

Excessive water feed. Mixing alcohol with a substitute sometimes leads to a tendency to run too much water, resulting in emulsification, poor performance of the dampening system, and related problems. A true alcohol substitute should require no alcohol at all.

Picking resulting from low ink film thickness. Some alcohol substitutes require ink and water to be balanced at a lower point than normal in order to hold open shadows and fine screen tints. There may be a need to decrease ink film thickness to as low as 0.15 mil, which is a deviation from the normal 0.2–0.4 mil for sheetfed printing. Generally, thinner ink films produce more stress on the sheet, which results in greater picking. However, tests have indicated that some alcohol substitutes cause less picking at low ink film thickness levels than does alcohol. Because of the water film required, alcohol substitutes tend to improve blanket lubrication, giving better sheet release from the blanket.

Suggestions for Running Substitutes

The following checklist features nine steps that are recommended to run alcohol substitutes successfully:

1. Submit a sample of your tap water to your chosen dampening solution manufacturer for analysis. This

sample will provide information for selecting the correct dampening solution and alcohol substitute chemistry for your dampening system and your printing plant's water characteristics.

2. Discuss your printing operation with your chemical supplier. Be specific about press models, inks, dampening systems, roller washes, blanket washes, and different types of paper used to make sure that they are totally compatible.
3. Check dampening roller pressure settings and durometer readings. This should include inking and dampening form rollers. Make sure plate-to-blanket pressure is also set properly.
4. Follow the manufacturer's mixing instructions. If the instructions recommend mixing between 3–8 oz./gal. of water, start with the minimum of 3 oz. Take a pH/conductivity reading and record the information as a starting point reference.
5. Run this mixture of dampening solution and monitor its printability. For example, how does the plate roll up? How does the press start up after feeder trips? Does the plate run clean and open without feeding excess amounts of dampening solution? Communicate this information back to the dampening solution manufacturer.
6. Check your dampening solution regularly. Paper coating, ink bleed, and blanket and roller cleaners can contaminate dampening solution. Take temperature, pH, and conductivity readings after every three hours of press operation. Record these readings in the press logbook. Keep the solution at the mixture that works best.
7. As the pressrun continues, observe the changes in pH and conductivity. When they reach a point where printing problems begin, such as plugging or scumming, the dampening solution is probably contaminated. Record your finding in the press logbook and remix a fresh batch of solution.
8. Drain and clean your dampening system weekly.
9. Have the refrigeration system on your water circulation systems checked and serviced by a qualified technician regularly (after 1,000 hours of operation).

Maintenance

Like all mechanical devices, the dampening system should be properly lubricated and cleaned. Worn bearings or adjustments must be repaired or replaced, and corroded or uneven roller stocks must be turned down. Worn or bent spindles must be repaired. No press operator can obtain good dampening with rollers that are not cylindrical.

The dominant maintenance problem on conventional dampening systems is caused by the roller covers. They become greasy and ink-permeated during running, consequently failing to carry water adequately. When covers become dirty, hard, or threadbare, they must be replaced. Paper sleeves are easier to change than cloth covers.

When removing a covered roller from the press for any reason other than to replace the cover, the press operator must make sure that the ends of the roller are not reversed when the roller is reinserted. A roller reversed end for end will rotate in the opposite direction in relation to its cover, and the cover will be twisted. A cloth cover will become baggy and begin to lint, and a paper-strip cover may actually begin to creep. To prevent these problems, some press operators mark the operator's side end of all covered rollers.

A mixture of one part 85% phosphoric acid to thirty-two parts 14° Bé gum arabic, called **1:32 gum etch,** can be used to desensitize a chrome-plated roller to make it water-receptive. After the gum etch is applied, the roller's surface should be polished with a dry cloth.

The smooth metal surface of the oscillator can become greasy. The press operator can sometimes see it because the film of dampening solution on the oscillator's surface will be broken. Such a roller should be thoroughly rinsed with a grease-cutting solvent. The solvent should then be washed away with water, and the roller gum-etched. The gum etch should be rubbed down to a smooth film and allowed to dry. The roller should then be dampened to see if the dampening solution beads. If it beads, the cleaning operation should be repeated. If the solution does not bead, the roller is ready for operation. Several proprietary solutions are available to clean the oscillator.

If organic growth occasionally occurs in the recirculating system, a preventive measure is to clean the system at least once a week. Such maintenance should include draining the fountain, refilling it with plain water, and redraining it. Fungus arresters can also be used to prevent organic growth. A solution of 10% bleach and 90% water is often used to flush recirculators and pans at the end of the work week. The system must be flushed thoroughly to remove all traces of bleach before it is refilled with dampening solution.

Operating Problems

The greatest problems that face the press operator in the operation of the dampening system are uneven dampening across the plate and inconsistent dampening during a run. Uneven dampening across the plate has a number of causes. The two most common causes are dirty dampening rollers and improper roller settings.

With seamless molleton dampener covers, if the roller is removed from the press and accidentally replaced in a reversed position, the twist reverses and the cover becomes baggy, resulting in uneven dampening.

Improperly adjusted dampening form rollers and ductors cause many problems. It is absolutely necessary to see that all contact points are adjusted properly. Each form roller and the ductor must be checked at least at four points. Each end of each form roller must properly contact both the plate and the oscillator. Each end of the ductor must properly contact the oscillator and the fountain roller.

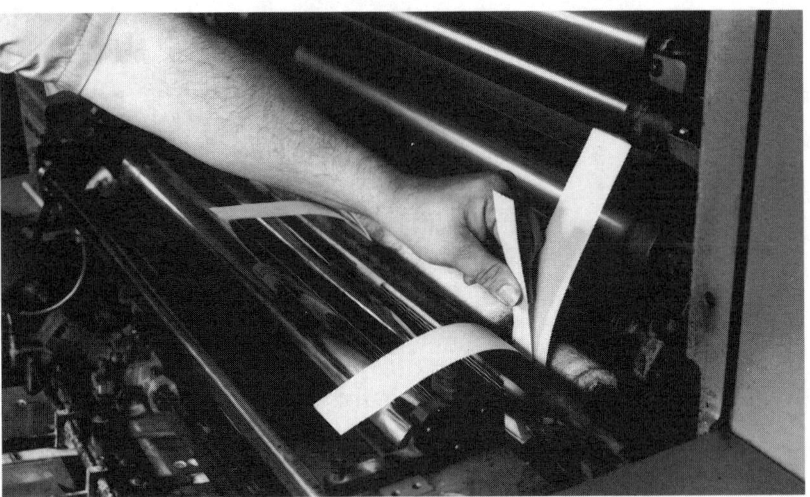

Using a sandwich of plastic strips to determine if the form roller is properly set

If the spindle bearings are good; the spindles and the stocks are straight, round, and true; and the covers are clean and unworn; proper adjustment is not difficult. If the system is in good order, properly adjusted, and properly operated, even dampening across the plate is ensured.

Poor dampening at the roller ends causes many problems. The plate may catch up (start taking on ink in nonimage areas) at the sides or the ends of the cylinder. The ends of form rollers are often smaller than the rest of the roller if the ends of the molleton sleeves are drawn down too tightly. Poor contact with the plate often results.

Uneven dampening can cause serious problems. A large part of a job can be ruined before uneven dampening is discovered. If the plate becomes too dry locally or all over, **catchup**—ink in nonimage areas of the plate because of a lack of dampening solution—is likely to occur on the plate, and those sheets must be discarded. Even when there is no actual catchup, there may be a strengthening of color or a slight thickening of halftones that prevents those sheets from matching the others or the proof.

Uneven dampening throughout the run is generally caused by poor operation of the dampening system. It can stem from frequent stopping of the press or sudden changes in atmospheric conditions. A sudden change in relative humidity may cause a setting that was good at 9:00 A.M. to be extremely poor at 11:00 A.M. It is seldom that an early-morning setting will do for a whole-day's run in a plant that is not air-conditioned. A draft from an occasionally opened door may also affect dampening characteristics.

It is not unusual for a plate's demand for dampening solution to change during a day's run. After 15,000–20,000 impressions, the desensitizing film on the plate may change to such an extent that extra dampening solution is needed to keep it clean.

Generally, most dampening problems result from too much solution on the plate. Too much solution results in excessive emulsification into the ink. The press operator often increases the ink flow to compensate for this occurrence. However, increasing the ink flow only compounds problems. The result is a poor job, perhaps beyond salvaging, and often a ruined plate. Too much dampening solution on the plate affects the entire inking system. When dampening solution gets on the rollers of the ink train, the gum and acid desensitize the rollers and they refuse to take ink. Running more ink will not cure the condition. Ink can become emulsified in the dampening solution, causing *tinting* in the nonimage areas of the plate. The ink can also emulsify so much dampening solution that it prints light and results in grainy halftones and weak solids.

Running too much dampening solution along with too much ink compromises the drying characteristics of the job. The ink on such a job will smear for days after printing. The moisture picked up by the paper will further retard drying, because the moisture is trapped between the sheets and raises the humidity of the air that is trapped with it.

Too much moisture transferred to the paper from an overdampened plate also causes register problems. Paper expands across the grain between colors. Excessive expansion of this type requires a shift in packing, which may ruin register and also cause slurring. If the moisture pickup of the paper is uneven or if the moist paper dries out around the edges of the piles between printings, achieving close register will be almost impossible.

A problem that resembles tinting is **bleeding,** which is generally due to incompatibility between the ink and dampening solution. When this problem occurs, the dampening solution has broken down the ink, causing tiny water-soluble ink pigments to bleed into the dampening solution. This pigment is eventually absorbed into the paper, causing a uniform tone across the sheet.

The basic requirements of good dampening are as follows:

- A well-desensitized plate
- A clean dampening system that is properly adjusted
- The proper dampening solution
- A sound knowledge of the system and how it works

The press operator has very little to do with the kind of plate to be used, except to recognize a poor plate and report it. The press operator should know when the plate is at fault and be able to distinguish between a poor plate and poor handling of the dampening system.

The dampening system should always be kept clean and properly adjusted. Covers should be soft and water-receptive. Metal rollers should be clean and desensitized so that they will carry an unbroken film of dampening solution. Only enough solution to keep the plate clean should be run. Dampening feed should be carefully adjusted and controlled throughout the run. Only the necessary amounts of alcohol, gum, and acid should be used. The pH and conductivity of the solution should be tested frequently. Manufacturer's instructions for the proper setting of dampening rollers should be strictly followed.

5 Sheet Control

One of the overlooked requirements of successful offset press operation is the smooth and consistent flow of paper through the press. The following conditions must be met for satisfactory flow of paper:

- The paper must be reasonably flat and free from any pronounced tendency to curl, and it must be properly piled and lined up in the feeder.
- Proper adjustment and timing of all sheet-handling elements must be maintained.

Poor sheet control can necessitate frequent press stops, resulting in color variation and ink/water imbalance. Plate problems can stem from press downtime. Getting the press back into balance can result in paper waste.

Sheet control on sheetfed presses involves four basic subsystems:

- Feeder section, where paper is removed from the top of a pile table, forwarded on a feedboard to front stops, laterally and horizontally positioned on the feedboard, and fed into the first printing unit
- Infeed section, where the sheet is transferred from the registering devices of the feedboard to the first impression cylinder of the printing press
- Sheet transfer section, where the sheet is moved between impression cylinders of a multicolor press.
- Delivery section, where printed sheets are jogged and stacked one on top of another.

The first portion of the sheet control system that the press operator is concerned with is the feeder section. Two basic types predominate:

- Stream feeder, where a number of sheets of paper traveling slower than press speed overlap on the feedboard

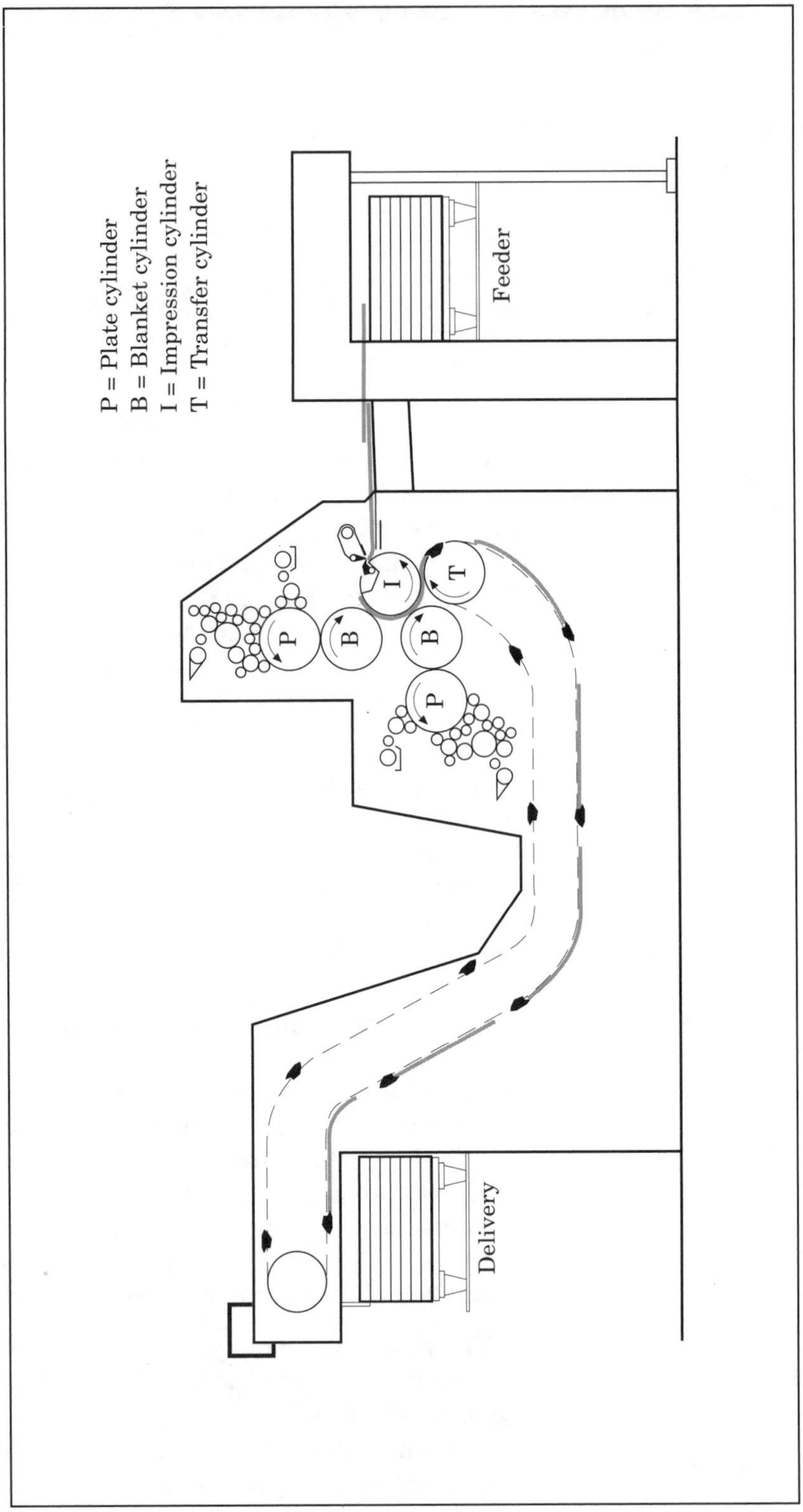

Sheet flow through a two-color press that has a common impression cylinder

Courtesy MAN Roland Inc., Sheetfed Press Div.

P = Plate cylinder
B = Blanket cylinder
I = Impression cylinder
T = Transfer cylinder

Feeder

Delivery

Sheet flow through a two-color convertible perfecting press

Courtesy MAN Roland Inc., Sheetfed Press Div.

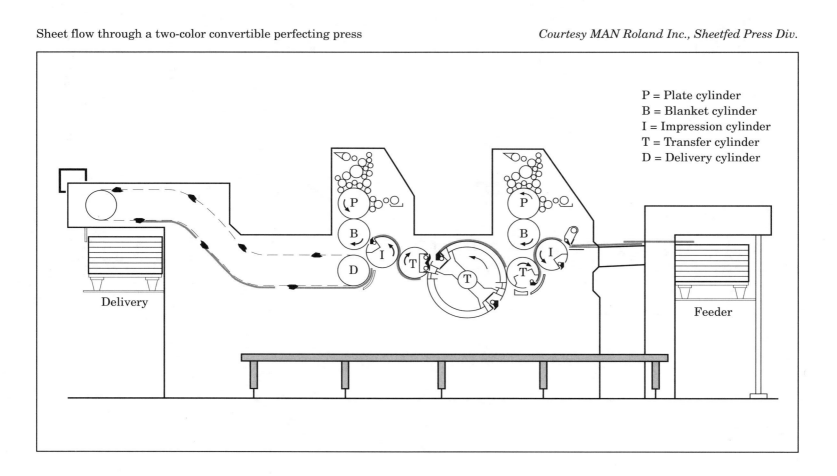

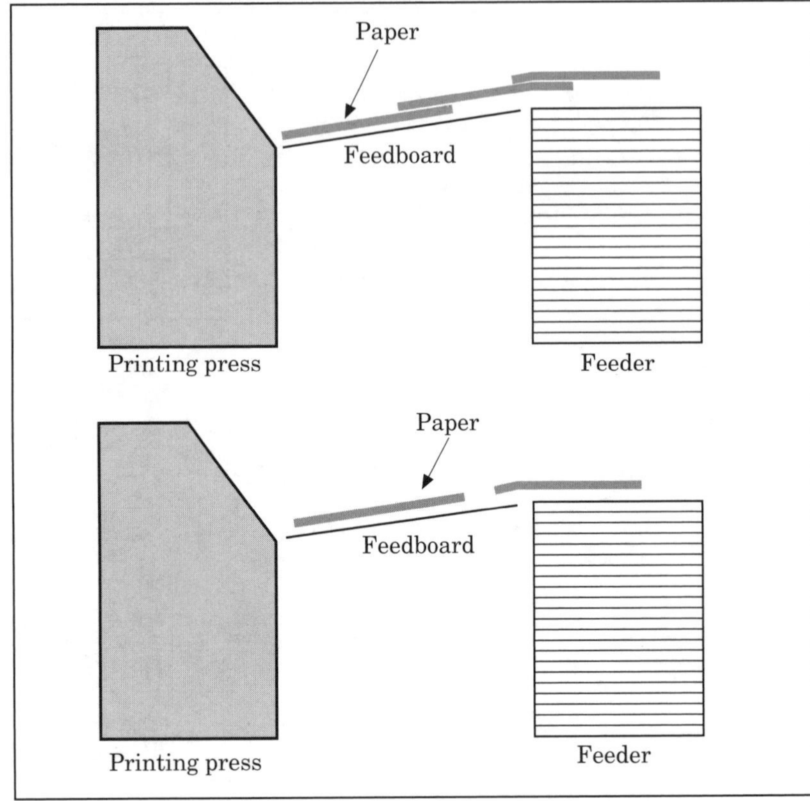

A stream feeder *(top)* and a single-sheet feeder *(bottom)*

- Single-sheet, or successive-sheet, feeder, where only one sheet of paper (traveling at press speed) is on the feedboard at any instant

Stream Feeder

A stream feeder is better able to control the press sheet before its insertion into the first printing unit. Since each sheet of paper is traveling slower than the press, the sheets are easier to control and there is less sheet bounce. The stream feeder is more widely used. Much of the information pertaining to it is also applicable to the single-sheet feeder.

A feeder section of either basic type of feeder can be divided into several distinct segments that work together:

- Pile table, a raisable platform where the paper to be printed is loaded
- Sheet-separation unit, a device that uses both air and a vacuum to separate the top sheet from the pile
- Feedboard, or feed table, a platform or ramp on which the sheet to be printed is transported to registering devices that properly position the sheet and time its entry into the printing unit

Feeder section of a sheetfed press

Pile Table

Stock to be fed into a press must first be neatly fanned and loaded onto the pile table to prevent subsequent feeding problems. Variation in pile position from top to bottom—sometimes as much as an inch or more—may require the press operator to stop the press. Therefore, the press operator must keep the paper pile in the proper position.

Positioning the table. To initially position the pile table, the press operator lowers the table to its lowest position and aligns its center with the center of the feeder. To determine the position of the stock, the operator folds a sheet of stock exactly in half and places it on the pile table with the crease ¼ in. (6 mm) off center, toward the side opposite the device that laterally positions the sheet when it is on the feedboard. The pile guide, which must be perpendicular to the pile table, is securely positioned against the edge of the paper that is used for lateral positioning.

Checking stock. Before the pile is loaded, the stock must be checked against the job specifications. Some of these are size, color, weight, texture, moisture content, quantity, and grain direction. Also, all stock packet labels and ream markers should be removed and retained in case the final count is

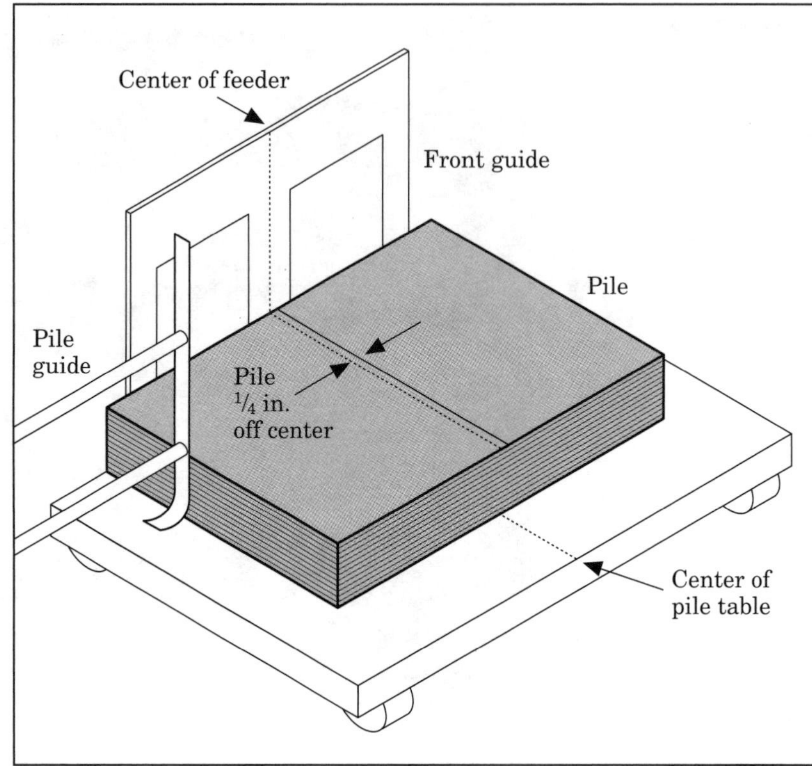

Pile positioned ¼ in. off center away from side guide being used

debatable. Occasionally, the paper supplier will indicate the preferred side-guide and gripper edges.

Wavy-edged or curled paper can cause feeding problems on a sheetfed press. Therefore, stock should be preconditioned to the pressroom's relative humidity and temperature before the job is printed.

Loading the feeder. To load the feeder, each lift (a manageable amount of paper) is fanned and positioned against the front and side pile guides. Excess air is smoothed out after each lift. The side sheet steadiers are placed approximately 0.02 in. (0.5 mm) from the paper pile. Before the pile table is raised to feeding height, all ream markers are removed, and the edges and corners are checked to make sure none were bent during loading.

Bending your knees while keeping your back straight is a safe way to lift or load paper. Only as many sheets as can be easily handled should be lifted.

Continuous feeder. Some feeders can be operated continuously, without the press being stopped so that the next pile of

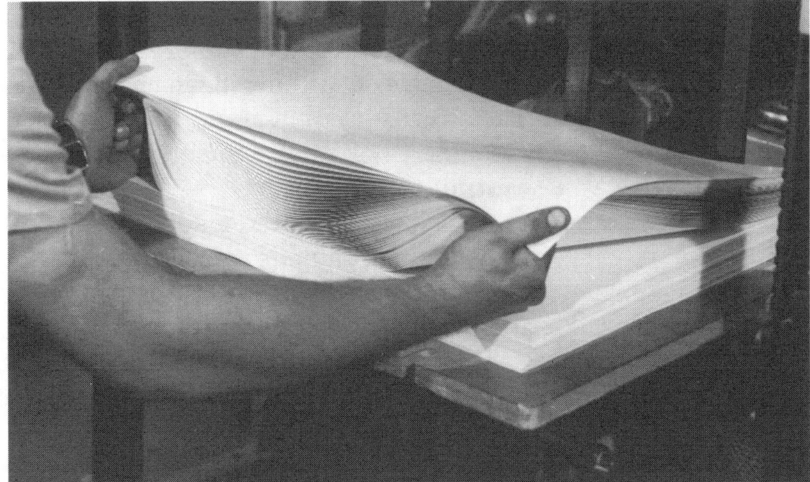
Press operator fanning a lift of paper and positioning it against the front and side pile guides

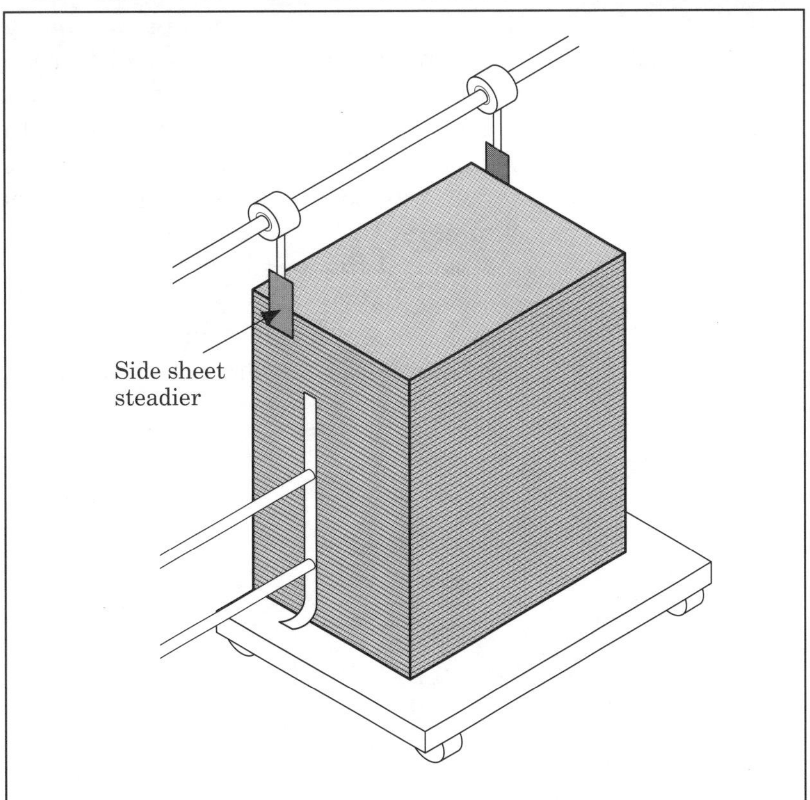

Positioning side sheet steadiers

paper can be loaded. The exact means of reloading the pile without stopping the press varies, but typically either a secondary pile table attached to its own secondary pile hoist system or a series of rods, or swords, that fit through grooves is used.

In the system using swords, when all but a thousand or so sheets have been fed, the press operator inserts the swords into grooves that have been cut in the top of the pile table. The swords are now under the remaining paper and rest on secondary hoist bars. Sheets continue to be fed and the pile continues to rise (supported by the swords) while the pile table is lowered and reloaded. When loading is complete, the reloaded pile table is raised until the top sheets of paper on it touch the swords. At this point, the swords can be removed.

The only precaution in the operation of a continuous feeder is to avoid changing the position or height of the top sheets during a pile change.

Another form of continuous feeder is the **roll sheeter,** a device that cuts paper on a roll into sheets and sends them to the press feeder. Roll sheeters are being used on an increasing number of presses, especially for long pressruns. A roll sheeter saves the printer money because the most economically sized sheet is fed into the press. In addition, a roll sheeter combines the economies of roll stock with the quick makeready and low waste of sheetfed printing. Roll sheeting eliminates the need to stack paper piles.

Most roll sheeters are electronically synchronized to the press so that the press still runs at full speed. Usually, changeover from roll to sheet stock is quick and easy, taking less than 5 min. in some cases. Such a quick and easy

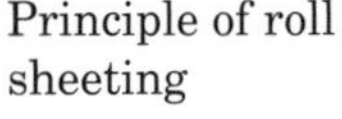
Principle of roll sheeting

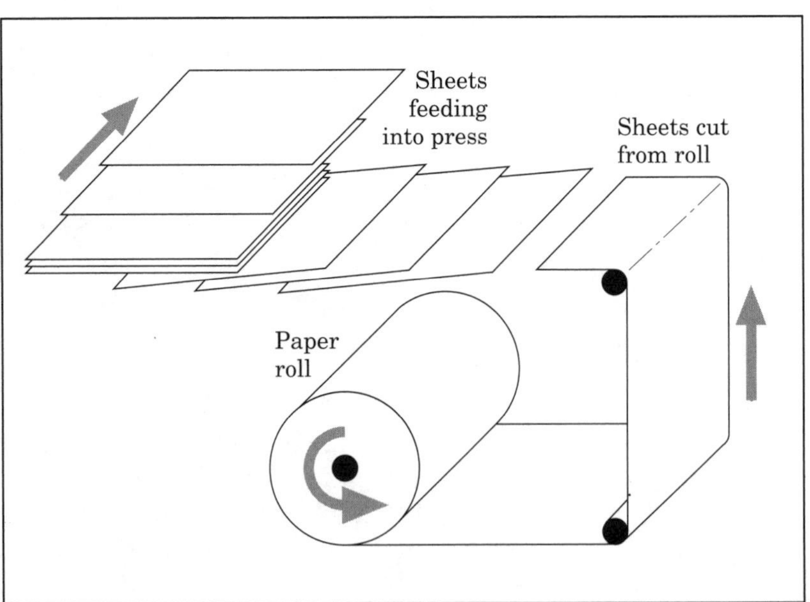

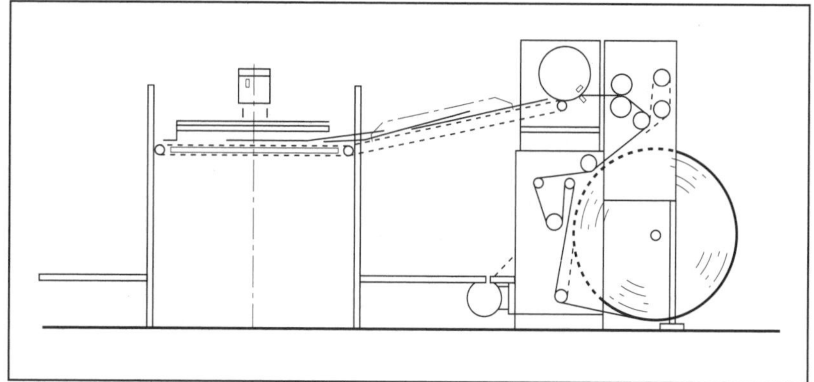

Roland-Mabeg roll sheeter
Courtesy MAN Roland Inc., Sheetfed Press Div.

changeover makes the press more flexible and less dependent on the availability of sheet stock. Most roll sheeters are accurate to within ±0.01 in. (±0.25 mm).

Many roll sheeters have a decurling bar to make the sheets flat so that they feed into the press easier.

A sheeter that feeds paper grain long into the press is preferable to one that feeds paper grain short (cross grain).

Sheet-Separation Unit

The sheet-separation unit consists of devices that separate the top sheet from the paper pile and forward the sheet to the feedboard.

Air-blast nozzles force air beneath the top five or six sheets of the pile. Rear pickup suckers then lift the top sheet. The feeder pressure foot drops down onto the pile, where it steadies the top sheets of the pile while the air-blast nozzles blow

Sheet-separation unit on a MAN Roland press

Sheet-separation unit

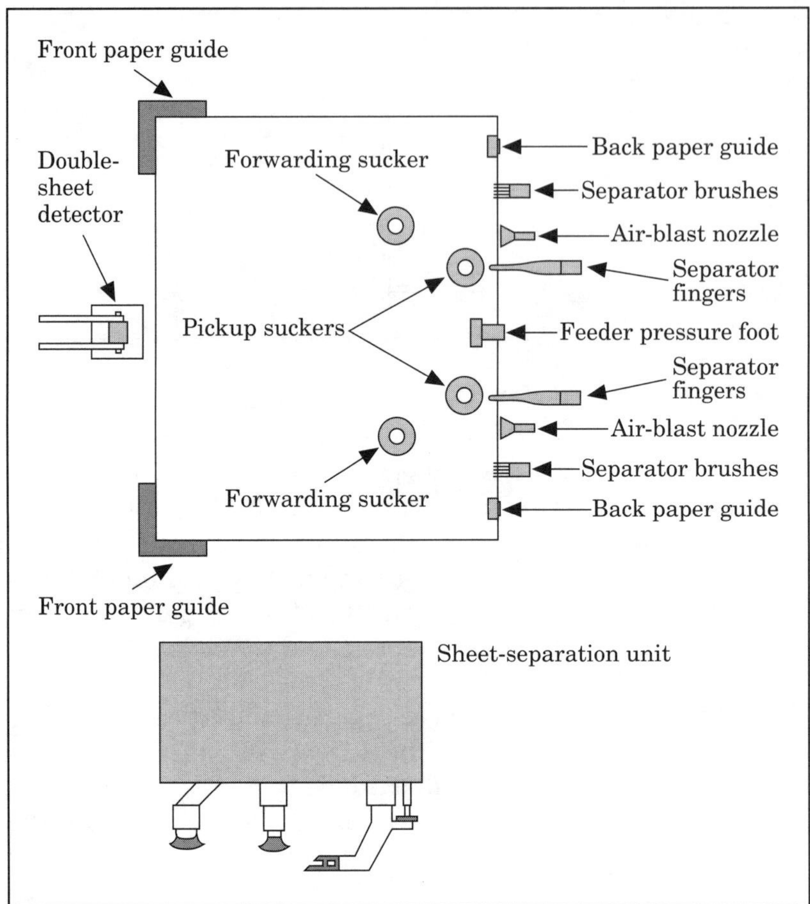

a cushion of air beneath the lifted sheet. Forwarding pickup suckers then transfer the sheet to the forwarding rollers. (On smaller presses, a single set of suckers is used to pick up and forward the sheet.) While this is happening, the rear pickup suckers are already lifting another sheet off the top of the pile. The overlapping, or feeding of sheets in a "stream," leads to the name stream feeder.

Both the vacuum for the suckers and the air for the air-blast nozzles can be regulated and should be set according to the size and type of stock and recommendations in the press manual. Some presses also have gauges that indicate air blast and vacuum pressure. The arrangement of holes in the suckers also varies according to stock used.

Pile height. A critical factor for trouble-free sheet feeding is correct pile height, which is usually $\frac{3}{16}$ in. (5 mm) below the forwarding flaps at the front of the pile. If the pile height is

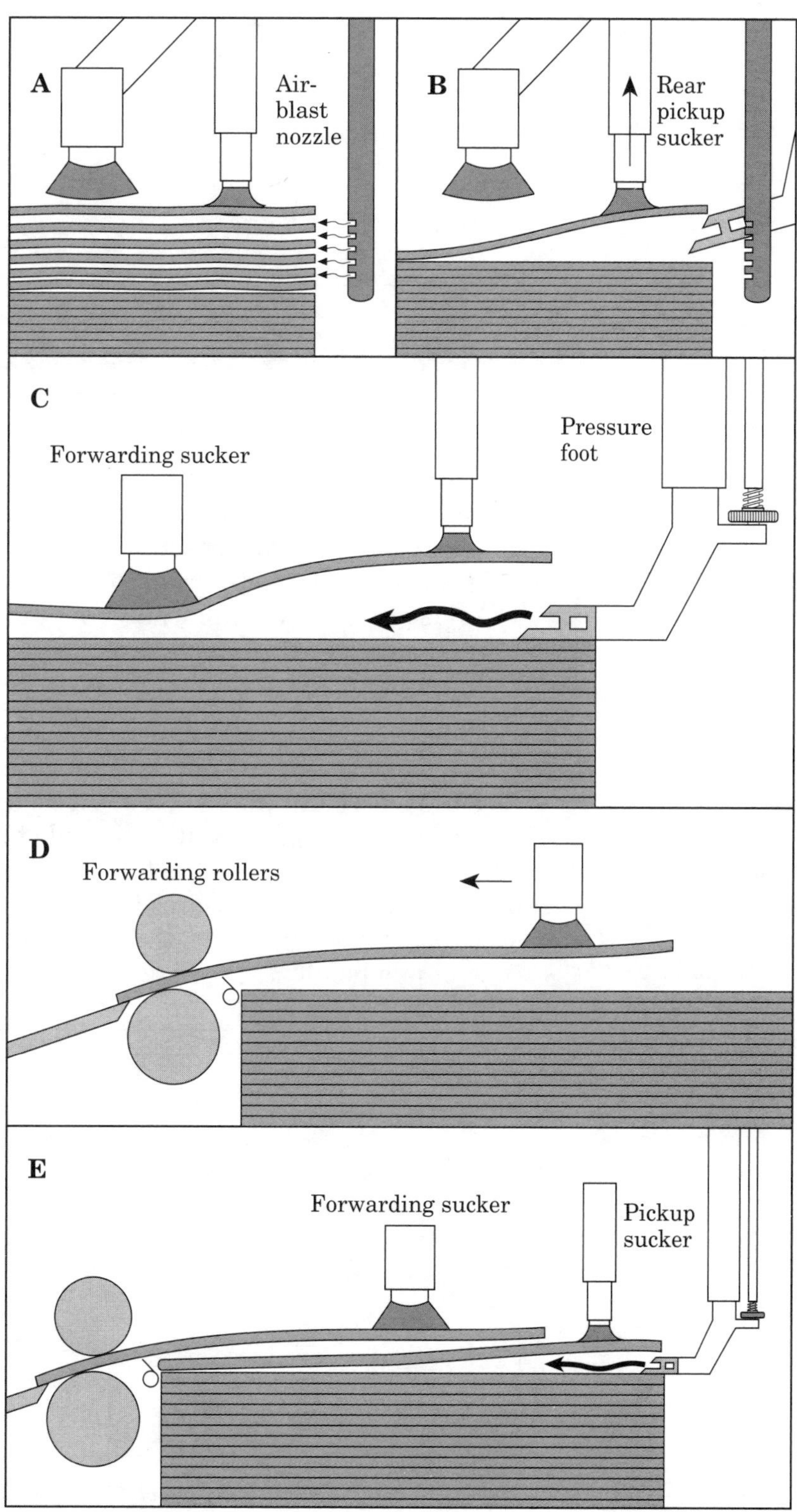

Principle of sheet separation on a stream feeder: (A) air-blast nozzles separate top sheets of pile, (B) rear pickup suckers lift top sheet while feeder pressure foot drops down onto pile, (C) pressure foot blows air beneath top sheet so that forwarding suckers can pick it up, (D) forwarding suckers transfer sheet to forwarding rollers, and (E) rear pickup suckers, pressure foot, and forwarding suckers work together to feed a stream of sheets

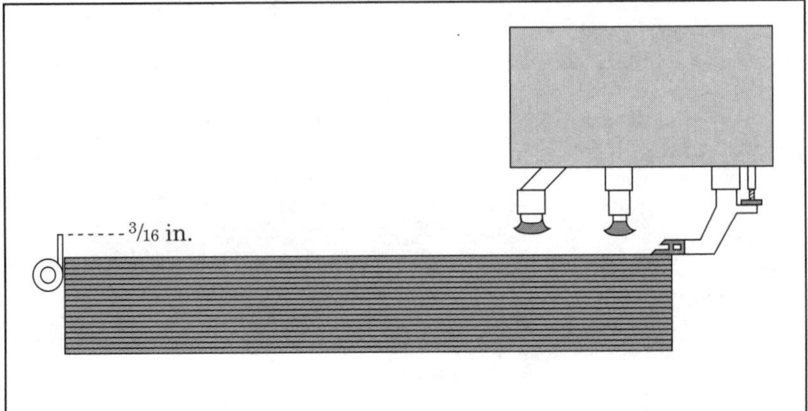

Positioning the top of the pile 3/16 in. (5 mm) below the top of the forwarding flap

not correct, the sheet-separation unit may not be able to separate the topmost sheet from the pile, or it may feed two or more sheets to the feedboard.

Three main methods are used to control pile height:

- Adjusting the feeder pressure foot up or down
- Tilting the separation unit
- Adjusting the separation unit up or down

The pressure foot's position is adjusted by means of a screw. Some presses do not have an adjustable foot, in which case the entire unit must be moved up or down to the desired height. On some presses, it is possible to pivot or tilt the separation unit. If the pressure foot is adjustable, this pivoting or tilting action compensates for uneven stock. If the pressure foot is not adjustable, the tilting action must be used to control pile height.

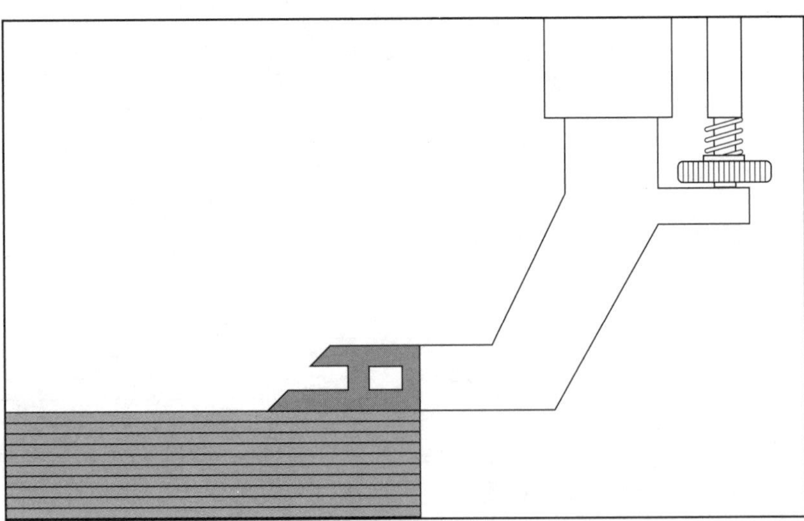

An adjustable feeder pressure foot

Feeder pressure foot blowing air beneath the top sheet of the paper pile

A sheet-separation unit that can be moved up or down

Note the absence of an adjustable feeder pressure foot.

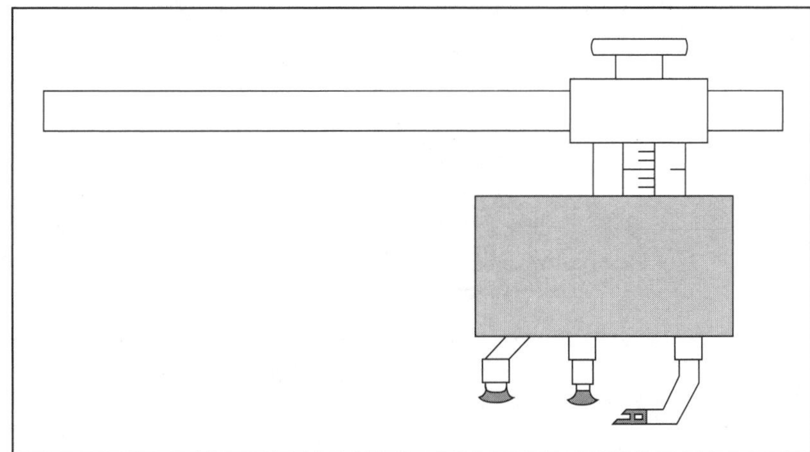

A sheet-separation unit that can be tilted up or down

Note the presence of an adjustable feeder pressure foot.

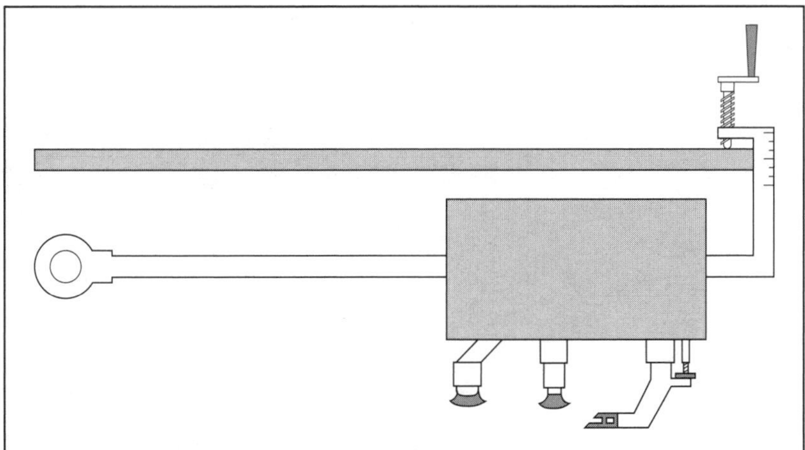

Sheet steadiers. Rear sheet steadiers are positioned at the outside quarters of the pile, with the weights riding freely on the pile. A sheet folded in four columns makes it easier to judge where the outside quarters are; the rear sheet steadiers

Use of the tilting ability of a sheet-separation unit to compensate for uneven stock

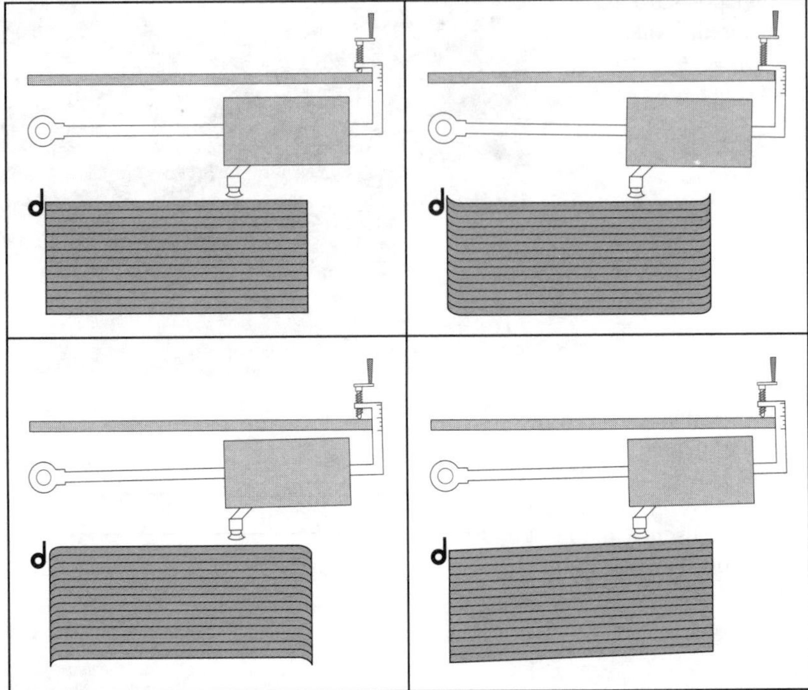

are positioned on the outer creases. Side sheet steadiers are positioned so that they almost touch the pile edges, approximately 0.02 in. (0.5 mm) away.

Positioning sheet steadiers

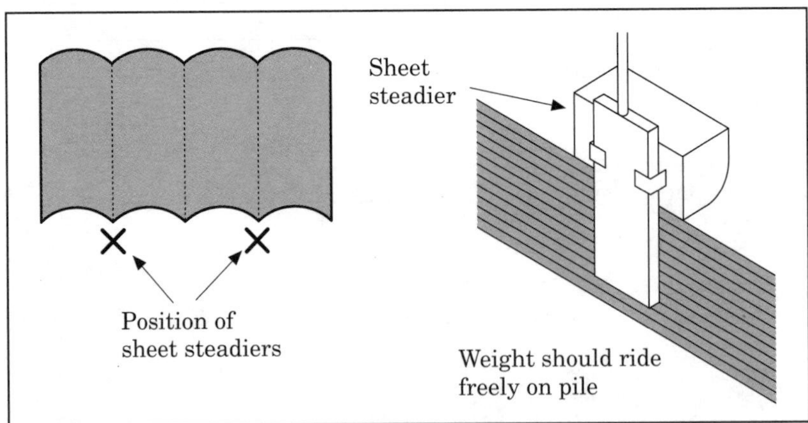

Separator brushes and fingers. Separator brushes or fingers prevent the suckers from picking up more than one sheet at a time. They should be positioned about 3/16 in. (5 mm) in from the edge of the pile and 1/16 in. (2 mm) above it, or just touching it. Stock weight and caliper—thickness—affect the exact location of the brushes and fingers.

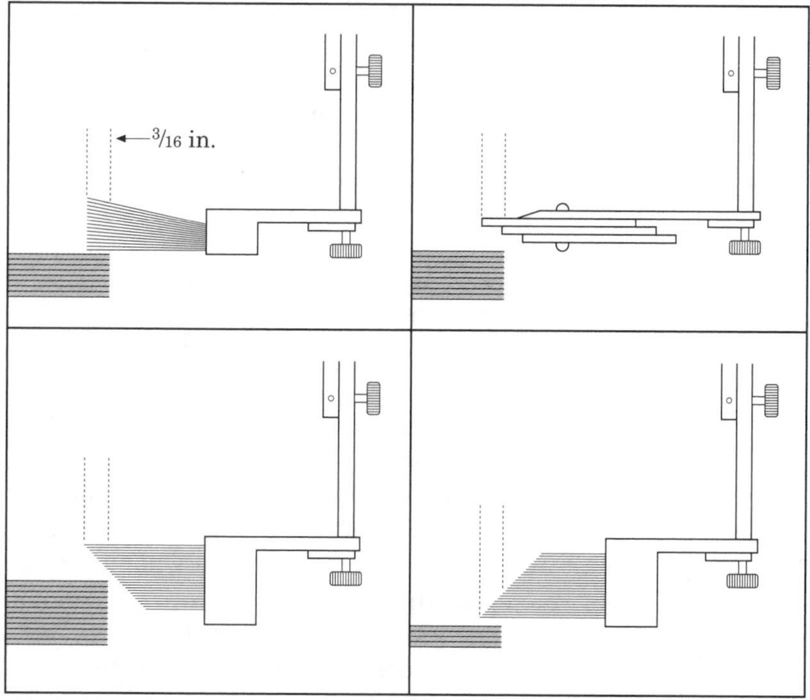

Positioning separator brushes and fingers approximately 3/16 in. (5 mm) into the pile

Rear pickup suckers. Also requiring adjustment are the pickup suckers, the devices that lift the top sheet off the pile. After being brought to their lowest position by turning the handwheel, they are adjusted so that they are parallel to the pile. On some presses, the pickup suckers tilt when they pick up a sheet. This tilting action helps prevent double sheets by slightly raising the back edge of the top sheet to permit air

Rear pickup suckers lifting the top sheet of paper from the pile

from the air-blast nozzles to better separate it from the sheet of paper just below it. Stock thickness also affects the angle of tilt that is required. In addition, stock thickness also affects the type of sucker and sucker holder that is used. The press manual should be checked to assist in the selection of the proper sucker and sucker holder for the material to be printed.

Forwarding suckers. The forwarding suckers, the suction devices that forward the sheet to the forwarding rollers, also require adjustment. They are brought to their lowest position by turning the feeder handwheel. For paper, the recommended minimum height for the suckers above the pile is 1/16–3/16 in. (2–4 mm); if possible, the forwarding suckers should be angled inward to prevent sagging of the sheet. For board, the suckers should be just touching the pile or up to 1/16 in. (1 mm) above it. They should be parallel to the pile, not angled inward. Some forwarding suckers are self-adjusting for height. Like the rear sheet steadiers, the forwarding suckers also are positioned on the outside quarters of the pile.

Air blast. The rear air-blast nozzles also require adjustment. Before the airflow is adjusted, the air pump is turned on, the feeder section engaged, the air to the separation unit turned on, and the feeder handwheel turned until the rear air-blast nozzles blow. Proper air flow will create an "air bulge" under the top 6–10 sheets of the pile. The air-blast nozzles can be adjusted up or down to separate the proper number of sheets.

When the rear pickup suckers first grasp a sheet of paper, the air blast through the feeder foot and/or the air-blast nozzles should provide an air cushion beneath the sheet.

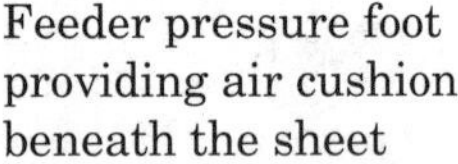
Feeder pressure foot providing air cushion beneath the sheet

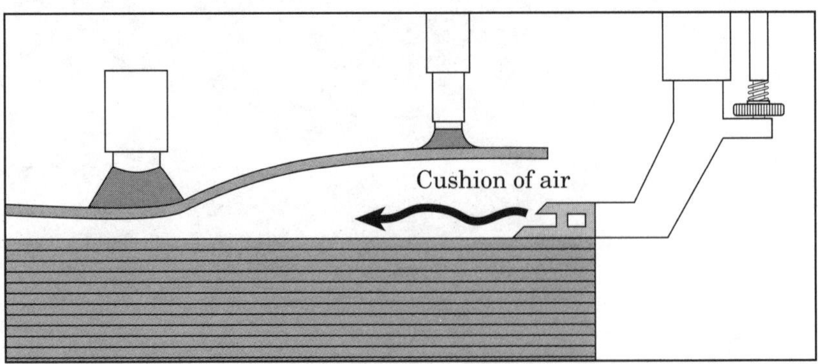

Properly adjusted air flow should separate the gripper edge of the sheet from the pile.

If all parts of the sheet-separation unit have been properly adjusted and the pile is at the proper height, the sheet of paper will be transferred to the forwarding rollers.

Ideally, the air compressors and vacuum pumps for the press should be located in a special room outside of the pressroom. This will lessen noise and, more importantly, dirt in the pressroom.

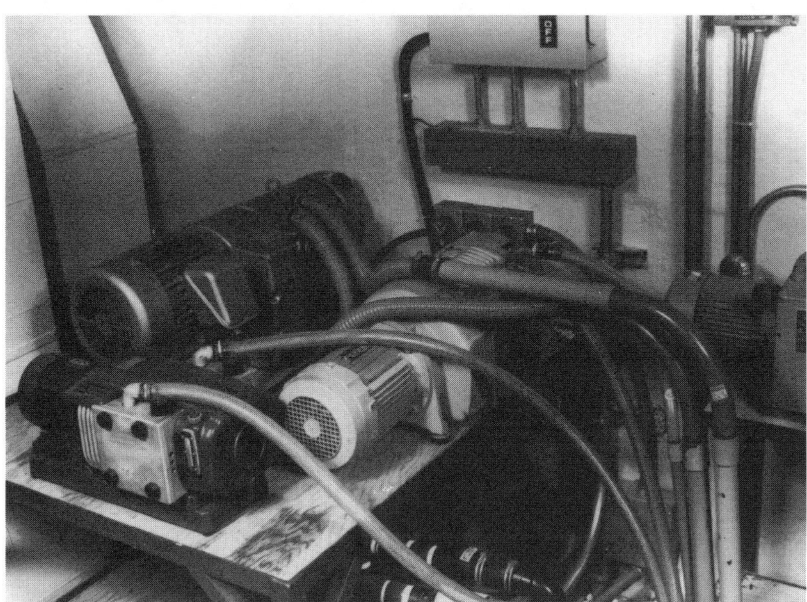

Air compressors and vacuum pumps in a special room outside of the pressroom

Feedboard

Once the forwarding rollers grasp the sheet of paper, the sheet of paper begins to be transferred to the feedboard.

If the sheet-separation unit is incorrectly adjusted, the suckers may pick up and forward two or more sheets of paper simultaneously. Therefore, located between the forwarding rollers is a double-sheet detector, or two-sheet caliper, a device that can be set to stop the feeding action of the sheet-separation unit if more than one sheet of paper is being forwarded.

If the separation unit is functioning properly, a series of hold-down rollers, balls, rotary brushes, and/or flat brushes running on feed tapes transport each sheet down the feedboard. The sheet is driven and held against the front guides, a series of stops that halt the forward movement of the sheet on the feedboard. Then, a side guide pulls the sheet against a register block, which stops the sideways movement of the

Feedboard of a sheet-fed press, showing the various devices to control the press sheet as it moves toward the front guides

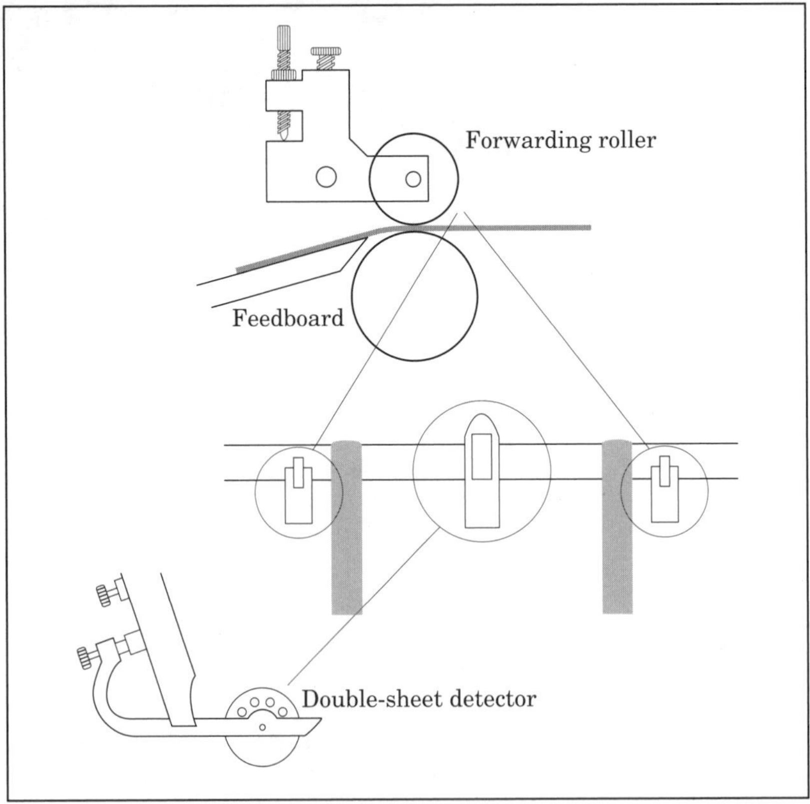

Forwarding rollers and double-sheet detector

sheet. The front guides and the side guide position each sheet exactly, thus achieving lateral and circumferential register on the feedboard.

Feeder tapes, hold-down rollers, front guides, and side guide on the feedboard

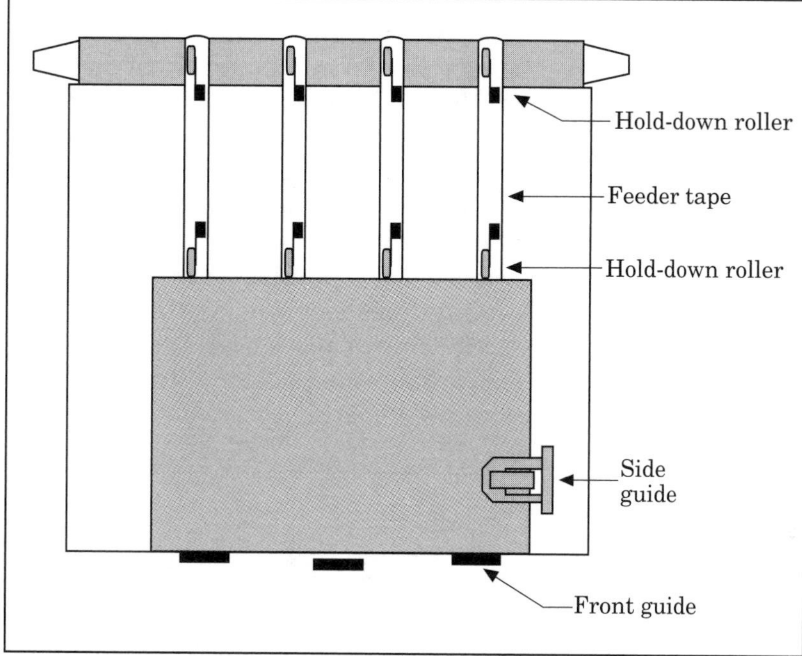

Forwarding rollers. Forwarding rollers must be accurately positioned. If the press has two forwarding rollers, they should be positioned on the outside quarters of the sheet. Folding a sheet of paper in four columns and positioning the forwarding rollers on the outside creases is a simple way to properly position the two forwarding rollers. If the press has four forwarding rollers, a sheet of paper should be folded into eight columns and the forwarding rollers positioned on the first, third, fifth, and seventh creases from the left side of the press sheet.

In addition to being properly positioned, the forwarding rollers on some presses should be properly tensioned. If necessary, the handwheel of the feeder is turned until the forwarding rollers drop onto the rear tape roller and begin to be driven. A strip of 0.004-in. (0.10-mm) paper is used to gauge the tension of the forwarding rollers. The strip is placed beneath the roller being set and then pulled sideways from under the roller. A light drag on the paper strip corresponds to the proper tension. Tension of all forwarding rollers should be the same—light and uniform. Poorly set rollers affect the timing of the sheet to the front guides. A feeler gauge is necessary to check the gap between the adjusting screw and wheel holder on some presses. Proper clearance is usually found in the press manual.

Double-sheet detector. The number of sheets passing beneath the caliper roller depends on the length of the stock being run. If a maximum sheet size is being printed, there are three overlapping sheets. If a minimum sheet size is being printed, there are two overlapping sheets. Hence, the term "double-sheet detector" when used in conjunction with a stream feeder is a misnomer. If a maximum sheet size is being printed, the double-sheet detector is set to trip if four or more overlapping sheets are passing under it. Similarly, if a minimum sheet size is being printed, the detector is set to trip if three or more overlapping sheets are passing under it. The double-sheet detector, then, could be described as an *extra-sheet detector.*

Double-sheet detector with electrical contacts

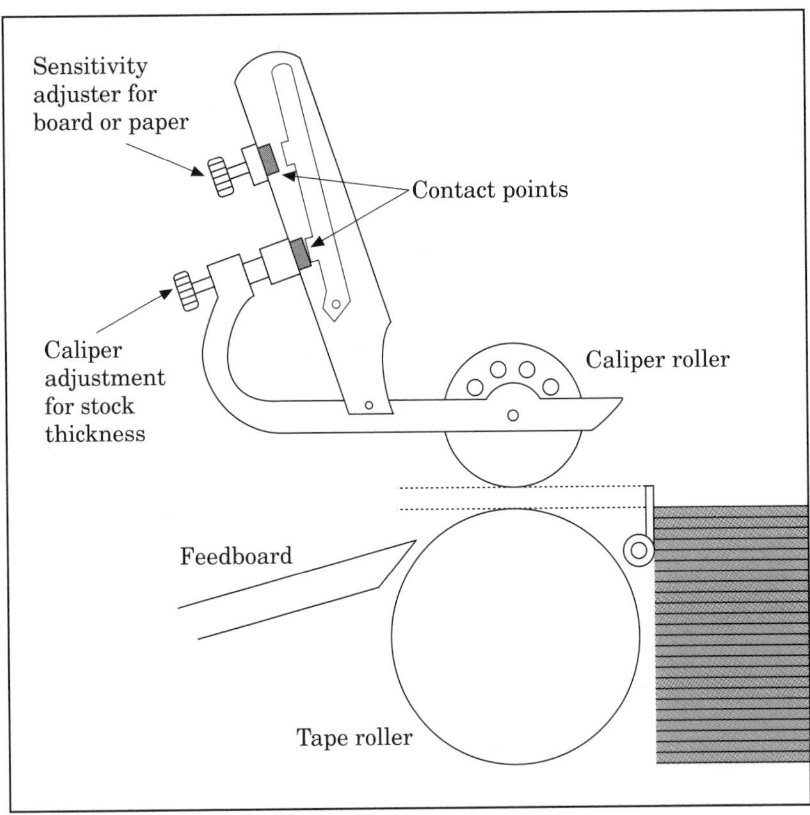

Clearance is also dependent on stock caliper (thickness). Consequently, the double-sheet detector is set using multiple strips of paper of the proper thickness. The number of strips of paper necessary is determined by feeding at least four sheets of paper to the feedboard and then counting the number of sheets of paper overlapping under the caliper roller.

- **Three-sheet clearance.** If three sheets overlap under the caliper roller, four 2×12-in. (50×300-mm) strips of the stock being printed are used to set the double-sheet detector. The caliper roller is adjusted to provide clearance for three overlapping sheets but to disengage if four sheets pass beneath it.
- **Two-sheet clearance.** If two sheets overlap under the caliper roller, three 2×12-in. (50×300-mm) strips of the stock being printed are used to set the unit. The caliper roller is adjusted to provide clearance for two overlapping sheets but to disengage if three sheets pass beneath it.

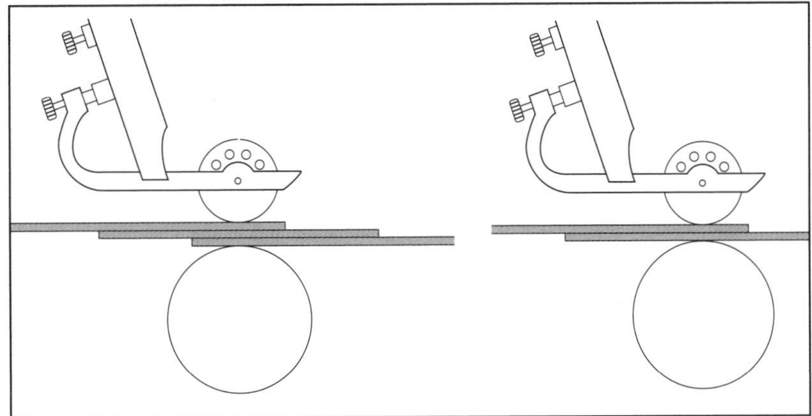

Double-sheet detector set for three-sheet clearance *(left)* and two-sheet clearance *(right)*

Detectors operate either electronically or mechanically. Some electronically operated detectors have a set of contacts that control the sensitivity to paper or board. False detection due to tail-end slap of board often occurs when the press operator changes from paper to board. Therefore, when the stock is changed, the detector must be adjusted accordingly.

Some mechanical detectors have a friction brake to prevent the caliper roller from turning too easily. This brake must not interfere with the roller when paper strips are being inserted. The sensitivity controls of an electronic detector serve the same purpose as the friction brake—to regulate the rotation of the caliper roller.

Many press operators feed sheets down the feedboard and then lower the sheet detector until the feeder trips. The sheet detector is then adjusted for clearance of the paper stream.

Feedboard devices to transport sheets to the front guides. After the press sheet is separated from the pile, it is transferred to the forwarding rollers and then to a series of devices on the feedboard that move the sheet to the front guides. The devices and their position on the feedboard vary from press to press. Depending on press manufacture, these devices may be rollers, balls, brushes, rods, bars, or wheels riding on tapes. Their function is to move a sheet of paper in a straight line until it is stopped by the front guides. In order for the paper to move in a straight line, the transport devices and feed tapes on the feedboard must be properly adjusted. In addition, these devices must be kept clean, because ink buildup can cause the sheet to become cocked on the feedboard.

Sheet guide rods, or **hold-down rods,** are positioned so that they hold down the back corners of the sheet as it enters the feedboard. Properly positioned rods guide the sheet under the forwarding wheels and double-sheet detector.

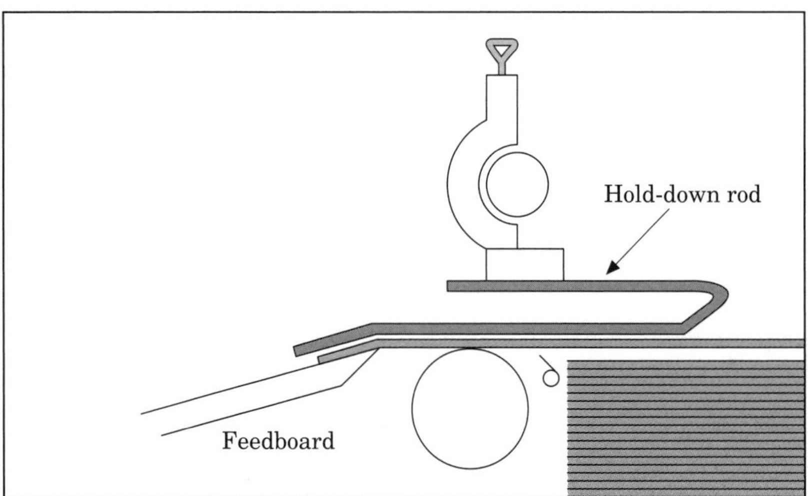

Positioning hold-down rods at the back corners of the sheet as it enters the feedboard

Feed tapes must be properly spaced and properly tensioned. In general, feed tapes are spaced approximately 4–6 in. (100–150 mm) apart. Spacing of tapes depends on the number of tapes on the press and the size of the sheet being printed. If a press has four feed tapes, a press sheet folded in four columns aids in positioning the tapes. The two inside tapes are positioned in the center of the inner quarter panels, and the two outside tapes are positioned almost in the center of the outside panels but a little closer to the outside of the sheet. If the press has six feed tapes, a press sheet folded in eight columns aids in positioning the tapes. One tape is positioned on each of the following creases of the press sheet (from the left): first, second, third, fifth, sixth, and seventh.

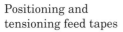

Positioning and tensioning feed tapes

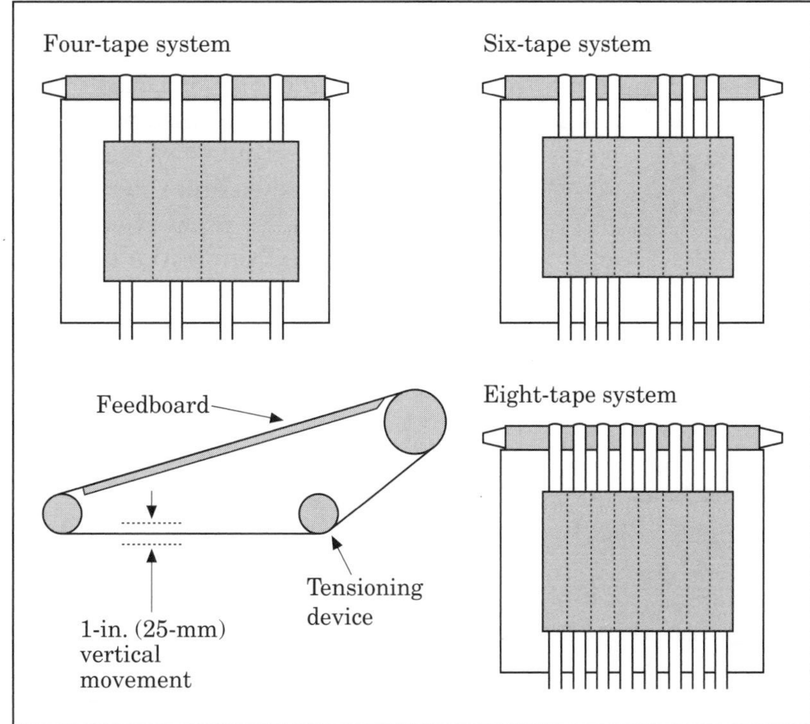

To properly transport a press sheet, the feed tapes must drive with a firm, uniform tension. As a general rule, vertical movement of the tapes should be limited to 0.5–1 in. (13–25 mm). Feed tapes should be kept clean, and worn tapes (e.g., frayed edges) should be replaced.

Before the hold-down rollers can be accurately set to the tail edge of the sheet, the front guides are set to their central or recommended (forward or back) position for correct gripper bite. (See the section discussing front guides for information on how to set them.) Once the front guides are set, the feeder is engaged, the air pump is turned on, and the feeder hand-wheel is turned until one sheet is picked up and forwarded. The sheet is transported along the feedboard until it is stopped against the front guides. Different procedures are used to set the feedboard for paper and board.

Setting the feedboard devices for paper. Good register is the result of hold-down wheels and rotary brushes driving in line with a front guide. Good side-guide register is the result of hold-down rollers not driving the sheet when it is against the front guides; i.e., when the sheet is touching the front guides, the rollers must not be riding on the sheet.

Therefore, hold-down rollers are spaced so that they almost touch the tail edge of the sheet when it is against the front guides, but not so close that they impede with the side-guiding of the sheet. Flat brushes are positioned at the back edge of the sheet so that they hold it against the front guides. Rotary brushes and rollers run on the feed tapes and the rear quarter of the press sheet. Hold-down fingers are positioned near the front of the press sheet to guide it into the front guides and to keep the corners flat. Hold-down balls are adjusted to freely run on the feed tapes and the press sheet; lightweight balls (usually glass or plastic) are used for paper.

Setting the feedboard devices for paper

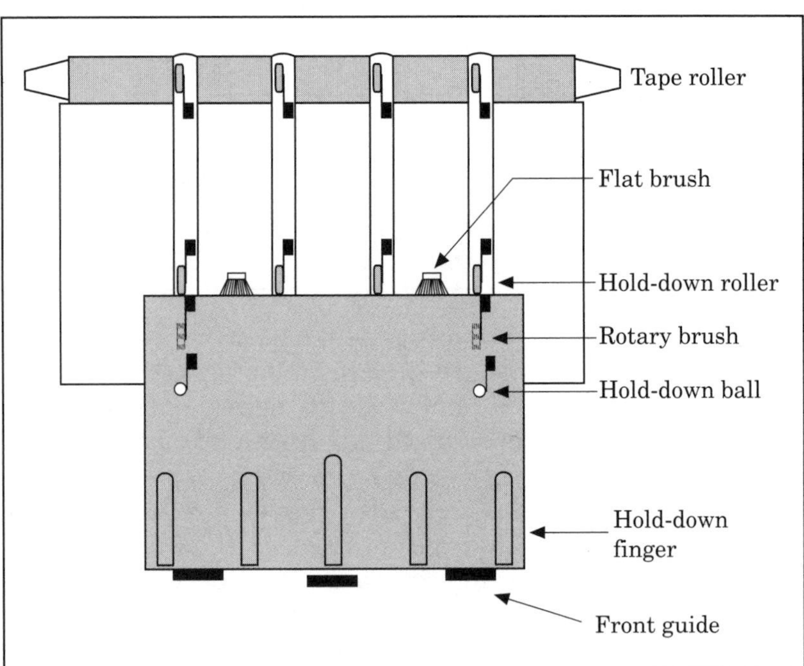

Hold-down rollers, in addition to being positioned just back from the rear edge of the press sheet, must be properly tensioned. A simple way to set the hold-down rollers is to first decrease the tension on each roller until it stops turning and then to increase the tension until it just starts to turn positively on the tape.

Setting the feedboard devices for board. Properly positioned rotary brushes just touch the tail edge of the board after it contacts the front guides. The brushes are adjusted by first releasing tension until they are no longer tape-driven

Relocation of hold-down rollers to transport minimum sheet size

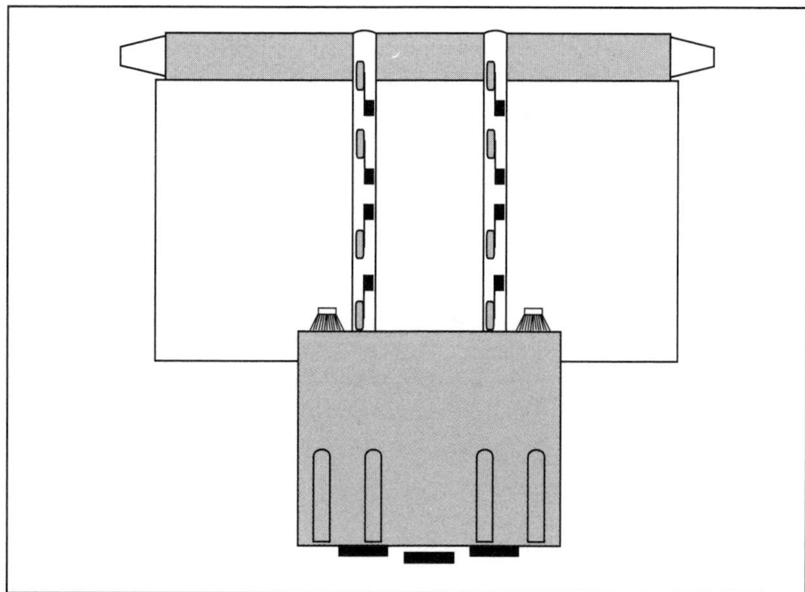

Setting the feedboard devices for board

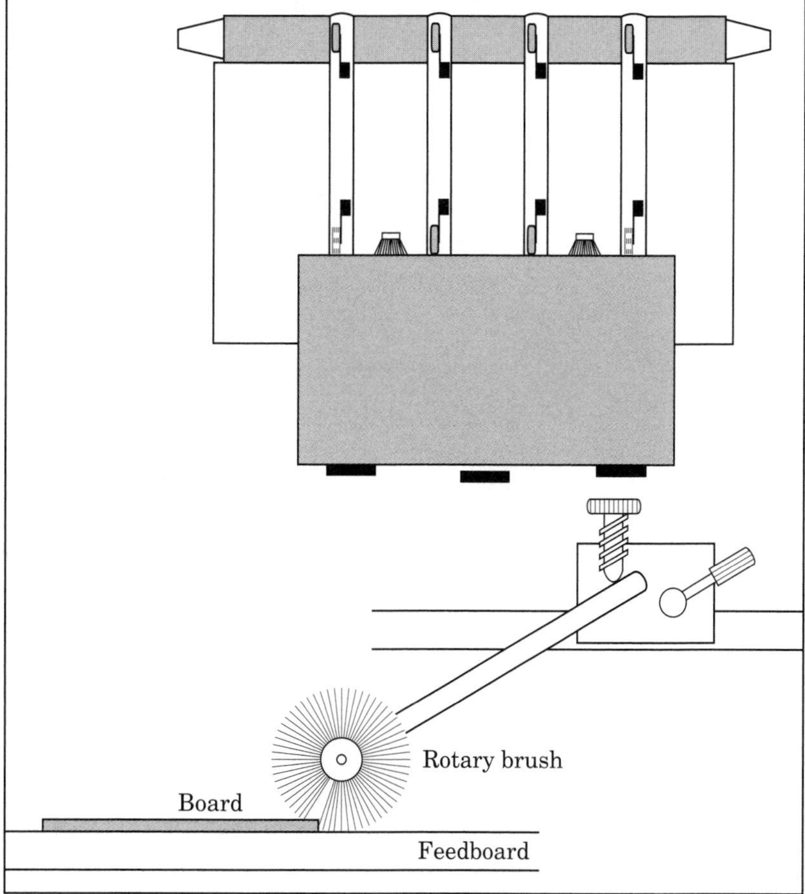

and then increasing tension until they just begin to be tape-driven. Heavyweight balls are used as hold-down rollers. Flat brushes, hold-down rollers, guides, and fingers are positioned in the same way that they are for paper.

Sheet bridges. Several evenly spaced sheet bridges are installed across the gap in the feedboard to prevent the stock from following the tape roller. One sheet bridge is positioned at each outside edge of the sheet, and two or more are positioned under the sheet, depending on its size.

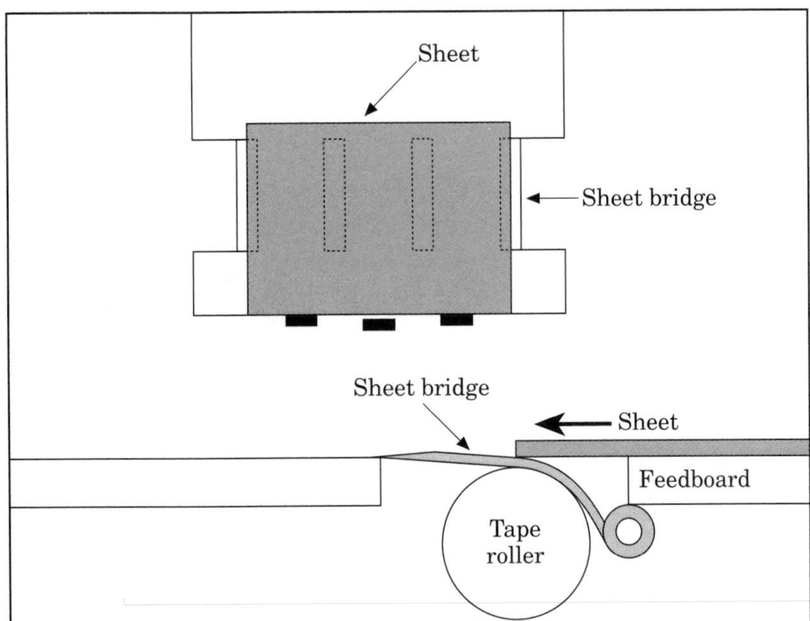

Using sheet bridges to prevent the paper from following the tape roller

Suction devices. The feedboards of some presses are equipped with suction, or vacuum, devices. One type of device consists of a series of suction holes that hold the sheet flat when it is at the front guides. Another type consists of two or more nozzles that aid in transporting the sheet to the front guides. The printing of a small sheet requires the blocking off of all suction holes not covered by the sheet. Suction devices are used in place of, or in combination with, hold-down fingers.

The correct amount of vacuum is determined by transporting a press sheet to the front guides or moving it over the introducing nozzles, inching the press until the vacuum holds the sheet, increasing vacuum until the sheet becomes distorted, and then decreasing it until the distortion disappears.

Suction devices found on some feedboards

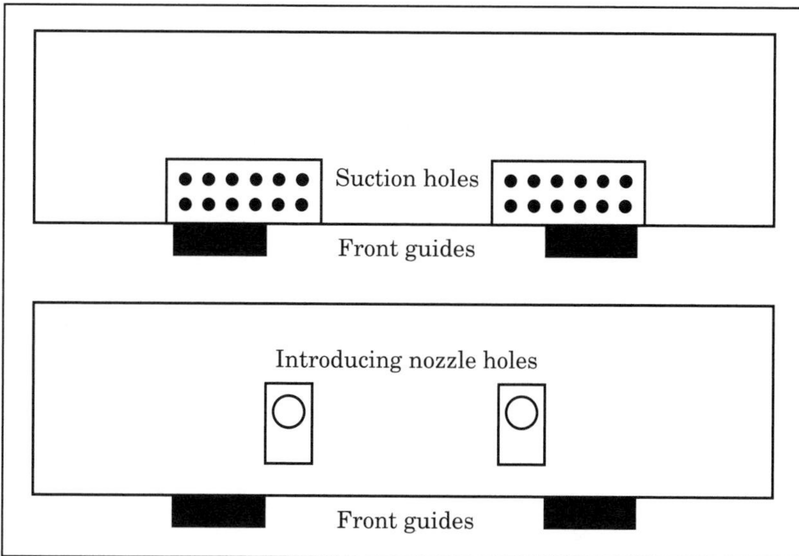

Safety bar. Some presses have a safety bar, or crash bar—a device that detects foreign objects on the feedboard and prevents their passage into the printing unit. Foreign objects include wooden pile wedges and crumpled sheets of paper. Clearance between safety bar and feedboard, which is adjustable, varies from 0 to ⅜ in. (0 to 10 mm). In general, safety bar clearance equals the stock thickness plus ¼ in. (6 mm).

Early and late sheet detectors. In addition to the safety bar, most presses have a device that detects either the early or late arrival of sheets at the front guides. Four basic types of sheet detectors are used:

- **Mechanical type,** which detects late sheets. A sheet reaching the front guides at the proper time prevents a pin from entering a slot in the feedboard. However, if the sheet is late reaching the front guides, the pin drops into the slot, and the feeding action of the press stops. A mechanical sheet detector is easily damaged due to paper-caused wear or poor adjustment.
- **Electromechanical type,** which detects early sheets. The electromechanical sheet detector consists of normally open electrical contacts. A sheet arriving too early at the front guides causes the contact points to close, and the feeding action stops. An electromechanical sheet detector is also easily damaged due to paper-caused wear or poor adjustment.

Various types of early and late sheet detectors

Electromechanical

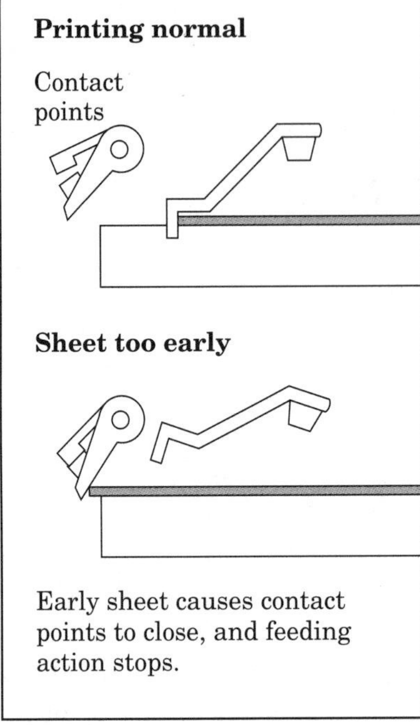
Printing normal
Contact points
Sheet too early
Early sheet causes contact points to close, and feeding action stops.

Mechanical

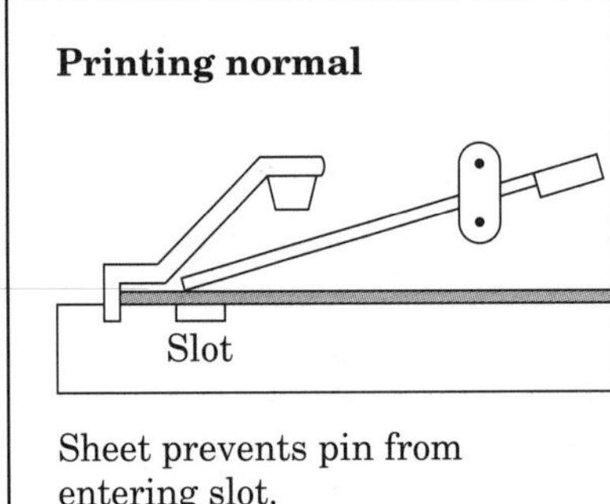
Printing normal
Slot
Sheet prevents pin from entering slot.

Sheet too late

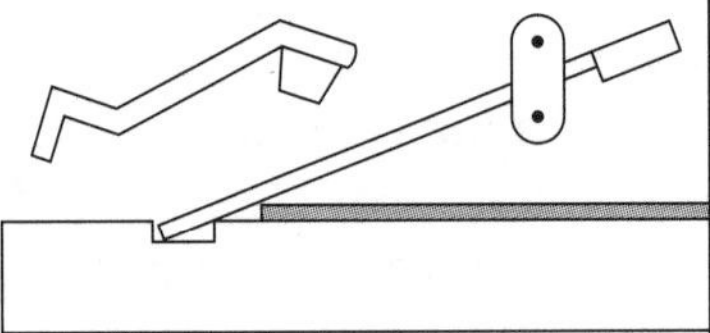

Late sheet causes pin to drop into slot, and feeding action stops.

Photoelectric

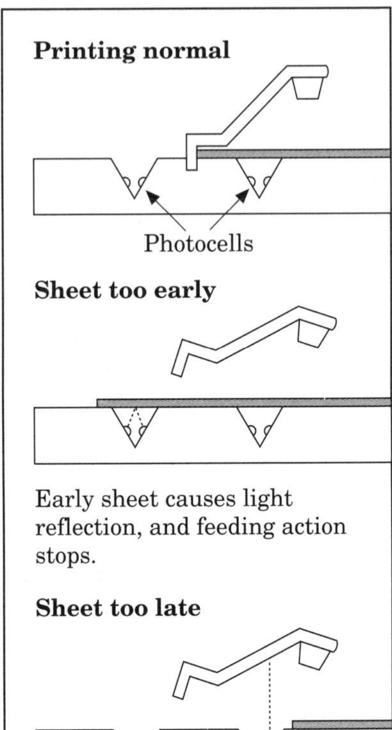
Printing normal
Photocells
Sheet too early
Early sheet causes light reflection, and feeding action stops.
Sheet too late

Late sheet interrupts light reflection, and feeding action stops.

Pneumatic

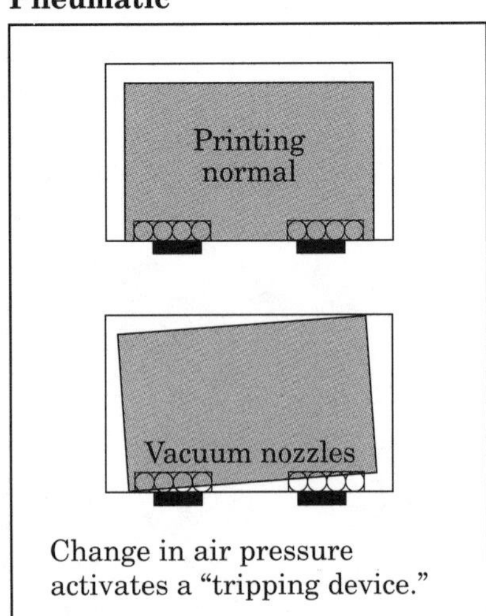
Printing normal
Vacuum nozzles
Change in air pressure activates a "tripping device."

- **Photoelectric type,** which detects both early and late sheets. This type of detector consists of two photocells, one to detect early sheets and one to detect late sheets. Each photocell is paired with a lamp that does not shine on the photocell. If the front guides are up, an early sheet reflects light from the lamp of the "early detector" to its photocell, stopping press rotation and feeder operation. If the front guides are down and the sheet is late, no light reflects from the lamp of the "late detector" to its photocell, stopping feeding action. The operation of each photocell is timed to the position of the front guides. To operate properly, the photocells must be kept clean.
- **Pneumatic type,** which detects sheets located improperly at the front guide. Consisting of a series of vacuum nozzles, the device detects an improperly located sheet whenever air pressure changes. A change in air pressure activates a tripping device that stops feeding action. Porous stock may cause false detection.

No matter what type of detector is used, it must be cleaned daily. In addition, the detectors should be tested periodically. Testing usually involves the insertion of paper strips over the detectors to simulate an "early" or "late" sheet. The press manual usually contains information necessary to perform an accurate test.

Front guides. Front guides either pivot from above the feedboard or from below. They square the sheet in relation to the printing cylinders and determine the front margin. A consistent front margin contributes to the accurate and repeatable positioning of images on press sheets. The accurate positioning of images—either in relation to images on other press sheets or in relation to an image already printed on that

Front guides

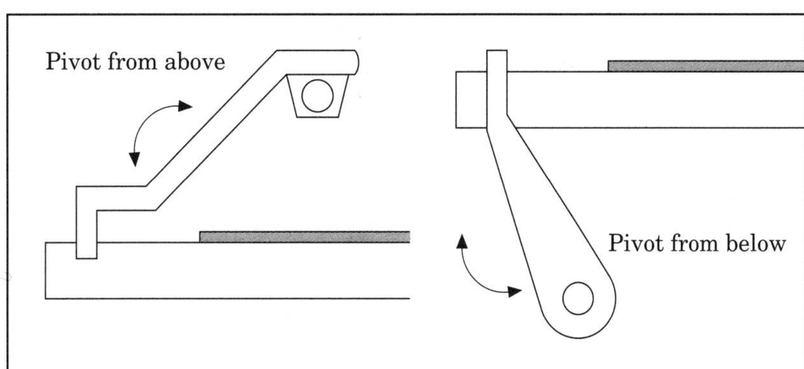

press sheet—is called **register.** An inconsistent front margin contributes to misregister, incorrectly positioned printed images.

Sheet register on the feedboard requires three points to control the press sheet: two front guides and the side guide. Most presses have more than the two front guides required to register a sheet; the other guides are positioned in one of two ways:

- Slightly away from the sheet but close enough to maintain support
- As far away from the sheet as possible to avoid interfering with sheet register

The exact number of front guides on a press varies from manufacturer to manufacturer. However, factors affecting the number of front guides are the maximum sheet size and the thickness of the stock.

Placement of the front guides along the lead edge of the press sheet is critical. If the two front guides used for sheet register are too close together, the sheet often rests only on one of the two, resulting in a slightly twisted or cocked press sheet. If the front guides are too far apart, they inadequately support the center of the press sheet.

Lightweight stock under 30 in. (750 mm) in width and board stock require two front guides for register and perhaps one for maintaining support at the center. A press sheet folded in four columns aids the press operator in positioning the front guides laterally if they are movable. The front guides used for sheet register are positioned on the outside creases and are adjusted to their central position. If a guide is used to maintain sheet support, it is positioned on the center crease and adjusted so that it is 0.003 in. (0.08 mm) from the sheet; placing a sheet against the front guides aids in positioning the third guide slightly away from the sheet. Any remaining guides are positioned to their forward-most position; i.e., away from the paper. Whenever front guides are moved to compensate for changes in sheet size, they must align with the feed plate and infeed grippers. The front guides on almost all presses are adjustable.

Lightweight stock over 30 in. (750 mm) requires two front guides for register and two for maintaining support of the center. A press sheet folded into eighths aids the press operator in positioning the front guides. The front guides used for sheet register are positioned on the outside creases and are adjusted to their central position. The two guides used to maintain sheet support are placed on the third and fifth creases from the left edge of the sheet; they are adjusted until they clear the sheet by 0.003 in. (0.08 mm). Any remaining guides are adjusted to their forward-most position.

Bite refers to the amount of sheet—margin—under the paper gripper of the impression cylinder. For tight-register work, gripper bite must be correct. Front guides in their central position provide the proper amount of bite. Front guides in the forward position result in maximum gripper bite but also tend to cause sheet transfer problems. Front guides in the back position result in minimum gripper bite, which often leads to a sheet tearing out of the grippers due to insufficient holding power.

Front guide height above the feedboard varies according to stock thickness. Regardless of whether the front guide incorporates a smoother (a device that helps to keep the sheet flat), the basic procedure for adjusting front guide height remains the same. For either a single-sheet or stream feeder, two 12×3-in. (300×80-mm) strips of the stock to be used are inserted under the front guide, which is then adjusted until it clears the two strips. A third strip is then inserted, with the front guide height adjusted until the third strip drags when pulled away from the front guide. For board stock, the front guide is set to clear the board plus two sheets of 0.004-in. (0.10-mm) paper.

Side guide. The third point of the three-pointed sheet-registering system is the side guide. Three basic methods of side-guiding predominate:

- Roller action
- Foot (plate) action
- Pneumatic (suction) action

Although the mechanisms vary, each pulls the sheet against the **register block,** or **register plate,** a device that stops the lateral (sideways) movement of the sheet. (The side guide for a single-sheet feeder pushes the sheet toward the center of the feedboard.)

Like the front guide, the side guide must be properly positioned to guarantee register of the press sheet. The register block of the side guide is reset to its zero or center position using the micrometer-like side-guide adjustment. After a press sheet is forwarded to the front guide (using the feeder

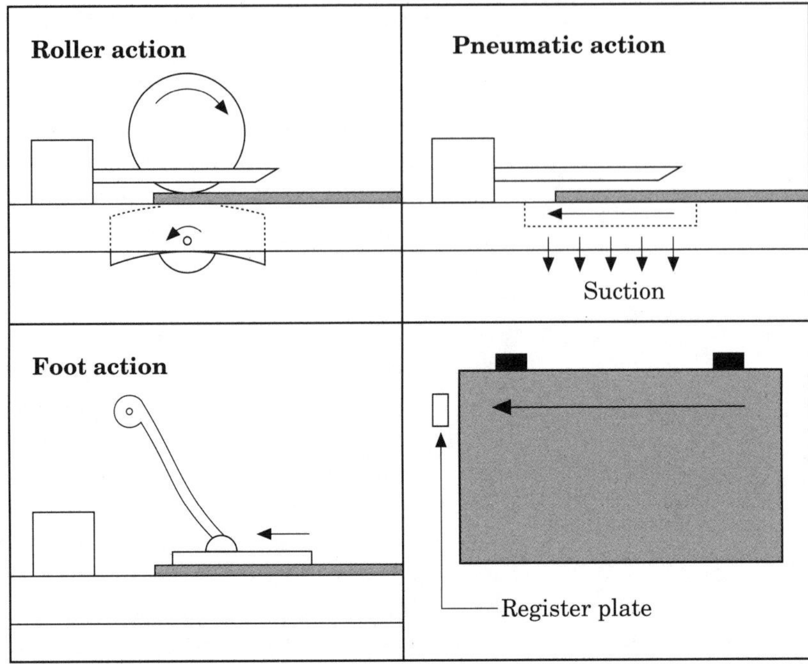

Basic methods of side-guiding: roller action *(upper left),* foot action *(lower left),* and pneumatic action *(upper right)*

All three methods pull the sheet against a register plate *(lower right)*

handwheel), the register block is moved until it is ¼ in. (6 mm) from the sheet, and it is locked in that position.

The register block must be adjusted until it is parallel to the edge of the sheet. A new offset printing plate or a metal square aids in paralleling the register block to the sheet and in squaring the register block to the front guides.

The smoother attached to the register block must be adjusted to compensate for stock thickness. The press is inched until the smoother is at its lowest position. Two 12×3-in. (300×80-mm) strips of the stock being printed are inserted under the smoother plate, which is adjusted in height until it clears both strips. A third strip is then inserted, with the height being adjusted until the third strip drags when pulled away from the side guide. For board stock, the height is set to drag on one sheet of board and three strips of 0.004-in. (0.10-mm) paper. If the smoother is too high, a sheet may buckle when pulled against the register block, causing misregister. Refer to the operator's manual for specific instructions.

Roller- and foot-action side guides. The puller roller and foot of the roller- and foot-action side guides need proper levels of tension. Too much spring tension applied to the puller roller or foot may cause the sheet to buckle against the register block. Tension, initially set to its lowest level, should be increased by one-half turn as each sheet passes the register block. When a sheet pulls over to the register block, tension is at its proper level. The tensioning device should then be locked in place.

In addition, the side-guide spring used must be appropriate for the thickness of the stock being printed:

- Lightweight stock requiring a lightweight spring
- Medium-weight stock requiring a medium spring
- Board and heavyweight stock requiring a heavy spring

Pneumatic-action (suction-action) side guide. A pneumatic-action, or suction-action, side guide has a **suction plate,** a device that holds the sheet by vacuum and then moves the paper against the register block. The suction plate used in this system must be appropriate for the stock being printed; e.g., a board-type sucker when board is being printed.

Proper levels of vacuum are necessary for the pneumatic side guide. Vacuum, initially set at its lowest level, is gradually increased as sheets pass the register block. When a sheet pulls over to the register block, the level of vacuum is correct.

Single-Sheet Feeder

Sheet control for a single-sheet, or successive-sheet, feeder is basically the same as for a stream feeder except in a few key areas.

Pile and Side Guide Positioning

The side guide for a single-sheet feeder is usually a push type. Therefore, the paper pile is positioned off-center ⅛–¼ in. (3–5 mm) toward the side guide being used so that the sheet is pushed across the center of the feedboard as it is side-guided. Rear sheet steadiers are located on the outside quarters of the pile so that they just touch it.

Sheet-Separation Unit

With a single-sheet feeder, sheet separation occurs at the front (gripper) edge of the paper pile. Air is blown against the top several sheets of the pile, causing an air bulge that separates these sheets from the pile. Suckers located almost over the gripper edge of the sheet drop down and hold the top sheet due to vacuum. They move forward, putting the gripper edge of the sheet between some type of wheel/roller forwarding combination at the head of the feedboard. The entire sheet is forwarded onto the feedboard before the suckers remove the next sheet from the top of the pile.

Proper pile height—approximately ⅜ in. (10 mm) below the separating fingers—is critical to trouble-free feeding. The separating fingers are positioned ⅜ in. (10 mm) below the top of the air-blast nozzles when they are in their raised position.

Another critical adjustment factor is the air-blast nozzles. They are raised or lowered until they separate the top 6–10 sheets from the pile. Sufficient air blast creates a bulging of the sheets, making it easier for the pickup suckers to forward only one sheet to the feedboard.

The angling of the pickup suckers varies depending on the stock being printed. A greater angle is necessary for feeding paper than for feeding board. Angled pickup suckers help to minimize the feeding of double sheets. Therefore, the suckers are angled as much as possible while still maintaining positive pickup. Any suckers not being used to pick up the sheet are turned off.

Double-Sheet Detector

On a properly operating single-sheet feeder, only one sheet passes under the double-sheet detector at any time. Consequently, the detector is set to prevent the passage of two sheets.

On some presses, a simple choke prevents the feeding of double sheets. The choke is set to jam two or more sheets against the feedboard. As a result, these sheets fail to reach the front guides, and the press trips off impression.

Infeed Section

After a press sheet is registered on the feedboard, it is moved in various ways from the feedboard to a set of grippers on the first impression cylinder. Then, the grippers on the impression cylinder close on the sheet and transport it through the first unit, where the sheet is printed. The front guides move aside to allow this transfer. The timing and adjustment of the devices in the infeed section are critical.

Three types of infeed are commonly encountered:

- **Swing-arm system.** Front guides stop the sheet and move out of the way at the proper time. Grippers on a swing-arm mechanism close on the sheet and transfer it to the impression-cylinder grippers.
- **Rotary-drum system.** Front guides stop the sheet and move out of the way at the proper time. Grippers on a rotating drum close on the sheet and transfer it to the impression-cylinder grippers.
- **Overfeed system.** Front guides on the feedboard preregister the sheet and move out of the way at the proper

time. Feed rolls or vacuum belts drive the sheet against stops (front guides) on the impression cylinder. The rolls or belts continue to drive the sheet, causing it to buckle. Grippers on the impression cylinder close on the sheet. The controlled buckling of the sheet ensures proper register.

Principal types of infeeds

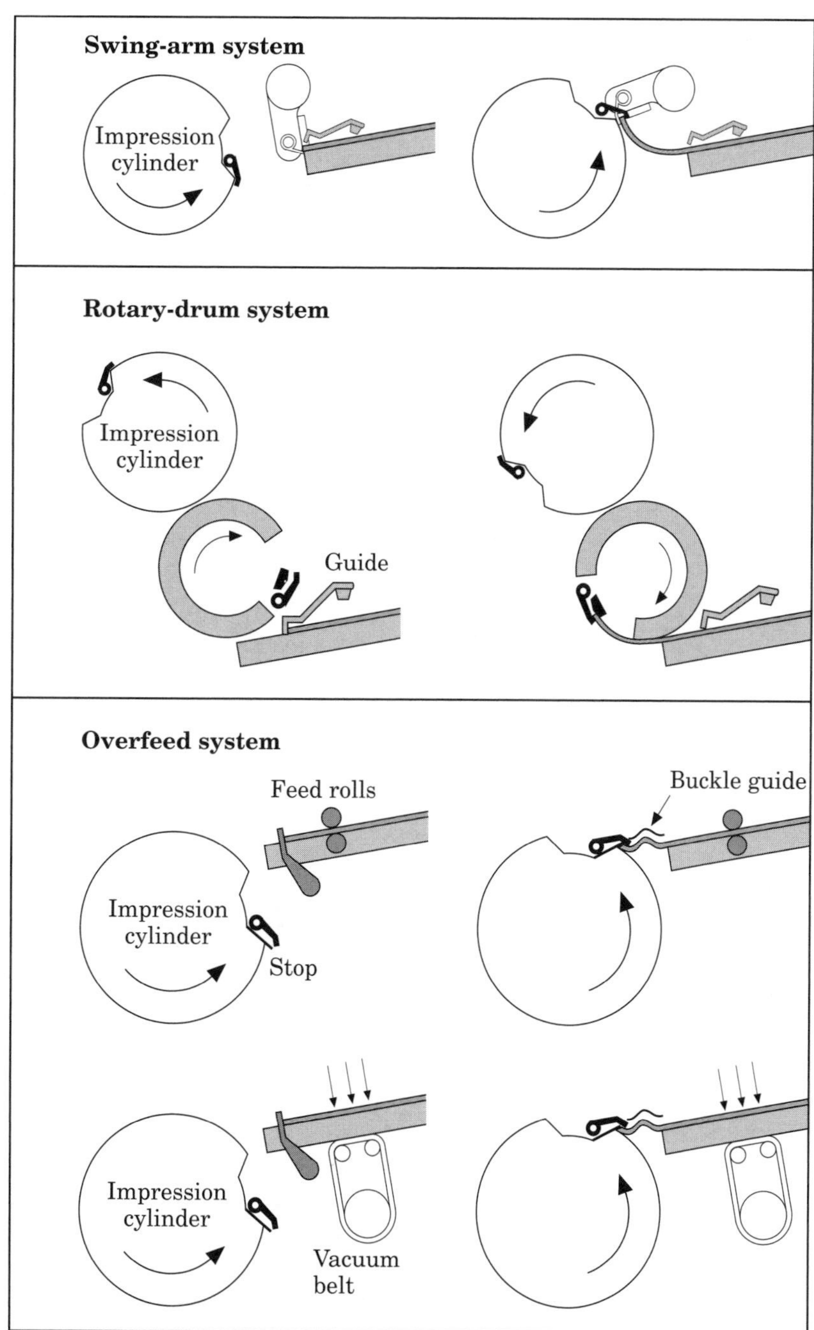

Infeed Gripper Clearance

Infeed grippers that are noncompensating (unable to automatically adjust themselves for stock thickness changes) require a simple adjustment when stock thickness is being changed; e.g., from paper to board. This adjustment provides clearance between gripper pad and feedboard and varies for each type of press. The operator's manual typically includes the recommended clearance and method of adjustment.

On one press, the recommended clearance between pad and the feedboard is 0.008 in. (0.20 mm) plus the stock thickness. If 0.004-in. (0.10-mm) paper is being printed, the clearance from gripper pad to feedboard is 0.012 in. (0.30 mm)—0.008 in. plus 0.004 in. (0.20 mm plus 0.10 mm).

Impression-Cylinder Stops

With the overfeed system only, the stops (front guides) on the impression cylinder are sometimes intentionally bowed to control distortion of the sheet, or fan-out, expansion of the sheet near the tail edge. Before the next pressrun is started, the stops are returned to their central position.

Adjusting the stops on the impression cylinder permits depth of gripper bite to be increased or decreased slightly.

On a feed-roll overfeed system, changing to a very heavy caliper board requires adjustment of the tension between feed rolls. Textured stock that could crush also requires proper feed-roll tension. Improper tension between feed rolls often causes creases or wrinkles at the tail edge of the sheet.

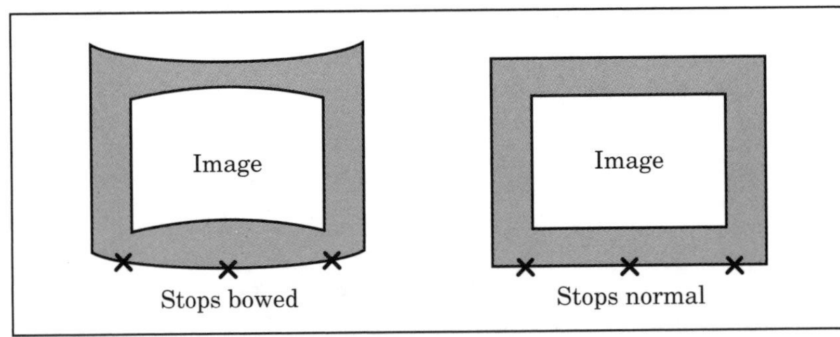

Effect of bowing the front guides (stops) on an overfeed system

Gripper Bowing

A gripper-bowing device compensates for the effects of fan-out by intentionally bowing the gripper bar as much as 0.008 in. (0.020 mm) at its center. Such a device is usually part of an infeed drum, but some presses include the device throughout the transfer system.

Passing a sheet through the impression nip irons out the sheet, causing it to fan out toward the tail corners. If the grippers are not bowed, the sheet relaxes to almost its former

Effects of fan-out

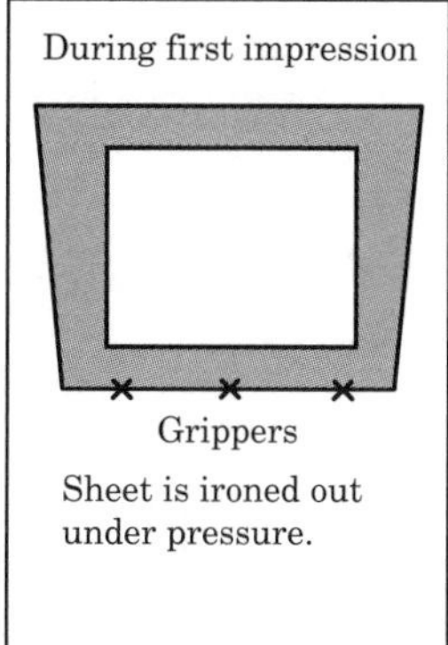
During first impression
Grippers
Sheet is ironed out under pressure.

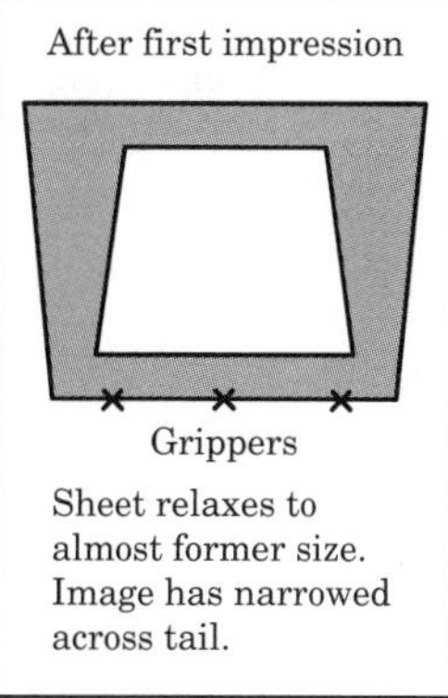
After first impression
Grippers
Sheet relaxes to almost former size. Image has narrowed across tail.

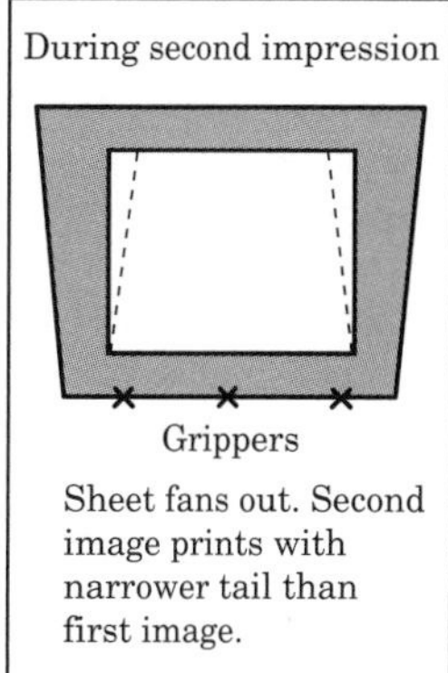
During second impression
Grippers
Sheet fans out. Second image prints with narrower tail than first image.

size after the first impression, resulting in an image narrowed across the tail. As the second impression is being printed, the sheet fans out again, but the second image prints with a narrower tail than the first image.

The use of a gripper-bowing device often minimizes the effects of fan-out. The gripper-bowing device is adjusted to bow the sheet gripper edge out, so that fan-out is exaggerated. This bowing, in turn, exaggerates the narrowing of the image at the tail of the sheet, compensating for further fan-out on the second impression and subsequent image narrowing at the tail of the sheet. During the first impression, the gripper pads are bowed out, resulting in a bowed-out sheet and exaggerated fan-out. After the first impression, the sheet relaxes and the image narrows more than usual at the tail. The grippers on the second impression are not bowed but are in their central position. During the second impression, the sheet still fans out, but the second image fits the first image because the first image is narrower than usual.

Bowing the gripper edge in is also possible. Bowing-in causes a widening of the image at the tail.

Using a gripper bowing device to control fan-out

During first impression
Grippers
Sheet is bowed back. This exaggerates fan-out.

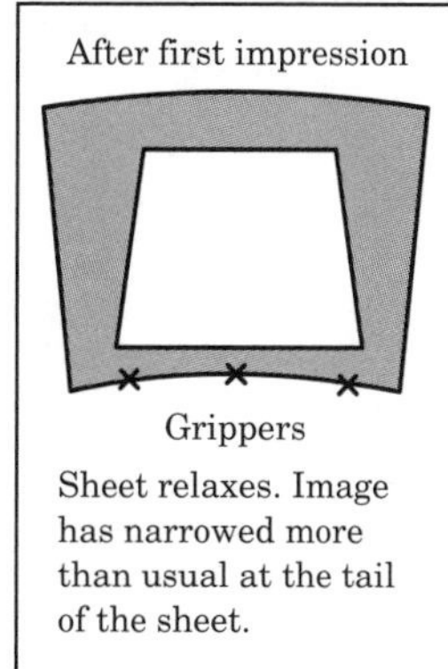
After first impression
Grippers
Sheet relaxes. Image has narrowed more than usual at the tail of the sheet.

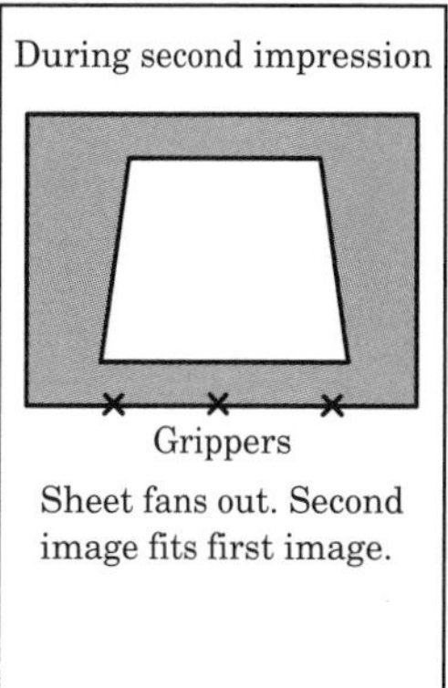
During second impression
Grippers
Sheet fans out. Second image fits first image.

Bowing of the gripper bar of the first impression cylinder to compensate for a distorted sheet

Some gripper bars can be bowed in the center, moved forward or back, or angled.

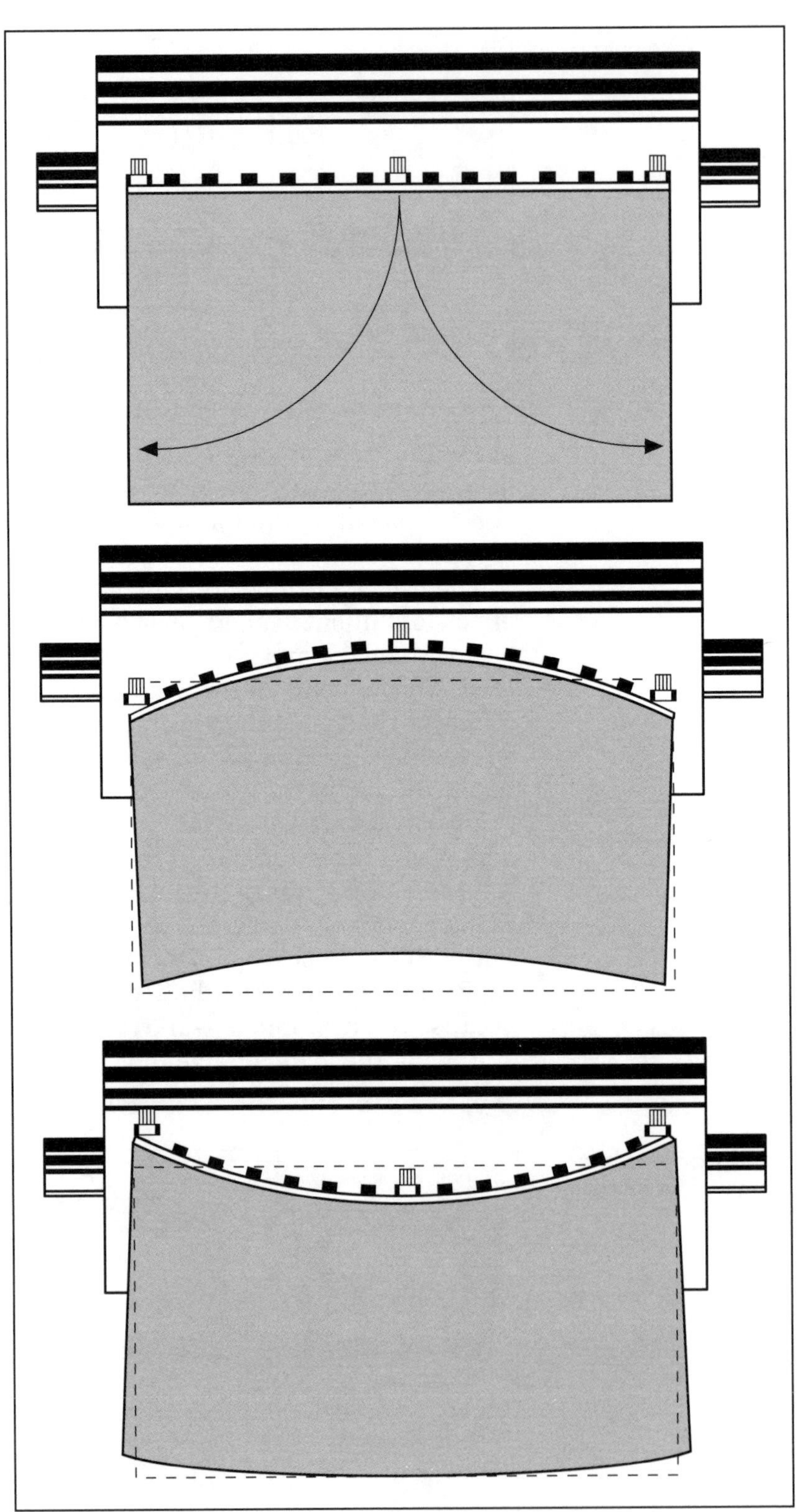

Gripper Bite

Impression-cylinder grippers that are too tight damage the lead edge of the paper and cause problems in the delivery. Wrinkling of the sheet often results when one gripper is set too tightly and the next one is set too loosely. Therefore, properly tensioned grippers are essential for good registration.

Sheet Transfer Section

The sheet transfer section transports the press sheet between the impression cylinders on a multicolor sheetfed press. Depending on the number of printing units, the number of sheet transfer sections varies. For example, a four-color press has three sheet transfer sections.

Three principal methods of sheet transfer are common:

- **Chain transfer,** where sets of grippers riding on a chain transport the sheet from one impression cylinder to the next. When the sheet is transferred from the chain grippers to the impression cylinder grippers, and vice versa, the sheet is held by both gripper systems for a short distance. Chain transfer lessens the chance of ink smearing because the paper contacts fewer surfaces. Specially designed metal shields minimize air turbulence in a chain transfer system.

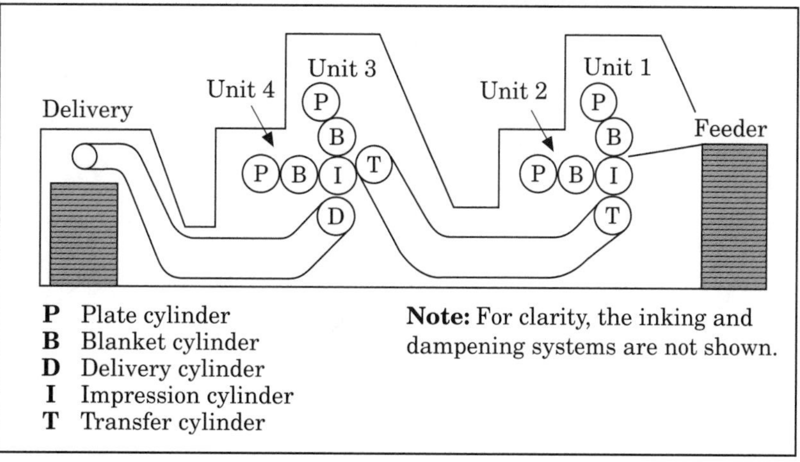

Chain transfer system with common impression cylinders

- **Single-drum transfer,** where a set of grippers on a large-diameter transfer cylinder transport the sheet from one impression cylinder to the next. The diameter of the transfer cylinder varies considerably with press design. For example, one press design has a common-impression cylinder three times the size of the plate or blanket cylinder and a transfer cylinder four times the size of the plate or blanket cylinder. (See also "Transfer Cylinder" in chapter two.)

Single-drum transfer system

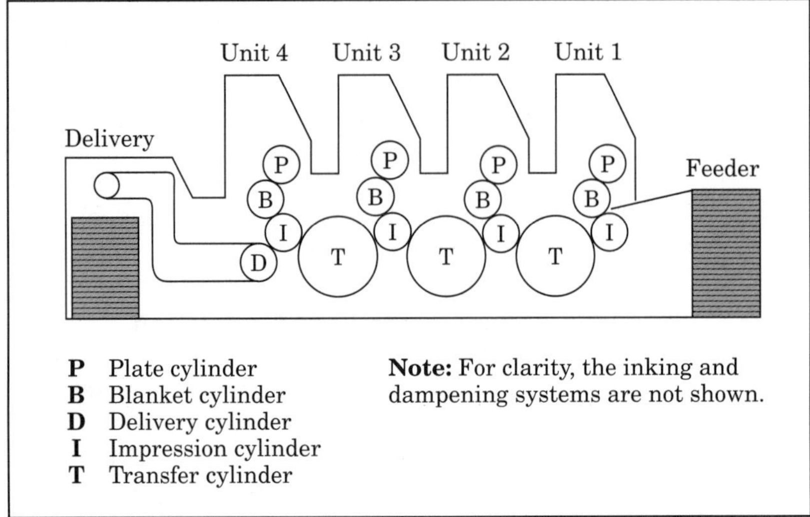

- **Three-drum transfer,** where three transfer cylinders—are used to transport the sheet from one impression cylinder to the next. Each has a set of grippers.

Three-drum transfer system

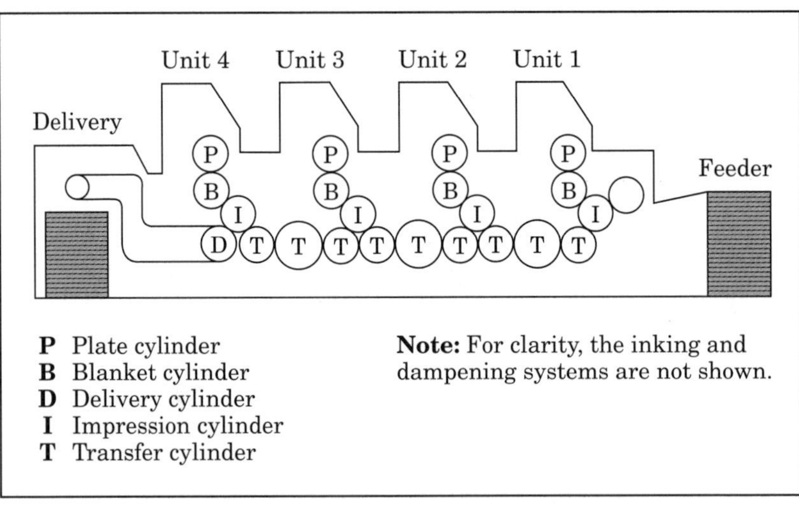

Antimarking devices are positioned in print margins of the press sheet. A special air-cushion drum on some presses can be used to float the sheet above the drum's surface without the tail edge fluttering, thus preventing marking of the printed image, or a special net-like covering can be attached to transfer cylinders that contact the wet side of the press sheet. (See "Transfer Cylinder" in chapter two.)

If the sheet transfer system has gripper-bowing devices, it is often necessary to reset them for a new job.

Delivery Section

The delivery section begins as the sheet leaves the final impression cylinder. Delivery grippers take the printed sheet from impression-cylinder grippers and transport it to the delivery pile, or table. The grippers typically travel on gripper bars. The grippers release the sheet onto the pile, where various devices (joggers) arrange the sheets into a neat, uniform pile.

Delivery section

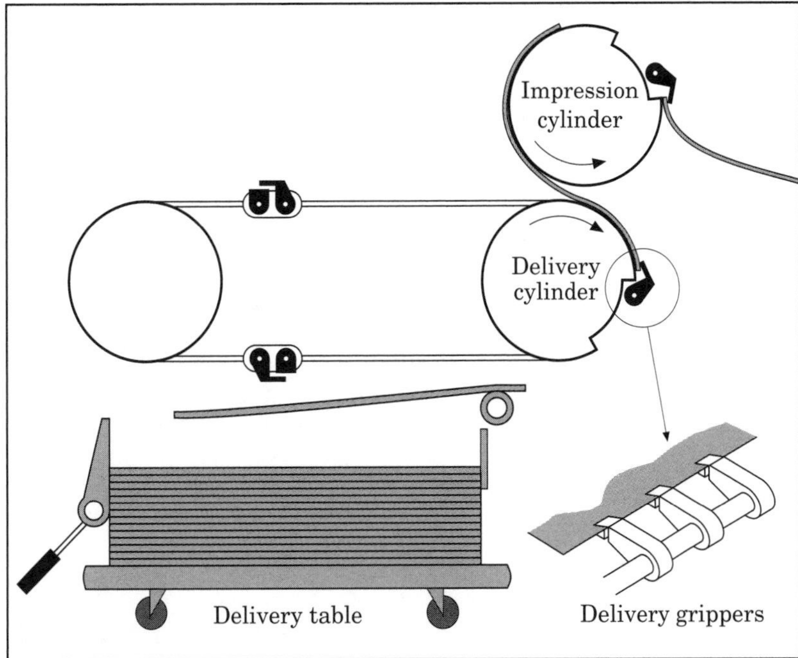

A sheet decurler, which is a device that is designed to take troublesome curl out of press sheets, is often located between the last press unit and the delivery.

Operating principle of a typical sheet decurler

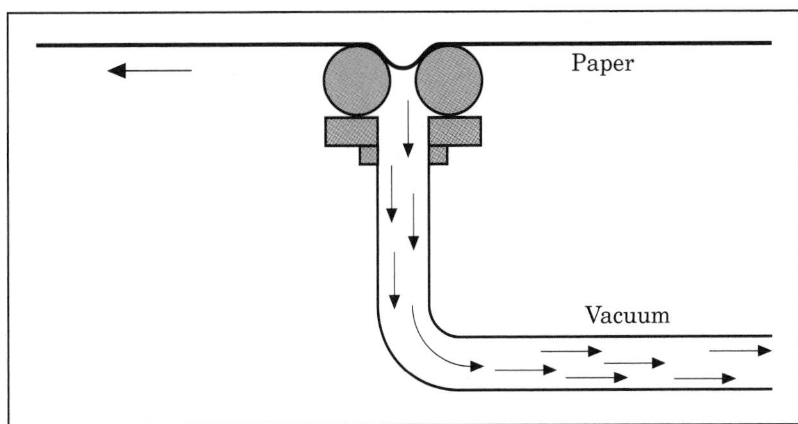

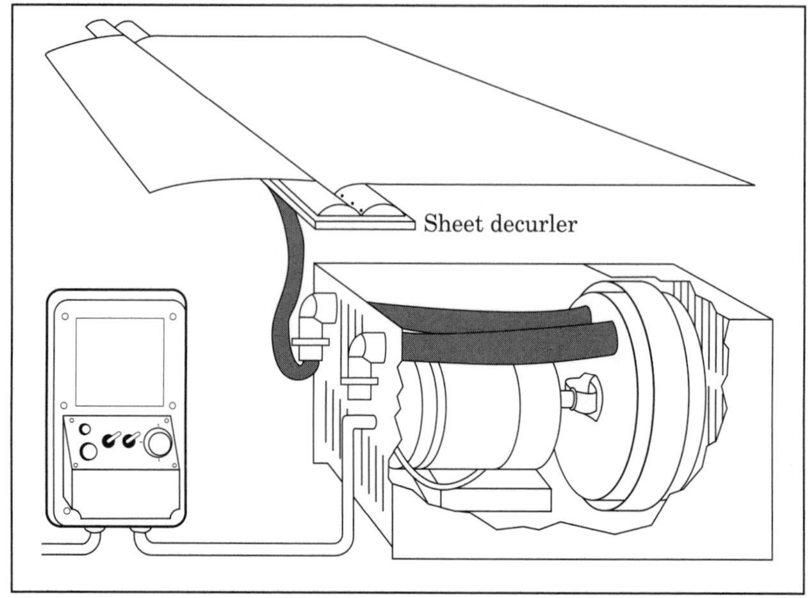

Sheet decurler
Courtesy Baldwin Graphic Products

Jogging the Delivery Pile

Three movable devices (two side joggers and a rear sheet guide) and one fixed device (a front gate) jog the sheet into a pile, but the neatness of the pile depends on the proper

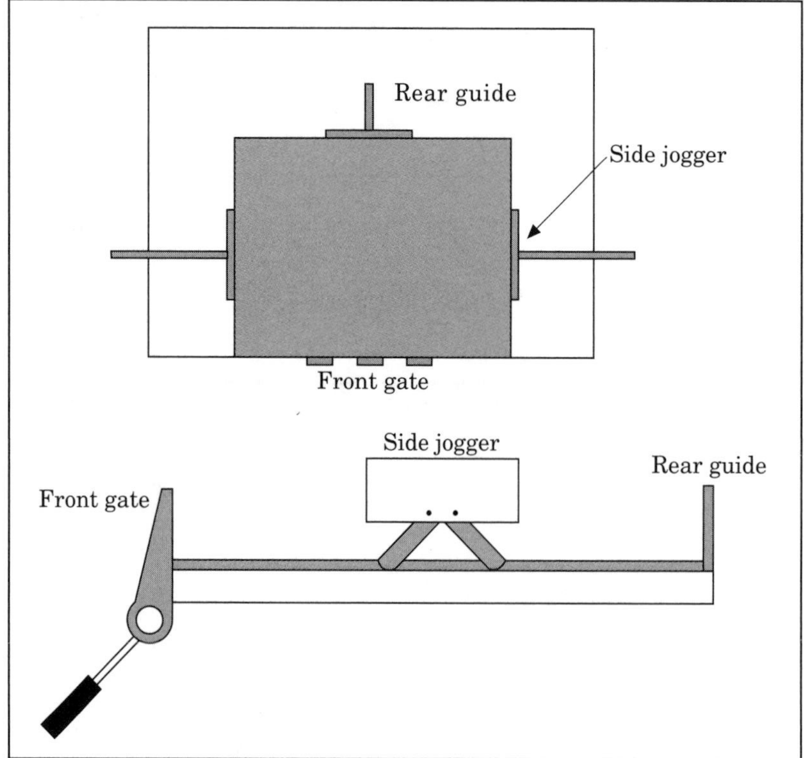

Setting the joggers in the delivery

positioning of the devices. Joggers are set to the exact size of the press sheet. An improperly set jogger—either with the side joggers set too close together or too far apart or with the rear sheet guide set too far forward or too far back—results in an improperly stacked pile of sheets. A properly jogged delivery pile helps to avoid errors in the trimming and finishing operations.

Following is a procedure for setting the joggers:

1. Forward a sheet onto the feedboard using the feeder handwheel. Make sure that the impression control is in the "off" position.
2. Inch the press forward until the sheet just begins to be transferred from the impression cylinder grippers to the delivery grippers.
3. Move the side guide joggers to their outermost positions. Move the rear sheet guide to its rear-most position.
4. Inch the press forward until the sheet drops onto the delivery.
5. Inch the press forward until the joggers are at their innermost jogging position.
6. Put the press on "safe." Loosen the set screws of the rear guide and move it so that it holds the sheet against the front gate. Tighten the set screws.
7. Loosen the set screws on each side jogger and move the joggers so that they touch the edge of the sheet. Tighten the set screws.
8. Inch the press forward, checking that the rear guide and side joggers are neatly boxing in the sheet.

Sheet-Guiding Devices

Several types of devices assist the grippers in moving the press sheet from the impression cylinder to the point just before the delivery gripper release.

Common sheet guiding devices include skeleton wheels, star wheels, covered cylinders, and air-cushion drums, depending on the press.

Skeleton wheels are movable wheels that are positioned in nonprinting areas of the press sheet. Properly positioned skeleton wheels evenly support and help to peel the sheet from the last impression cylinder.

Positioning of sheet-guiding devices is usually done from under the feedboard or from the delivery. If counter guide rails are used, they are positioned to support the back of the sheet. Final location of sheet-guiding devices depends on the position of images on the printed sheet.

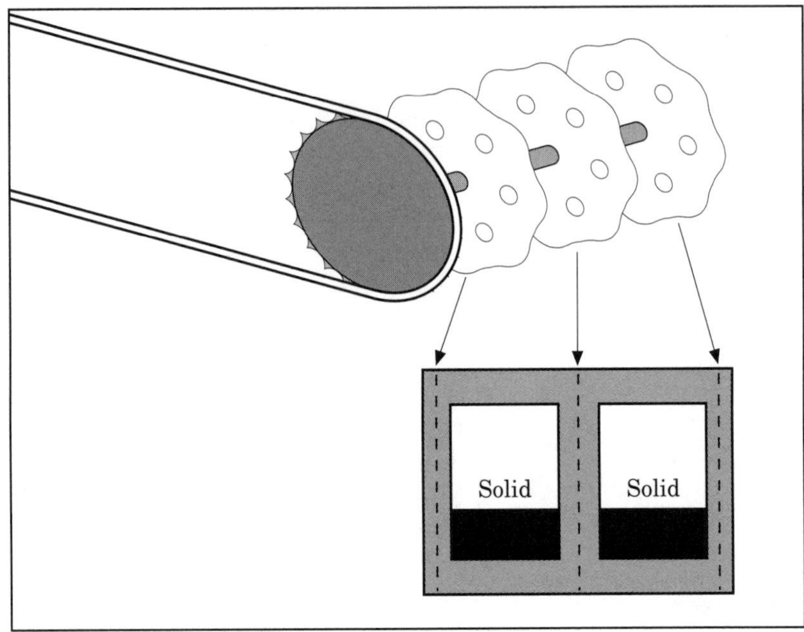

Positioning skeleton wheels to contact the nonimage areas of the sheet

Delivery-Assist Devices

Several devices assist the joggers in neatly stacking the printed sheets. Commonly used devices include suction rollers, blow downs, and pile wedges.

Suction slow-down rollers. Suction rollers slow down and steady the sheet as it enters the delivery. They are usually positioned just behind the rear sheet guide and beneath the chain delivery. Only those suction rollers that the sheet passes over should be used, with all others being turned off. Test-running the press helps to determine the proper vacuum setting.

Blow-downs. Near the top of the delivery are the blow-downs, a series of air holes that assist in dropping the sheet onto the delivery table. Air is blown on the top side of the sheet, forcing it downward. Fans are also used for this purpose. The proper level of air depends on press speed and on the weight and type of stock. Test-running the press helps to determine the proper air pressure.

Wedges. Wooden or plastic wedges are used at startup to produce a neat pile. By holding up the rear (trailing or tail) edge of the sheets, wedges help to counter tail-end hook (a sharp curl at the back edge of the sheet). Since wedges can cause marking, they must be carefully used.

Sheet blow-downs and suction rollers, which assist in delivering the press sheet

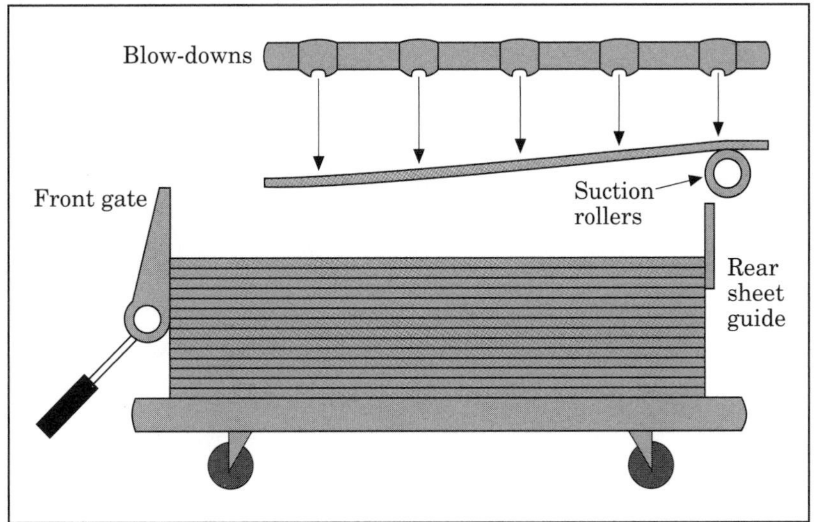

Wedge used to hold up the rear edge of the press sheet

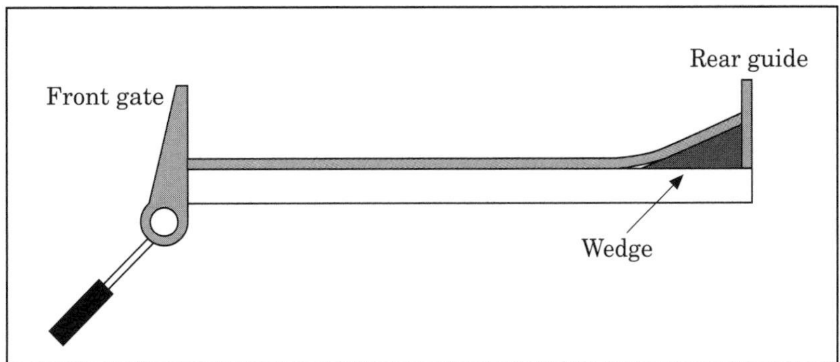

6 Packing and Printing Pressures

Neither ink nor water will transfer without proper pressure between the transferring elements. The plate cylinder and blanket cylinder surfaces must run with pressure between them to effect cylinder transfer; running contact is not enough. There must also be adequate pressure between the blanket and the paper.

Pressure is more than essential in lithography; it is critical. Tolerances are small. The press operator's margin of error in squeeze is as little as 0.002–0.003 in. (0.05–0.08 mm).

The procedure for setting cylinder pressures is called packing. The noun "packing" also refers to the paper or plastic sheets that are put under the blanket and plate.

As discussed in chapter 2, the bodies of the plate and blanket cylinders are lower than the surface of the bearers. The exact difference in height—called the **cylinder undercut**—varies from manufacturer to manufacturer. For specialty printing applications, the cylinder undercuts can be custom-cut. Often, the amount of undercut is specified by the plant ordering the press. Knowing the exact amount of undercut on the plate and blanket cylinders is essential to setting proper pressures in the printing unit.

Cylinder undercut, the amount that the cylinder body is beneath the bearers

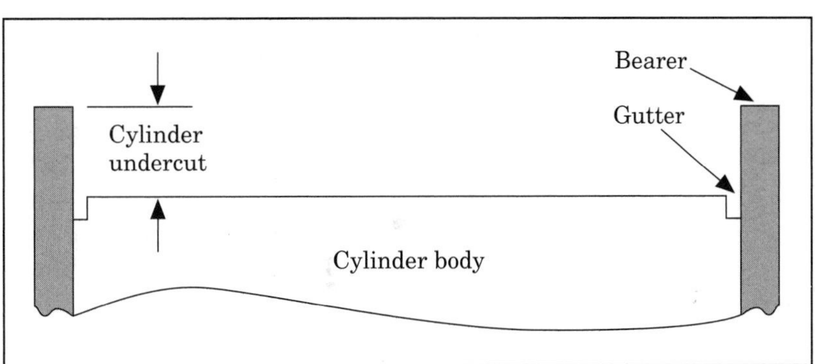

Packing sheets are put under the blanket and plate to increase the diameters of the cylinder bodies. (The true diameter of the cylinder is the same as the pitch diameter of the gears.) There are three primary reasons for altering cylinder diameters:

Gears of plate and blanket cylinders meshing at the pitch line diameter

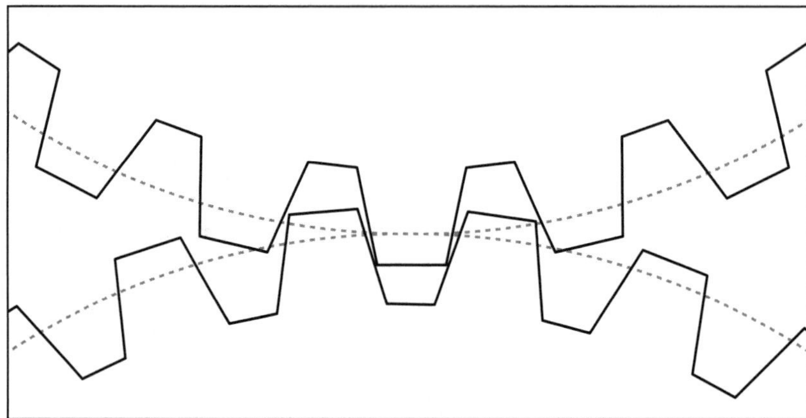

- **To compensate for different plate and blanket thicknesses.** Packing makes it possible to use a fairly wide range of plate and blanket thicknesses on one press. Packing sheets themselves are available in a variety of thicknesses.
- **To adjust the pressure between plate and blanket.** In order to transfer ink from the plate to the blanket, either the plate or blanket, or both, must be packed above bearer height. Pressure between plate and blanket is increased by adding packing sheets and decreased by removing packing sheets. The pressure between plate and blanket, and blanket and impression cylinder, is referred to as *squeeze.*
- **To compensate for paper growth, or stretch, during multicolor printing.** Paper stretches when it is printed. By changing the ratio of the plate and blanket cylinder diameters, a stretched print can be matched.

Packing Material

Any material having enough dimensional stability and uniformity of thickness to raise a plate or blanket to proper height and keep it there can be used for packing. However, few materials meet these requirements. Probably the most common material currently used is specially manufactured kraft paper. Kraft paper is a highly calendered (smoothed), water-resistant paper with negligible compression. It is made in a variety of thicknesses so that the press operator, by choosing the right sheet or sheets, can create nearly any packed height that is required. Kraft packing paper is manufactured to reasonably close caliper tolerances, which is extremely important to the press operator.

Packing paper, however, does not offer the ultimate dimensional stability on the press. Polyester or similar plastic is much tougher and is coming into wide use as a packing material under plates—especially frosted polyester. Polyester also has high resistance to lithographic chemicals. It is more expensive than kraft paper but, with reasonable care, can be reused. However, it should never be used under a blanket. Some press manufacturers offer kits that allow press operators to "permanently" mount the plastic packing material with spray adhesive to the plate cylinder. This method is particularly helpful if numerous plate changes are made per shift.

Press sheets or any other papers not designed for the purpose make poor packing materials. Their thicknesses are not uniform enough to meet the critical standards required in press packing. It also compresses easily.

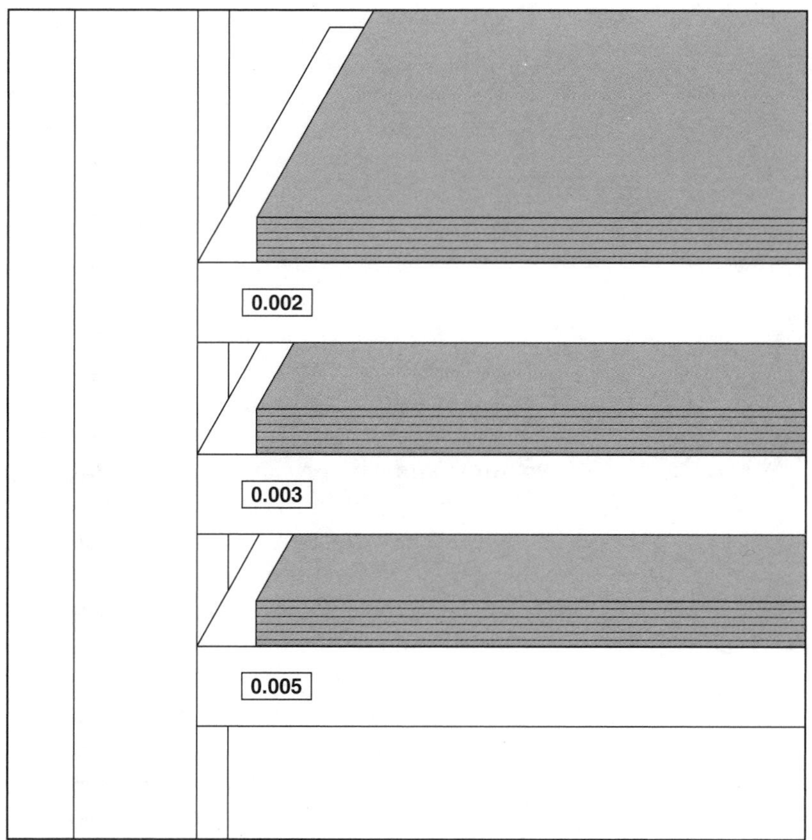

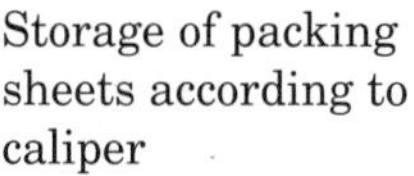
Storage of packing sheets according to caliper

Packing sheets should be cut square and sized for the press, and stored according to caliper using a separate shelf for each thickness. Sheets of similar caliper should also be color-coded or stamped for ease of identification. If the press operator has to search for packing sheets, measure their thickness, and cut them to size while the press waits, makeready can be very costly.

Opinions vary regarding optimum packing width. Some press operators prefer packing of the same width as the plate and blanket for easier alignment. Others like packing to be anywhere from 1⁄16 in. (2 mm) to ½ in. (13 mm) narrower than the plate or blanket, hoping that the dampening solution does not affect the packing sheets.

Packing cut slightly narrower than the blanket

Notice that the blanket is packed above bearer height.

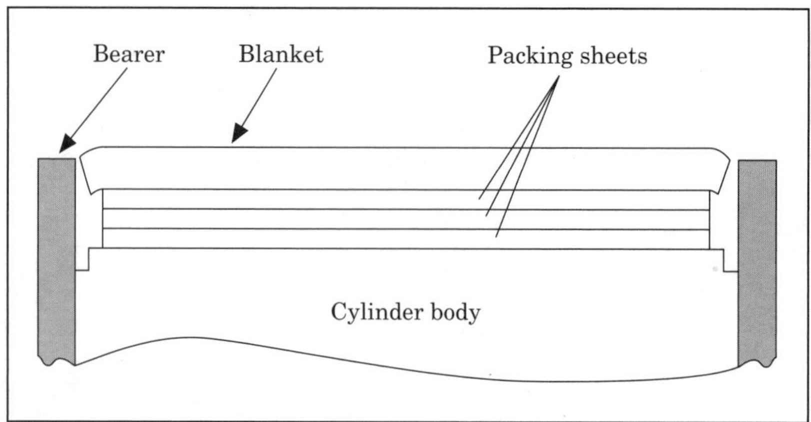

Water that gets under the edges of the plate and blanket soaks into the packing paper, causing it to swell. Packing thickness can increase by several thousandths of an inch (or hundredths of a millimeter) and raise the edge of both the blanket and the plate, increasing the pressure between them.

Cylinder Pressures

Unfortunately, pressures on a printing press are not measured and stated in pounds per square inch. No practical means has yet been found for measuring the pressure between two cylinders on a running press. As a result, pressures are described in the most convenient measure available: thousandths of an inch (or hundredths of a millimeter) of "squeeze." Squeeze on a bearer-contact press is the combined height of plate and blanket over their respective bearers, while squeeze on a non-bearer-contact press is the combined height of plate and blanket over their respective bearers minus the distance between the bearers.

How much pressure does a given amount of squeeze exert? That is difficult to say because pressure is not directly proportional to squeeze.

There is a simple principle behind the procedure used by the press operator to develop squeeze in the plate-to-blanket nip. Assume that an unpacked plate cylinder and unpacked blanket cylinder on a bearer-contact press are turning together with their bearers in firm contact with one another. Although the bearers are in contact, there is no pressure between the cylinder bodies because the bodies do not touch. The distance between the cylinder bodies is equal to the amount of undercut on the plate cylinder plus the amount of undercut on the blanket cylinder.

To develop plate-to-blanket squeeze, the press operator, in effect, increases the diameter of the cylinder bodies. The plate and its packing raise the height of the plate cylinder, and the blanket and its packing raise the height of the blanket cylinder. The total thickness of the material that is put on both cylinders determines the amount of squeeze, assuming compression of neither materials nor cylinder bearers.

Assume that the cylinders on a bearer-contact press are packed so that the plate and the blanket are exactly even with the surface of their respective cylinder bearers. How much squeeze is there? None, theoretically. The cylinders are just touching and there is no squeeze between them. There is no pressure between the working surfaces until the press operator adds materials with thicknesses more than the total undercut of the two cylinders. If, however, just one more sheet of 0.001-in. (0.025-mm) packing is added under the plate, the squeeze between the two cylinders is 0.001 in. If an identical sheet is added to the blanket cylinder, the squeeze becomes 0.002 in. (0.05 mm). The effective surface of each cylinder body is 0.001 in. above their respective cylinder bearers for a total of 0.002 in.

The squeeze at the printing nip is not just the amount that the blanket cylinder is packed in relation to the bearers. The actual squeeze also includes the thickness of the paper being printed and the pressure exerted by the impression cylinder. In calculating packing, the press operator starts by packing the plate and blanket cylinders according to the recommendations of the press manufacturer, or to the appropriate height for that press determined by experience. Depending on the thickness of the substrate being printed, the impression cylinder is positioned closer or farther away from the blanket cylinder to provide the proper amount of squeeze at the printing nip.

Squeeze between plate and blanket is less than that at the printing nip. The press operator's ultimate concern is with pressure and not squeeze, for it is pressure that determines the effectiveness of ink transfer. At the plate-to-blanket nip, a rigid surface (the plate) and a resilient surface (the blanket) are squeezed together. A given amount of squeeze at the plate-to-blanket nip exerts more pressure than the same amount of squeeze applied between the two resilient surfaces (the blanket and the paper) at the printing nip.

Determining the Proper Packing

What is the proper packing? The answer to this question is not simple. It is affected by blanket, bearer compression, and the quality-vs.-productivity requirements of the job.

Many manufacturers of conventional blankets specify a squeeze of 0.002–0.004 in. (0.05–0.10 mm), with a 0.003-in. (0.08-mm) squeeze being the most common. The squeeze that provides the highest-quality reproduction is the proper one. However, sometimes it is better to slightly overpack the blanket cylinder by about 0.001 in. (0.025 mm) to compensate for the compression of the blanket that occurs during the pressrun.

Effect of Blanket on Packing

The blanket is an extremely important operating factor affecting packing and squeeze. The type of blanket used—conventional or compressible—makes a difference. Compressible blankets make it possible to obtain good printing with considerably higher squeeze. This gives the press operator a little more margin for error in packing the press.

Compressible blankets do not all compress equally. The press operator should keep in mind that different compressible blankets can produce a great variety of printed results. Packing is a means to control pressure. The squeeze pressure relationships for different blankets can vary considerably. For example, assume that the minimum pressure required to transfer a certain ink is 200 lbs./in.^{2} (14 kg/cm^2). In examining the compression-vs.-pressure characteristics of different blankets, it can be demonstrated that to achieve 200 lbs./in.^{2} may require less than 0.003-in. (0.08-mm) squeeze on one blanket and as much as 0.007- or 0.008-in. (0.18- or 0.20-mm) squeeze on another blanket. The difference in compression produced by a given pressure depends upon the hardness and compressibility of the blanket in question.

Effect of Bearer Compression on Packing

Another factor that affects the packing as measured on a bearer-contact press is bearer compression, or bearer deformation. Normally, press bearers that run in contact exert considerable pressure on each other. This pressure helps the press run more smoothly. Because it causes the bearers to compress at the nip, it creates problems when trying to predict the proper packing ratio for the press. For example, assume that the minimum squeeze between plate and blanket for present press conditions is 0.004 in. Assume also that the bearers compress 0.0005 in. each. If the plate and blanket are both packed exactly 0.002 in. over bearer, the actual compression between plate and blanket will be 0.005 in. rather than 0.004 in. The extra 0.001 in. of squeeze is due to the fact that the packing measurements are made relative to the uncompressed bearer. Bearer compression on newer presses is not excessive and probably runs in the range of 0.001 in. total compression for the two bearers involved. On older presses, however, bearer compression can run considerably higher, even as much as 0.002 in. compression per bearer. This would mean a total of 0.004 in. squeeze gained in a printing nip due to bearer compression.

The press operator uses the amount of undercut on the cylinders as a basis for calculating the amount of packing needed. The manufacturer's original specifications should be followed, and a packing gauge must be used to verify the packing of the cylinder.

When the press is put on impression and the bearers have been properly set, there is considerable pressure between them. These relationships can change, especially when press cylinders are small in diameter. For one thing, hard steel bearers do not remain perfectly circular, but deform under pressure. This changes the amount of undercut on the cylinders at the nip. The problem is greater on older, lightly built presses equipped with relatively small bearers.

Therefore, the press operator has to determine the effective cylinder undercut when the press is running under pressure. The procedure to determine effective undercut takes time but only has to be done once. The press is packed in normal fashion, and a plate that prints both solid and screened images is mounted on the plate cylinder. The press is run until ink and water are balanced. Then, packing is removed (starting under the plate), until the solids no longer print. At this point, the packing is reinserted, 0.001 in. (0.025 mm) at a time, until the press is again printing a good, full-strength solid. The press is now properly packed with minimum pressure.

The packed height is measured using a packing gauge. The indicated squeeze is the minimum for printing with the given paper, ink, and blanket combination, on the press in question, using the packing gauge normally used by the press operator. This figure automatically takes into account any bearer deformation occurring on the press.

The bearers on any press deform; the amount depends on the construction of the press cylinders. Change in the radius of the bearers is important because in effect it increases the amount of squeeze at the printing nip. The above procedure for determining squeeze automatically compensates for this problem.

The method described above also eliminates some potential difficulties inherent in using a packing gauge. The objective of the procedure is to adjust press packing until a visible standard of performance is achieved: a good, full-strength solid. The press operator then uses the packing gauge to measure the conditions on the press that yield this standard of performance. What do these measurements mean? The press operator's aim is to be able to reproduce those packing conditions at will. If the gauge is properly used, it indicates whether this has been done. The packing gauge used should be tested to see if its readings are sufficiently consistent to be used in the pressroom.

Effect of Quality and Production Factors on Packing

Another factor affecting the final packing ratios is the relationship between the quality requirements and the production requirements of the job. High-quality printing requires the correct amount of squeeze and, therefore, very tight control over packing. If emphasis is on production, however, overpacking is used to guarantee that a small decrease in the height of the blanket will still maintain ink transfer. As the emphasis shifts from quality to production, the tendency to overpack increases.

Measuring Packing Material Thickness

Packing a press is an important operation. It should never be done haphazardly. Every item of thickness should be checked carefully. There are many chances to make a mistake. Only by precisely measuring plate, blanket, and packing can the press operator be sure to obtain the proper squeeze. A deadweight bench micrometer, such as a Cady gauge, is a good all-purpose measuring device for use in the pressroom.

Plate Thickness

Although plate thickness seldom varies to any appreciable amount from one plate to another, it is advisable to gauge several plates in a new shipment to determine if there is any

Digital bench micrometer
Courtesy E. J. Cady & Co.

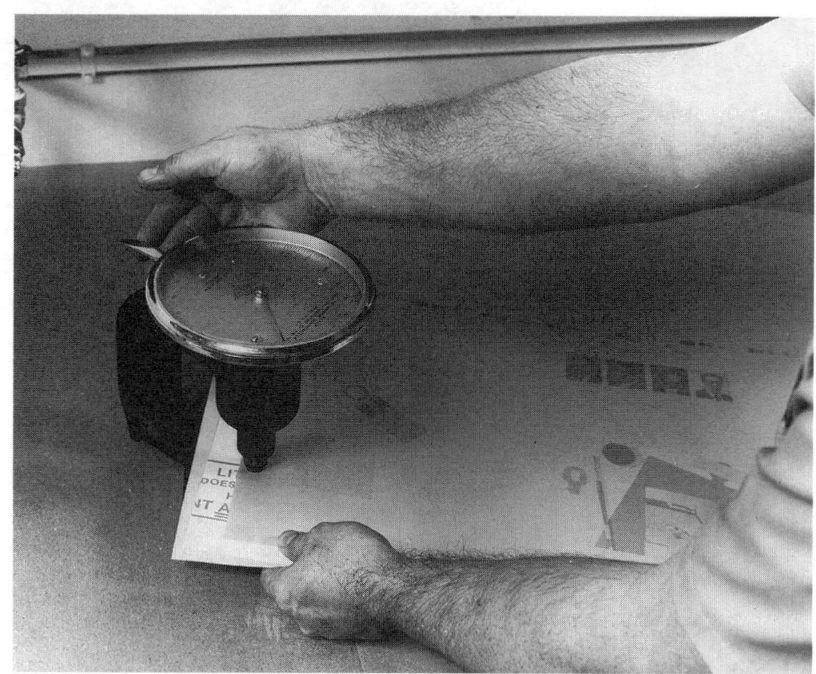

Press operator measuring the combined plate and packing thickness using a deadweight bench micrometer from E. J. Cady & Co.

deviation in plate gauge within the shipment. If any deviation is discovered, each plate in the shipment will have to be gauged before it is mounted on the press. A preliminary check of plate thickness gives the press operator a known starting point when calculating packing. Plate thickness, once determined, remains constant because plates are not affected by atmospheric or press moisture.

Blanket Thickness

Accurate measurements are needed to give the press operator an idea of what is required. The thickness of everything used in packing should be checked, no matter how many times a particular brand of plate or blanket is used. This is especially true for blankets. Each one should be checked with a bench micrometer (a deadweight gauge, such as the Cady gauge) and its average thickness marked on the back.

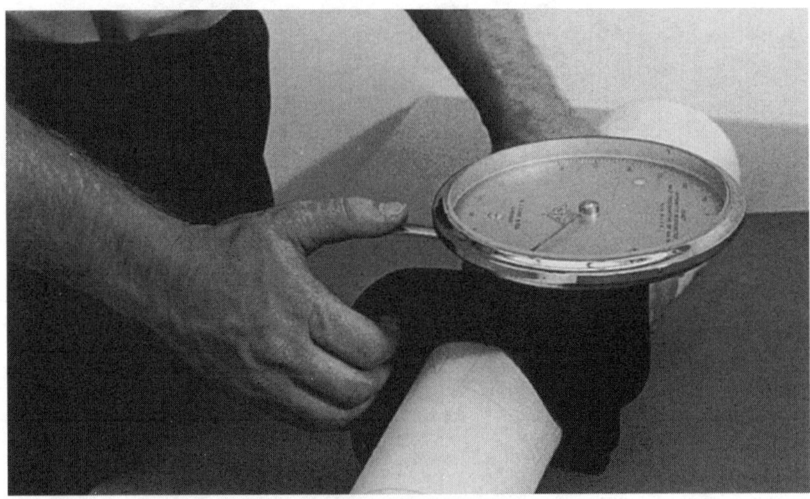

Press operator using a deadweight bench micrometer from E. J. Cady & Co. to measure blanket thickness

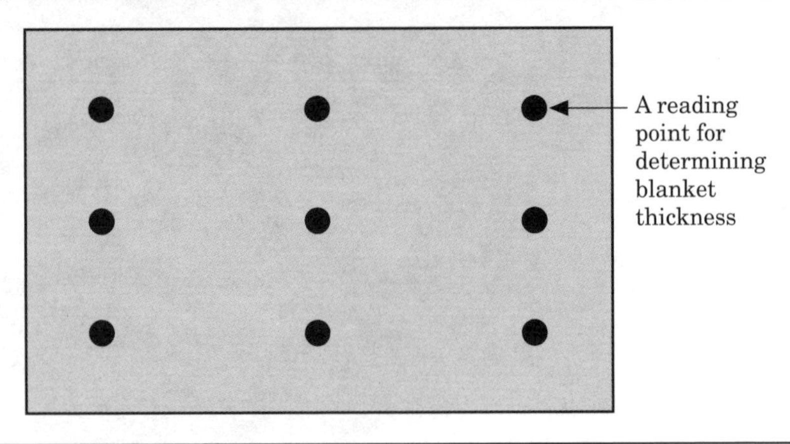

The nine reading points for blanket thickness

Thickness readings of a blanket should be taken in at least nine places to get an average as well as to determine any deviation in the surface thickness of a single blanket.

Packing Thickness

Packing sheets should be measured, even though the packing manufacturer indicates the caliper of the sheets. The following procedure is the best one to follow to measure them:

1. Open the package containing the packing sheets and permit the packing sheets to come into equilibrium with the temperature and relative humidity of the pressroom.
2. Measure the thickness of the packing sheets.

The higher-quality packing sheets are affected less by humidity.

Packing Gauge

In checking cylinder packing, there is no substitute for a good packing gauge designed for graphic arts use. The gauge gives the press operator an accurate reading of how far over or below bearers the cylinders are packed. This is not to say the press operator shouldn't get accurate measurements on the materials used in packing the cylinders.

A packing gauge placed against the plate, with its feeler foot resting on the plate cylinder bearer, gives a reading of the height difference between the surface of the plate and the surface of the bearer. A reading should be taken from both ends of the plate cylinder. The height of the blanket in

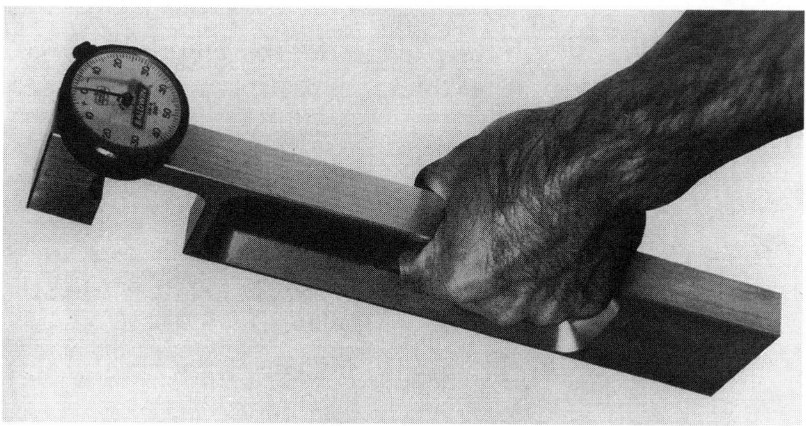

Packing gauge
Courtesy Baldwin Graphic Products

reference to the surface of the blanket cylinder bearers should also be measured using a packing gauge. The gauge manufacturer's instructions should be followed in order to properly zero the gauge in reference to the bearers.

Arithmetic of Packing

Properly measuring the thicknesses of the various materials involved in packing is the first step toward successfully packing the press. Calculating the necessary amount of packing is the second step.

Plate-plus-Packing Height

The plate-plus-packing height is the total thickness of the plate and its packing. It is determined by (a) adding the plate height above bearers (as specified by the press manufacturer or determined through experience) to the cylinder undercut or (b) subtracting the plate height below bearers from the cylinder undercut.

The total thickness of the packing sheets needed is obtained by subtracting the plate thickness from the plate-plus-packing height.

For example, a press manufacturer specifies that the plate height above the bearers should be 0.003 in. (0.08 mm). The press manufacturer also specifies the cylinder undercut as 0.019 in. (0.48 mm). What would be the plate-plus-packing height if the press is packed to these specifications?

0.019 in.	Cylinder undercut
+ 0.003 in.	Height above bearers
0.022 in.	Plate-plus-packing height

0.48 mm	Cylinder undercut
+ 0.08 mm	Height above bearers
0.56 mm	Plate-plus-packing height

If the plate in the above example is 0.014 in. (0.36 mm) thick, what thickness of packing sheets is necessary?

0.022 in.	Plate-plus-packing height
– 0.014 in.	Plate thickness
0.008 in.	Packing sheet thickness

0.56 mm	Plate-plus-packing height
– 0.36 mm	Plate thickness
0.20 mm	Packing sheet thickness

To reduce packing creeping, use two 0.004-in. (0.10-mm) sheets of packing instead of one 0.008-in. (0.20-mm) sheet.

Blanket-plus-Packing Height

The blanket-plus-packing height is the total thickness of the blanket and its packing. It is determined by (a) adding the blanket height above bearers (as specified by the press manufacturer or determined through experience) to the cylinder undercut or (b) subtracting the blanket height below bearers from the cylinder undercut.

The thickness of the packing sheets necessary is obtained by subtracting the blanket thickness from the blanket-plus-packing height. For example, a press manufacturer specifies that blanket height below the bearers should be 0.001 in. (0.02 mm), and the cylinder undercut should be 0.075 in. (1.91 mm). What would be the blanket-plus-packing height if the press is packed to these specifications?

0.075 in.	Cylinder undercut
– 0.001 in.	Height below bearers
0.074 in.	Blanket-plus-packing height

1.91 mm	Cylinder undercut
– 0.02 mm	Height below bearers
1.89 mm	Blanket-plus-packing height

If the blanket in the above example is 0.065 in. (1.65 mm) thick, what thickness of packing sheets is necessary?

0.074 in.	Blanket-plus-packing height
– 0.065 in.	Blanket thickness
0.009 in.	Packing sheet thickness

1.89 mm	Blanket-plus-packing height
– 1.65 mm	Blanket thickness
0.24 mm	Packing sheet thickness

Calculating Squeeze on a Bearer-Contact Press

Squeeze on a bearer-contact press is calculated by determining the height of the plate in relation to the plate cylinder bearers and the height of the blanket in relation to the blanket cylinder bearers. The two heights are added, with the resulting value being the squeeze.

For example, a press manufacturer specifies that the plate height above bearers should be 0.003 in. and the blanket height above bearers should be 0.001 in. What is the squeeze?

0.003 in.	Height of plate above bearers
+ 0.001 in.	Height of blanket above bearers
0.004 in.	Squeeze between plate and blanket

For example, a press manufacturer specifies that the plate height above bearers should be 0.003 in. and the blanket height below bearers 0.001 in. What is the squeeze?

0.003 in.	Height of plate above bearers
+ (–0.001) in.	Height of blanket below bearers
0.002 in.	Squeeze between plate and blanket

In the above example, since the blanket is packed below the bearer, its height is a negative number.

Calculating Squeeze on a Non-Bearer-Contact Press

Squeeze on a non-bearer-contact press is calculated by adding the height of the plate in relation to the plate cylinder bearers to the height of the blanket in relation to the blanket cylinder bearers and subtracting the distance between the plate cylinder and blanket cylinder bearers. For example, a press manufacturer specifies that the plate height above bearers should be 0.007 in. and the blanket height above bearers should be 0.003 in. In addition, the distance between bearers is 0.008 in. and not adjustable by the press operator. What is the squeeze?

0.007 in.	Height of plate above bearers
+ 0.003 in.	Height of blanket above bearers
0.010 in.	Combined height of plate and blanket

0.010 in.	Combined height of plate and blanket
– 0.008 in.	Distance between bearers
0.002 in.	Squeeze

With some non-bearer-contact presses, the distance between the plate cylinder bearers and the blanket cylinder bearers can be adjusted. Therefore, with such a press, follow the manufacturer's recommendations for adjustments and packing.

Consequences of Improper Packing

A squeeze of 0.002–0.004 in. (0.05–0.10 mm) is all that is necessary to transfer ink from the plate to a conventional blanket to paper. When grainless plates, hard blankets, and coated paper are used, a squeeze of 0.002 in. is usually sufficient. With compressible blankets, a squeeze pressure between 0.005–0.008 in. (0.13–0.20 mm) is typical.

With a conventional blanket, excessive squeeze (typically any squeeze greater than 0.004 in.) results in a variety of problems. Similarly, if the squeeze is insufficient (typically any squeeze less than 0.002 in.), other problems arise. Excessive squeeze results in more serious problems: initial and often detectable dot gain, deterioration of print quality, and plate damage.

Note: Always follow the blanket manufacturer's instructions relating to proper squeeze pressure.

Excessive Squeeze

The press's tolerance to variation in packing is not great. Any squeeze between plate and a conventional blanket greater than 0.004 in. (0.10 mm) is usually considered excessive. Excessive squeeze causes premature plate wear. It is not the squeeze itself that causes this wear, but the fact that there is slippage between the plate and blanket at the point of contact. The slippage may result in a uniform dot gain in areas that carry enough ink to lubricate the surfaces. The visual effect on a 70% tint may be a slur. On lighter tints the slippage may be intermittent and cause streaks.

Excessive squeeze creates friction that wears plate images, breaks down the thin desensitizing film, and actually flattens the grain. On long pressruns, the plate may go blind and scum at the same time. Excessive squeeze between plate and blanket sometimes overcomes the traction between the bearers, causing the cylinders to slip. Gear streaks then appear on the blanket and sometimes on the bearer surfaces. Excessive squeeze between impression cylinder and blanket contributes to slur, paper curl, and picking. This pressure is independent of packing; there is a control on every press to adjust the impression. GATF recommends to always try to print with the minimum amount of impression pressure.

Causes of excessive squeeze. Improper packing is the major cause of excessive squeeze between plate and blanket cylinders. The packing and blanket gauges must be read carefully when measuring the plate, blanket, and packing. Care must also be exercised when making packing calculations. Following a few precautions minimizes the probability of mistakes. One precaution is to post a sign over the work table of each printing press, simply recording the depth of the cylinder undercuts. The sign could read something like the following:

Plate Cylinder Undercut	0.19 in.
Blanket Cylinder Undercut	0.075 in.

Another precaution against mistakes is to use sheets that are made expressly for packing. Putting each thickness of packing material on a separate shelf and color-coding similar thicknesses of packing material are two more ways to safeguard against errors.

Another common cause of excessive squeeze is inaccurate measuring of blanket thickness. It is almost impossible to find the true thickness of a blanket with the ordinary machinist's micrometer, which generally gives a reading of 0.001–0.002 in. (0.05–0.08 mm) less than the true thickness. This is enough to cause trouble. A special deadweight blanket thickness gauge has been developed for measuring blankets; this device is called a Cady gauge. Its use minimizes the chance of overpacking the blanket.

Perhaps the least suspected and yet the most dangerous cause of excessive squeeze is untrue cylinders. Cylinders that show no indication whatsoever of any surface damage may have low spots in them. These depressions are sometimes as deep as 0.005 in. (0.13 mm) without being discovered. A rag, sponge, or wad of paper passing between contacting cylinders can cause such depressions. If a cylinder has a depression, the packing can be increased in order to get the low spot to print. However, all other areas will have excess pressure.

The same thing is true when a blanket is slightly damaged. If a blanket is badly crushed, it is either repaired or discarded. But if the low spot is not easily noticeable, the press operator is apt to overpack it with one large sheet so that the low spot prints satisfactorily. However, all other areas will have excessive pressure.

Still another cause is unparallel cylinders. Misalignment causes light printing on one side of the press. Trying to correct this by adding all-over packing produces serious excess pressure on the other side.

Insufficient Squeeze

Squeeze less than 0.003 in. (0.08 mm) between the plate and blanket results initially in a light or faded print. There are several causes of insufficient squeeze:

- Inaccurate measuring of blanket
- Improper calculation of amount of packing needed
- Compression of blanket and packing during mounting
- Compression of blanket and packing during pressrun

The first cause of insufficient squeeze is easily avoided if the correct measuring devices and techniques are used. The second cause is avoided if the press operator makes calculations carefully; press-mounted signs indicating proper packing thicknesses and a hand-held calculator are desirable aids. The use of a torque wrench when tightening a blanket compresses the blanket a uniform amount.

The fourth cause is the worst. When printing starts, the quality of the print is high, but as the pressrun continues, the quality deteriorates as the blanket and packing compress, reducing the squeeze to below 0.003 or 0.002 in. (0.08 or 0.05 mm). To compensate for the poor print, the press operator often increases the ink (and water) to the plate. The quality of the print might improve, but the problem of insufficient squeeze has not been solved. Insufficient squeeze reduces the amount of ink transferring to the blanket from the plate. The initial symptom of insufficient squeeze is that the ink density of the print becomes light and the solids and type appear grainy in spots. After the symptom appears and the incorrect increase of ink and dampening feed, further symptoms appear:

- Rough, fuzzy edges on halftone dots, type, and line images resulting from insufficient ink transfer pressure and an excessively thick ink film
- Snowflaky printing—tiny open holes in areas that should be solid, full-density ink—due to excessive amounts of water droplets (from dampening solution) in ink
- Dampening rollers dirtied by water picking up tiny ink particles resulting from running excess dampening solution

In addition to the above symptoms, there are numerous problems that result indirectly from improper squeeze and directly from either increased ink feed or increased water feed: stripped rollers, glazed rollers, blind images, slow ink drying, decreased ink tack, poor trapping, filled-in halftones and reverses, poor register, tinting on later units of a four-color press, coating piling, and paper curling.

None of the above problems would occur if, instead of increasing ink and dampening feed, the press operator would stop the press and measure blanket height using a packing gauge. Checking blanket height is the first thing that the press operator should do when printing starts to look light after 500 or 1,000 impressions. Adding the proper thickness of packing paper restores the squeeze to the proper level.

An incorrect remedy for light printing due to insufficient squeeze is to increase the blanket-to-impression-cylinder pressure. This action, however, compresses the blanket still more, which further decreases the squeeze between plate and blanket. Excessive pressure is also placed between blanket cylinder and impression cylinder. Every time the gaps in the two cylinders meet, the excessive pressure is released, leading to vibrations throughout the cylinders. These vibrations, in turn, produce streaks.

Print Length Adjustment

Paper often stretches slightly between colors on a single-color or multicolor press. Consequently, the print must be made intentionally longer on the next color. On a sheetfed press, paper is run with the grain across the press. The paper stretches across the grain. Therefore, the stretch is around the cylinder. To match a stretched print, the press operator changes the diameter ratios of the cylinders. If the blanket diameter is larger than the plate diameter, the print will be longer. The reverse is also true: the higher the plate in relation to the blanket, the shorter the print. To match a stretched sheet on a bearer-contact press, then, it is only necessary to take packing from under the plate and put it under the blanket.

Print Length Adjustment on a Bearer-Contact Press

The following procedure is used to shorten print length on bearer-contact presses:

1. Increase plate height by adding packing.
2. Decrease blanket height by the amount of the packing change.
3. Increase the pressure between the blanket and impression cylinders by the amount of the packing change.
4. Decrease the inking and dampening roller setting to the plate by the amount of the packing change, if necessary.

The following procedure is used to increase print length on bearer-contact presses:

1. Decrease plate height by removing packing.
2. Increase blanket height by the amount of the packing change.
3. Decrease the pressure between the blanket and impression cylinders by the amount of the packing change.
4. Increase the inking and dampening roller settings to the plate by the amount of the packing change, if necessary.

Print Length Adjustment on a Non-Bearer Contact Press

The following procedure is used to shorten print length on non-bearer-contact presses, assuming that the distance between the plate and blanket cylinders is adjustable:

1. Increase plate height by adding packing.

2. Decrease the pressure between the plate and blanket cylinders by the amount of the packing change.
3. Increase the pressure between the blanket and impression cylinders by the amount of the packing change.
4. Decrease the inking and dampening roller settings to the plate by twice the amount of the packing change, if necessary.

The following procedure is used to increase print length on non-bearer-contact presses, assuming that the distance between the plate and blanket cylinders is adjustable:

1. Decrease plate height by removing packing.
2. Increase the pressure between the plate and blanket cylinders by the amount of the packing change.
3. Increase the pressure between the blanket and impression cylinders by the amount of the packing change.
4. Increase the inking and dampening roller settings to the plate by twice the amount of the packing change, if necessary.

Note: No blanket cylinder packing change is necessary when adjusting the print length on a non-bearer-contact press.

Limits on Enlargement

How much enlargement is safe? Excessive transfer of packing from plate cylinder to blanket cylinder often results in slurring or doubling due to the variation in the surface speed of the two cylinders. Halftones also fill-in, and the plate wears rapidly. Therefore, the question "How much enlargement is safe?" depends upon the packing conditions at the start of the pressrun. If initial plate packing conditions resulted in zero slippage, a packing shift of 0.004 in. (0.10 mm) would not cause excessive slippage. But, if initial packing conditions resulted in some slippage, the additional slippage caused by the 0.004-in. packing shift could easily exceed allowable slippage and could cause slurring and gear streaks.

When presses are packed precisely to specifications, the resulting cylinder circumferences produce equal print length. In color work, it is sometimes necessary, however, to deviate from these specifications to obtain color fit. Fortunately, a fairly wide tolerance is permissible in the packing conditions, except for squeeze. Without this latitude, it would be very difficult for the press operator to fit multicolor images when the paper stretches.

A general recommendation: if the paper on a multicolor job is expected to stretch and it is being run on a one-color press, it is best to pack the press for a relatively short print on the first color; i.e., some packing would be shifted to the plate cylinder initially.

Calculating Print Length Gain for Different Substrates

The following procedure can be used to judge the print length for a given substrate, or paper stock:

1. On the sides of a flat plate, scribe two lines near the lead edge and two lines near the trailing edge. These lines should be scribed so that they print in the trim area of a press sheet.
2. Measure the distance between the lines.
3. Mount the plate on press and print several sheets.
4. Measure the distance between the lines on a press sheet.
5. Subtract the distance between lines on the plate from the distance between lines on the press sheet. Divide this number by the distance between lines on the plate. The answer will be the average print length gain per inch for that substrate.

This test can be repeated for other substrates to determine how to pack the press to compensate for print length gain. Through experience, the press operator will be able to predict print length gain and be able to make the necessary changes in packing to correct for it.

Approximate position of scribed lines in the trim area

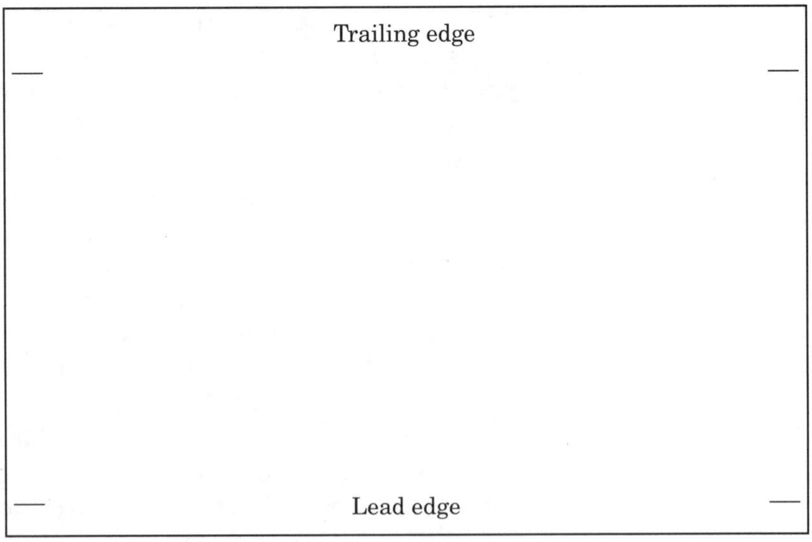

Trailing edge

Lead edge

7 Blankets

Blankets cause many problems, but they have the one redeeming feature that has made offset lithography what it is: they can transfer ink to paper (fairly rough paper) with high fidelity (good solids and very fine dots).

The blanket's importance is often overlooked, but it is as important as any other part of the lithographic printing system. Because it is the last image transfer point, it directly affects the quality of the printed job.

Blanket Manufacture

The use of rubber for offset blankets goes back to the invention of the modern offset press by Ira Rubel in 1909. Rubel knew of the excellent image-transfer capability of rubber surfaces, and he made this capability the central design feature of the first offset press.

The first commercially used offset blankets were made of natural rubber, which was somewhat less than ideal in this application. These blankets had a tendency to swell, stretch, blister, and become tacky. They had poor resistance to solvents and oils. In addition, rubber—a naturally occurring substance—could not be produced to uniform specifications and close tolerances.

The development of synthetic rubbers in the 1930s made it possible to overcome the disadvantages of poor solvent and oil resistance associated with natural rubber. The use of synthetic rubbers also made it possible to control formulations and to produce close-tolerance blankets in uniform batches.

The synthetic rubbers that are most commonly used today are Buna-N and, to a lesser extent, neoprene. The specific formula used is generally kept secret by the blanket manufacturer. In addition to the basic rubber compound, the formula contains additives to toughen and reinforce the blanket surface. Softeners and plasticizers are also added to give the blanket resiliency. Finally, a vulcanizing agent, usually sulfur, is included to cause the molecules of the rubber compound to cross-link during the vulcanizing process.

Manufacture begins with the weaving of the fabric backing. The material used is a very high grade of long-staple cotton. The tolerances on the finished fabric are extremely rigid (especially in terms of thickness and strength).

Warp threads on the fabric side of a blanket

Before the rubber is applied, the fabric backing is stretched in the same direction as the tension to be applied when the blanket is mounted on the press. Prestretching minimizes the amount that the blanket stretches when it is mounted on the press. The backing fabric is woven to be much stronger lengthwise (around the cylinder) than across its width. Colored threads are woven into the backing to indicate the direction of greatest strength. (The direction of maximum strength is called the **warp;** the direction of minimum strength is called the **weft.**) On the press, blanket strength is needed in the around-the-cylinder, or warp, direction. The warp threads should always run from leading to trailing edge. If they run from side to side, the blanket stretches beyond recovery and runs loosely, causing doubling and slurring.

The prestretched fabric is coated with a thin layer of adhesive cement, and another layer of prestretched fabric is placed on top of the first. A three-ply blanket has three such fabric layers. Most offset blankets are three- or four-ply, although two-ply blankets are also made. Three-ply blankets are usually between 0.062 in. (1.57 mm) and 0.066 in. (1.68 mm) thick. Four-ply offset blankets generally fall in the 0.072-in. (1.83-mm) to 0.076-in. (1.93-mm) thickness range.

After the fabric layers have been cemented together, the rubber surface is applied to the backing in sixty to eighty individual coats, each carefully laid down. The entire operation is carried out in a temperature-controlled, dust-free atmosphere. Conditioned air is necessary in meeting thickness tolerances. Standard tolerance on blanket thicknesses is about ±0.0005 in. (±0.013 mm).

The blanket is then powdered, festooned, and cured (vulcanized). This last operation causes rubber molecules to cross-link, giving the finished blanket its strength and dimensional stability. A good blanket stretches less than 2.5% in the around-the-cylinder direction and has a tensile strength of about 300 lb./in., which is very high. Because of this, excessive tension from end to end is not nearly as much of a problem in mounting blankets as is uniform tension across the blanket width.

Performance Requirements

A "good" printing blanket, like good ink and paper, results from tradeoffs between a number of opposing characteristics.

Sheet Release

Release is the readiness of the blanket to give up the paper after it leaves the nip. The smoothness of the blanket surface is a factor; very smooth blankets tend to have poor release. Even so, it is fairly clear from research that smoothness is not the only factor that contributes to blanket release.

Press operators agree almost universally that a hard blanket gives the best release. Whatever theoretical justification there is for this contention has not yet been supported by research findings. One stumbling block has been finding a reliable means of measuring hardness that allows comparison between blankets. Durometers require a sample thickness many times greater than the thickness of the rubber surface layer on blankets. This makes the value of blanket durometer readings questionable.

The blanket is just one of several factors affecting sheet release. Press speed, ink tack, printing pressures, and paper surface also affect sheet release. The increasing use of lightweight paper, faster press speeds, and higher-tack inks makes the importance of a blanket with good sheet release characteristics all the more critical.

Resilience and Durability

Resilience and durability are two other important qualities. **Resilience** is the ability of a blanket to return to its original thickness after pressure on its surface has been removed. Resilience is usually most important to the press operator as **smash-resistance,** the ability of a blanket to *recover* from being momentarily subjected to excessively high pressure. **Durability,** on the other hand, is the blanket's ability to withstand the pressure, tension, and physical abuse it continually undergoes on the press.

Surface Smoothness

Surface smoothness is another important quality. The nature of blanket manufacture creates microscopic contours on the rubber surface. Some have suggested that this graining is important in removing water from the plate. Others argue that optimum blanket performance is obtained with a polished, grainless surface. In any event, nearly all blankets sold commercially have a slightly grained surface. It is important that the grain is not so great that it affects printing, especially in solids. Grain is another reason why a light washing of the blanket surface is inadequate for keeping the surface clean. The surface should be free from pinholes, pits, or other defects.

Solvent Resistance

A blanket must have an affinity for ink but should be resistant to the ink vehicles and the solvents used to clean it. To perform satisfactorily, the blanket must not swell when contacted by a solvent. Solvent-resistance properties vary considerably, which means that only solvents compatible with the blanket are suitable for cleaning it.

Stretch and Tensile Strength

A blanket should undergo minimum stretch on the press. However, it is normal for a newly mounted blanket to stretch slightly. As a result, the initial blanket tension decreases and the blanket becomes slightly loose. Therefore, it is not uncommon that the blanket has to be "taken up" (retightened) after the first 3,000 or 4,000 impressions. After that, the blanket should remain dimensionally stable (i.e., not stretch) on the press for the rest of its run life, assuming that it has been properly mounted. The blanket with the least tendency to stretch after the initial stretch has been taken up is the one most satisfactory from the standpoint of maintaining uniform conditions during the pressrun. If it is necessary to retighten a blanket at regular intervals, printing pressure may be excessive, lockup tension may be insufficient, or the blanket may be stretching excessively from being overtensioned.

Compressible Blanket

Use of the compressible blanket has become widespread in recent years. Like a conventional blanket, a compressible blanket has a surface of synthetic rubber and a fabric backing of several plies. But in addition to the fabric layers, the backing includes one or more layers of a compressible material, such as adhesive–foam rubber, cork, or nonwoven fibers.

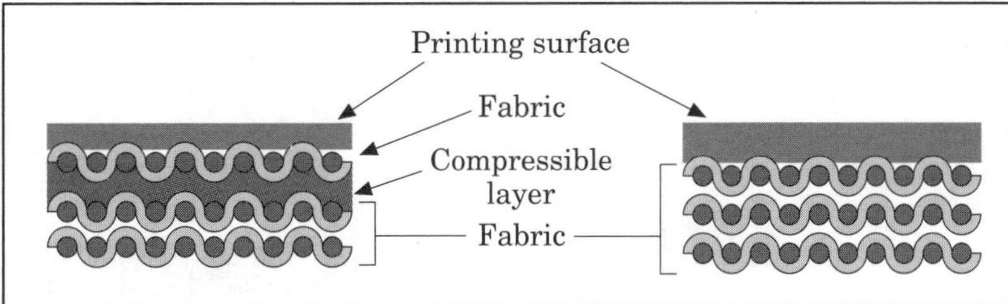

Cross-section of compressible blanket *(left)* and conventional blanket

One advantage of a compressible blanket is its wider packing latitude. With either type of blanket, an increase in packing also increases pressure. However, with a compressible blanket, the pressure increase is not as great. In effect, over a given range, a change in packing produces a relatively small change in pressure. Consequently, the press operator has somewhat wider packing tolerances. This is important because improper pressure can lead to a host of process problems: plate wear, dot spread, ink film graininess, mottle, dot slur, gear marks, blanket low spots, changes in image length, and paper pick. Although packing latitude is greater with a compressible blanket, the manufacturer's directions for packing both types of blankets should be followed.

A photomicrograph showing the printing surface, compressible layer, and carcass of a compressible blanket *Courtesy DAY International Printing Products Co.*

Compressible blanket

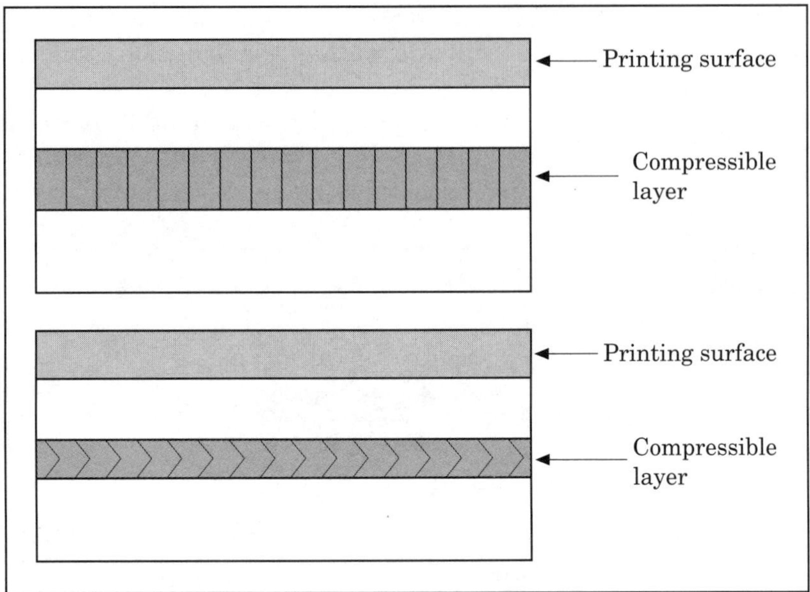

Reduced slippage at the nip is a second advantage of a compressible blanket. (**True rolling** is a term often used to describe the condition of no slip in the printing nip.) With a conventional rubber blanket, bulges form on either or both

The results of test conducted by a blanket manufacturer on how blankets react to pressure

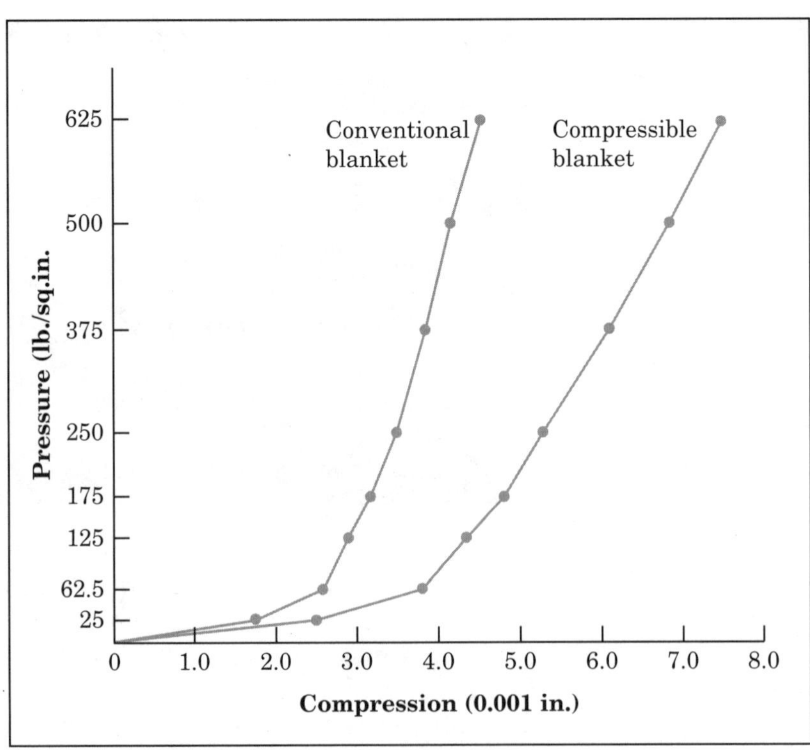

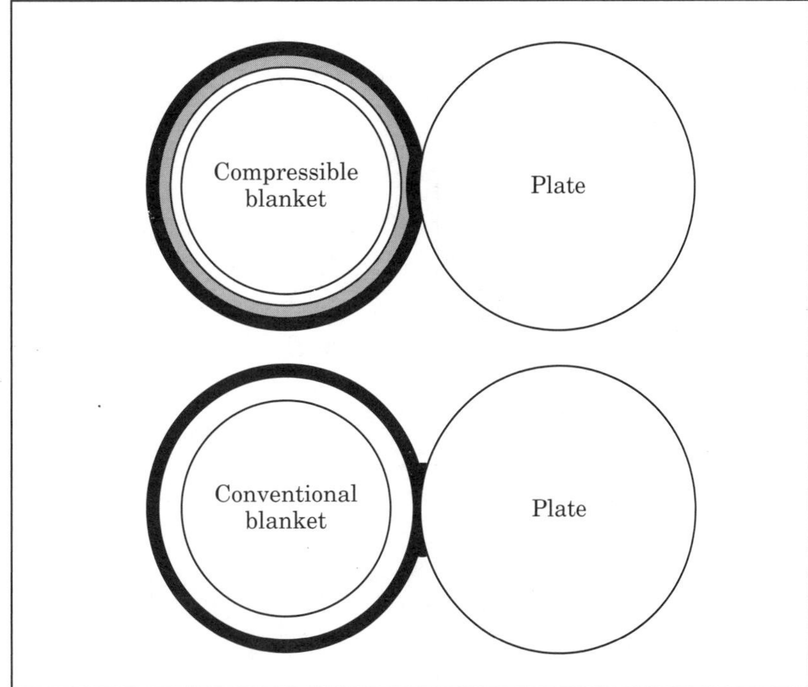

The deformation of compressible and conventional blankets at the nip between the plate and blanket

sides of the nip. Because the blanket deforms, its surface speed through the nip is different from the surface speed of the plate. In other words, there is usually slippage between the plate and a conventional blanket, which can lead to slurring. A compressible blanket does not deform in the same way. Less rubber is displaced as the blanket travels through the nip. The speed differential between plate and blanket is considerably reduced.

Some manufacturers say that using a compressible blanket leads to longer plate life. Reducing slippage between plate and blanket means that the polishing action of the blanket against the plate is reduced.

Whenever an unwanted solid object goes through the press (such as a ream marker or a double sheet), a **smash,** or an undesired localized compression of the blanket's surface, results. A compressible blanket resists smashing better because of the compression layer's ability to compress. Smash recovery, depending upon the severity of the smash, may be within 2–10 sheets. **Compression set** is the permanent reduction in thickness of any of the blanket's component parts.

Another advantage of a compressible blanket is that any thickness variation tends to "even out" in the blanket-to-plate and blanket-to-impression-cylinder nips.

Compared to conventional blankets, compressible blankets usually produce sharper dots and halftones, better register, less paper distortion, and fewer washups.

Compressible vs. conventional blankets

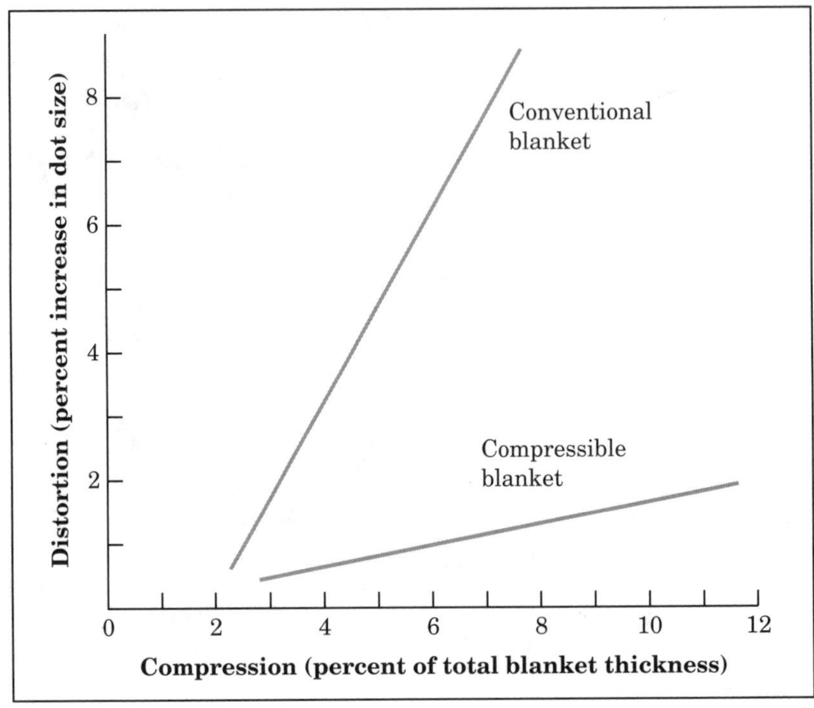

Blanket Selection

In choosing a blanket, the press operator should select a thickness that minimizes the amount of packing needed. The blanket should also be wide enough to run from gutter to gutter. This helps to prevent chemicals and other contaminants from working their way under the blanket during the pressrun.

Blankets come in different colors. At one time, the blanket's color indicated its hardness. This is no longer true.

Many blanket manufacturers now question the usefulness of thinking in terms of blanket "hardness." Durometer tests provide inadequate measures of blanket hardness because the rubber layer is too thin to make accurate measurements. Also, the readings are affected by the relative compressibility of backing materials.

Quick-Release Properties

Many blankets are sold today as "quick-release" blankets. The quick-release properties of a blanket are probably associated with the surface roughness of the blanket. The rougher the surface, the less tendency there is for the paper to adhere to the blanket. However, as the roughness of the surface increases, the blanket's ability to reproduce fine dots and smooth solids decreases.

Blanket Thickness

Today's blankets usually have their thickness marked on the back. This figure may be accurate, but it does not convey enough information about the blanket to the printer.

One of the problems with depending on these figures is that the printer does not know which instrument was used to make the measurement. Due to different instruments and different measuring techniques, it is quite reasonable to assume that a measurement of 0.065 in. (1.65 mm) by one manufacturer may not agree with the same measurement by another manufacturer.

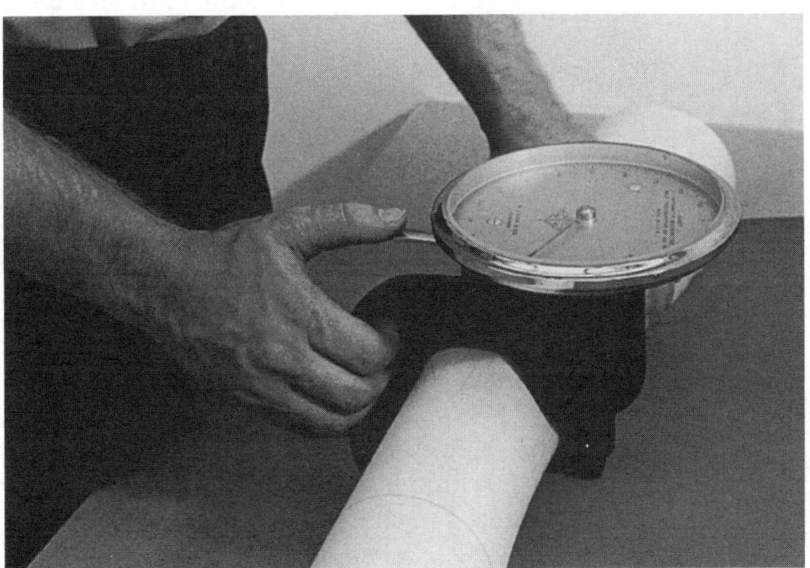

Press operator using a deadweight bench micrometer from E. J. Cady & Co. to measure blanket thickness

A single figure stamped on the back of a blanket does not ensure uniformity. Each printer should have an agreement with the blanket supplier regarding acceptable **nonuniformity,** or overall variation, of a given blanket. Although blanket manufacturers talk in terms of uniformity of ±0.001 in. or ±0.002 in. (±0.025 mm or ±0.05 mm), such a figure may refer to the uniformity of an entire shipment of blankets. The printer's problem is nonuniformity within a given blanket, which can produce a problem that the printer cannot resolve. Checking each blanket's thickness necessitates a standard procedure. This procedure involves making a fixed number of measurements at the center and edges for each blanket received, using a deadweight micrometer, such as a Cady gauge. The average reading of all measurements should be marked on the blanket back to enable accurate computations of required packing thickness. The difference between the highest and the lowest readings should also be noted, and if this difference exceeds the agreed-upon tolerance, the blanket should be returned to the supplier.

Proper Care of Blankets

Today's blankets perform very well under press-related stresses and pressures. They also resist well the chemicals applied to their surface: ink, solvent, water, acids, gums, and salts, for example. However, they must be cared for properly.

The blanket should be rolled up carefully when being transported. It must not be folded, because the crease will permanently damage the blanket's face.

Blanket Storage

Off-press abuse—even of a seemingly minor kind—can ruin a blanket.

Exposure to light is a good example of off-press abuse. Directly exposing a blanket to sunlight will, over a period of time, crack and craze the rubber surface, making it unusable. Fluorescent light and heat can have a similar effect. Blankets should be stored in a dark, dry, cool place.

The tube in which a blanket is shipped is a good storage place. The tube should be stored on end. The press operator should never put too many blankets in a single tube, however. The innermost blanket will be very tightly wound, and prolonged storage under high stress may ruin the fabric backing.

Blankets can be stored flat. If they are, they should be stored so that rubber contacts rubber and fabric contacts fabric. Prolonged contact between a rubber surface and a fabric backing can cause the fabric pattern to emboss on the adjacent rubber surface.

Some manufacturers recommend flat face-to-face storage, and others recommend standing tube storage.

Blanket Solvents

The press operator must make sure that the solvents used to clean the blanket are compatible with the ink *and* blankets. The ideal solvent should have a high solvency power for ink and the other compounds that frequently find their way onto the blanket during printing. It should have no damaging effects on the resiliency or printability of rubber. It should be nontoxic and have a flash point above room temperature, yet not so high that it takes a long time to evaporate.

Many commercial solvents come close to filling this bill. Any solvent should be approved by the blanket manufacturer to make sure that it is compatible with the materials in the blanket and does not cause swelling or premature aging. Roller and plate suppliers should also be consulted before using a new solvent.

The accompanying illustration shows how much a certain blanket swelled when exposed to different solvents. It can be seen that some solvents have an extreme effect on blankets while others have little or no effect.

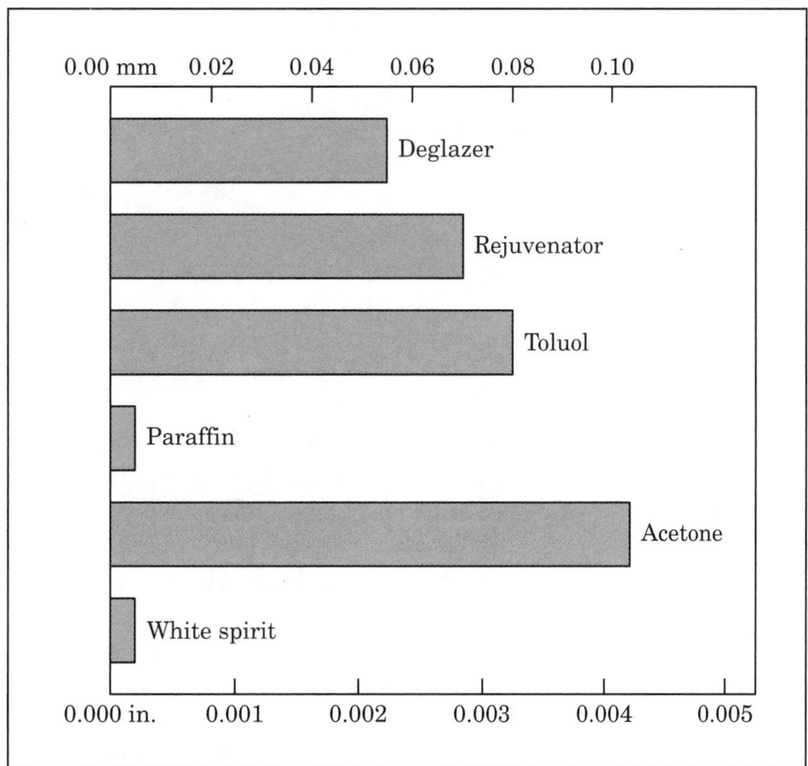

Swelling of a blanket caused by exposure to various solvents for a period of 5 min.

Repeated use of a solvent easily absorbed by the rubber causes deterioration. Washes with high kauri-butanol (KB) solvents should be avoided. A solvent with a high KB number is more easily absorbed by the rubber and evaporates more slowly. Rate of evaporation is important. A low rate forces delays in reinking after a blanket wash. Retained solvent increases the tackiness and frictional coefficient of the blanket.

Solvents containing benzol or toluol damage natural rubber, making it softer, tackier, and gummier. They should not be used. The use of solvents like kerosene and mineral spirits, which have a high boiling point and take a long time to dry, should be avoided.

Some substances that swell blankets include chlorinated and coal tar solvents, ketones, and esters. Aromatic solvents such as toluene, xylol, turpentine, and pine oil also cause swelling. Benzene, perchloroethylene, trichloroethylene, carbon disulfide, and carbon tetrachloride should not be used because of their high toxicity and ability to dissolve rubber. All chlorinated solvents are toxic.

The previous discussion concerning matching the KB of the blanket wash to the blanket also applies to the ink itself. Sending an ink sample along with a blanket order ensures compatibility.

Material Safety Data Sheets should be on file for all pressroom solvents.

Washing and Reconditioning the Blanket Surface

A clean blanket is essential to high-quality printing. Scrubbing a blanket removes the hardened surface left on the blanket by the various gum and ink vehicles used during printing. Scrubbing also diffuses the oils and driers just below the blanket's surface, greatly increasing the life of the blanket.

When washing blankets, the press operator should be careful not to splash solvent along the blanket edges, because they may not be sealed. The top layer of the blanket is probably solvent-resistant; the under layers are probably not. Excess solvent attacks the adhesive that bonds the fabric plies together. Cutting blanket packing to less than full blanket width makes it difficult for excess ink to build up at the edges in the first place. It is important that the solvent-treated portion of the blanket be wiped dry with a clean lint-free cloth as soon as possible.

Proper reconditioning of a blanket requires some work as well as attention over a period of time. The first step is ink removal by means of a solvent. Once ink is off, the blanket is washed with water to remove gum residue. At this point, the blanket is usually removed from the press and placed on a table for scrubbing. (Pumice should not be used to clean the blanket's surface, because it could produce scratches.) The blanket surface is cleaned until it has the velvety feel of live rubber. A hand blanket scrubber, such as a pocket-shaped scrubbing pad containing a cellulose sponge, may be used to remove heavy build-ups.

Press operator cleaning the blanket with solvent on a wadded rag

Notice that the press operator is wearing rubber gloves as protection against the solvent.

Press operator using a clean lint-free cloth to dry the blanket

The back of the cleaned blanket is then soaked for a day or so to restore the fibers, and the blanket is hung up to dry. A mixture of one part glycerine to four parts water generally restores blankets better than plain water. Never return a blanket to the press until it is *absolutely dry.*

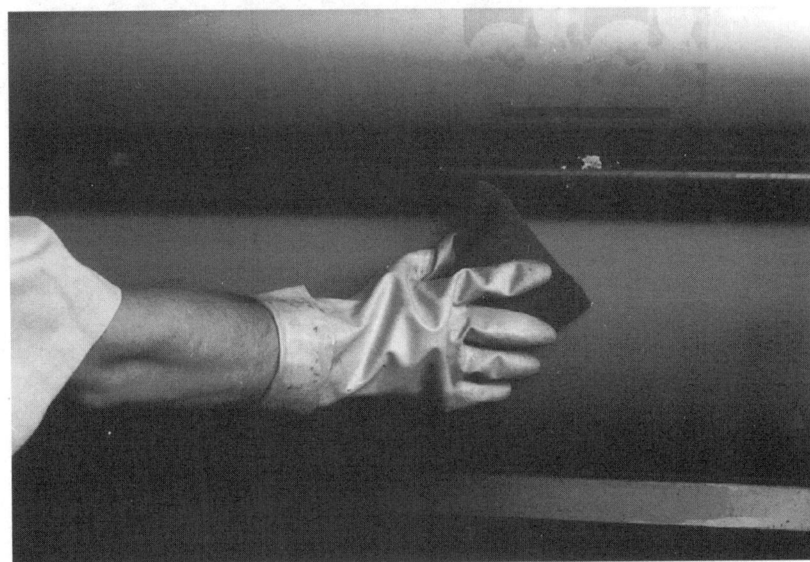

Press operator using hand blanket scrubber

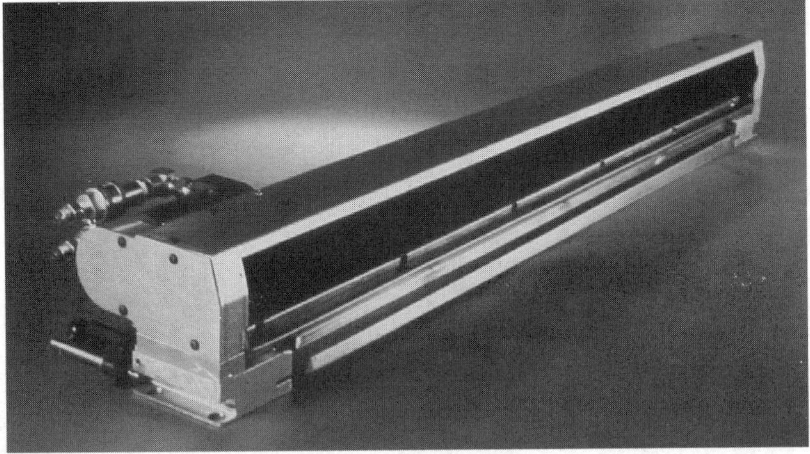

Automatic blanket washer
Courtesy Oxy-Dry Corporation

Blanket Mounting Bars

In many instances, blankets can be ordered with mounting bars attached. Otherwise, the press operator must mount a bar to it.

The blanket must be evenly tensioned when it is stretched on the cylinder. The first step toward ensuring uniform tensioning is to make sure that the blanket is perfectly square. Usually, blankets are properly cut and squared before being

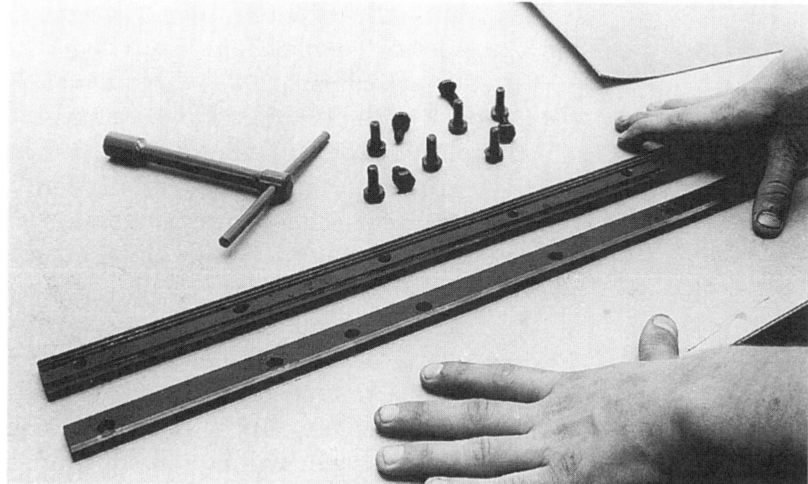

The blanket bars, bolts, and T wrench used to attach the bars to a blanket

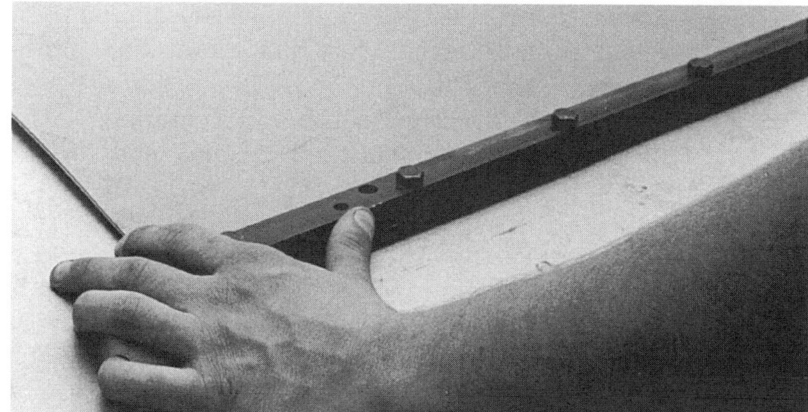

Blanket bars being fastened by aligning the holes in both bars with the holes in the blanket and then inserting the bolts

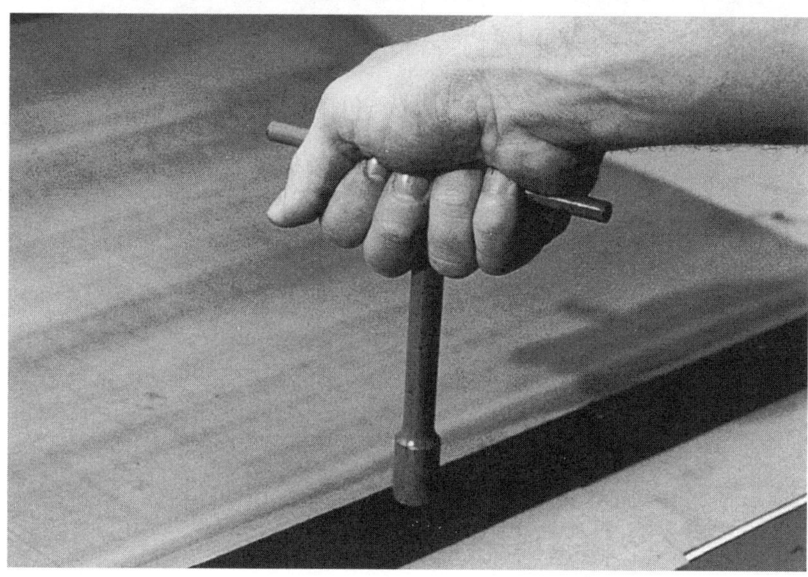

T wrench being used to tighten the bolts starting from the center and working towards the ends

shipped, but it is a good idea to check squareness anyway. The sides of the blanket should be parallel to the warp threads, which run in the direction of the arrow printed on the back of the blanket. (The warp threads on some blankets are colored for easier identification.) The warp threads have to be at a 90° angle to the lead edge and back edge of the blanket. A large carpenter's square can be used. If the ends are not perpendicular, they should be carefully trimmed.

An unsquare blanket probably will be mounted to bars in an unsquare manner. If the ends of the bars are closer together on the right side than the left (because the warp threads are not perpendicular to the bars), the blanket will have more tension on the right side when on the press and, more importantly, will be pulled thinner on that side. For the right side to print under this condition, the left side must print with excessive pressure, resulting in poor print quality and worn plates. It is a part of the press operator's job to check that the blankets are square.

Every press should be equipped with one or two spare blankets, mounted on bars, ready to be put into the press at an instant's notice.

Blanket Mounting

Blankets are usually three- or four-ply for commercial work. Three-ply blankets are generally mounted on blanket cylinders with undercuts of 0.075 in. (1.9 mm) or less. Four-ply blankets have an extra layer of fabric backing for greater strength and are mounted on larger presses with undercuts of more than 0.075 in. Three-ply blankets generally are not mounted on cylinders with undercuts designed to accommodate a four-ply blanket. A three-ply blanket mounted on such a cylinder requires an extra 0.010 in. (0.25 mm) or so of packing. On the deeper-undercut cylinders, some press operators prefer using a four-ply blanket and less packing to avoid the problem of packing creep.

The previous chapter of this book discusses packing in detail. Only packing paper is used under a blanket; Mylar causes numerous problems when used as a blanket-cylinder packing material. (Some press manufacturers specify the use of a special "underlay" blanket in addition to packing sheets.) Press operators typically attach the packing to the cylinder body and then mount the blanket instead of attaching the packing to the back of the blanket. Before packing is positioned, the cylinder body and bearers should be cleaned, and any rust should be removed.

Blanket packing should *always* extend all the way from leading edge to trailing edge. This practice ensures good plate-to-blanket and blanket-to-impression-cylinder contact all around the cylinder and maximizes the printing area on the form. Blanket packing should be cut about $\frac{1}{16}$–$\frac{1}{8}$ in. (2–3 mm) narrower than the blanket to prevent packing swelling. Blanket packing is allowed to extend slightly into the cylinder gap so that the blanket helps to hold the packing in place and to prevent it from creeping while the press is running.

Many press operators use paint to indicate the exact center of the blanket cylinder to aid in placing blankets and packing. By marking the exact center of the blankets and packing, the press operator can match the cylinder, blanket, and packing marks and accurately center blankets and packing with minimal effort.

The blanket bars mounted at the leading and trailing edges of the blanket are inserted into the blanket lockup mechanism. When tightening the lockup at the trailing edge, the press operator should take care not to pull the blanket thin at one spot or another. One factor is the strength of the press

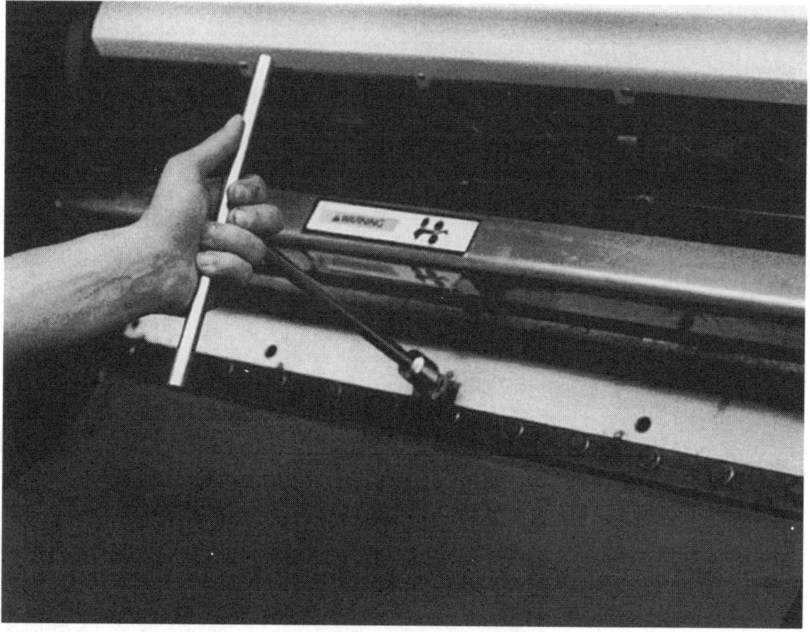

Lead edge of blanket being locked into the clamp or reel bar

operator. Another is the blanket itself; blanket “A” may stretch lengthwise and therefore decrease in thickness 0.001 in. (0.025 mm), whereas blanket “B” might decrease 0.002 in. (0.05 mm). These factors make it difficult to properly mount

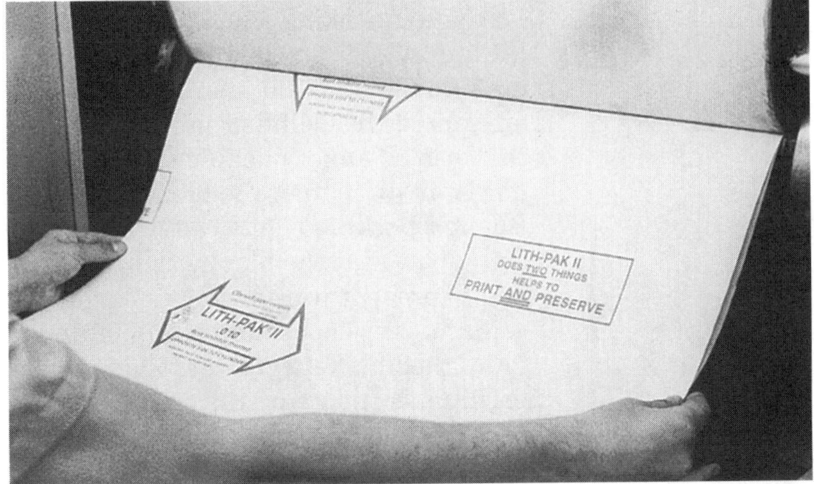

Proper thickness of packing being applied to back of blanket

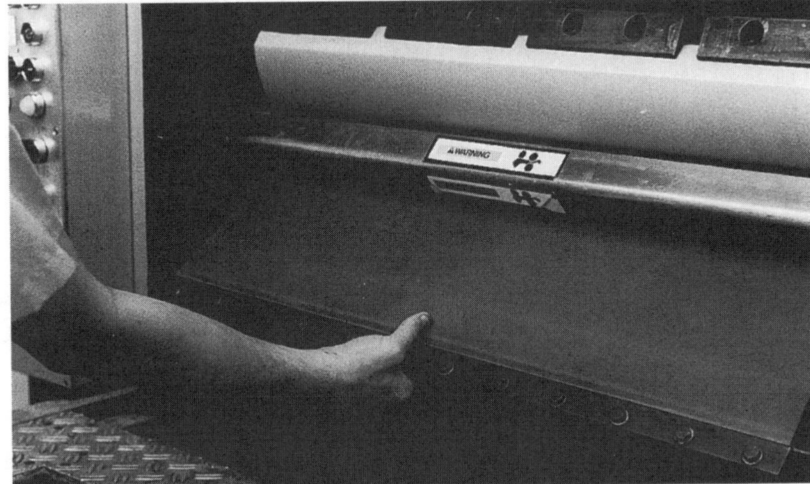

Press operator holding the blanket and packing together while slowly inching the press until the trailing edge reel bar is accessible

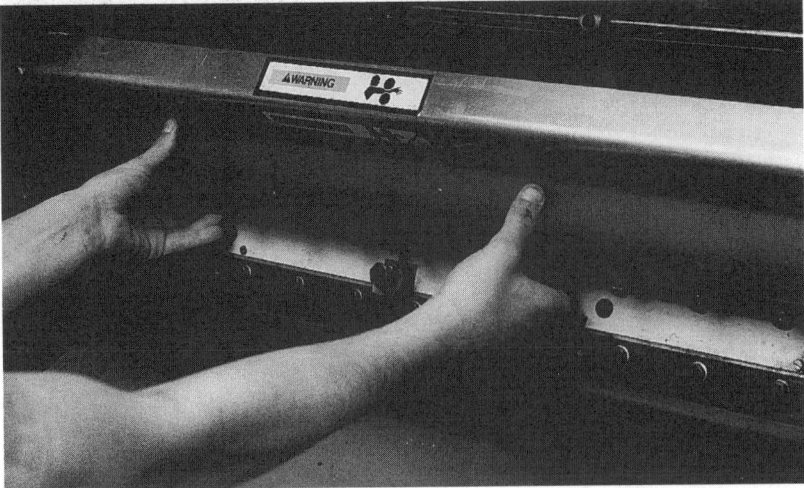

Trailing edge of blanket being inserted into reel bar

a blanket. Doing it properly is something that comes only with experience, although using mechanical aids is helpful. A torque wrench can be used to apply a known amount of tension to the mounted blanket. A torque wrench has an indicator giving an exact reading of how much torque the press operator is putting on the blanket reel.

Micrometer-adjustable torque-sensing wrench

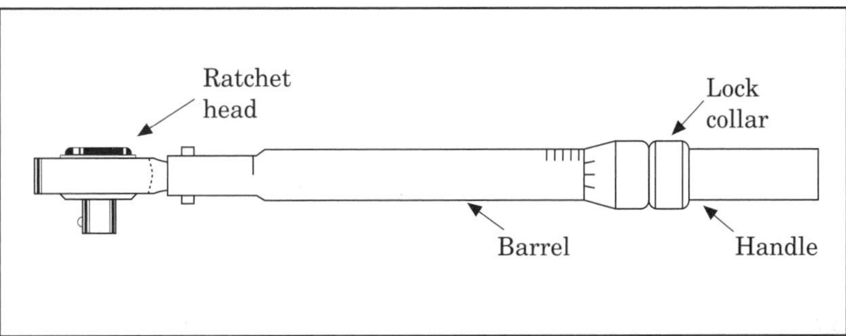

Overtensioning a blanket damages it. A procedure recommended for properly tensioning a new compressible blanket follows:

1. Overpack the blanket by 0.002 in. (0.05 mm).
2. Print approximately 500 sheets and retighten the blanket using a torque wrench.
3. Print another 500 sheets and again retighten the blanket. A quality compressible blanket should require no more tightening during a pressrun.

Some manufacturers provide recommended torque values for blanket tensioning. However, in most cases, the press operator should determine the correct value by using a press-mounted blanket that is producing high-quality printing as the standard for that press/blanket combination. Following is a simple procedure for determining the torque value of a properly mounted blanket:

1. Adjust the torque wrench to its lowest reading.
2. Place the wrench on the blanket reel, and apply pressure to the wrench as if tightening the blanket.
3. If the wrench *does not* make a clicking sound when pressure is applied, the torque exerted on the blanket will be indicated by the setting of the torque wrench. If the *wrench* does make a clicking sound, increase the setting of the torque wrench by the smallest increment possible.
4. Repeat steps 2 and 3 until the torque value of the blanket is determined. Record this value. All press units should receive the same amount of tensioning.

Recovering from a Blanket Smash

In some plants, a routine procedure is followed for keeping blankets in good repair. In these plants, the supervisors not only insist upon thorough, frequent scrubbing but also have a routine for handling damaged blankets. If a blanket is smashed during a run, no time is wasted on repairing it at that time. It is quicker and easier to install a spare blanket on the press. If the printing surface of the blanket is cut or damaged, the blanket should be replaced. However, slightly damaged or slightly cut blankets can be used when scoring or perforating on the press.

If a blanket is smashed but the surface is not cut, soaking the back side of the blanket often saves the blanket. When a blanket is smashed, most of the damage is done to the cloth fabric under the rubber. The rubber returns to its original thickness, but the cloth fibers remain compressed. The cure is to bring fabric fibers back to their original size.

1. Remove the blanket from the press and scrub the back thoroughly.
2. Place the entire blanket in a container of water, and soak it for a day or so. (A little wetting agent, such as glycerine, helps.)
3. After the soaking, hang the blanket by the clamp bar and let it dry thoroughly. (Some blankets become wavy after being soaked, but they usually smooth out when stretched around the blanket cylinder.)

If the blanket is too big for any available container, an alternative procedure is used:

1. Clean off the back of the blanket, and hang it up by the clamp bar.
2. Use a sponge to soak the back with water. Rewet the blanket every hour or so. Rewet the damaged areas especially. Continue this periodic rewetting for a couple of days depending on the condition of the blanket.

Either treatment restores the original thickness of the blanket in most of the smashed areas. The success of these treatments depends on how badly the blanket was smashed. *These treatments do not work if the rubber is cut or the cloth fabric under the rubber is torn or shredded.*

Use of Slightly Damaged Blankets

In most cases, if the printing surface of the blanket is damaged—e.g., cut—the blanket should be discarded. However, at least one slightly damaged blanket should be keep on hand whenever scoring or perforating is done on the press. The scoring or perforating dies would damage a new blanket, but since no printing occurs on that blanket, the use of an old blanket is acceptable.

The scoring or perforating dies are self-adhesive tapes designed to be attached to the surface of the impression cylinder. Usually, an image is printed on the last impression cylinder, and the dies are attached to that cylinder using the printed image as a guide. Another method involves attaching the perforating tape or scoring tape to a printed sheet of paper, which is later attached to the impression cylinder:

1. Attach (tape) the die(s) to a printed press sheet, called a **carrier sheet.**

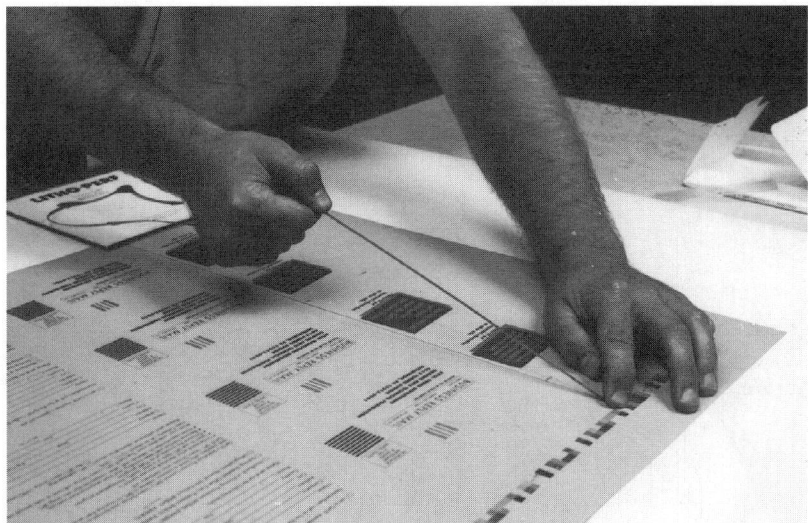

Press operator placing a perforating die on the press sheet

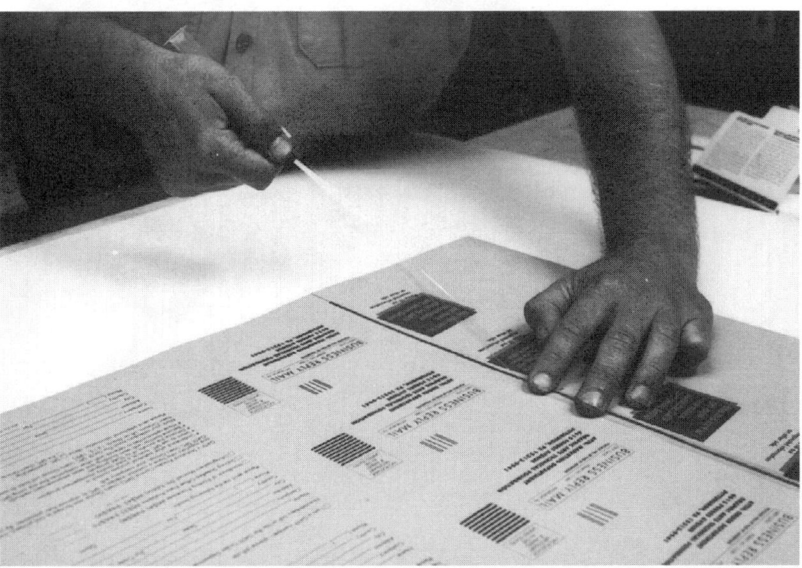

Press operator taping the perforating die to the press sheet

2. Adjust the impression cylinder to compensate for the carrier sheet and stock thickness.
3. With impression off, feed the sheet through the press until its lead edge is in the grippers of the last impression cylinder.
4. Lift the trailing edge of the sheet, and apply rubber cement to the back side of the press sheet so that the sheet becomes cemented to the surface of the impression cylinder.
5. Inch the press until the grippers open on the press sheet. With a razor knife, cut and remove the portion of the sheet that is held by the grippers, and then rubber-cement the lead edge of the sheet to the impression cylinder.
6. Run the printed press sheets through the press. The perforations and scores will be in register.
7. After scoring and perforating is completed, remove the press sheet from the cylinder surface. **Caution:** Wear rubber gloves when handling rubber cement and its thinner.

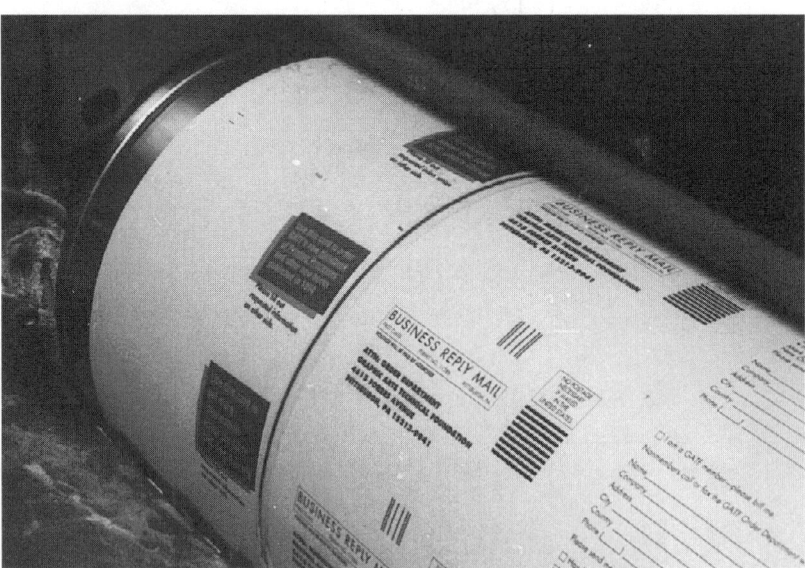

Press sheet and perforating die attached to impression cylinder

8 Plates

The lithographic press operator is concerned with plates in two ways. One is the physical action of mounting, adjusting, and removing the plates. The other is assuring that the delicate chemical separation of image and nonimage areas is completely maintained during the pressrun. This requires more careful attention in lithography than in any other printing process. In rotogravure, the image areas are cut into a metal surface. In letterpress, they stand out solidly above the surface. But the level surface of the lithographic plate requires a chemical distinction between image and nonimage areas. When a properly made plate is run on the press, the dampening rollers keep the nonimage areas of the plate moist so that these areas do not accept ink. The ink rollers then transfer ink only to the dry image areas, on which there is no water. The press operator does not need to know all the techniques required to make a plate, but understanding the nature of the lithographic plate and how it carries its image is helpful in maintaining the image satisfactorily.

Types of Plates

There are several types of photolithographic plates, but they share one key feature: during platemaking, a photochemical process divides the plate surface into two different types of areas characterized by two different chemical properties. **Image areas**—the parts that are to print—are made oil-receptive **(oleophilic)** and water-repellent **(hydrophobic). Nonimage areas**—the parts that are not to print—are made water-receptive **(hydrophilic)** and oil-repellent **(oleophobic).** Therefore, when the printing plate is contacted by the dampening rollers, only the nonimage areas accept the water-based dampening solution and become wet. When the dampened plate is contacted by the inking form rollers, only the image areas accept the oily lithographic ink.

The objective of the plate manufacturer is to make the image areas as ink-receptive and water-repellent as possible and to make the nonimage areas as water-receptive and ink-repellent as possible. The press operator must try to keep them that way. Lithographic plates are made of various base materials, but most of them are made of grained aluminum, usually anodized and then silicated to create a durable water-receptive surface. Most of them are **surface plates,** in which an ink-receptive light-sensitive coating applied to the plate surface remains on the plate in the image areas after processing, while in the nonimage areas' coating is removed from the water-receptive layer.

Plates are usually imaged by exposure through a photographic film (although some are exposed by laser directly from information output by computers). In the United States, most plates are exposed through a negative; such plates are called **negative-working,** or **negative, plates.** In a negative-working plate, the light that strikes the plate forms the image areas; therefore, laser-imaged plates are negative-working.

When a negative-working surface plate is exposed through a negative, the light-sensitive coating hardens and becomes insoluble in the image areas. During development, only the unexposed, unhardened coating over the nonimage areas dissolves, leaving the water-receptive aluminum uncovered. In the usual kind of negative-working surface plate, called **subtractive**, the exposed coating is very tough and durable on press. This material remains on the plate as the image areas but is removed ("subtracted") from the nonimage areas when the coating is dissolved away. However, the bared aluminum in the nonimage areas, although it is already water-receptive, must be made even more so. This **desensitization** is accomplished by **gumming,** the application of a thin, uniform coating of a gum arabic or similar solution that protects the surface from oxidation and makes the surface very water-receptive. The kind of negative-working surface plate that requires the addition of an image-reinforcing material during development is called **additive.** Although most of these additive plates are **wipe-on** plates that are coated by the platemaker, presensitized additive plates are also available.

It may be useful for a press operator to know something about certain other types of plates besides the more commonly used ones described above. A plate that is exposed through a film positive is called **positive-working.** Presensitized positive-working plates are similar to subtractive negative-working plates except that the insoluble image areas are unexposed while the nonimage areas become soluble during exposure and are then removed during development. Positive-working plates are always subtractive. Many of these plates can be thermally cured at high temperatures to harden the image areas for better press life.

Very durable positive- and negative-working surface plates that last for more than 1,000,000 impressions under normal conditions are available. For even longer pressruns, multimetal plates are available. They are made of two or even three laminated metals. One of the metals—usually electroplated copper because of its ability to accept ink—provides the image areas. Another metal—aluminum, stainless steel, or chromium, because of the ease with which they accept water—forms the nonimage areas. If a third metal is used, it serves simply as a base metal to support the two top metals. Multimetal plates can be either negative- or positive-working. The top metal carries the coating of photosensitive material.

Negative-working multimetal plates are usually **bimetal:** copper electroplated on a nonimage metal. Exposure light penetrates the transparent image areas of the negative and hardens the photosensitive coating. During processing, the unhardened coating of the nonimage area dissolves, baring the copper. Then an etch removes the copper from the nonimage metal—aluminum or stainless steel.

Most positive-working multimetal plates are exactly like the negative-working multimetal plates except that the coating becomes soluble when exposed to light. During development, the exposed coating is dissolved away to uncover the copper. Then, the copper is etched away leaving the water-receptive aluminum or stainless steel as the nonimage area.

But whatever the type of plate and however it is made, its action on the press is very much the same. For best results, follow the manufacturer's instructions and use only recommended products and chemicals. The type of plate will be mentioned subsequently only if it affects troubleshooting or other matters of plate handling on the press.

Plates for waterless lithography. Plates for waterless lithography are constructed of an aluminum base, a primer, a photopolymer layer, an ink-repellent silicone rubber layer, and a transparent protective film on top. The plate can be hand- or machine-developed in a special processor. Care must be taken handling the plates; any scratches in the silicone rubber layer can become an unwanted image area.

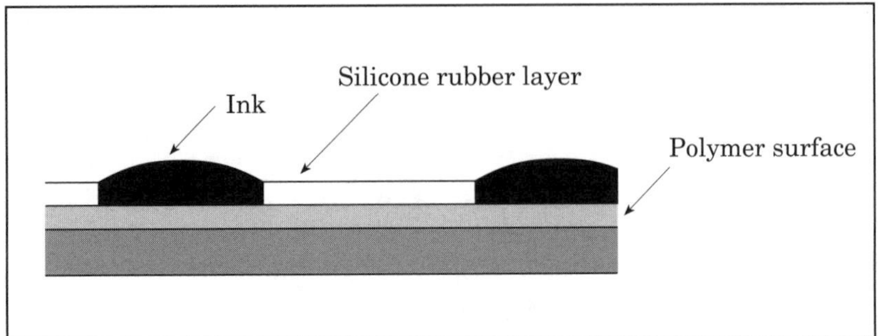

The Toray Waterless Plate
Courtesy Toray Marketing & Sales (America), Inc.

A positive-working waterless plate is processed by first exposing it to UV light through a film positive in a vacuum frame. The exposure causes the silicone rubber layer to bind to the light-sensitive layer in the nonimage area. The top protective layer is then peeled off, and a developer that removes the silicone rubber layer from the light-sensitive layer in the image areas is applied to the plate surface.

Processing of negative-working plates begins in the same way. However, with a negative-working plate, exposure to UV light through a film negative *weakens* the bond between the light-sensitive layer and the silicone rubber layer in the exposed image areas. After the exposure, the protective cover film is peeled off and a pretreatment solution is applied. This solution strengthens the binding between the silicone rubber and light-sensitive layers in the plate's unexposed nonimage areas. The silicone rubber layer is then removed from the light-sensitive image layer in the plate's exposed areas.

Waterless plates can be used for high-quality commercial printing on both sheetfed and web presses and tend to print with a minimal amount of dot gain. Waterless plates are said to print sharp and be capable of high screen rulings in the 200–600 lines-per-inch (lpi) range.

Direct-digital plates. With advances in imaging technology, a number of lithographic printing plates are now exposed in an imagesetter or "platesetter" using digitally driven, low-power lasers. This class of plate is called a **direct-digital plate** because it is exposed directly from digital data, instead of being exposed through a film intermediate. This technology is usually referred to as **direct-to-plate** or **computer-to-**

plate (CTP) technology. (The term "direct-to-plate" can also refer to a plate created from reflection copy mounted on the copyboard of a camera-like platemaker, but in that case the preferred term is "photo-direct plate.")

When a plate is exposed with a laser beam, the light scans across the plate rapidly, while the plate moves slowly under the beam. With a laser, each tiny printing spot may receive an exposure of only microseconds in duration.

Several different approaches to CTP technology have been announced including silver-based, electrophotographic-based, and photopolymer coatings that can be sensitized to the three dominant lasers in use today (laser diode for infrared, argon ion for blue-green, and helium neon for red) with coating sensitivities that satisfy graphic arts imaging speeds.

Plates can also be imaged directly on the printing press. In the original Presstek technology used with the Heidelberg GTO-DI, a specially designed plate was imaged on the plate cylinder using a spark-discharge plate-imaging process. This plate has three layers: a silicone surface, an aluminum ground plane, and a 7-mil polyester base. The imaging head, consisting of an array of sixteen tungsten-needle electrodes, generates sparks that remove the silicone surface and the aluminum ground plane in the image areas. The exposed polyester base attracts ink, while the silicone surface repels ink, thereby making it a waterless system. The resolution of this imaging technology is 1,016 dots per inch (dpi).

In 1993, Presstek released a new plate system, called PEARL, which replaced the original spark-discharge system. PEARL uses an array of sixteen infrared laser diodes, rather than a spark, to remove the silicone surface. The plate used with PEARL consists of three layers. The bottom layer is either 6-mil polyester or metal. The middle layer is no longer aluminum; it is now an infrared-absorbent material. The top layer is still silicone, but the silicone has been reformulated for strength and durability.

Preparing for Plate Mounting

Before plates are mounted, presized and calipered packing material should already be stored in a rack. Litho packing or Mylar is used instead of printing paper, which compresses easily and absorbs too much moisture. Packing width should be exactly the same as the plate width or slightly narrower (e.g., 1⁄16–1⁄8 in., or 2–3 mm); wider packing absorbs dampening solution from the dampening rollers. If packing has to be cut down, an old plate can serve as a guide.

Handling and Inspecting the Plate

Whenever a plate is handled, it should be held at the gripper and tail edges to avoid damaging the gum protecting the nonimage areas. The plate should be placed on a clean, dry, flat surface to check it against the instruction ticket and copy. It should be inspected for defects, such as scratches and unwanted images.

Minor deletions are made following the plate manufacturer's recommendations, and then etch and gum are applied to the erased area. Sometimes, minor image-area additions can be made by scratching the plate and then applying ink or tusche. A new printing plate should be made for any major correction.

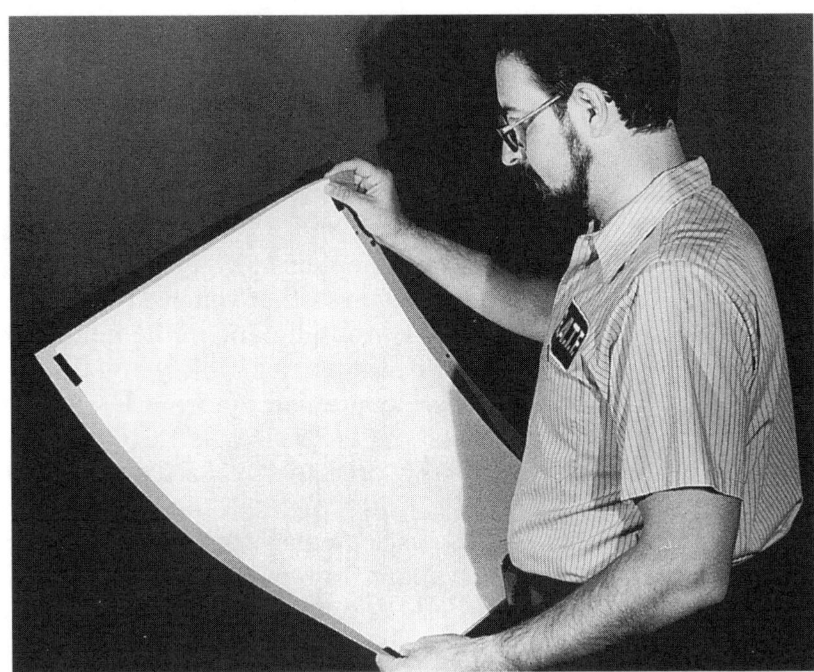

Press operator holding the plate at the gripper and tail edges

Notice the paper protecting the image area from scratches.

Determining Packing Requirements

To determine the total thickness of packing that will be needed, the thickness of the plate must be measured. A deadweight bench micrometer, mounted flush with the bench surface, is recommended for the pressroom because it can be used to measure both compressible and noncompressible materials. If the pressroom is not equipped with one, a paper micrometer is preferred over a machinist's micrometer because its anvil has a larger area, which measures compressible materials more accurately.

With the plate on a flat surface, its thickness is measured in at least three places, and its average thickness is calculated.

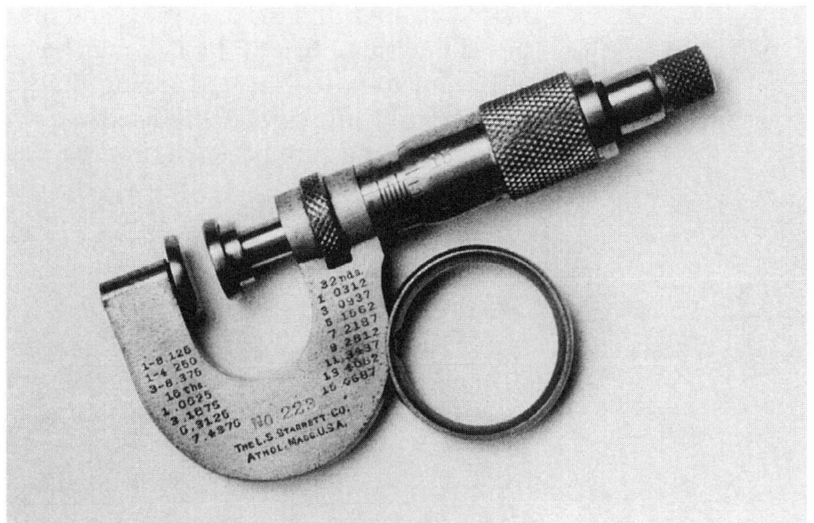

Paper micrometer

Note the enlarged anvil.

If a machinist's or paper micrometer is used, it must be held firmly and flat on the plate when measurements are being made.

Total packing thickness required is determined from the measured plate thickness in the following way. The press specification plate or press handbook indicates the **cylinder undercut** (the difference between cylinder body radius and bearer radius) and the **height above bearers** (the distance between the top surface of the plate and the bearers when the press is properly packed). Some press manufacturers specify that the plate should be packed even with the bearers, but most often, the plate is packed slightly above the bearers. The sum of these two figures equals the combined thicknesses of the plate and the proper packing. If the cylinder undercut is added to the height above bearers and the plate thickness subtracted from that sum, the difference is the proper total packing thickness, or amount of packing needed:

  Cylinder undercut
+ Height above bearers
– Plate thickness
―――――――――――――
  Packing thickness

Preparing the Plate Cylinder

Most sheetfed presses have plate cylinders that can be moved circumferentially (around the cylinder) and laterally (across cylinder) and plate clamps that can be adjusted in one or more directions. Therefore, before the plate is mounted, the plate cylinder and plate clamps are returned to their "zero" positions. In addition, the cylinder body must be cleaned.

Preparatory to plate mounting, the plate cylinder bolts for circumferential register are loosened and the plate cylinder is moved to its zero position, in accordance with operating manual instructions. It is important to remember that all bolts must be retightened carefully.

Plate cylinder equipped with a pin register system

The trailing edge (tail) plate clamp is zeroed by being placed in its lowest position (toward the cylinder body). It is then centered between the cylinder bearers, and its side bolts are finger-tightened. If the press is of the kind that has the tail plate clamp split into two or three sections, each section is zeroed according to operating manual instructions. The lead clamp is zeroed according to the press operating manual procedure. This action properly positions the start-of-print line. The lead clamp is centered, and its side bolts are finger-tightened.

Cleaning the cylinder body with a solvent helps to remove dried ink, gum, or old packing particles. Any rust should also be removed. A light application of oil to the cylinder helps to prevent rust and holds the packing in place.

Plate Mounting

Procedures explained in the press operating manual are used to mount the plate. The following is a typical procedure:

1. Lock off the inking and dampening rollers to prevent them from contacting the plate during mounting. Put

the press "on impression" and inch it for two complete revolutions to ensure the pressure.

2. Insert the gripper edge of the plate into the leading clamp. If the press has a pin system, push the plate holes over the pins; if not, line up the plate centerline with the clamp centerline. Tighten the clamp bolts from the center outward.

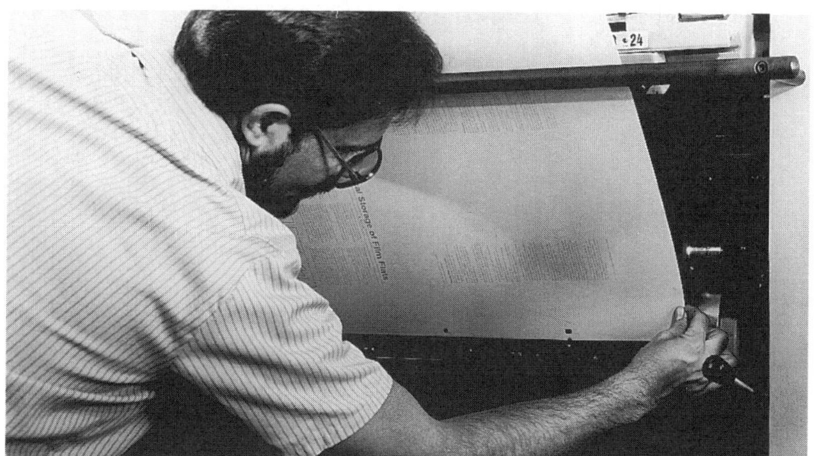

Press operator inserting gripper edge of plate into the leading clamp

3. Insert the calculated amount of packing behind the plate, making sure that no edge is bent over or extends beyond the side edge of the plate. Align the scribe marks on the plate with the preregister marks on the plate cylinder by adjusting the leading clamp tensioning bolts.

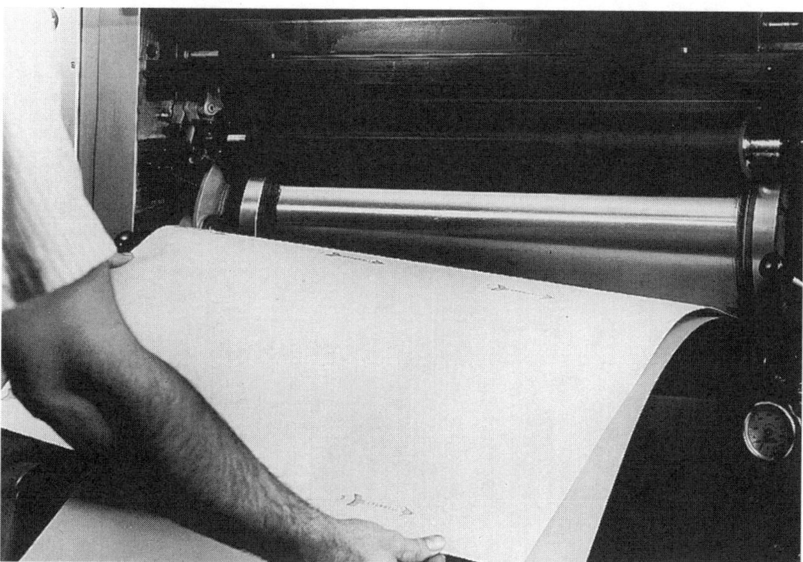

Press operator inserting packing behind the plate

4. Holding the plate and packing with one hand as illustrated, keeping tension on the plate, inch the press forward until you can insert the plate tail into the trailing clamp. The pressure between plate and blanket

Press operator inching the press while keeping tension on the plate and packing

cylinder should be "on" to help roll out the plate as it goes around the cylinder. *The primary objective is to get the plate to fit snugly against the cylinder.*

5. After inserting the plate tail into the trailing clamp, close the clamps; but before tightening them, slowly inch the press forward until the plate tail is at a point just *before* the point of contact between the plate and

Press operator inserting the tail edge of the plate into the trailing clamp

blanket surfaces. This action seats the plate into the clamp and minimizes sideways movement of the plate tail clamp. Tighten the trailing clamp bolts, working from the center bolts to the outside bolts. If the press is equipped with speed clamps, which have quick-throw eccentrics, adjust them to bite hard onto the plate. Check the press operating manual for proper adjustment procedures.

Press operator tightening trailing clamp

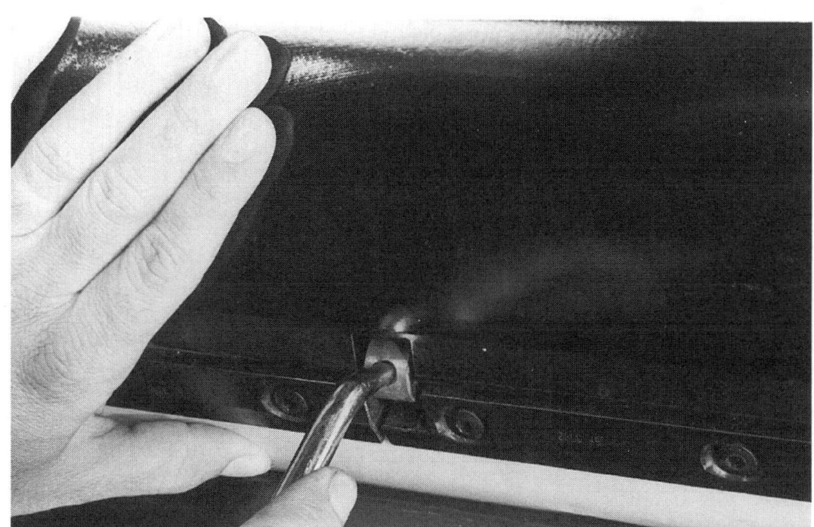

6. Draw up the plate as squarely as possible with the center tensioning screws. Tighten the tension bolts, not fully, but until a crease forms on the plate as it pulls around the edge of the cylinder gap.
7. Tap the plate with your knuckles near the end of the cylinder body. If the plate is not snug on the cylinder, it will sound hollow. If it does, continue tapping on the plate while simultaneously applying additional tension on the trailing clamp bolts until the plate and packing are tight against the cylinder body. Then put the press "off impression" and inch it forward two revolutions.

If a bulge is noticeable on either side of the plate, it is not squarely seated. Try relaxing some of the tension on the trailing clamp side bolts and moving the trailing clamps to push the plate tail to the center of the press. Then draw up tension on the trailing clamp. If this does not work, take the plate off and remount it.

When a plate must be removed, whatever the reason, loosen the securing bolts or quick-action eccentrics of the trailing-edge plate clamp. Ease the plate out of the clamp. Reverse-inch the press while keeping a firm tension on the plate tail and packing to avoid any scratching. Loosen the plate clamp bolts or quick-action eccentrics of the leading plate clamp and remove plate and packing.

Automated plate mounting. In the last few years, several press manufacturers have added automatic or semiautomatic plate mounting devices to their presses. The exact procedure involved in using these devices varies with the level of the device's automation, as well as from manufacturer to manufacturer. Therefore, consult the operating manual for the specific procedure. The basic procedure with one automatic plate mounting system includes the following steps:

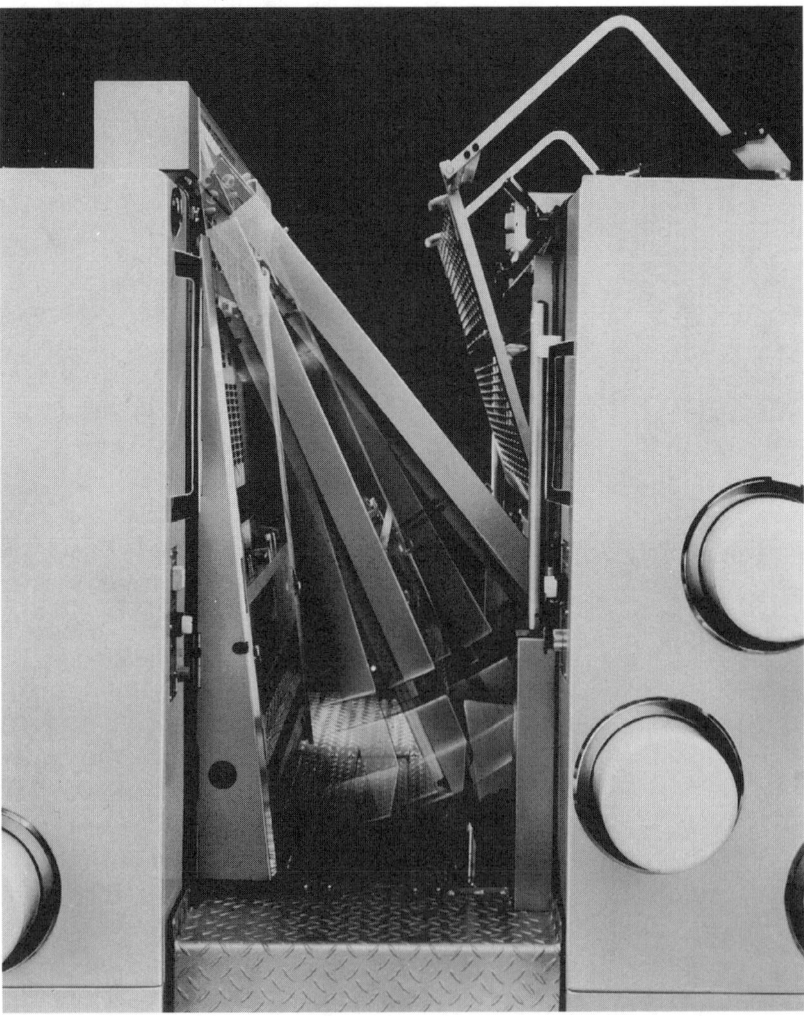

Komori Automatic Plate Changer (APC) *Courtesy Komori America Corp.*

1. Press operator loads new plates into a plate cassette.
2. Press operator selects a unit that needs a new plate and depresses a pushbutton to start the mounting procedure.
3. Safety guard automatically opens, and rear of plate loader moves toward the plate cylinder.
4. Plate clamp opens, and old plate is discharged into the loader.
5. New plate leaves loader, is inserted into position, and is mounted on the plate cylinder.
6. Plate clamp closes, loader retracts to original position, and safety guard closes.

A device for automatic plate mounting
Heidelberger Druckmaschinen AG

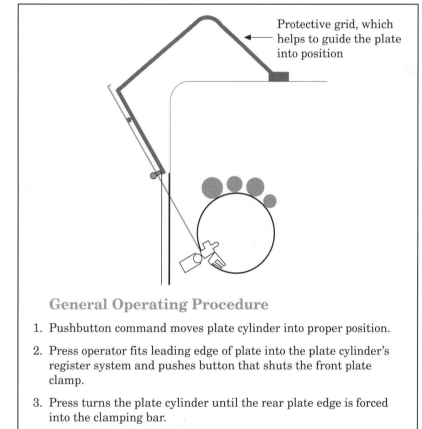

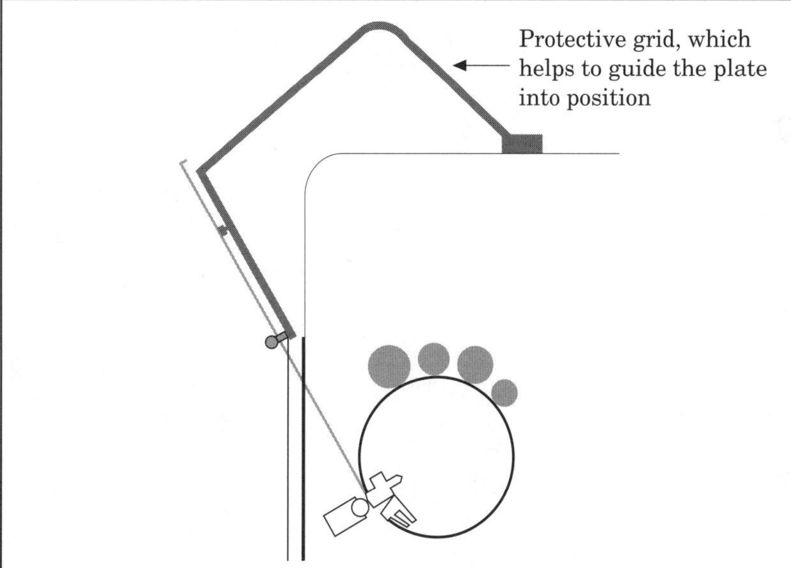

General Operating Procedure

1. Pushbutton command moves plate cylinder into proper position.
2. Press operator fits leading edge of plate into the plate cylinder's register system and pushes button that shuts the front plate clamp.
3. Press turns the plate cylinder until the rear plate edge is forced into the clamping bar.

Measuring the Height of a Mounted Plate

After a plate has been mounted, the height of its surface above the bearers should be measured even though the amount of packing to make it the correct height was calculated. A hand-held packing gauge is needed to make this measurement. Such a gauge may have a magnetic or nonmagnetic body.

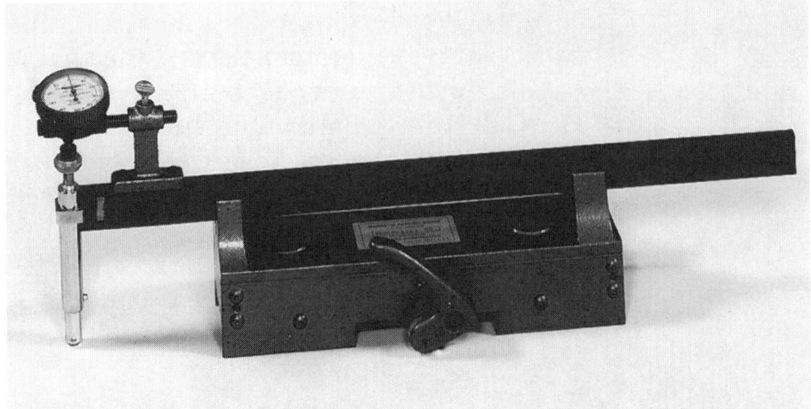

Magnetic packing gauge
Courtesy Roconex Corporation

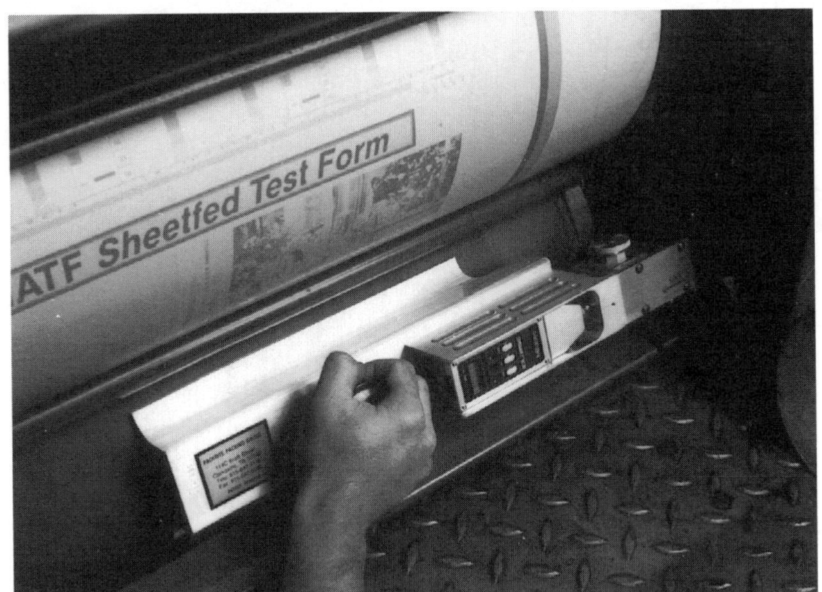

Press operator using the 3000 Series Packrite™ packing gauge to measure the height of the blanket in relation to the blanket cylinder bearers

Note the alignment saddle that allows the gauge to easily self-center.

Before using the packing gauge, clean the bearers thoroughly, being sure to remove any gum or ink particles. To avoid scratching or damaging the plate, place a single sheet of lightweight paper over it.

Follow this procedure to use a magnetic packing gauge:

1. Place the gauge base onto the paper that is protecting the plate on the cylinder and move the ends back and forth until the base seems to be solidly seated on the cylinder.
2. Place the indicator bar into the base slots with the feeler foot on the plate.
3. Make sure that the base is seated properly by adjusting the packing gauge dial to indicate a zero reading, then

turning the feeler foot around and checking for a zero reading from the other side. If it does not show a zero reading, reset the base. Repeat until the reading from both sides of the base is zero.

Press operator zeroing a magnetic-base packing gauge on the plate

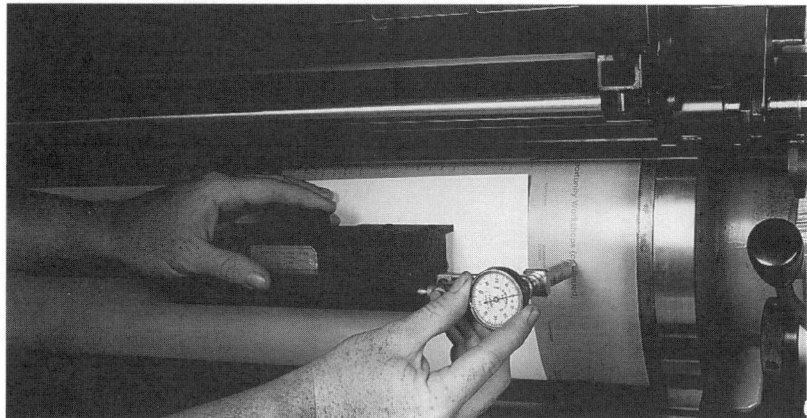

4. Slide the indicator bar over and onto the bearer. A positive reading on the dial indicates how far the plate surface is above the bearer height. (A negative reading indicates how far the plate surface is *below* the bearer height.)

Press operator measuring the height of the plate surface in relation to the bearer

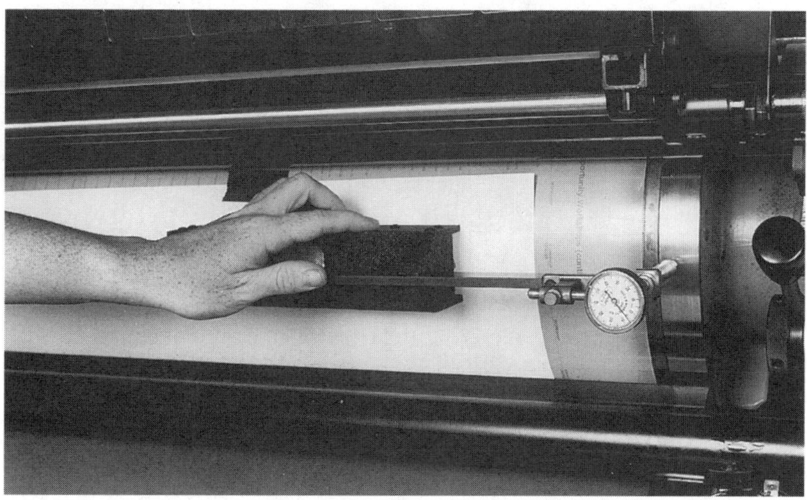

Prepare for the use of the nonmagnetic packing gauge in the same manner as for the magnetic gauge, and then follow this procedure:

1. Place the packing gauge body and feeler foot onto the plate and turn the dial until it reads zero.

Press operator zeroing the nonmagnetic-base packing gauge on the plate

2. Move the gauge over so the feeler foot rests on the bearer. A positive reading on the dial indicates how far the plate surface is above the bearer height. (A negative reading indicates how far the plate surface is *below* bearer height.)

Press operator measuring the height of the plate surface in relation to the bearer

Making and Keeping the Plate Runnable

When the press operator receives the plate, the nonimage areas are coated with gum. After the plate has been mounted, the gum should be washed off the nonimage areas with water. Image areas on most plates as received are so ink-receptive and water-repellent that no protection is needed. Then the plates should be rolled (inked) up, and the **lay** (position of the printed image on the sheet) determined.

The printed image must be exactly square in relation to the paper or previously printed colors. Sometimes the plate may need to be repositioned by tilting or cocking the plate cylinder clamps. Repositioning the plate is preferable to adjusting the front sheet guides, which alters the amount of "gripper bite" and thus may cause register problems.

The following procedure can be used to reposition the plate:

1. With a pencil or marking pen, rule a line that extends from near the side edges of the plate onto the cylinder body (or use the preregister marks if they are on your press).
2. Rule another line on one side of the cylinder body that indicates how far the plate is to be moved.
3. Release the trailing clamp tension bolts so the plate can be pulled forward on the desired side.
4. Push the clamp sideways one-third the distance the plate needs to be drawn forward, using the trailing clamp side bolt. Make sure that the other side bolt is clear of the bearer. The plate should now be loose and bulging on the desired side.
5. Tighten the leading clamp tension bolts to align the marks. If the plate does not pull forward easily (excessive force will split it), decrease the tension of the trailing clamp and push it a little more sideways.
6. Draw up the tension at the trailing clamp when the marks line up satisfactorily. Tap-test the edges of the plate to make sure it is snug on the cylinder.

Once good plates are properly running, the image and nonimage areas are protected by the printing process itself. But when the press is stopped more than one hour, the plates should be gummed and the image areas left inked up. For longer stops, including overnight shutdowns, ink drying must be prevented by either washing the ink off with a suitable solvent or using a finisher recommended by the plate manufacturer. Ink remaining on the plate can dry so hard that it will not accept ink, thus blinding the plate.

A commonly used finisher is an asphaltum-gum etch (AGE), which deposits a film of protective gum arabic on the nonimage areas and asphaltum on the image areas. Asphaltum, which is somewhat greasy, preserves the ink-receptivity of the image areas for a long period. When the plates are ready to be run again, they are washed off with water. This removes gum from the nonimage areas while leaving asphaltum on the image areas, so they will readily accept ink.

Caution: Use only the finisher recommended by the plate manufacturer. AGE, for example, could cause gum blinding in the image areas of certain brands of plate.

Plate Problems

Lithographic plates are subject to two main problems: they scum and they go blind. Scumming occurs when the nonimage area becomes sensitized to ink, and blinding occurs when the image area of the plate fails to accept ink.

Scumming

Scumming occurs when ink adheres to part of the nonimage areas of a plate. The term "nonimage areas" applies not only to the large areas where there is no image but also to the open areas between halftone dots. Thus, when a halftone begins to fill in, it is said that the plate is beginning to scum.

The mechanism of scumming. The nonimage areas are **desensitized** during the platemaking operation: that is, they are treated so that they are water-receptive. This treatment is usually accomplished with a thin adsorbed film of a hydrophilic gum, such as gum arabic.

When plates are running clean, the gum film may gradually wear off, but it is replaced with gum from the dampening solution. If for some reason this process does not occur smoothly, ink varnish may become adsorbed onto the nonprinting areas. The result is a scummy plate. Ink and paper constituents may contribute to scumming.

Prevention of scumming. With the anodized aluminum plates being used today, scumming is not the major problem it once was because aluminum is a metal that is easy to desensitize. Nevertheless, scumming is still a problem.

To prevent scumming, the plate must be properly desensitized when it is made and always opened with water at the start of a run. If a plate on the press is to stand for an hour or more, it should be gummed to protect the nonimage areas. If these procedures are followed, a plate should run clean, unless a very greasy ink is being used.

When a plate begins to scum, something should be done at once. If ink becomes firmly attached to parts of the nonimage areas of the plate, it is difficult to reverse the process and make these areas water-receptive again. The plate should be treated with a good desensitizing plate cleaner or etch. Some pressure must be used on the scummed areas to remove the ink so that it can be replaced with the desensitizing gum. Such a plate etch should finally be dried on the plate, since any desensitizing etch protects better if it is dried. A procedure such as this should be tried at least twice before adding more etch or fountain concentrate to the dampening solution.

Ink dot scum on aluminum plates. Sometimes aluminum lithographic plates develop a peculiar type of scum, called "ink dot scum." Such scum consists of thousands of tiny, sharp dots of ink. The areas between the ink dots are still well desensitized.

Ink dot scum is associated with the pit corrosion of aluminum. When aluminum corrodes, the corrosion occurs in many little spots, which become pits. When the desensitizing gum is removed from these pits, they can hold ink.

This type of scum can often be produced by covering a plate with water and allowing it to evaporate slowly. The scum may appear in a band on a plate opposite a wet dampener roller.

If ink dot scum has not progressed too far, it can be eliminated by treating the plate with a desensitizing solution consisting of phosphoric acid and gum arabic.

Plate Blinding

A plate is blind if it will not produce an image. This may be caused by the erosion of the image area from the plate or by the covering of the image area with gum or another hydrophilic material. If the image is worn off the plate, the problem may simply be called plate wear and is caused by the abrasion of image areas.

Blinding usually refers to the presence of an image on the plate that will not accept ink. A plate goes blind when the image areas do not accept ink from the ink form rollers as well as they should. With modern plates and plate processors, blinding is greatly reduced, and plate life is greatly extended.

Abrasion of image areas. If parts of the image are actually abraded off the plate, the plate will be blind in these areas. Abrasion is one of the worst causes of blinding because little can be done to remedy the situation. It is commonly caused by hard, improperly set form rollers. Abrasion of the image areas can also be due to excessive pressure between the plate and the blanket. It can also be caused by abrasive particles in the ink or paper. Sometimes, the pigment particles used in the coating on a coated paper are hard and abrasive in nature. Paper fibers, too, can be somewhat abrasive. When newsprint is run on a lithographic press, the fibers often accumulate on the rubber blanket. Such accumulation (called "linting") often leads to blinding of the image areas, due to the abrasive action of these fibers.

Another source of abrasion is dry antisetoff spray. When sheets treated with this spray for the first color are run through the press again for the second color, the dry spray particles on the sheets can exert an abrasive action on the second color plate.

The increased thickness of a swollen blanket causes excessive pressure between the blanket and plate, which may lead to abrasion of the plate and ultimately to image blinding.

Poor adhesion of image areas to the metal. Sometimes a plate starts to print satisfactorily and then begins to go blind as the run proceeds. One reason for this development can be poor adhesion. The light-hardened coating must adhere to the metal; the lacquer, if one is used, must adhere to the coating; the developing ink must adhere to the lacquer.

If the chemical or physical adhesive bond is poor, the result is a partial blinding of the image areas. Sometimes the press crew must have another plate made, and either the procedure or the chemicals must be changed to avoid a recurrence of the problem.

Partial desensitization of image areas. During development, lithographic plates are treated with a solution of a water-soluble gum. Gum arabic or some other desensitizing gum is also used in dampening solution. Occasionally, gum adheres to part of the image areas of the plate. If this happens, these areas accept water instead of ink. The result is that the plate is blind: the plate will not print in these areas. Any change in press conditions that favor the gum may lead to a partial blinding of the image areas. Some of these conditions are as follows:

- **Running the ink film too thin.** This condition makes it easier for the gum to break through the ink film and become attached to the material underneath. If the color must be reduced, it is much better to add a transparent extender to the ink and then to print a thicker ink film.
- **Too much water in the ink.** If the ink becomes waterlogged, it is much easier for the gum to replace it on the image areas of the plate.
- **Too much gum in the dampening solution.** The more gum that there is in the dampening solution, the more gum that will become emulsified in the ink. This gives the gum a better chance to adhere to the image areas.

- **Too much acid in the dampening solution.** The acid makes the gum a better desensitizing agent so that it can adhere more easily to the image areas if it gets a chance.

There is another way in which the image areas of a plate can be partially desensitized to ink. If press ink is allowed to dry on the image areas of the plate, these areas often do not accept ink properly when the plate is run again. If a plate is to be left overnight or stored for a rerun, the plate should be rubbed with a good finisher before shutting down the press.

Solvents in the ink or plate cleaner. Most light-hardened coatings and the lacquers used over them are highly resistant to the solvents in most lithographic inks and plate cleaners. Such cleaners must not be used on unbaked, positive-working presensitized plates. If these plates have been exposed to light for any length of time, an alkaline cleaner can attack the image areas, causing the plate to go blind.

The light-sensitive materials in ultraviolet inks are polar in nature and attack the coating on some types of plates. For this reason, diazo presensitized and wipe-on plates cannot be used with ultraviolet inks. Many photopolymer plates are satisfactory for printing ultraviolet inks.

9 Paper

Manufacture

One of the costliest printing materials used by the press operator is paper. An understanding of its manufacture, although not essential, helps the press operator to interpret paper behavior on press.

Raw Materials

Fiber. The principal raw material used in papermaking is wood fiber obtained from trees or from recycled paper. Other plants, such as sugar cane or bamboo, are also used as fiber sources. A fiber with a hollow tubular or quill-shaped structure is required for papermaking. Nonwood plants provide a minor source of fiber for papermaking, but many of the nonwood fibers are important to the manufacture of specialty papers.

Trees are replenishable, easily harvested, and easily transportable, making them the ideal source of cellulose in papermaking. Cellulose fibers have a very high tensile strength and a great affinity for water, meaning that the fibers can be bonded together strongly in a network to form paper. The size and shape of fibers, which vary with type of tree and even within a given tree, have an important influence on paper properties.

Nonfibrous materials. In addition to a fiber that can network with other fibers to form a sheet, a wide variety of nonfibrous substances are added during papermaking to alter the properties of paper.

Fillers (finely divided, relatively insoluble inorganic materials or minerals) are added prior to sheet formation for a variety of reasons, such as to increase opacity and brightness, reduce ink strike-through, and decrease the harshness of the papers. The addition of fillers also improves softness, reduces bulk, increases smoothness, makes paper more uniformly receptive to printing inks, improves printability, and contributes to greater dimensional stability. Clay (from refined natural kaolin clay), titanium dioxide, and calcium carbonate are the most commonly used fillers.

Paper often has internal sizing added to it to retard the penetration of water or other fluids. Rosin and papermakers' alum are two materials commonly used for internal sizing. Paper may also be sized by coating it with a solution of starch.

The addition of starches, gums, and synthetic polymers to the paper prior to sheet formation enhances fiber adhesion, dry strength, and filler retention.

Dyes and colored pigments tint white papers and produce colored papers.

Pulping Methods

Pulping permits papermaking fibers to be separated from wood. Several methods are used; the three basic methods are mechanical pulping, chemical pulping, and semichemical pulping (a combination of mechanical and chemical pulping treatments). Each method produces pulp that imparts different properties to paper.

The principal types of mechanical pulp are **groundwood,** produced by forcing pulpwood against a revolving, abrasive grinding stone; **refiner mechanical pulp (RMP),** produced by passing wood chips through a disk refiner instead of pressing the wood against the grinding stone; and **thermomechanical pulp (TMP),** produced by preheating wood chips with steam prior to passing them through a disk refiner. The heat generated by disk refining and preheating the wood chips softens the lignin that holds the fibers together, permitting fiber separation with little fiber damage. Each of the mechanical pulping methods gives a high yield of pulp because the lignin and other materials are retained.

Chemical pulping liberates the cellulose fibers from the lignin that bonds them together. During chemical pulping, chemicals dissolve the lignin and hemicellulose in wood to free cellulose fibers from the wood. The bleaching of chemical pulp removes residual lignin and hemicellulose. Chemical pulping has a yield of 45–55%, compared to the yield of 90% or more common with mechanical pulping methods. Chemical pulping processes use acids, such as sulfurous acid, and alkalis, such as lye (caustic soda).

Semichemical pulps are produced by first mildly cooking wood chips with chemicals, most commonly sodium sulfite or a small amount of an alkaline salt, such as sodium carbonate, bicarbonate, or hydroxide. The cooking partially removes and softens the lignin, weakening the bond between fibers. After cooking, the chips are passed through one or two disk refining steps for fiberizing. A wash removes the chemicals. Semichemical pulping retains a considerable amount of lignin, and consequently, yields are typically 60–80%. Bleaching reduces the yield, as it does with any pulping method.

Bleaching of Pulp

Unbleached wood pulp ranges in color from cream to dark brown; a brown paper bag is made of unbleached pulp. Bleaching removes residual lignin in the pulp without causing severe chemical damage to the cellulose fibers. Bleaching a pulp makes the resulting paper whiter, which improves printing contrast. Whiter pulps produce colored papers that are more brilliant.

Stock Preparation and Refining

The fibers obtained by pulping must receive further treatment before they can be used to make high-quality paper. This treatment is called **stock preparation,** and it entails fiber refining and the mixing of fibers with nonfibrous materials to produce a paper of the desired properties. Paper is formed on the papermaking machine, but many of the characteristics of paper are determined during stock preparation.

During refining, beaters, conical-type refiners (jordan), or disk refiners are used to subject the fibers to varying degrees of brushing, cutting, fraying, and shortening actions depending on the properties desired in the paper. As a result, the fibers swell and soften and their surfaces develop fine hairs, all of which promote bonding to make a stronger paper.

During stock preparation, the cellulose fibers are mixed with fillers, internal sizing, dyes and colored pigments, and other additives that impart properties to paper.

Paper Machine

The paper machine converts the papermaking **furnish**—the mixture of fibrous and nonfibrous materials created during stock preparation—into paper.

In the **wet** or **forming section** of the paper machine, the diluted furnish is formed into a mat of fibers, from which most of the water is removed by gravity or vacuum. In a fourdrinier paper machine, one side (the bottom) of the fiber mat is in contact with a wire (a finely woven mesh of bronze or plastic material) and is called the **wire side.** The top side of the fiber mat is called the **felt side.** The felt side has shorter fibers, more fines, and more fillers, contributing to the two-sidedness of paper produced on a fourdrinier machine. In a twin-wire paper machine, the paper is formed between two converging wires, with water being drained through both sides of the sheet. As a result, the paper does not exhibit two-sidedness, but the top side is still referred to as the felt side. With a cylinder machine, the paper is formed on a wire-covered cylinder. When the fiber mat reaches the top of the rotating cylinder, it is transferred to the underside of a felt.

Paper machines also have a **press section,** where as much water as possible is removed from the web by pressing and suction, and a **drying section,** where the remaining water is removed, this time by evaporation caused by hot drying cylinders.

Paper leaving the dryer has a moisture level from 2 to 8%, depending on its desired end use.

A paper machine also has a **calender,** a series of all-metal rollers running in contact that evens out the thickness of the paper, increases its density, and makes it smoother.

Finishing

Finishing, in a discussion of papermaking, refers to operations that begin at the paper machine reel and end when the paper is packaged for shipment. The finishing operations that are of particular interest to press operators are sheeting, supercalendering, and embossing.

Some sheetfed offset presses are equipped with a roll sheeter. However, most paper reaching the pressroom has been sheeted at the papermill. Rolls are converted to sheets on the sheeter, which has a rotary cutting unit. The single rotary cutter has a fixed-position bedknife and a second knife mounted on a rotating cylinder, and the double rotary cutter has two knives mounted in cylinders that rotate in synchronization. Sheet length depends on both the speed of rotation of the rotary cutter and the speed of the web.

Supercalendering is another finishing operation. Unlike the paper machine calender, the supercalender has both metal and soft, resilient rolls. The hard metal rolls press into the resilient rolls at the nip, producing a polishing action that imparts varying degrees of smoothness and gloss to the paper.

Embossing gives paper a pattern finish. Like a supercalender, the embosser consists of a metal roll that rolls against a soft-surfaced roll. Unlike the supercalender, the metal roll carries an embossed pattern, which is imparted on

A supercalender

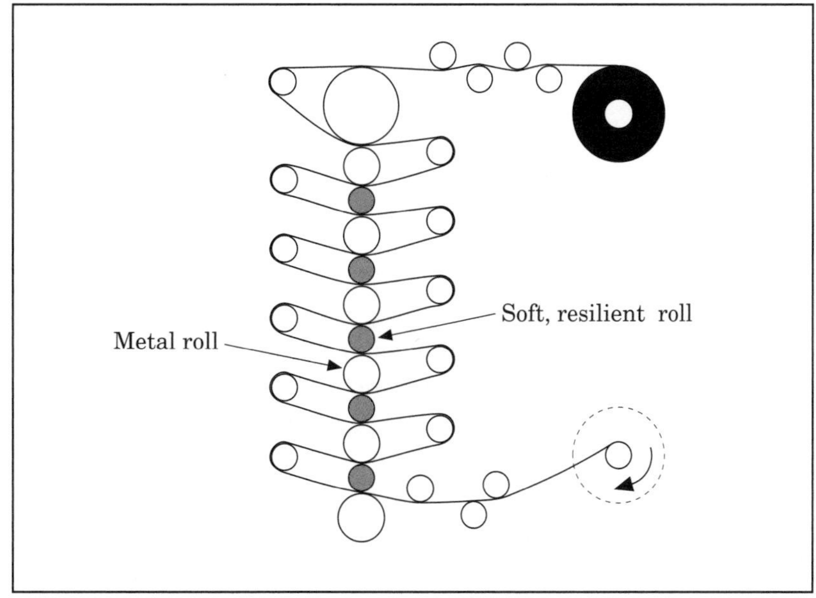

the soft-surfaced roll through direct running. The paper that passes through the nip between these two rolls receives the embossed pattern.

Coating

The press operator often uses the printing press to put a varnish coating on the paper after it has been printed, usually for protective or aesthetic purposes. However, the papermaker also may apply a coating to the surface of paper to make the paper more suitable to its end use. A pigment coating, for example, improves the paper by filling voids in its surface. Coating increases the paper whiteness, paper opacity, ink holdout, water resistance, gloss, and pick resistance.

Paper Weight

The weight of printing paper is designated as basis weight or grammage.

Basis weight is the weight, in pounds, of a ream of paper cut to its basic size, in inches. With few exceptions, a **ream** of paper is 500 sheets. **Basic size** is the sheet size in inches of a particular type of paper. Each basic size has been adopted because of widespread practice and usage.

Basis weight is sometimes specified per 1,000 sheets. If so, the basic weight is typically followed by a capital M, representing 1,000 sheets. For example, a particular bond paper having a basis weight of 20 lb. would be designated "40M," indicating that 1,000 sheets weigh 40 lb. The weight of paperboard is per 1,000 sq. ft.

Four common basic sizes for paper

Paper type	U.S. sheet size	Metric sheet size
Bond and writing	17×22 in.	432×559 mm
Cover	20×26	508×660
Newsprint	24×36	610×914
Book	25×38	635×965

In the metric system, grammage is the word used to express the weight of paper. **Grammage** is the weight in grams of a single sheet of paper having an area of 1 m^2. Grammage is abbreviated as g/m^2. (One pound contains 454 g, and one meter equals 39.37 in.) Conversion factors are used to convert basis weight to grammage, and vice versa.

Factors to convert basis weight to grammage, and vice versa

Basic ream size	To convert from grammage to lb./ream, multiply g/m^2 by:	To convert from lb./ream to g/m^2, multiply lb./ream by:
17×22 in.	0.266	3.76
20×26	0.370	2.70
20×30	0.427	2.34
22×38	0.438	2.28
22½×28½	0.456	2.19
25½×30½	0.553	1.81
23×35	0.573	1.74
24×36	0.614	1.62
25×38	0.675	1.48

Paper Requirements for Sheetfed Lithography

Paper for lithography must meet certain requirements:

- **High surface and internal bonding strength,** to withstand the tackier ink films of lithography
- **Good, but not excessive, water resistance,** to prevent softening and weakening of the paper surface (which can result in picking and fiber or coating transfer to the blanket) and to prevent excessive moisture pickup from the dampening system (which causes curl and paper dimension changes)
- **An exceptionally clean and strongly bonded surface,** to counteract the tendency of the blanket to collect loosely bonded material from the paper's surface

- **Compatibility with the chemistry of the ink and dampening system,** to prevent any active materials in the paper from reacting unfavorably
- **Ability to withstand repeated separation from an inked and moistened blanket,** to prevent stretching, curling, and releasing of surface material

Paper must be accurately trimmed and square. It must not have bowed edges, which can cause misregister and wrinkling on the press and inaccurate trimming.

Paper Properties

Several paper properties are particularly important to the press operator. Among these are gloss, opacity, grain direction, ink absorbency, moisture content, dimensional stability, and surface strength.

Gloss

Gloss is the high reflectance of light from a smooth surface. Paper with high gloss increases the gloss of the printed ink film. Brilliance and intensity of color are similarly enhanced. Paper absorbency and ink holdout can affect the gloss of an ink film. Therefore, for color to remain uniform throughout a pressrun, the paper must have minimal variations in gloss, which is the responsibility of the knowledgeable papermaker.

GATF Research Project Report 6060, *A New Method of Rating the Efficiency of Paper for Color Reproduction,* discusses the effect of gloss and absorbency on print color. Variations in gloss and absorbency, as well as texture, opacity, brightness, and color neutrality, affect the appearance of the color of the same ink on different papers. Differences in gloss and absorptivity of paper are major factors in variations of printed ink color. Differences in them can shift the hue or grayness of the primary ink (cyan, magenta, and yellow), cause a hue shift of secondary overprinted colors (red, green, blue), and require changes in the amount of color correction needed. As a result, color reproduction depends on properly prepared color separations, ink, and paper.

Opacity

Opacity, the extent to which light transmission is obstructed, is an important consideration in a printing paper. Insufficient opacity causes excessive show-through, which reduces printing contrast and lowers print quality.

Grain Direction

Grain direction in paper results from water-suspended fibers flowing onto the moving paper machine wire. In referring to the grain of paper on a printing press, the terms "grain long" and "grain short" are used. With **grain-long paper,** the grain parallels the long dimension of the press sheet. With **grain-short paper,** the grain parallels the short dimension.

Grain-long paper is preferred for printing register. However, grain-short paper has greater stiffness, better blanket release, and less tendency to develop embossing and tail-end hook. Heavier-weight paper conforms better to the curvature of the cylinders if it is run with the grain parallel to the press cylinder axis.

Binding considerations also affect the preferred grain direction. Grain parallel to the bound edge of a book is preferred. Grain perpendicular to the bound edge can cause buckling and distortions at the spine and make the pages stiffer and more difficult to turn. However, with paper used in a loose-leaf binder, having the grain perpendicular to the binding edge results in a paper that has greater strength and stiffness for turning.

Paper folds more easily with the grain (i.e., parallel to the grain direction) and tends to crack less. However, the strength at the fold is greater if the paper is folded across the grain. For right-angle folds, the more difficult fold should be made with the grain.

The preferred grain direction for printing register is often different than that preferred for folding and finishing. Consequently, the various considerations have to be compared to determine which direction the paper grain should run.

If the grain direction of a sheet of paper is unknown, a square sample cut from the sheet can be placed in water or moistened on one side. The axis of curl is parallel to the grain direction. It is helpful to indicate on the square which side parallels the long dimension of the sheet and which side parallels the short dimension.

Curl test of paper grain

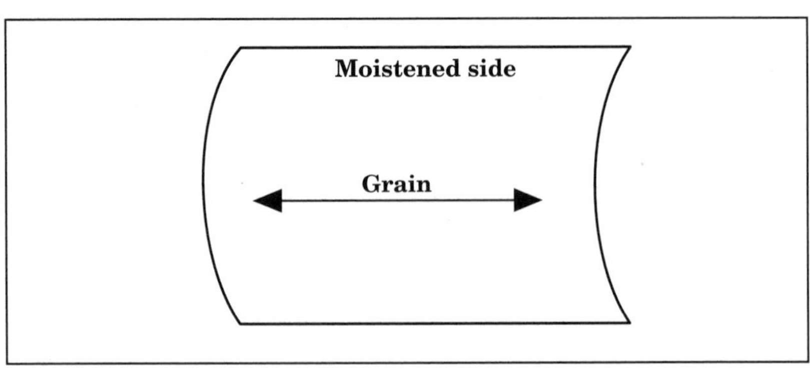

Another way to determine grain direction requires two strips of paper, ½×6 in. (13×150 mm). The sheets are cut at right angles to each other and parallel to the sheet's edges. The strips are aligned at one end and then alternately placed one on top of the other. The strip cut grain short bends more easily and, consequently, falls away from the other strip when placed on the bottom. Grain direction of the press sheet is determined from the grain direction of the strips.

Flex test of paper grain

Since paper is stiffer across the grain, two strips of the same width cut at right angles from a sheet can show grain direction

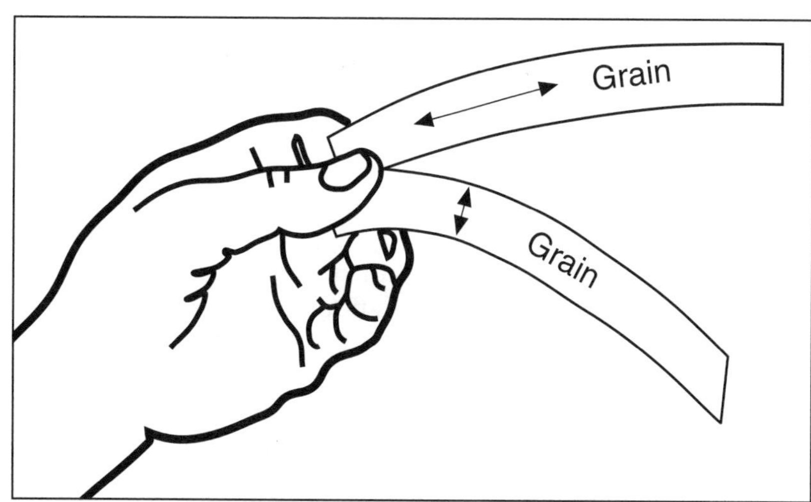

Ink Absorbency

Ink absorbency determines at what rate and in what amount printed ink penetrates the paper. Ink vehicle penetrates into the voids, capillaries, and pores, depending on the absorbency of the paper. Ink holdout, related to ink absorbency, is the extent to which paper resists or retards the penetration of the freshly printed ink film.

Ink absorbency and ink holdout influence ink drying, ink setoff, and blocking. High ink absorbency prevents setoff and ink blocking. Low ink absorbency means high ink holdout and high gloss. Uniform absorbency from sheet to sheet is as important to the press operator as uniform absorbency within a sheet.

Moisture Content and Relative Humidity

The moisture content of paper influences numerous paper properties, particularly its dimensional stability. In addition, paper can pick up moisture from the surrounding atmosphere, such as in the paper storage area and the pressroom.

Cellulose fibers are **hygroscopic,** i.e., they have a strong attraction for water molecules. Fibers become larger upon absorbing moisture, and they become smaller upon giving up moisture. Therefore, a change in moisture content of paper results in dimensional changes. Consequently, a major cause of register problems, curl, and paper distortion during printing is a change in the moisture content of paper.

The moisture content of the paper should be in equilibrium with the relative humidity of the pressroom. However, for multicolor and multipass printing, a moisture content slightly higher than its equilibrium value minimizes dimension changes between printings.

If the moisture content is too low, the paper tends to be hard and brittle, decreasing resiliency and smoothness under printing impression. Paper having optimum moisture content prints better because the moisture increases the paper's resiliency, which helps it to flatten out and conform to the printing surface under impression.

Dimensional Stability

Dimensional stability refers to the ability of a sheet to maintain its dimensions with changes in its moisture content or applied stress. All cellulosic papers expand or shrink with changes in their moisture content. Papers with little refining, high porosity, or large amounts of fillers tend to have good dimensional stability. Tightly bonded, strong sheets have less. Since sheetfed printing exposes paper to moisture from both blanket and atmosphere, dimensional stability is an important consideration when a paper is printed. The best R.H. to maintain dimensional stability of the paper is 35–50%.

Surface Strength

The surface of a printing paper is exposed to numerous forces during printing. A paper with high surface strength is necessary to resist these forces. **Surface strength,** or **pick resistance,** is the ability of a paper to resist a force applied perpendicularly, such as that in the splitting of an ink film, to its surface before picking or rupturing occurs. **Picking** is the removal of surface fibers and coating in the printing nip. Picking usually appears as the complete removal of a piece of paper or coating from the surface. **Wet picking** results when a surface's strength is affected due to dampening.

Paper Handling

Not only must paper be handled carefully during shipment but it must also be handled carefully in the plant.

Paper must be brought to pressroom temperature before opening so that it does not curl due to the gain or loss of moisture. Paper should remain tightly wrapped until it is ready for the press, and it should be wrapped tightly after printing to keep the press sheets from developing tight or wavy edges.

An instrument called a **hygroscope** is used to measure the moisture content of a pile of paper relative to the humidity of the pressroom. Readings from a hygroscope help the press crew to determine if paper conditioning is necessary.

Temperature Conditioning

Temperature conditioning means that the paper is not unwrapped until it reaches the same temperature as the pressroom where it will be used.

In some printing plants, paper is stored in the pressroom. Consequently, it is at pressroom temperature when it goes to press. Because the paper is stored in the pressroom, temperature conditioning is unnecessary.

In other plants, however, paper is kept in a warehouse or separate storage area. Paper is brought to the pressroom only as needed. Temperature conditioning is necessary because the temperature of the storage room is usually different from that of the pressroom.

Temperature conditioning chart for paper (American units)

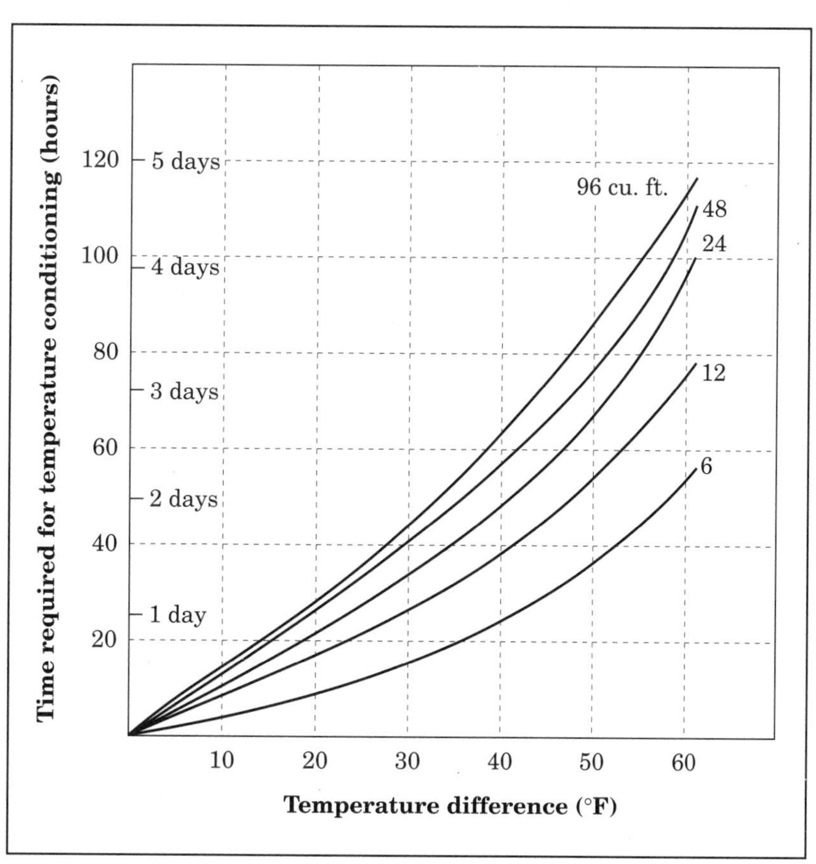

Temperature conditioning chart for paper (metric units)

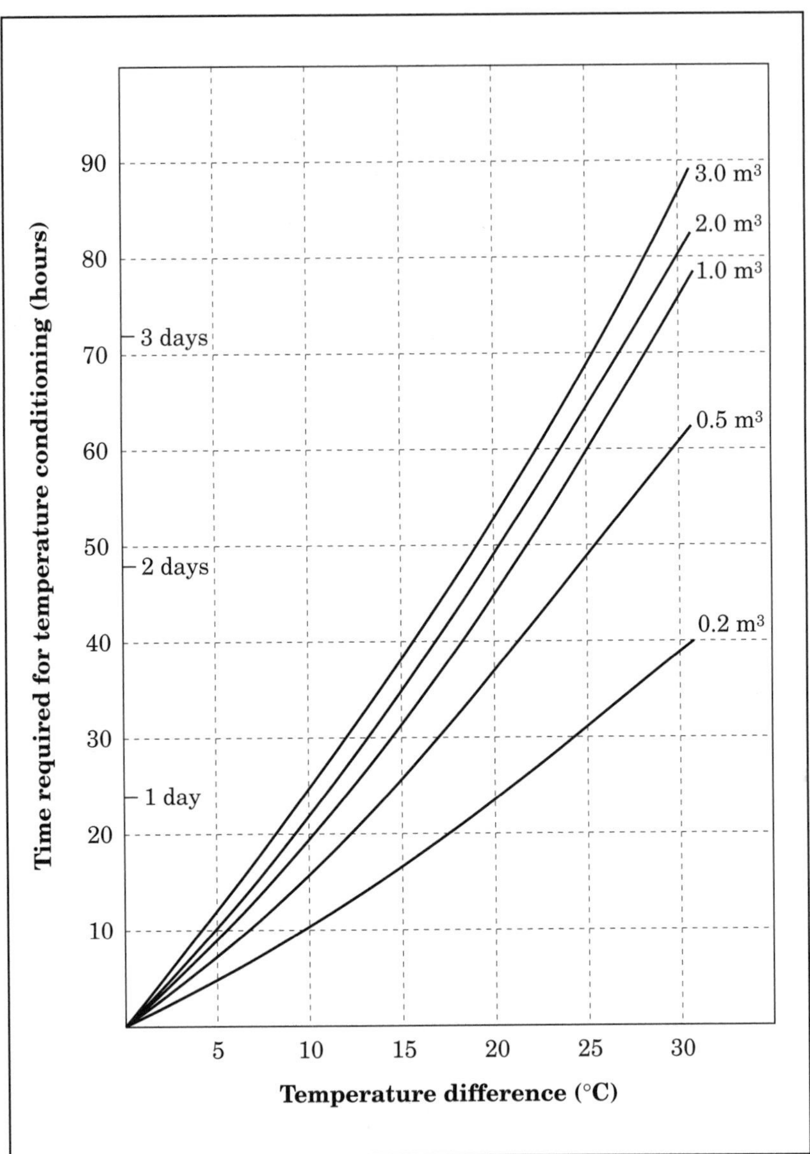

Temperature changes, which occur when paper from a cold warehouse or truck is delivered to a warm pressroom, cause trouble even if the paper is wrapped and sealed to protect it from humidity changes. When cold paper is unwrapped in the pressroom, moisture condenses on the edges of the paper. As a result, the exposed edges of the paper absorb moisture and become wavy; the paper is often referred to as **wavy-edged paper.**

If the temperature of the paper is higher than the temperature of the pressroom when unwrapped, the surrounding air becomes warmer and its relative humidity is lowered. The paper's exposed edges will lose moisture to the atmosphere and shrink; the paper is often referred to as **tight-edged paper.**

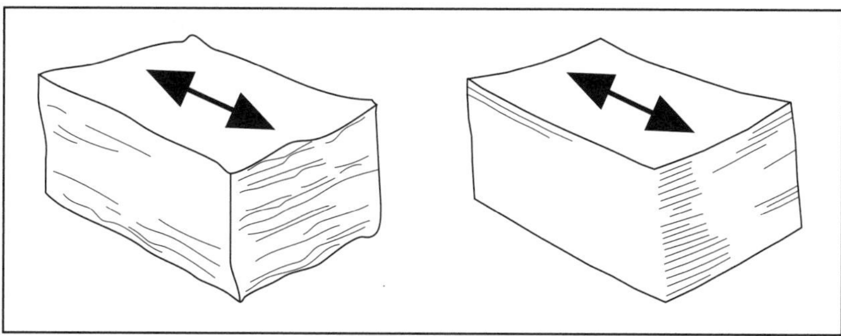

Wavy-edged paper *(left)* and tight-edged paper *(right)*

Chilling the air with an air cooling unit dries the air and creates tight edges in the paper. Air conditioning requires control of both temperature and humidity.

Air Conditioning

Paper is manufactured so that it stays flat and does not develop wavy or tight edges before or during printing in a normal pressroom atmosphere. An air-conditioned pressroom greatly reduces moisture problems.

If the pressroom R.H. (and temperature) is kept at a constant level, the printer can order paper that is in reasonable balance with a specified relative humidity.

The R.H. of most paper manufactured in the United States and Canada is in the range of 35–50%. The R.H. of an air-conditioned pressroom should be maintained at a selected value within this range.

Paper with an R.H. 5–8% higher than the pressroom R.H. is desirable for high-quality, close-register printing requiring more than one pass through the press. Paper with this R.H. loses moisture to the pressroom atmosphere at about the same rate that it picks up moisture from the press, assuming that the pressroom R.H. is controlled. Since moisture change is minimal between successive printings, the printing of tight-register work is more easily accomplished.

Paper cannot be produced to meet the R.H. requirements of pressrooms in which the R.H. and temperature are not controlled. Papermakers produce papers that meet the R.H. conditions of the average pressroom. If the pressroom is not temperature- and humidity-controlled, the paper should still be temperature-conditioned.

Guide for decision on printing sheetfed paper, assuming paper at 45% R.H.

Nature of printing	Pressroom R.H. (%)	Recommendation
No register, danger of wrinkles only	33–53	OK to print
	Less than 33 or more than 53	Change R.H. of pressroom
Loose register (2–3 rows of dots)—single printing on two- or four-color press	37–53	OK to print
	33–36 or 54–55	Marginal
	Less than 33 or more than 55	Change R.H. of pressroom
Close register (one row of dots)—single printing on two- or four-color press	40–53	OK to print
	35–39	Marginal
	Less than 35 or more than 53	Change R.H. of pressroom
Loose register (2–3 rows of dots)—two or more printings	41–53	OK to print
	37–40	Marginal
	Less than 37 or more than 53	Change R.H. of pressroom
Close register (one row of dots)—two or more printings	45–53	OK to print
	40–44	Marginal
	Less than 40 or more than 53	Change R.H. of pressroom

Storage

To ensure that paper is received in proper condition, all deliveries should be checked upon arrival. Wrappings or cartons having minor tears should be repaired. Skids with punctures, tears, or breaks in the protective wrapping should be rejected. The truck driver or train man should note the damage on the way bill and initial it. Printers should photograph damaged skids and cartons before they are removed from trucks or railroad boxcars. The photograph acts as proof of the paper condition upon arrival. In addition to protecting the printer, the photograph helps the papermill track down the causes of damaged paper. If paper wrappings must be removed for sampling or testing purposes, the wrapped paper should be brought into temperature balance before opening and then rewrapped immediately. Careful handling of paper minimizes unloading damage.

Ideal warehouse and storage conditions minimize the movement and rehandling of paper from the time it is received by the printer until it arrives at the press. Each time paper is moved, either to gain access to other skids of paper or to be transported to the press, the likelihood of handling damage is increased.

Paper must not contact concrete or damp basement floors. The moisture damages and distorts the paper. Consequently, platforms or racks that elevate the paper above the floor are recommended. Papers should be stored *away* from any object (such as a radiator) that heats the paper, but warehouses should be heated in winter.

After paper is printed, protective plastic covers should be placed tightly over the pile to minimize changes in R.H.

Reusable plastic skid cover, available from Poly-Kleen Co.

Paper Problems

Lithographic paper problems can be classified broadly into three groups: register problems, printability problems, and runnability problems. Close register, so essential to multicolor work, is obtained only by close control of the moisture in the paper. Preconditioning paper to pressroom conditions and controlling pressroom relative humidity and temperature reduce register problems. Printability problems include hickeys, piling, ghosting, back-edge curl, and surface rupture.

Runnability problems include curl, sheet defects, and static electricity. Sheet decurlers installed in the delivery minimize curl. Many sheet defects that affect runnability are relatively uncommon: sheets with turned-over corners, sheets stuck together, sheets with edges that are crimped together due to a dull cutting knife, and out-of-square sheets. Static, however, is a common problem. Static electricity causes sheets to cling tightly to each other or to parts of the press. Consequently, static electricity interferes with sheet pickup and forwarding, prevents proper sheet transport on the feedboard, causes variations in positioning at the grippers and side guide, and results in jogging problems at the delivery. Proper control of humidity eliminates most static problems. Use of a static eliminator in the delivery is also helpful.

Register Problems

Misregister problems occur if the paper's moisture content changes during a pressrun. A moisture change causes the paper to change its dimensions in both directions, although more so across the grain. Misregister due to moisture change is an unlikely problem with single-pass printing on a multicolor press. However, where two or more passes per side are involved, dimensional change due to moisture change between successive printings can be serious. Therefore, use as little dampening solution as possible, or use a wetting agent in the dampening solution to reduce the amount of water needed to keep the plate clean, and run the paper grain-long.

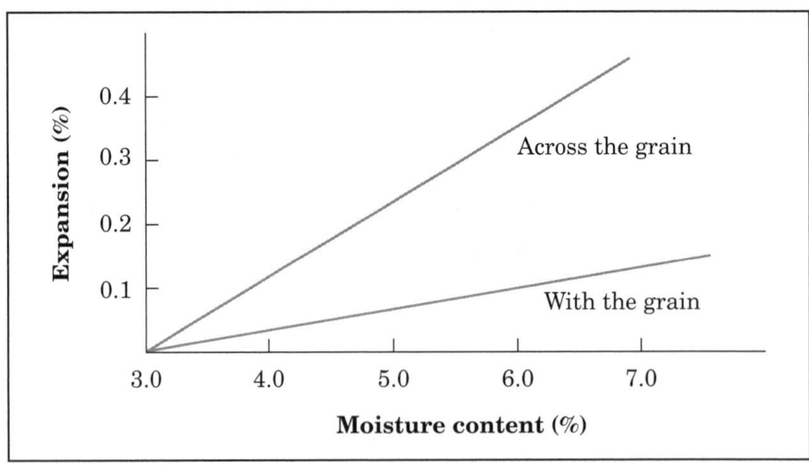

Expansion of paper with and across the grain as moisture content increases

In offset printing, the mechanical forces of the press tend to stretch the paper in the direction of its travel. The following four recommendations help to minimize sheet stretching:

- Reduce the pressure between impression and blanket cylinders to the minimum required for acceptable printing.
- Reduce the tack of inks as much as possible if large solid areas are being printed.

- Use blankets that have good release properties, to avoid overstretching the paper.
- Print solids close to the gripper edge.

If some subjects on a press sheet register and others do not, or if the misregister varies from sheet to sheet, the problem is called **random misregister.** This condition usually occurs when printing heavily embossed papers or papers with a puckered or cockle surface. Reducing the blanket-to-impression cylinder pressure helps lessen the misregister but the transfer of ink to the paper may be incomplete. A solution to this problem is to run heavily textured papers through the press once without printing.

Misregister along the back edge of the press sheet is usually caused by tight- or wavy-edged paper, so proper handling of the paper *before* printing helps to eliminate register problems *during* printing.

Hickeys

A hickey is an imperfection in printing due to a particle on the blanket or, sometimes, the plate.

Hickeys are of two types. The first, a **doughnut hickey,** consists of a small, solid printed area surrounded by a white halo, or nonprinted area. The other, a **void hickey,** is a white, unprinted spot surrounded by printing.

Doughnut hickeys are caused by ink-receptive, solid particles on the plate or blanket. Ink skin is a common cause of a doughnut hickeys.

Blanket contamination from paper usually produces void hickeys. Occasionally, coating debris accepts ink and produces doughnut hickeys. However, repeated dampening causes the particle to become water-receptive, and the doughnut hickey eventually changes to a void hickey.

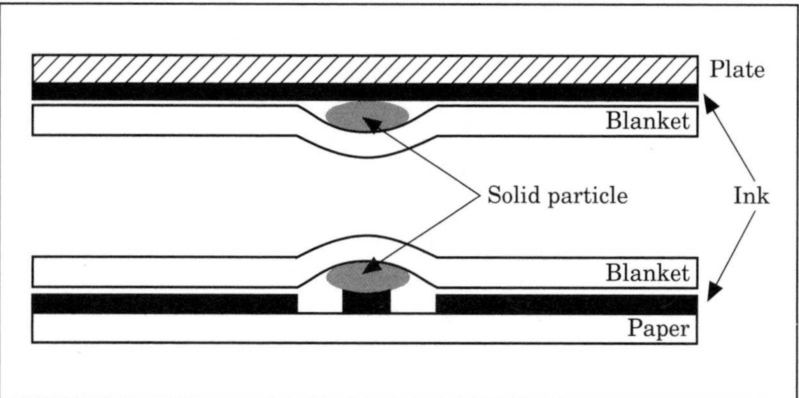

A solid particle (such as dirt), enlarged, on the blanket, producing a hickey on the printed sheet

Water-receptive particles on the plate or blanket produce void hickeys. Because of their thickness, they prevent the plate or blanket from receiving ink in their immediate surrounding area.

Piling

The accumulation of material on the blanket in such quantity that it interferes with print quality is called **piling.** Piling in the nonimage areas is often caused by fillers and coating particles that become attached to the blanket. Improper ink and water balance can also cause nonimage area piling.

Back-Edge Curl

Back-edge curl, or **tail-end hook,** is a curl in the paper at the back edge of a press sheet as a result of printing heavy solids close to the back edge during offset printing. The heavy solid causes the sheet to stick to the blanket.

Back-edge curl is avoided if large solid areas are printed on the front half of the sheet. The use of quick-release blankets and sheet decurlers lessens the problem of back-edge curl.

Surface Rupture

Picking, plucking, tearing, and similar problems occur when paper or coating is not strong enough to withstand the pull of the inked rubber blanket. The principal causes are insufficient bonding strength in the paper or excessive ink tack.

Picking is the removal of pieces of paper surface by the ink. They stick to the blanket or plate, causing spots in the printing.

Tearing occurs when the ink pulls a continuous strip of the paper surface, leaving a delaminated area in the press sheet. (The term "ply delamination" is reserved for a phenomenon that occurs on blanket-to-blanket web presses.)

Splitting occurs when large areas of the paper surface are torn loose from the press sheet and stick to the offset blanket. Splitting usually starts in a solid printed area and continues to the trailing edge of the sheet. It sometimes develops into a V-shaped tear.

The following recommendations eliminate or minimize the problems of surface rupture:

- Reduce the ink tack.
- Change to a blanket with better release properties or with a rougher surface.
- Decrease press speed.
- Decrease the pressure between the impression and blanket cylinders.

Recycled Paper

Using recycled paper as a fibrous source is not new. There is evidence that it was practiced before 1637 by the Chinese. Over 25% of all paper and paperboard manufactured in the United States is recycled. The world average is 30%. The amount of wastepaper recycled depends upon the economics of collecting wastepaper as opposed to the economics of growing trees and pulping them. Collecting wastepaper for recycling is relatively expensive. Pulpwood, however, is a major farm crop in the United States, and agricultural advances have managed to keep the costs of producing it low while increasing the yield.

Few recycled paper products are strictly made completely from wastepaper. Most recycled papers have some virgin paper content. Recycled paper is made from various percentages of virgin paper and from two main categories of wastepaper: preconsumer waste and postconsumer waste. **Preconsumer waste** (i.e., paper that never reaches the consumer) comes from trimmings, clippings, and other paper mill waste, such as that from small unusable butt rolls or obsolete inventories. Preconsumer waste also consists of unprinted paper from the printer, such as trimmings from press sheets and unused or rejected paper stock. **Postconsumer waste** is finished material (e.g., magazines and newspapers) that is recycled or disposed of as solid waste after its product life span is completed.

Approximately 80% of the paper recycled in the United States is used to manufacture paperboard. Much of this comes from post-consumer sources like old corrugated containers, mixed wastepaper, and old newspapers, catalogs, and directories. Wastepaper recycled into paperboard is generally not deinked.

Recyclable wastepapers are classified into five major groups according to their reuse as fibrous sources by the paper industry. About half of all U.S. recycled wastepaper consists of discarded fiber and corrugated containers, which are recycled into linerboard, corrugated containers, and other paperboards. Mixed papers unsuitable for recycling into white papers are used to manufacture paperboard and construction paper and board. Old newspapers and over-issue news represent a significant percentage of the total wastepaper recycled. While in past years this source was mainly recycled into paperboard, it has been used increasingly since 1970 to manufacture deinked newsprint, and its use will continue to grow in various U.S. regions. Pulp substitutes as generated by printing and paper converting plants and consisting primarily of nonprinted, white uncoated paper are recycled into fine printing and writing papers as well as sanitary and tissue paper products. Another source of recyclable paper for high-grade deinking consists of tabulating cards, coated papers, and printed white papers.

The recycling of wastepaper to make fine, white printing and writing paper requires *deinking,* which is the removal of ink and other unwanted materials, or contaminants. Higher grades of wastepapers with fewer contaminants are required for deinking. Examples are tabulating and card stocks and waste such as milk cartons, envelope cuttings, and printing wastes generated directly by converting operations.

After cooking and coarse screening, the pulped wastepaper is usually completely defibered. Cleaning, including centrifugal cleaning to remove unwanted material, and fine screening follow. Washing and bleaching are the final steps. The individual steps of deinking vary, depending upon the type of wastepapers used and the intended end products.

Flotation has been used for deinking in Europe for many years. After cooking, defibering, and coarse screening, the diluted wastepaper slurry enters flotation cells. Ink particles are removed by using air and chemicals that produce an ink-bearing froth that rises to the top level of the cell, where it is skimmed off.

When selecting a recycled paper, review the optical properties of the paper, just as you would with any printing paper. Recycled papers are available in everything from the finest premium coated paper to low-quality uncoated groundwood stocks. If the physical and optical properties of the stock are satisfactory, there should be no more problems when printing recycled paper than when printing virgin stock.

If large or expensive jobs will be printed on unfamiliar stock (including stock made from 100% virgin fiber), be sure to submit samples to your ink supplier and ask for the appropriate ink for that stock. Paper color variances can affect ink color, so it is always good practice to obtain drawdown proofs of the ink on the stock. For example, lower ink mileage with increased dot gain is normal for rough, absorbent stocks.

10 Ink

Unlike flexography and letterpress, which print from a raised or "relief" surface, and rotogravure, which prints from an engraved or "intaglio" surface, lithography uses a planographic plate to separate the image from the nonimage areas. The image area of the plate is preferentially wet by ink, and the nonimage area is preferentially wet by water. Therefore, unlike other inks, lithographic ink must be formulated to work with water. In offset lithography, the ink on the plate is transferred to a blanket. In direct lithography, which is sometimes used to print newspapers, ink is transferred directly from the plate to the paper.

Ink is a complex mixture of pigment, varnish or vehicle, and modifier or additives. The important properties of ink are drying properties, color, color strength, opacity or transparency, and body or working properties. All of these properties must be selected to suit the particular job and, most importantly, the paper or other material being printed.

Ink is discussed comprehensively in GATF's book *What the Printer Should Know about Ink.* Ink problems, as well as possible solutions to them, are discussed in great detail in GATF's *Solving Offset Ink Problems* book.

Ink Making

The actual manufacturing of ink is relatively simple, but ink formulations themselves are complex. Advanced science is involved in creating them. When dry pigments are used, varnish and pigment(s) are weighed and stirred together in a tub using high-speed dispersion equipment to mix the pigments with the varnish. This mixing operation, wetting the pigment and mixing the ink ingredients thoroughly, saves subsequent milling time. Most sheetfed inks are now made from "flushes" in which the pigment is dispersed during manufacture.

Three-roll mill

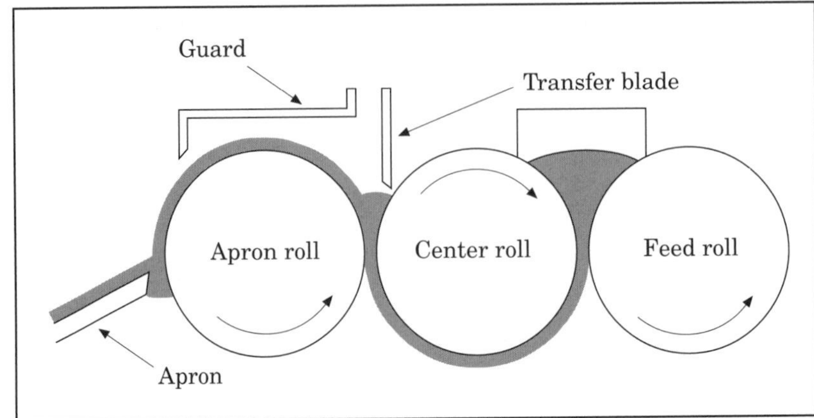

Next, the mixture is ground on a three-roll mill where it is sheared as it passes between rollers. As can be seen by examining the illustration, the rollers of the three-roll mill, which turn at different speeds and in different directions, shear the ink film between them. This shearing breaks up

Bead mill
Courtesy Buhler-Miag, Inc.

the pigment agglomerates into microscopic particles so that each becomes completely surrounded and wet by the varnish. Milling also “classifies” the pigment, permitting finely dispersed pigment to flow through the mill and retaining or holding back coarser pigment particles. Ground ink is taken off the high-speed roll by a blade, as shown in the illustration. A thorough job of grinding may require as many as three passes through the mill, depending on whether the pigment is soft or hard and how easily it is wet by the varnish.

Milling is a costly procedure, and inks can be cheapened by reducing the amount of milling. This causes several problems including lower color strength and larger pigment size. Large pigment particles in the ink can cause problems, such as scratches to the plate and plate wear. Since the pigment is the most expensive part of the ink, and uniform dispersion is accomplished by extensive milling, which is also expensive, better inks cost more.

Progress in recent years has resulted in the production of inks that are stable in the can. However, it is still a good practice to make sure that new inks arriving in the ink room are not placed on the front of the shelf and used first. Rather, a system of “first-in, first-out” should be used to ensure that the oldest inks are used first. This prevents inks from becoming so old during storage that they must be discarded.

Constituents of Inks

Since formulation of inks is the ink manufacturer’s responsibility, the subject is presented only briefly here.

A sheetfed ink contains the following materials:

- Pigment: carbon black, phthalo blue, rubine, or other
- Varnish: long-oil alkyd, phenolic, or urethane litho varnish
- Drier: cobalt and manganese salts
- Solvent: heatset oil, 535°F (280°C)
- Modifier: wax compound for rub resistance

These standard inks dry primarily by *polymerization,* a chemical reaction that is initiated by oxygen and catalyzed by cobalt and manganese ions from the drier.

Pigments

A **pigment** is a finely divided solid material that gives an ink color. Lithographic ink pigments vary widely in chemical composition, their principal requirements being that they (1) do not dissolve or bleed in the press dampening solution, (2) are unchanged in color or tinctorial strength by chemicals in the dampening solution, (3) produce inks that will not be broken down by the plate moisture, and (4) do not possess abrasive properties that would damage printing plates. These requirements narrow the field of acceptable pigments.

They can be either opaque or transparent. The body and working properties of an ink depend not only on the type of vehicle and its viscosity but also on the nature and amount of pigment it contains. In addition to color and opacity, important pigment characteristics include particle size, specific gravity, refractive index, texture, wettability, and free surface energy.

The **particle size** of pigments suitable for inks ranges from about 0.01 to 0.5 microns, which corresponds to 0.000004–0.00002 in. (0.0001–0.0005 mm). Among the process colors, carbon blacks are the finest and chrome yellow particles are the coarsest, one of several reasons that diarylide yellows are preferred. In general, pigments of fine particle size work best and, with the exception of blacks, produce the more transparent inks. Coarser pigments not only produce more opaque inks but also tend to pile on the ink rollers, plate, and blanket. Special formulation is often required to make such inks transfer properly. Large pigment particle size causes fairly rapid plate wear.

The **specific gravity** of a pigment is the ratio of the weight of one of its particles to the weight of an equal volume of water. Heavy pigments generally require less varnish per pound than light pigments, and the volume and mileage of a pound of their inks are less.

Refractive index is a measure of the ability of a pigment particle to bend or refract light rays. If the pigment and vehicle have the same refractive index (vehicles also have a refractive index), the film is transparent. If the refractive indexes are different, the light rays are bent and scattered and the film is opaque. The greater this difference, the more opaque the film is. Pigments vary in refractive index much more than vehicles. Opaque pigments like titanium dioxide and chrome yellows have high refractive indexes.

Texture is the hardness or softness of a pigment in its dry form. If it rubs out easily to an extremely fine powder between finger and thumb, it is soft. If much pressure is needed, or if the powder feels gritty, it is hard. Texture determines the ease of grinding or dispersing a pigment in its vehicle—in other words, the number of passes through the mill necessary to produce a good ink. Recent research indicates that sharp or gritty pigment particles can greatly accelerate plate wear. This can be true even for particles that are acceptably small.

Wettability is the ease with which a pigment can be completely wet by the *ink vehicle.* In offset inks particularly, complete pigment wetting by the ink vehicle is necessary to prevent breakdown and dispersion in the dampening solution. At least one press problem can be traceable to poor pigment wettability. In waterlogging, water begins to wet the surface of pigment particles, and as a result, the pigment and vehicle separate, usually leaving pigment caked on the rollers.

Free surface energy involves the molecular forces at the surface of the pigment particle. These forces determine whether the particle "prefers" to be wet by oil or by water. Pigment surface forces probably play a part in determining whether a pigment will grind to a short or a long body in an oily vehicle.

Because pigments vary much in particle size, specific gravity, wettability, and free surface energy, each pigment poses a different problem in ink formulation. The inkmaker requires many varieties of ink vehicles, extenders, and modifiers in order to produce good working inks in all colors.

There are two broad classes of pigments: organic and inorganic. The term **organic** means "derived from living organisms." Organic pigments contain hydrogen and carbon and usually one or more of the following chemical elements: oxygen, nitrogen, sulfur, and chlorine. Organic pigments include furnace black, lampblack, and channel black for black inks, diarylide yellows and Hansa yellows for yellow inks, phthalocyanine for cyan inks, rubine for red-shade magenta inks, rhodamine for blue-shade magenta inks, and red lake C in red inks. Inorganic pigments include titanium dioxide, chrome yellow, molybdate orange, cadmium yellow and cadmium red, iron blue, and ultramarine blue.

Vehicle

Pigment particles are dispersed in a complex liquid mixture known as the **ink vehicle.** The vehicle consists of a varnish, solvent, and additives required to give good performance. The nature of the vehicle determines most of the working properties of the ink and some of its optical qualities as well. The vehicle disperses the pigment and, after drying, bonds the pigment particles to the paper.

A variety of substances including drying oils, synthetic resins, and modifications of natural rosin are used in ink vehicles. Among the drying oils used to produce varnishes for lithographic inks are linseed oil, tall oil (from kraft pulping of wood), soybean oil, safflower oil, and chinawood oil (tung oil). Refined ("food-grade") soybean oil is used in some sheetfed offset inks to replace a portion of the more expensive vehicle, such as linseed alkyd.

Additives

The inkmaker adds various materials to the ink to make it press-ready for sheetfed lithographic printing.

One additive is a **slip compound** that improves scuff resistance of the printed ink film. Waxes are used in the compound, which is either a micronized dry powder or a fine dispersion of several waxes in an appropriate oil vehicle.

Also added to many inks are **wetting agents,** which promote the dispersion of pigments in the vehicle. The wetting agent selected by the inkmaker must be carefully chosen, to avoid excessive emulsification of dampening solution into the ink and other problems.

Setoff is controlled by the addition of **antisetoff compounds,** which prevent setoff either by protecting the ink surface or by shortening the ink (decreasing its gelling time). Compounds containing wax or grease shorten the ink, which decreases its setting time.

Shortening compounds reduce ink flying, or misting. The addition of a wax compound shortens the ink. Press operators should not add such materials to an ink except on the advice of the inkmaker because they can interfere with the proper flow on the press.

Reducers, such as #0000 litho varnish, boiled linseed oil, or a light linseed isophthalic alkyd, reduce the tack of an ink. It is much easier to reduce tack than increase it.

Stiffening agents, such as body gum (#8, #9, and #10 linseed varnish) stiffen an ink that is too soupy and that fails to print cleanly and sharply. It lessens the tendency of an ink to cause scumming or tinting and helps to prevent chalking on coated stocks.

Antiskinning agents are antioxidants that counteract the drying of sheetfed inks so that they do not skin over in the can.

The printer should make every effort to obtain inks that are press-ready direct from the can. Not only is altering the ink a nuisance, but it often causes more problems than it cures. If it becomes necessary to add anything to the ink, it should be done only on advice of the inkmaker.

Drying Agents, or Driers

An additive omitted from the previous section is the drying agent. Most printing inks benefit from the addition of a **drying agent,** or **drier,** which acts as a catalyst to convert a wet ink film to a dry ink film. Drying agents are, most frequently, salts of cobalt and manganese. Mixed driers are more effective than single driers. For years, the conventional drier has been a three-way type composed of cobalt, lead, and manganese salts. Due to environmental regulations concerning the use of lead, two-way driers using cobalt and manganese or three-way driers using zirconium instead of lead are being used increasingly.

Cobalt, a very active drier, is referred to as a **top drier** since it gives a very hard surface to the ink. Manganese, less active than cobalt, is a **through drier** since it dries the ink film throughout and does not form a hard surface.

If metal salts are suspended in liquids such as petroleum solvent, the resulting driers are referred to as **liquid driers.** The largest class of printing ink driers currently used consists of soluble drier containing resins and plasticizers to achieve the desired body or viscosity; these are referred to as **paste driers.**

Although drying agents are already included in the ink by the manufacturer, extra driers can be added by the printer. When driers are added at the printing stage, it is important not to exceed the manufacturer's recommendations for each ink. Using too much drier will not greatly improve an ink's drying rate; in some instances, it may actually slow it down.

Drying of Sheetfed Inks

The **drying** of a sheetfed ink is the process by which it is transformed from an original semifluid or plastic to a solid. On paper, drying takes place in two stages that, though separate and distinct, occur to some extent simultaneously. These stages are (1) setting by absorption and (2) solidification of the liquid vehicle by oxidation and polymerization.

Setting

Proper setting of ink is dependent on a correct relationship between the absorbency of the paper and body of the ink vehicle. If the ink vehicle is too fluid or the paper is too absorptive, or both, the pigment remains on the paper surface with insufficient binder, and the print "chalks." On the other hand, if the ink vehicle is too viscous or the paper does not absorb sufficiently, or both, the ink will not set properly, and the result will be setoff, sticking, or, in extreme cases, "blocking." Ordinarily, the paper is selected on the basis of

An ink film setting on uncoated paper

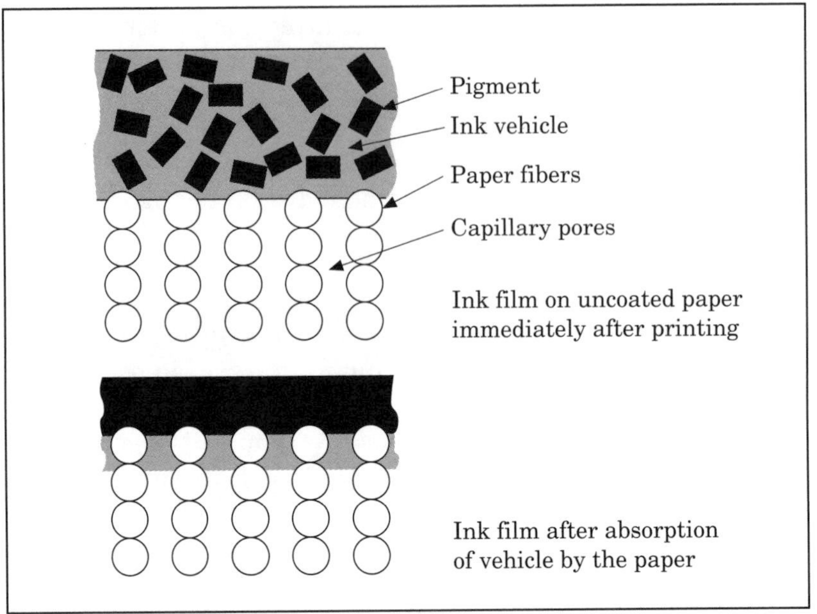

An ink film setting on coated paper

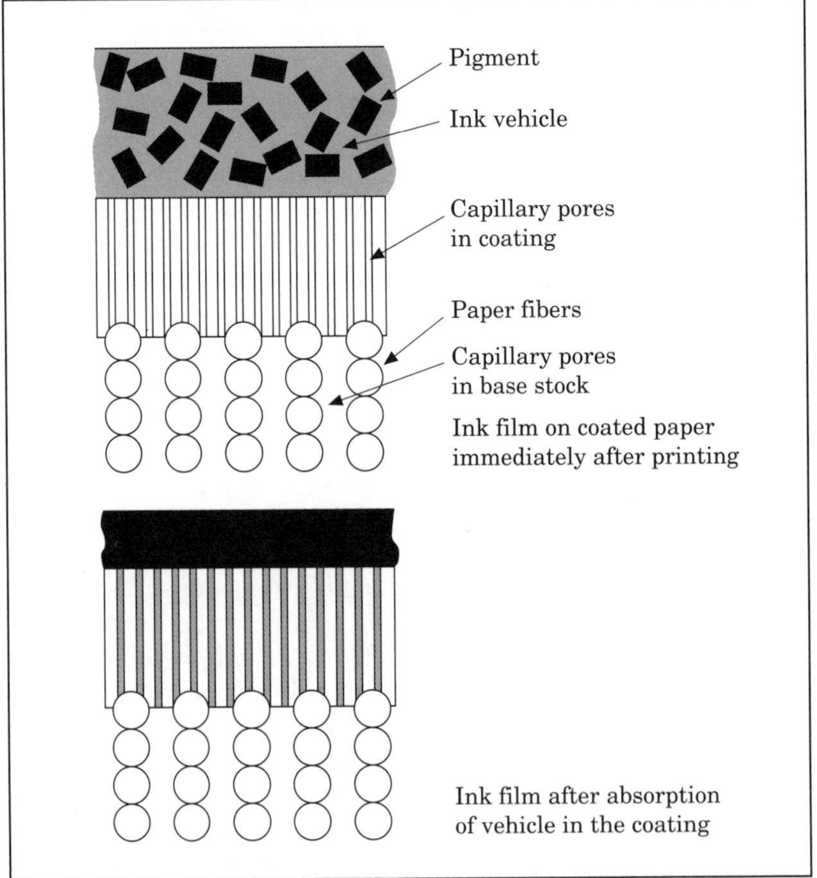

the requirements of the printed product, and the ink is adjusted to the paper. Sometimes a paper will be changed to correct a setting problem; however, most often, the ink is varied or changed to accommodate the paper.

Drying by Oxidation and Polymerization

The principle of polymerization is illustrated in the accompanying diagram. Those varnishes that are derived from drying oils, such as linseed oil, chinawood oil, or soya oil, react with oxygen in the air to form a chemical called a **hydroperoxide.** In the presence of a cobalt or manganese salt, called an initiator or a catalyst (a drier), the hydroperoxide reacts with another oil molecule, forming a molecular chain that continues to grow. As the chain gets longer and longer, it flows less and less readily until, after 2–4 hr., enough chains are formed to prevent ink flow. It will not smear when it is rubbed; it is dry.

Polymerization

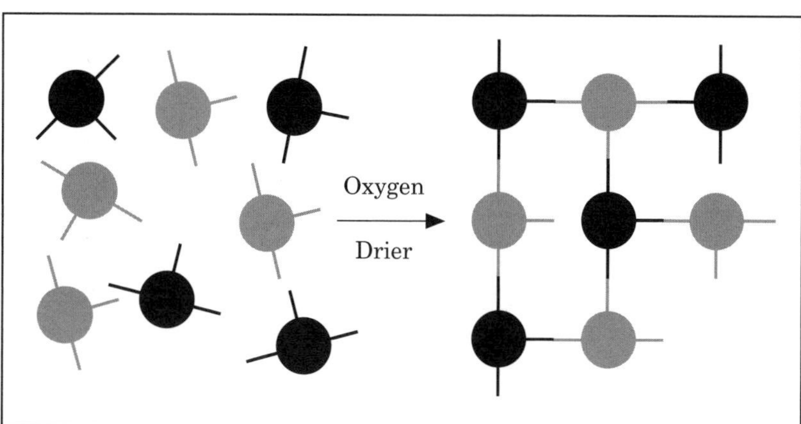

Factors Affecting Ink Drying Rate

Several factors affect the drying rate of inks containing drying-oil varnishes. Among these factors are the nature of ink pigment and other ingredients, nature of paper, temperature, amount of moisture present, acidity of dampening solution, availability of oxygen for drying, and ink film thickness.

If an ink does not dry in a reasonable length of time, the ink alone is often blamed. However, not only the ink but also the paper, the press, and the atmosphere are involved.

The major factors related to *ink components* that affect the drying rate are:

- **Pigments.** Some pigments themselves help drying, while others absorb drier and remove it from the reaction.
- **Varnishes.** Some varnishes dry much faster and harder than others.

- **Type of drier.** Cobalt, manganese, and zirconium compounds are used. They are not equally efficient as driers.
- **Amount of drier.** More drier is not necessarily better. It is important to have the correct amount of drier in the ink, and this amount is best determined by the inkmaker.
- **Drier dissipation.** The drying rate of an old ink should be checked before the ink is used on a job. A drier may become dissipated, or inactive, if the ink has been on the shelf for more than one year.

Effect of drier content on drying time of ink

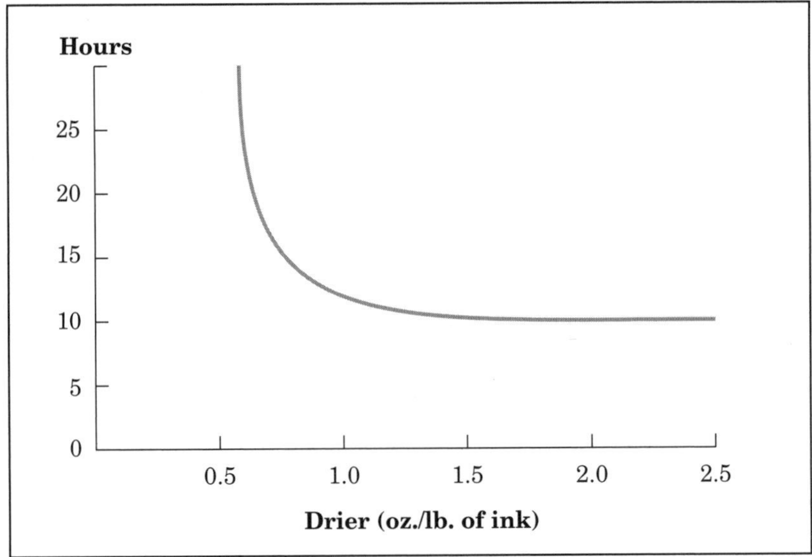

Some *paper characteristics* affecting ink drying are:

- **Absorbency of the sheet.** Absorbency of the paper does not affect real drying. However, the more absorbent the paper, the faster inks printed on it will set.
- **Paper or coating pH.** The more acid an uncoated paper is, the slower the printed ink dries. The more alkaline a coating is, the faster the ink dries. The coating on coated paper can also be responsible for the chalking of inks.
- **Moisture in the paper.** The more moisture there is in a paper, the slower the printed ink dries.

The method of controlling a press is particularly important in lithographic printing. It is necessary to have good ink/water balance for best printing conditions: enough ink should be used to get full color, with only enough water to keep the plate running clean. The following are important *press factors*:

- **Acid level of dampening solution.** Excess acid (pH too low) is the most common cause of ink drying problems. As the dampening solution is made more acid, inks with drying-oil varnishes take longer to dry because the acid reacts with the drier, destroying its effectiveness. As a general rule regarding ink drying, the pH is best maintained between 4.0 and 5.5, but always follow the recommendations of the dampening solution manufacturer regarding proper pH for the ink and paper being used.
- **Water in ink.** The more water that becomes emulsified in the ink, the slower the ink dries.
- **Kind of form.** Heavy solids cause more drying problems than light line work or halftones.

Temperature and relative humidity also affect the ink drying rate. The higher the temperature at which sheets are stored after printing, the faster the ink dries. An ink that requires 12 hr. to dry at 68°F (20°C) may dry in about 6 hr. at 80°F (27°C). On the other hand, excessive warmth generates blocking, dot gain, and other problems. As the relative humidity of the air increases, inks dry more slowly.

Effect of temperature on ink drying time

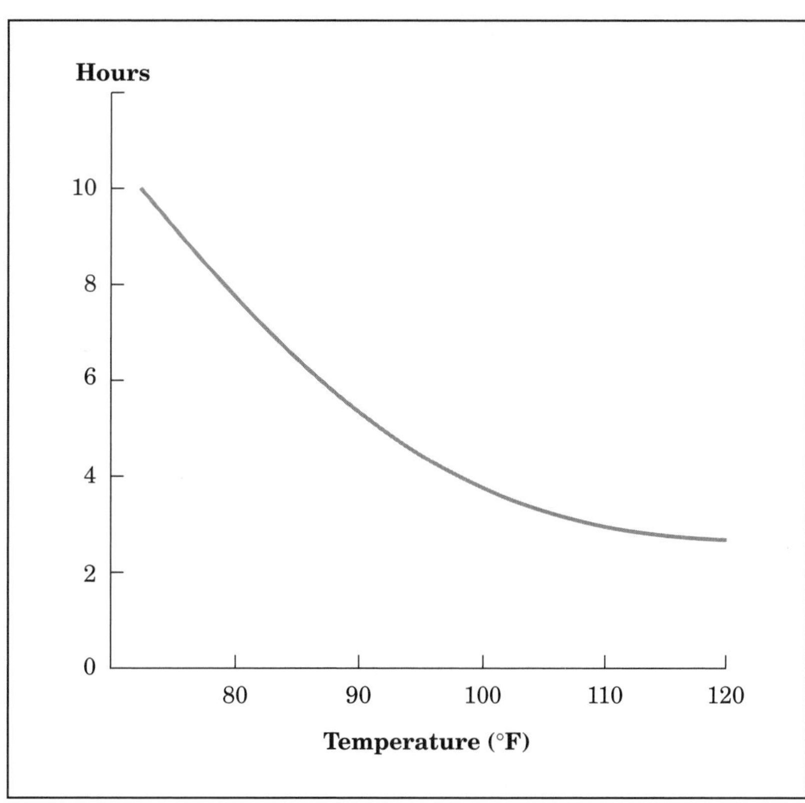

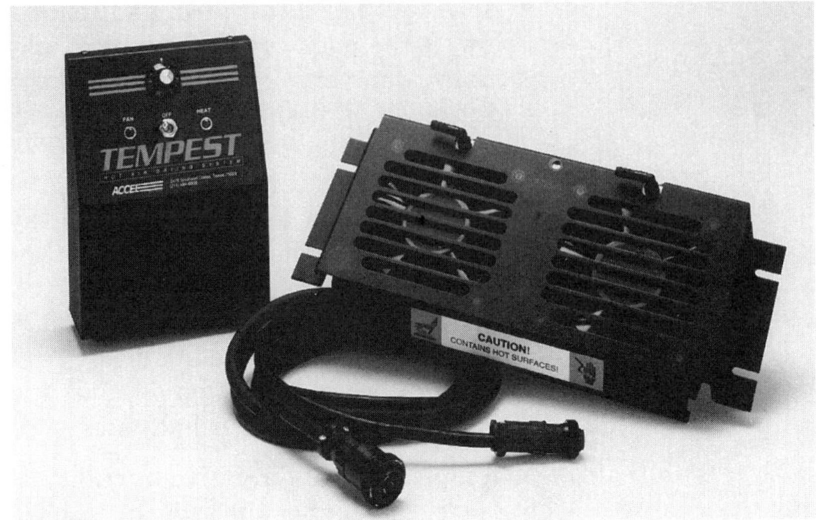

Tempest® hot-air drying system
Courtesy Accel Graphic Systems

Acceleration of Drying Using Radiation

Some sheetfed printing inks use ultraviolet (UV), infrared (IR), or electron-beam (EB) radiation to accelerate drying.

The UV ink drying system involves special inks *and* a series of special lamps that emit ultraviolet radiation. When UV inks are exposed to UV radiation, the polymerization reaction speeds up to a point where it is virtually instantaneous and complete. Some describe UV drying as "curing." These inks contain no solvent, so solvent-fume emission from the press is eliminated. One of the difficulties in formulating UV inks has been the successful use of the photoinitiators required to trigger their polymerization. These photoinitiators are expensive and difficult to use.

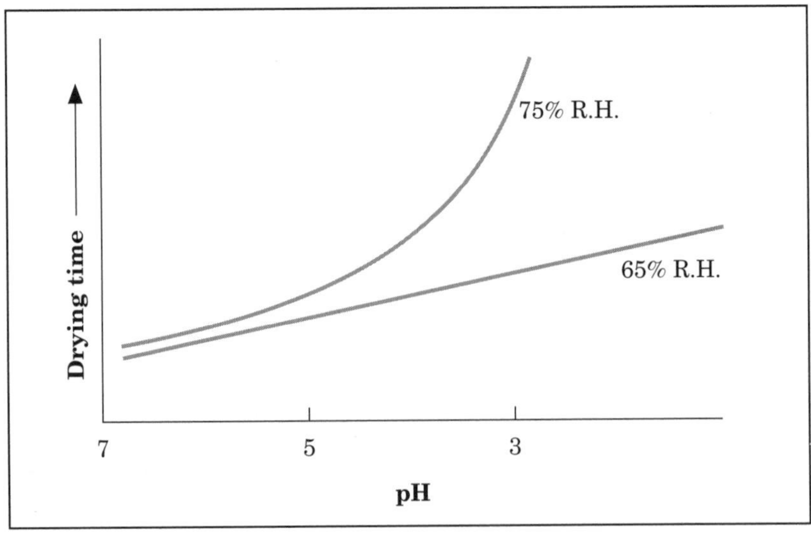

Effect of constant relative humidity (R.H.) and changing pH on drying time

Effect of relative humidity on the drying times of three inks

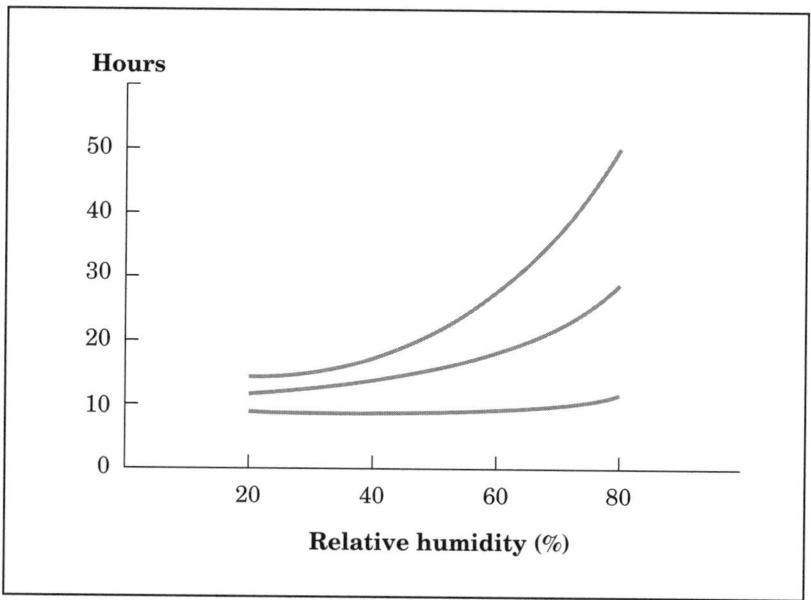

The EB drying system uses inks similar to those used for UV drying with the exception that photoinitiators are not required. A stream of electrons bombard the ink film and accelerate polymerization.

Infrared radiation does not usually cure inks. As commonly used, infrared radiators increase the setting speed of inks. When infrared radiation is used with quickset inks, the speed of setting is very fast. Special quickset infrared inks permit backing up a pile of prints 15 min. after they have been printed. Less spray powder is used with IR dryers, but the system must be kept under control to avoid embrittling the sheet or blocking the prints.

An infrared dryer
Courtesy Amjo IR / UV Curing Systems

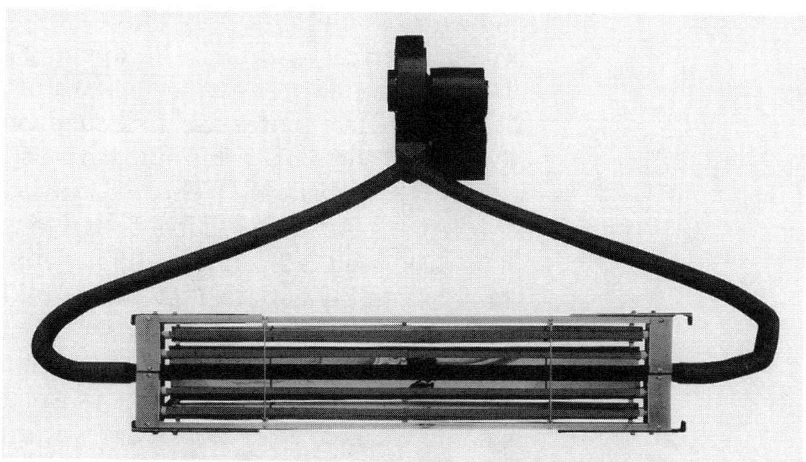

Quickset Inks

Quickset inks are formulated with a quickset varnish. A quickset varnish contains a low-viscosity, high-boiling-point hydrocarbon oil. When the ink is printed, the hydrocarbon oil is absorbed by the paper coating, and the viscosity of the printed ink film rises rapidly; that is, the ink sets.

Sheets printed with quickset inks can be handled more quickly than those printed with a nonquickset ink. In addition, quickset ink can set rapidly enough to increase the tack of the printed ink between units on the press. If they set sufficiently between units, it is possible to print process colors using four **unitack** inks; i.e., inks that have the same tack rating. This means that the printer can use one set of process colors in any printing sequence desired. However, better trap and color uniformity are achieved if the normal tack sequence is used (tack is highest on the first unit and decreases on subsequent units) and the printer uses only one color sequence or a different set of inks for each color sequence. When a normal tack sequence is printed, the ink film is usually thinnest on the first unit and increases in thickness with each succeeding unit, provided the inks are properly formulated and nothing has been added to the ink in the pressroom.

Waterless Offset Inks

Waterless offset inks contain many of the same things that conventional lithographic inks contain. The difference between them is that waterless inks have vehicles that allow them to have higher initial viscosities than those of conventional inks. Waterless offset inks also may have slightly lower tacks than those of conventional offset inks. The viscosity and tack differences between the two inks have to do with the differences between the two plates. Conventional offset lithographic plates operate on the principle that oil and water do not mix. They have a hydrophilic nonimage area that attracts water or dampening solution and an oleophilic image area that repels water and attracts oily ink. Waterless offset plates use a silicone material for the nonimage area of the plate. This silicone material has a low surface energy that resists ink if the ink's viscosity is high enough for it to be more attracted to itself than to the silicone material.

As discussed later in this chapter, the viscosity of a liquid changes rapidly with the temperature. In conventional lithography, the presence of water in the dampening solution on press cools the ink and helps it to maintain a viscosity that does not compromise its physical characteristics while it is being worked. The viscosity of waterless offset inks is maintained on press by a press temperature control system, either a plate cylinder cooling or ink oscillator (vibrator) cooling system. Waterless offset inks are formulated at varied viscosities in order to be adaptable to the geographic temperature environment of any printing press.

Optical Properties of Ink

The impression of color is a personal experience. It is received as light that is reflected, transmitted, or radiated from an object to our eyes. Light stimulates the nerve cells in our eyes and our brain to create the sensation of color. Being a personal experience, color identification varies between individuals, as well as the state of our health, our physical surroundings, and other physiological factors. The eye is sensitive to three colors, red, green, and blue. All of the various colors that we perceive are combinations of these three frequencies of light. In printing, the reflection of these three colors (red, green, and blue) from the surface of the paper are respectively controlled by application of the transparent inks known as cyan, magenta, and yellow.

Color

It is common to think of color as a property of objects and materials. Nothing, however, appears colored unless it is either illuminated or emits light. Pigments appear colored in white light because they absorb certain wavelengths and reflect or transmit others. They appear to change color if the spectral composition of the light is varied.

The three process color inks (cyan, yellow, and magenta) are transparent. Ideally each absorbs light from one-third of the spectrum and transmits light from the remaining two-thirds. Cyan has its characteristic color because it transmits blue and green light while absorbing (or filtering out) red light. Yellow transmits red and green light and absorbs the blue. Magenta absorbs green light and transmits the red and blue. Because process inks are transparent, one process color can be overprinted by another without changing the way each absorbs or transmits light. For example, magenta overprinted by cyan will produce blue because magenta filters out green light and cyan filters out the red.

Ordinary nonprocess inks are opaque and work differently. An opaque yellow ink, for example, reflects (rather than transmits) red and green light and absorbs blue light. When opaque inks are overprinted, the top color hides the bottom color, making them unsuitable for process-color printing unless the opaque color is printed first down.

Spectral reflectance curve of a "perfect" magenta ink

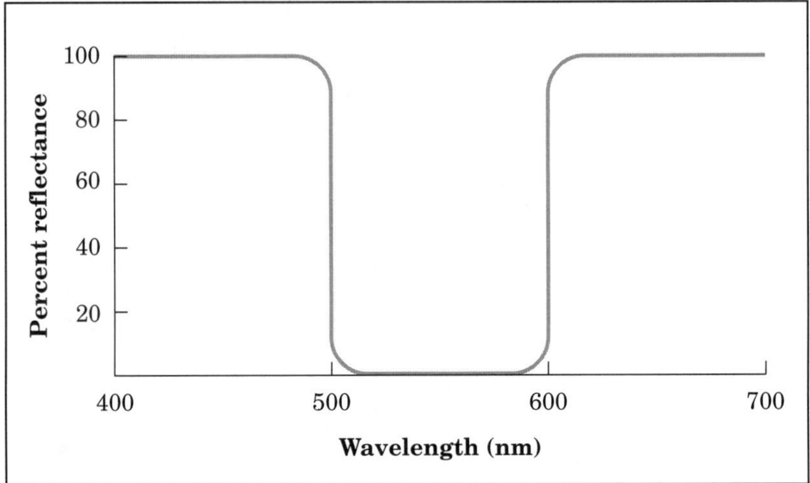

Spectral reflectance curve of a typical magenta ink

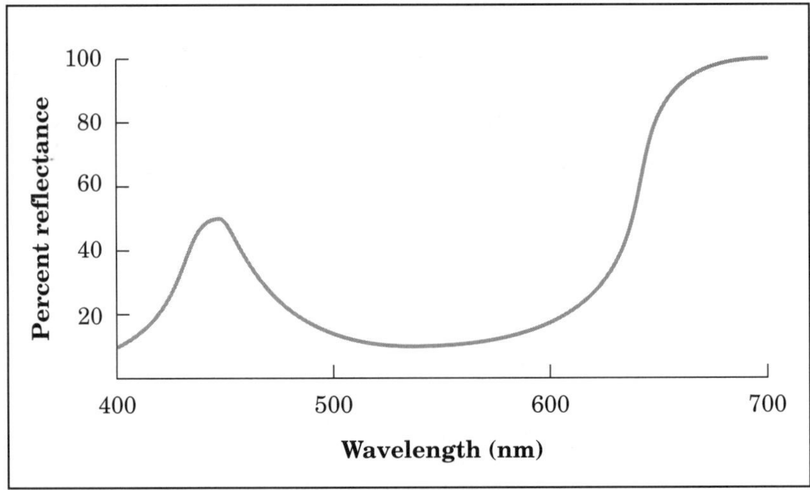

Spectral reflectance curve of a "perfect" cyan ink

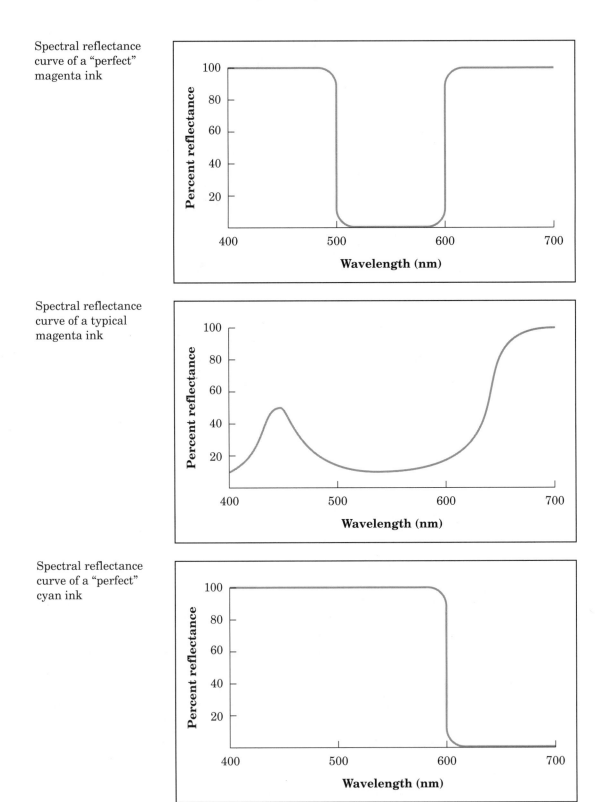

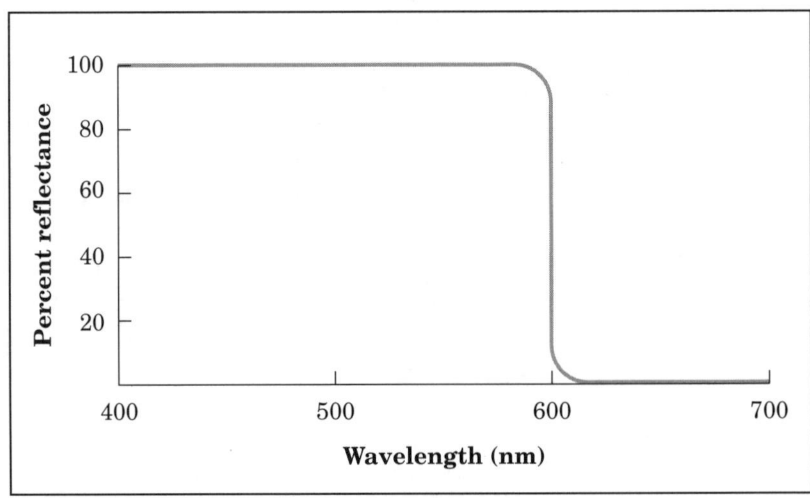

Spectral reflectance curve of a typical cyan ink

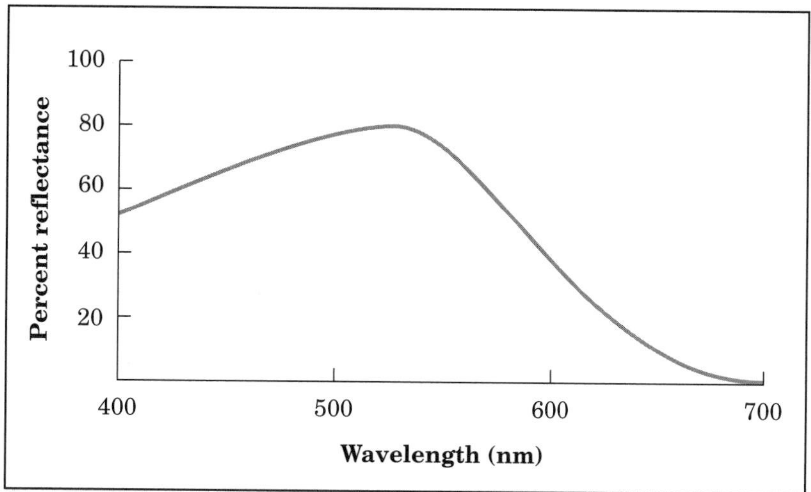

Spectral reflectance curve of a "perfect" yellow ink

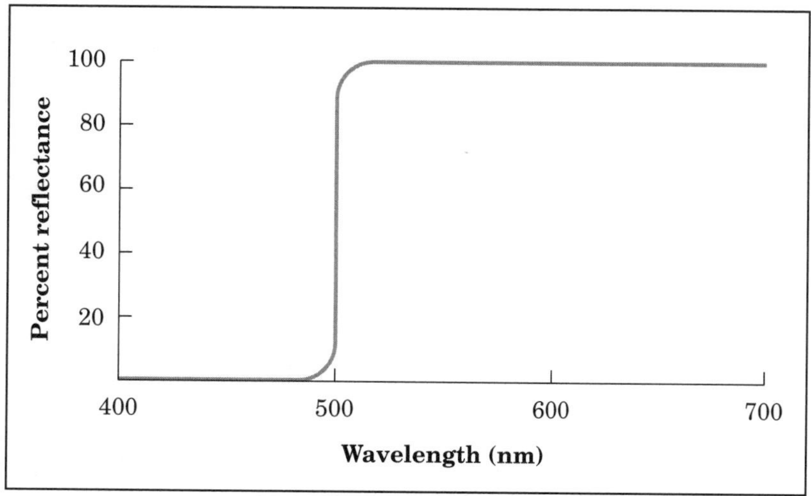

Spectral reflectance curve of a typical yellow ink

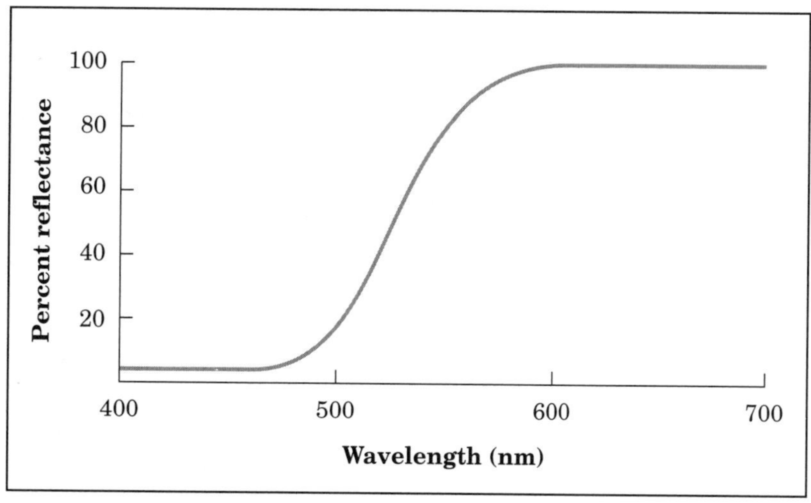

Printed ink films exhibit both masstone and undertone. **Masstone** is the color of a thick film of the ink. It is the color of light reflected by the pigment. **Undertone** is the color of a thin film of ink. It is the color of light reflected by the paper and transmitted through the ink film. In order to judge these two ink properties, the following procedure is followed:

1. Place two small samples of two different inks side by side on a piece of paper.
2. Use a drawdown knife to draw the samples down to adjoining films, first lightly for about 1½–2 in. (40–50 mm), then with heavy pressure for another 2 in.
3. Determine the relative masstone of the two inks by comparing the thick films and the undertone by comparing the thin films.

The difference between masstone and undertone applies to ink films as printed. For example, if an ink film is thick, the resulting color tends towards masstone. But if the ink film is thin, the undertone becomes predominant. A red ink with a bluish undertone may print a warm red if run with normal thickness but go to cold pink if run very thin. Such an apparent color change can cause problems on the press.

Color Strength

The **color strength** of an ink is its coloring power and is determined by pigment concentration, which determines the value of an ink and the amount of ink required to produce the desired color. Inexpensive inks contain less color; the printer must run more of them, which creates emulsification and drying problems, dot gain, and other problems. In lithographic inks, color strength must be great enough to produce the desired color in a printed ink film of normal thickness. Determination of an ink's color strength is difficult and best left to experts. A printer can often get the inkmaker to test a pair of inks of the same hue to determine which has the greater strength, or the ink can be sent to a testing lab.

Opacity

Opacity is the hiding power of an ink—the ability of its printed film to hide what is underneath. Some pigments have high opacity while others, particularly process ink pigments, are much more transparent. Two pigment qualities, refractive index and particle size, largely determine the opacity or transparency of ink. Opacity can be determined by making drawdowns over black or a contrasting color.

Even minor opacity in a process ink affects the way process colors reproduce. An opaque yellow run on the third unit can blank out much of the visual effect of cyan and magenta, and opaque inks should be avoided in printing process color.

Gloss

Although most of today's high-quality printing is done with high-gloss inks, the degree of glossiness is largely a matter of taste and preference.

Gloss is largely related to the varnish used in the ink, but high gloss is obtained when the resins in the ink film dry. Coarsely ground pigments can interfere.

Working Properties

Many common liquids like water, alcohol, and petroleum solvents are true "Newtonian" liquids. That is to say that any force applied to them will produce flow, and their rate of flow is directly proportional to that force. But other viscous materials, lithographic inks included, will not flow until a definite force is exceeded. The ink chemist describes this force as the "yield stress" or "yield value."

Offset inks are viscous fluid materials, or **viscoelastic,** because they behave both like fluids and like elastic solids. While it is not easy to separate these two types of behavior, the science of the subject forces us to shift from one type to another to explain why inks behave as they do on the press.

Body, length, tack, and thixotropy are ink properties that strongly affect how the ink feeds from the fountain, how it transfers and distributes on the rollers, and how it prints from the blanket.

Body

The term **body** means consistency. It is a rather loose, overall term referring mainly to stiffness or softness of the ink, although it often implies other things including length and thixotropy. **Thixotropy** is the characteristic of a material that causes it to change consistency on being worked. Working an ink on a slab with a spatula reduces its body and viscosity. After standing a while, the ink will return to its original viscosity.

Length

Ink must possess a certain degree of length in order to feed properly and transfer without piling. Too much length, however, may cause an ink to fly or mist. The ink formulator may test length by placing an amount of ink on a tilted slab. After 15 min., the ink's flow down the slab is measured.

More commonly, length is observed by tapping out a small sample of ink on a slab or dish. A short ink breaks after forming a short string, while a long ink forms a long string.

Short inks are sensitive to water pickup and have a tendency to become waterlogged. They also transfer poorly and tend to pile on the plate or blanket. Inks in this condition do not transfer properly and make color control difficult.

Thixotropy

As explained above, working an ink reduces its viscosity, and when the work is discontinued, the ink regains its original body or viscosity. This means that an ink becomes more fluid while it is on the press and sets up when it is on the sheet. This behavior is called *thixotropy.*

Effect of Temperature on Viscosity

The viscosity of all liquids changes rapidly with the temperature. The temperature coefficient of viscosity for inks may be –5% per degree Fahrenheit (about –9% to –10% per degree Celsius) or even greater. This means that a temperature increase of 10°F (5.5°C) can reduce the viscosity of the ink by 50% or more. (Raising the temperature 20°F reduces the viscosity by around 75%.)

The high negative temperature coefficient of viscosity has several implications for the printer. In the first place, if a multicolor press is not warmed to working temperature before printing starts, the color changes as the press warms up. Furthermore, should the temperature on one of the units change, owing to environmental conditions, the flow of ink changes on that unit, changing the color of the print. In waterless lithography, it is crucial to control the temperature of the ink to maintain its viscosity. This is accomplished by a press temperature control system.

In lithographic printing, if the press is cold when the paper is fed to it, the highly viscous ink may cause picking of the paper. The press and the pressroom must be up to temperature before attempting to feed paper into the press.

Tack

Tack is the resistance of a liquid to splitting. It is measured by determining the force required to split an ink film between two surfaces. Tack is an important property of an ink film because it can determine whether or not an ink will pick the paper surface or trap properly in multicolor printing, and it at least partially determines how sharp the printed image is.

In multicolor work involving the successive overprinting of wet ink films, it is necessary that the tack of ink films on the paper be higher than the tack of ink on the blanket. It is important to understand that the tack referred to is *tack at the printing nip.* The tack of fresh ink will in all probability bear little relationship to its tack at the printing nip of a lithographic press. *A number of on-press factors can either increase or decrease an ink's tack.*

The most important factors affecting tack are viscosity, press speed, and ink film thickness. In general, tack increases with viscosity and press speed. A high-viscosity ink run on a high-speed press will have a very high tack and can create problems such as picking of the paper surface. In this case, the picking may disappear by simply reducing press speed. Inkmakers have responded to the increased operating speeds of today's presses by formulating inks with lower tack.

The thinner an ink film, the more it will resist splitting. A thin film of ink has a higher tack than a thick film. Thus, when running process work, effective ink tack at the printing nip varies until the press operator establishes the required printed color densities by arriving at the proper ink film thickness. It is important to remember that the press operator varies ink film thickness to achieve the desired color. Thus, the ink film thickness on the press is related to color strength of the ink.

Emulsification also affects the tack of ink. Water works its way back into the roller train in the form of tiny droplets, which are milled into the ink films on the roller surfaces. Inks can sometimes pick up 30% or more water in this way and run with no problems. But a 30% pickup will significantly lower tack because a film of water has a much lower tack than an ink film. The amount of water picked up by the ink depends on the nature of the ink and the condition of the ink/water balance.

The following factors influence ink tack on the press: the tack of the ink when fresh, press speed, ink film thickness, water pickup (emulsification), thixotropy, solvent evaporation, and the temperature of the ink. When faced with a tack-related problem on the press, the press operator should check these factors immediately.

The tack numbers displayed on the ink can by the manufacturer are based on Inkometer readings taken in the laboratory. The press system exerts a strong effect on these ratings. Generally, a new ink having the same tack number as the old will perform in roughly the same way as the old ink if the press system has not changed. On the other hand, tack number should not be relied on as an indicator of ink performance in cases involving changes in press, speed, plates, paper, etc.

Color Matching

Many times, a customer requests a specific color other than black, cyan, yellow, or magenta. Depending on the amount of the ink required, the printer either orders the specific color from the inkmaker or mixes it in the printing plant. Obtaining the ink from the inkmaker is preferred if the color is a shelf ink or if the amount required is large. Small amounts of a particular ink can be mixed in the plant. Color charts from an inkmaker are extremely helpful.

In plants where a great deal of color matching is done, the press operator seldom mixes the ink. A better way—both economically and from a quality control standpoint—is to have a special person assigned to do color matching.

The simple rule of good color matching is to use the formula method. Every mixed color that is used in the plant should have each ingredient carefully weighed and recorded. This includes additives like driers.

When the proper shade is found, a large batch is mixed, following the formula. After the color is printed on the job, a small sample from the printed sheet is saved, and the formula and date are marked on the back. A sample should not be kept too long, perhaps one year for lightfast colors. In addition, the name and/or number of the job should be put on the sample in case of a reprint. The inks are then listed, with brand, name, number, and weight indicated.

Ink samples can be drawn out with a spatula, rolled out with a Quickpeek tester, or printed using a proof press and allowed to dry. Exposing one sample to atmospheric conditions overnight and enclosing the other in a book gives an indication of the drying behavior of the ink.

Sometimes, two or three small color samples are mixed if the color is expected to change during drying. For example, if a green made from a certain blue and yellow is expected to dry toward the blue side, a second sample would be made with less blue in it. The one drying closest to the desired color is used. If the color desired falls between two samples, a new sample can be mixed, using the formulas from the first two samples as the basis for the new formula.

A tint of a color is produced by adding an **extender,** a white transparent tinting medium, to a colored ink. The simplest form of color matching, as performed by the printer, is mixing an ink to obtain a required shade. The stronger color should always be added to the lighter colored ink in order to obtain a match more quickly and economically. The color should be viewed under different light sources to check for

metamerism—the phenomenon of colors that match under one light but do not under a different light.

Without a knowledge of color theory and without perfect color perception, an individual will resort to trial-and-error color matching. Fortunately, color matching systems are available that take the trial and error out of color matching.

Ink Handling on Press

Handling ink on an offset press is one of the press operator's most important skills. It seems simple to set an inking fountain to satisfy the demands of a plate. Apparently, fountain setting consists of opening up the keys that feed underinked areas and closing keys that feed overinked areas.

It is not as simple as it appears. An area may seem to require more ink, while the fact is that the area is overdampened. The effect looks about the same. Under a strong glass the difference can be seen, but it takes a little practice. The same thing is true regarding overinked areas. The amount of dampening has a more marked effect than the amount of ink. Usually, when tones start filling up, the press operator's first reaction is that dampening is excessive or the acid level in the dampening solution is incorrect. Often, the trouble is too much ink.

The first thing to be sure of, when manipulating the ink feed, is that the amount of dampening is correct. Dampening should be reduced to the point where the plate appears dry. Some plates require more dampening than others to keep them clean. Knowing how dry a plate can be and still run safely on the press is another skill acquired with experience.

Probably the worst thing that can occur on press, regarding ink, is too much dampening solution. The water in the dampening solution is worked into the ink (emulsified) and

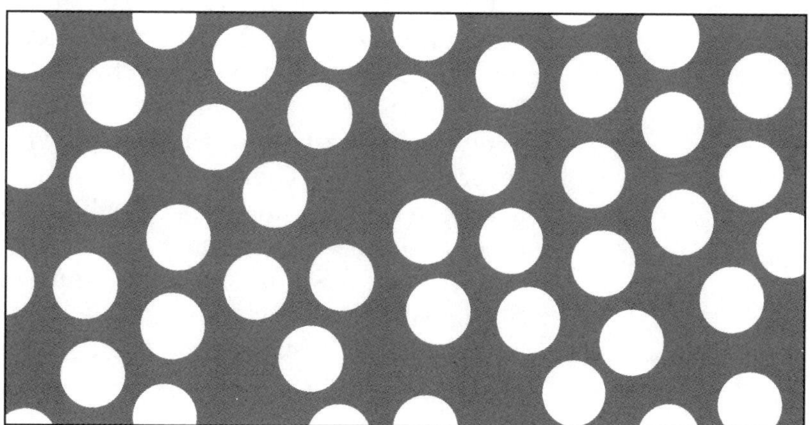

A water-in-ink emulsification

changes its characteristics. All inks emulsify water to some degree. Excessive emulsification causes problems, such as the caking of ink on rollers. Several conditions contribute to the emulsification of too much water in an ink:

- Too much dampening solution being fed to the plate
- Too much acid and gum in the dampening solution
- Too little ink on the ink rollers
- The nature of the ink itself

Once dampening is set at the proper level, the ink feed demands are set. Using a densitometer to measure the density of color patches on the press sheet helps in determining the proper amount of ink.

Too little ink on the plate is dangerous to the image, which requires ink to protect it from the acid and gum. Too much ink is dangerous to nonimage areas because it overcomes the desensitizing film and causes the plate to scum. The proper range of inking is small.

In handling ink, the press operator should take every precaution to avoid its contamination. Special care should be taken to prevent mixing dried ink (ink skin) into the fountain ink. To remove ink skin from a can, remove the oiled paper cover first. Then scrape off any ink skin formed around the edges. Use a broad knife to remove ink evenly from the surface rather than digging deeply into the can. When the required amount of ink has been taken out, smooth the surface with a broad knife and either replace the old oiled paper circle (the "skin sheet") or apply a new one. Press it into uniform contact with the remaining ink to prevent entrapping air bubbles. Ink that has been improperly stored should be discarded—not put onto the press where it can ruin print quality and press performance.

Be sure that the press is clean before inking up, especially if a light color or tint is to be run. Traces of a previous ink remaining on inking or dampening rollers can alter the hue, or dirty an ink. To avoid this condition, ink up the press with a light-colored ink or a transparent white ink and run it for several minutes. Then, scrape some of the ink off one of the drums to see how much its color has changed. Wash up the press and repeat until the ink is no longer contaminated.

A number of suitable press washup solvents are available. Strong solvents effectively remove ink but also swell rollers and blankets. Incorporation of a good detergent helps to remove ink without swelling the rubber. Formulation of a good press wash requires knowledge and experience, as does everything else. In addition to being a good ink solvent, it should also be safe from the standpoint of fire hazard and toxicity. Petroleum solvents, which are commonly used, should have flash points of at least 100°F (38°C) in order to meet underwriters' requirements. There are also two- and three-solution washup systems that remove not only ink, but also residues of gum arabic, which tend to cause stripping of rollers. Properly used, these and other proprietary washup solutions are more efficient cleaners than petroleum solvents. They reduce makeready times, wasted paper, and wasted ink.

Lithographic Ink Problems

The most aggravating problems in lithography are often interaction problems, which arise when there is more than one deficiency among the paper, ink, press, and press operation factors. Consequently, adjusting the press may solve the problem temporarily, only to have it recur later or to have it pop up as a "different" problem.

Even if the ink is not the primary cause of the problem, making adjustments to the ink is usually more practical than changing the paper or changing the form to be printed. Thus, a picking problem caused primarily by too much or too little ink on a marginally suitable paper will often be treated by softening the ink rather than by changing the paper or reducing the solids in the print.

The greatest number of ink-related problems are probably due to (1) ink that is not suited to the paper and (2) excessive acidity or dampening. Excessive acidity and dampening destroy or reduce the drier in the ink, and excessive acidity causes tinting and plate blinding.

Ink in the Nonimage Area

Ink in the nonimage area involves a variety of problems, some of which are easily confused.

Dot growth, slur, and doubling increase the area of paper that is printed and, in the printing of process colors, change the color of the print. Except for dot growth resulting from applying too much ink or ink that is too soft, these are not normally considered to be ink problems.

Catch-up, tinting, toning, and scumming are ink/plate/dampening problems that are often correctable on the press. **Catch-up,** or **dry-up,** is the name applied to ink appearing in the nonimage area because of either (1) insufficient dampening of the printing plate or (2) an excessively thick ink film compared to the dampening level. **Tinting** or **toning** results from ink emulsified in the fountain solution, while **scumming** is a permanent image—usually spots—in the nonimage area. To distinguish toning, scumming, and catch-up, the wet-thumb test is useful. To perform the wet-thumb test, the press operator puts the press on safe, inserts a finger in dampening solution, and then rubs it across the nonimage area of the plate and observes how the ink behaves.

Scumming can arise from a number of sources, including the ink. Several possible causes can occur simultaneously. Scumming can be caused by film and film processing, plates and plate processing, dampening solution, lighting, press adjustment, paper, or ink.

Ink in the nonimage area

Problem	Cause	Wet-thumb Effect	Solution
Catch-up	Plate too dry	Removes ink	• Increase dampening
Scumming	Poor plate	Does not remove ink	• Increase dampening • Replace plate • Clean up plate
Toning	Emulsification of ink	Removes ink	• Decrease dampening • Avoid detergents • Change inks • Check roller pressure
Tinting	Plate/paper problem	Does not remove ink	• Decrease dampening • Change paper • Use better plates
Ink dot scum	Plate corrosion	Does not remove ink	• Dry plates rapidly

Ink can cause scumming for several reasons. Addition of oleic acid to the ink can create a scummy plate. Uncontrolled or unexpected changes in the pigment or the resin treatment can also cause printing problems. Improper grinding that leaves grit in the ink will accelerate wear of the plate and result in scumming and/or plate blinding.

Piling in Image Areas

Piling is the accumulation of ink pigment or coating from the paper onto the blanket or plate. The major cause of image area piling is the shortness of ink caused by emulsification with water and dilution with dust, pigment, or other debris from the paper.

As an ink becomes emulsified it becomes short. Poorly ground or gritty ink tends to be short. Addition of pigment or dust from the paper aggravates the problem. Water is mixed into the ink at the form rollers, while paper dust and debris may be added at the blanket, and it is at the blanket that piling becomes worst.

Along with ink and paper, the blanket plays an important role in piling. If the surface of the blanket is very smooth, it

Sources of piling

Ink

- Poor selection of varnish promotes emulsification.
- Poor grinding results in gritty pigment.
- Excessive tack picks or causes linting or dusting of paper.
- Improper formulation promotes emulsification.
- Loss of ink solvent increases tack.

Paper

- Dusty or linty paper adds solids to ink.
- Insufficient binder or insolubilization of binder increases paper coating in the ink.

Dampening Solution

- Detergent or soap promotes ink emulsification.
- Excessive gum makes blanket sticky, promoting linting or dusting.
- Alcohol promotes precipitation of gum.

Blanket Wash

- Excess detergent can work its way into dampening solution, emulsifying the ink.
- Aggressive solvent creates tacky blanket that attacks paper.

Blanket

- Tacky blanket pulls dust out of paper.
- Excessively smooth blanket pulls dust out of paper.

Press

- Increasing press speed increases force on paper surface.
- Increasing back cylinder squeeze increases dusting of paper.
- Reducing ink film thickness increases forces removing dust from paper.
- Heated roller system evaporates ink solvents, increasing ink tack.
- Low temperature increases tackiness of ink.

forms a tight bond with the paper, pulling dust and pigment from the surface. Changing to a rougher blanket may help, but addition of a nonpiling additive (a glycol or a wax emulsion) to the dampening solution will also improve blanket release and often solve the piling problem. Dampening solution additives should be purchased from printers' suppliers.

Piling in Nonimage Areas

Nonimage piling, dusting, or **milking,** appears as white specks that accumulate in the nonimage areas of the blanket and occurs when the paper surface or coating becomes dissolved in the dampening solution. Nonimage piling worsens as the sheet travels through the press.

Linting

Removal of lint from the surface of uncoated paper is generally considered to be a paper problem, but it can often be solved by manipulating the ink. Decreasing the ink tack and increasing the flow of dampening solution are two of the ways to reduce linting.

Trapping

Variations in trapping result in color variation in lithography. Causes of trapping problems when attempting to trap on wet ink are entirely different than those when attempting to trap on dry ink. **Wet trapping** is the ability of a wet ink film to accept another wet ink film printed over it, while **dry trapping** is the ability of a dry film to accept a wet film printed over it. Chapter 13 discusses the procedure for measuring trapping using overprints of magenta, cyan, and yellow.

Wet trap. To assure good wet trap, two things must be kept under control: ink tack and ink film thickness. GATF has always recommended that inks vary by one or two tack units on multiunit presses. A thin ink film will not trap properly over a thick ink film, so that even if ink tack is properly controlled, ink film thickness must still be controlled (forms with light ink coverage should be run before heavy forms, and the color strength of the ink must be controlled). The small amount of time that an ink sets on a sheet between printing units affects wet trap. Two ink films separated by another printing unit generally trap better than two directly in line.

Inkmakers often offer **unitack inks,** that is, process inks all of the same tack. These can be made to work satisfactorily if ink film thickness is properly controlled, but even better results are achieved if the recommended tack sequence is observed. The inkmaker can then help his customers by varying the pigmentation level of the ink so that the operator must use the proper ink film thickness on press.

Dry trap. Some inks, notably the quick-, hard-drying inks based on chinawood or tung oil, dry to form a hard, impervious surface; the process is commonly called **crystallization.** High drier content is also believed to promote crystallization. Addition of hard waxes (for example, carnauba wax), which give a scratch- and abrasion-resistant surface to the dried ink, also interferes with dry trapping; thus, the inkmaker usually avoids their use.

If excessive drier is added to the ink, the nondrying oil in which the drier is dissolved can rise to the surface and produce a nonimage area on the dried ink film, an area in which ink will not trap.

As with all ink-drying problems, dry-trap problems are more easily prevented than cured. Getting the right ink in the first place is the best prevention. Some inks trap better than others, and if the printer is faced with a dry-trap problem, the inkmaker should be consulted.

Hickeys

Hickeys (small solid areas, sharply defined and surrounded by white halos) are sometimes referred to as ink skin hickeys, but any source of dirt (the press, the pressroom, raw materials, crew) can cause hickeys. In addition to common sources of dirt, there are many unusual sources, and the solution to a hickey problem often involves a careful, lengthy search. Paint, spray powder, and other materials falling from the ceiling frequently cause hickeys.

Gloss Ghosting

Gloss ghosting is also referred to as fuming ghosting or chemical ghosting. It is the transfer of a printed image (but not by setoff) from the front of one sheet to the back of another, not through the sheet. This type of ghosting results from one printed ink film altering the drying of a printed ink film on the adjacent sheet in the pile. It can be seen on metal that is printed on two sides, but slipsheeting the pile eliminates it. The ghost image is always the image of the other side of the page. There are several theories concerning the cause of gloss ghosting; all are complex, all supported by good evidence. Gloss ghosting may, indeed, arise from several different causes. As with other ink-drying problems, it is easier to prevent than to cure.

Gloss ghosting does not occur frequently, but it can be very expensive. In fact, gloss ghosting is very difficult to create in the laboratory. Although ink is involved, ink alone cannot be the cause, because ghosting often appears on some but not all prints of the same job. Paper, printing sequence, design, and level of gloss are also involved in ghosting.

Gloss ghosting is most apt to arise in quick-turnaround, high-quality jobs, which may explain the apparent increase in its frequency in those cases. It is seen only on highly glossy jobs; the human eye does not detect small differences in gloss at low levels. Work at GATF and elsewhere shows that the sooner sheets are backed up after printing the first-down side, the more severe the ghosting. It is recommended that production personnel schedule at least 24 hours of drying before backing up jobs that appear to be troublesome. The printer's salespeople may not favor this approach, but it is far faster than reprinting the job.

Regardless of the mechanism of its origin, the cure and prevention of gloss ghosting are the same. First of all, the printer should have the inkmaker supply an ink suitable for the paper to be run, and the printer should carefully follow good pressroom procedures. If the heavier form is printed first, ghosting will be reduced or eliminated. The ghost of a large solid is not visible in lines and alphanumeric characters.

It has also been shown that adding cobalt drier aggravates gloss ghosting. Printers and inkmakers often add cobalt when the job must be rushed. There is no evidence that infrared heaters cause gloss ghosting, but they do make it possible to back the job up sooner as do quickset inks, which may contribute directly to gloss ghosting.

Although application of a varnish over a ghost usually does not make it disappear and often makes it worse, if five clear varnishes of widely differing bodies are applied to a sample of the ghost on the workbench, it is often found that one of them will mask or obliterate the ghost. This varnish is a good choice for overprinting the ghosted sheets.

If a suitable gloss varnish cannot be found, the technique of applying and drying a matte or nongloss varnish and then following that with a gloss varnish has been found to be successful in overcoming ghosting.

Mechanical Ghosting

Mechanical ghosting includes ink-starvation ghosting and "repeat" ghosting. The ghost image is always carried on the same side of the sheet. Mechanical ghosting results from inadequacies of the inking systems found in lithographic presses. Some forms are almost impossible to print on lithographic equipment, and salespeople should help customers avoid such artwork.

When ink is removed from a form roller by a heavy form on the printing plate, the ink is not completely replaced by the ink splitting between the ink form roller and the oscillating roller. Differences in ink film thickness on the roller result in differences in ink film thickness on the paper and cause color differences.

Emulsification of the ink with water is equivalent to printing a thinner film of ink, which aggravates ghosting. Using alcohol in the dampening solution is helpful.

Ghost areas that run around the cylinder can often be reduced by increasing the travel (or side-to-side motion) of the oscillating roller. If mechanical ghosting is caused by improper diameter of the form rollers, these should be replaced by rollers of the diameter specified by the press manufacturer. It goes without saying that a press with four or five form rollers is capable of better ink distribution than one with two or three. Some printing characteristics are already established when the press is purchased.

The following recommendations help overcome mechanical ghosting:

1. Use opaque inks whenever possible.
2. Run a thicker ink film and increase it to the maximum allowable density for acceptable printing.
3. Reduce ink strength and run more ink or change to a weaker ink. A high-solid ink with good transfer properties yields good results.
4. Print an oversized press sheet with heavy solids in trim areas to reduce ink on the form rollers where coverage is light.
5. Rotate the print or print on an angle.
6. Run with the minimum amount of fountain solution needed to keep the plates clean.
7. Increase the pitch of the vibrator rollers for maximum side-to-side movement.
8. Use a less absorptive paper with better ink holdout.
9. Check all ink rollers and blankets for glazing, durometer, and stripe setting.
10. Put areas of heavy ink coverage near the lead edge of the press sheet.
11. Use oscillating form rollers.

12. Use angled takeoff bars. They help break sharp lines.
13. Turn the form, and grip the opposite edge, if possible.
14. Reposition the elements within the form.
15. Underprint a screen in the heavy coverage areas.

To evaluate a press system for mechanical ghosting, printers can obtain a GATF Mechanical Ghosting Test Form. For information on this and other process control devices, contact the GATF Process Controls Group.

Mottle

Mottle is irregular and unwanted variation in color or gloss caused by the ink being unevenly absorbed into the paper. It is characterized by a blotchy, cloudy, or galvanized appearance instead of a smooth, continuous ink film on the press sheet. It can usually be overcome by increasing or decreasing the body of the ink so that all of the ink is held out by the sheet or so that all of it is absorbed by the sheet. It is only when the ink body is just right to show differences in sheet absorbency that mottle becomes a problem.

In general, the heavier the paper, the greater the variation in absorbency. Mottle is seldom found on uncoated book paper, only occasionally on cover stock, and frequently on carton board.

Variations in binder migration in paper coatings sometimes create mottle on coated papers. Like the ink, the binder detects differences in paper formation or absorbency and exaggerates small differences in the base stock.

Coatings

The common definition of coatings as a layer or a substance spread over a surface for protection or decoration or a covering layer and/or film encompasses all primers, lacquers, barrier coatings, and overprint varnishes. Primers are based on nitrocellulose, vinyls, shellac, acrylics, or other polymeric resins. Lacquers include formulations based on nitrocellulose, acrylics, and styrene. Varnishes are usually associated with oil-based oxidizable systems, but they also include coating systems that dry by evaporation. Thermoset and similar coatings are included under the broader category of catalytic coatings. Obviously, the range of coatings used by printers and converters covers a variety of chemical formulations defined by functional applications.

Overprint varnishes are high-viscosity, nonpigmented or clear inks that are applied over the surface to increase gloss or protect the print. The ideal overprint varnish is colorless and transparent, yielding good gloss and scuff resistance when dry. Overprint varnishes also must be stable on the press, dry rapidly, and adhere well to the print. An overprint varnish contains the following materials:

- Varnish: linseed, tung oil alkyd, phenolic resin
- Drier: cobalt and manganese
- Modifier: wax
- Other: sometimes clay for viscosity control

Coating coalescence

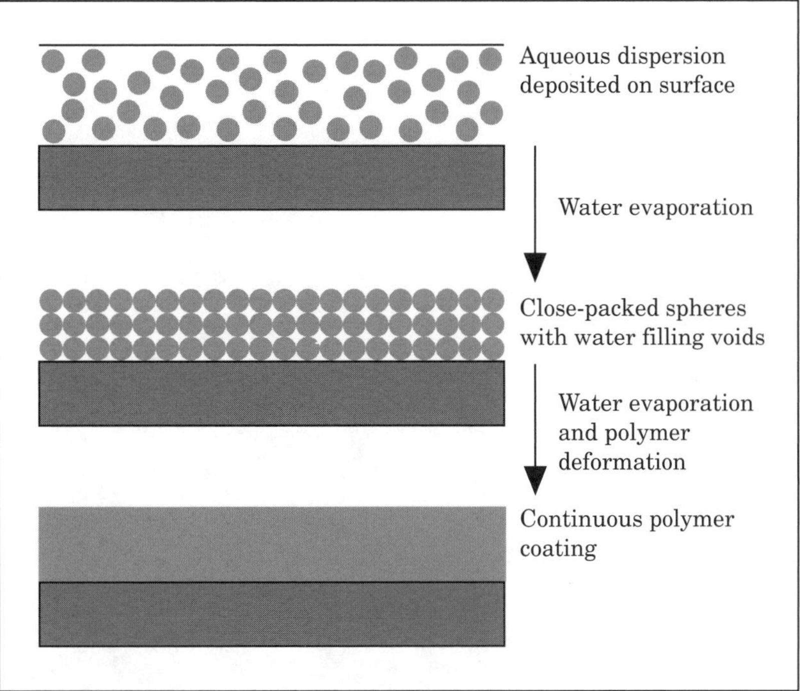

Varnishes, aqueous coatings, and ultraviolet (UV) coatings can be applied in line on sheetfed presses. Printers can choose to retrofit their presses and coat in line with blanket, plate, or end-of-press coaters, or they can purchase new presses that have dedicated coating units. The advantages of a dedicated coating unit are that the printer does not lose a print station to the coating system and the printer has more control of the weight of the coating and the quality of it.

Blanket coaters can use either a two-roll or three-roll transfer from the fountain to the blanket. Blanket coaters offer the following advantages:

- Coating is split once before being applied
- Very little time is taken to switch from print-to-coat and from coat-to-print because the coater is not connected to any of the other press functions

- Variable gap adjustment and roller speed direction, which allows control of coating weight

One drawback of blanket coaters is that they cannot be fitted to presses with common-impression cylinders because of their bulkiness. Another drawback is, of course, the loss of a print station while coating.

Blanket coater

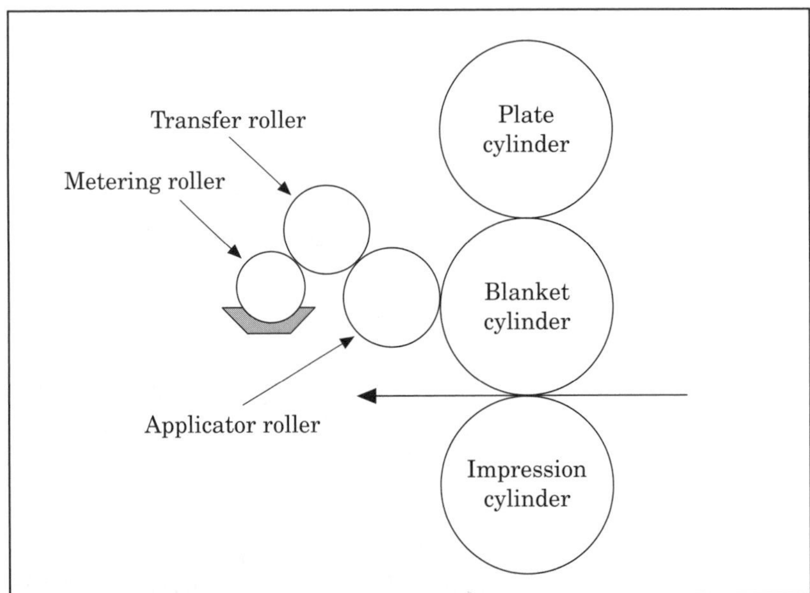

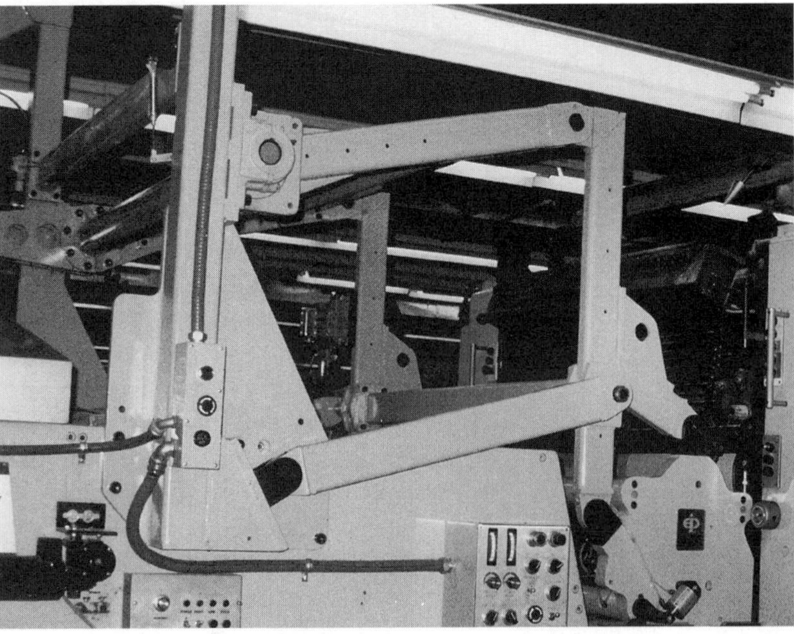

A retractable in-line blanket coater, which applies a continuous, uniform metered film of aqueous or UV coating directly to the blanket cylinder
Courtesy Epic Products International Corp.

Plate coaters feature a modified dampener system that will coat through the press's existing dampening system. Unfortunately this kind of coating system has more drawbacks than advantages:

- In comparison to the blanket coater, it takes longer to change over from print-to-coat and coat-to-print because the fountain must be cleaned
- As with the blanket coater, a print station is lost when the plate coater is in operation
- Coating weight can only be controlled by varying viscosity or coating gap, or adjusting the pan roller
- The secondary split between the plate and blanket before the coating is applied to the substrate decreases the amount of coating that can be applied

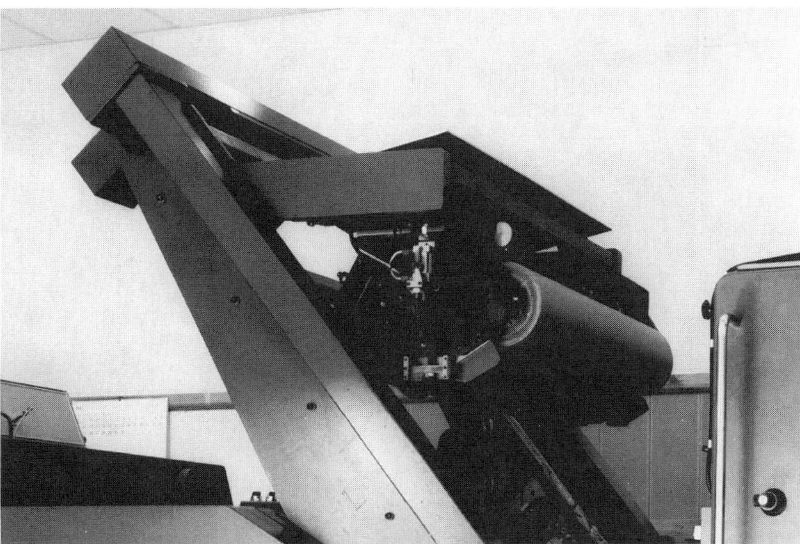

Super Blue® plate/blanket coater *Courtesy Printing Research, Inc.*

With end-of-press coaters, sheets pass from the press delivery grippers onto a vacuum-controlled conveyor and then into the coating nip of a three-roll coater. The advantages of an end-of-press coating system are the following:

- Variable roller speeds and gap adjustments, which allow complete control of coating weight
- Coating is not split before it is applied
- It does not require a dedicated print station, which is particularly advantageous for four-color presswork

Some of the disadvantages of this system are the fact that it is gripperless and can only run limited types of substrates, and its inability to produce a pattern coating.

11 Premakeready

Premakeready encompasses more than just those procedures that are performed to shorten makeready time and prevent downtime on the press. It also includes seemingly unrelated tasks that contribute to a press crew's productivity. Layout, tools, materials, teamwork, training, and inking and dampening system washup are the principal features of premakeready.

Printing Plant Layout

The layout of the printing plant, although apparently not related to premakeready, helps to reduce downtime and increases efficiency.

Space Allocation

When a printing plant is constructed or remodeled, several layout problems challenge management. Every operational station, including printing presses, must be properly positioned in the plant, with its location determined by its position in the sequence of normal operations. Each operational area must be allocated the proper amount of space, depending on the size of the equipment, the work area needed, and the amount of supplies stored in the area.

The space provided for a press depends on the type of press, the type of work to be printed, the pressroom turnover, the amount of paper that must be stored near the press, and several other factors.

Accessibility of Tools

Convenience is an important consideration in laying out a pressroom. Each press station should have a complete set of small tools, instruments, parts, and supplies that are not shared with any other station. Although sharing expensive items that are only used occasionally is practical, small often-used tools must be within easy reach. Operators should never have to walk two or three stations away to obtain the necessary tool.

Floor Layout and Aisles

Aisles between presses must be wide enough to permit a fork-lift truck to move paper from the storeroom to the feeder section of the press, and to move printed paper from the delivery to the bindery or shipping dock if it is going to an outside bindery.

Floor space is expensive and must be used efficiently. The access requirements, including room for efficient truck operation, and the floor load rating, which is stated in pounds per square foot (or metric units), should also be considered when allotting floor space.

Using a standard, single-size paper pallet permits the standardization of material handling equipment and makes better use of floor space. Safety and efficient stock retrieval are two other considerations in plant layout. Once available storage spaces and aisles have been determined, a good, long-wearing paint or tape should be used to clearly mark these areas. Trucks should be confined to aisles that are wide enough for maneuvering. Well-defined aisles and storage spaces make housekeeping easier.

Tools

Tools and measuring instruments that are needed for the next pressrun should be gathered while the present pressrun is still in progress, *not* during makeready. Often, crew members are idle at certain points during a pressrun. When not needed at the press, they can start gathering the tools and materials for the next job. This decreases downtime during makeready.

The numerous tools and measuring instruments required for makeready should be stored near the press. Some of the more important ones are listed below:

- Torque wrench, for tightening the blanket
- Assorted wrenches, for making press adjustments
- Deadweight micrometer, for measuring packing, plates, and blankets
- Packing gauge, for measuring plate and blanket heights on the press
- Magnifiers, for checking dot structure
- Densitometer, for measuring the density of the ink

During premakeready, the packing, plates, and blankets can be measured with the deadweight micrometer.

Materials

Stock Control

If stock control is poor or if the purchasing procedure is poor, the pressroom may run out of many small items from time to time. Each time, however, the press sits idle. Unfortunately, these missing items are not discovered until makeready, and an hour or two of press time is lost. As a consequence, the schedule is upset and overtime is necessary to get back on schedule.

Paper

Paper handling plays an important role in reducing press downtime. Preconditioning paper to the conditions in the pressroom is a part of premakeready.

Paper must arrive in the pressroom early enough to become temperature-conditioned. The press crew should not have to try out a pile of paper on the press to find out if it works. On multicolor or close-register jobs, the crew can spend hours of makeready time trying to get a poor sheet to fit. This generally happens when the paper goes through the press the second time, and the first-down color has fanned out across the back. It is too late to do anything about the paper then.

The moisture content of paper can be tested with a sword hygroscope. The pressroom should be air-conditioned, and its relative humidity controlled.

The paper must be inspected and tested before makeready begins. Wavy-edged paper can be detected as soon as the skid is unwrapped. The pH of the coating could be measured. The straightness of the gripper edge should be checked, and the gripper edge and guide edge should be checked to make sure that they are square to each other.

Inks

There is no economy in purchasing inexpensive inks if they cause problems on the press. An ink that lacks color strength has to be printed in such a thick ink film that dampening and plate problems occur. Inks should be tested, adjusted, and color-matched long before makeready time.

Blankets, Dampeners, and Rollers

Spare blankets, dampeners, and at least one spare roller set should be on hand at the press at all times. The spare blankets should be prepunched, if needed, and premounted in bars. The spare dampeners should be washed or re-covered; i.e., press-ready. The condition of press rollers should be monitored continually.

The way blankets are handled has a marked effect on press downtime. Blankets should be alternated so that one can rest while another is used. When a bad smash occurs, it is easier and faster to replace the blanket than to repair it. A moderately smashed blanket can usually be salvaged by soaking the fabric side of the blanket in water for several hours or days.

Blankets must be cleaned and deglazed every time they are removed from the press. Only the washup solution recommended by the blanket manufacturer should be used to ensure chemical compatibility and blanket longevity.

Packing

Packing sheets should be hard, smooth, water-resistant, easy-handling, and cut to the size of the plate. They should be kept separate according to caliper (thickness); a separate shelf for each thickness is desirable. If the press crew has to look around the pressroom for packing sheets, determine their caliper, and cut them to size while the press waits, makereadies will be very costly.

Soft, limp papers should not to be used. They contain so much air that accurate packing is impossible because the sheets compress excessively. Only specially produced packing sheets or Mylar®-like (polyester) plastics should be used to pack plate cylinders, and only the specially produced packing sheets should be used to pack blanket cylinders.

Material Testing and Reporting

The practice of material testing and reporting is not as far removed from premakeready as it may appear. For example, a plate that performs poorly during the start of a job can cause considerable press downtime.

Manufacturers test materials, but press operators must also test these products to determine if they perform in accordance with their own standards. A product may work fine in plant A but fail miserably the first time it is tried in plant B. The personnel in plant B may have to reuse the product several times to find out why it failed. This type of problem occurred when paper dampener covers were introduced and when presensitized plates were introduced. This problem probably occurs, to varying degrees, whenever a new product is introduced.

When something is new, it is usually different in some way and probably requires a change in handling technique. Therefore, a period of training, learning, and experimenting is needed. However, retraining or experimenting should not be done on production jobs.

Many large plants have established quality control laboratories for testing incoming inks, paper, and other materials. Quality control personnel also monitor jobs in progress, the performance of new materials, and the performance of equipment. Sometimes, small presses have been installed in the laboratory for testing, because even a small offset press can yield valuable product-performance information.

Pretesting as a part of premakeready. The pretesting of new materials is recommended. Any pretesting of materials constitutes premakeready because of the potential reduction of press downtime. Pretesting, whether performed on a small press or by some other means, provides information about the performance of plates, paper, ink, blankets, blanket cleaners, washup materials, and various other printing materials. All testing and experimenting should be done where and when it is inexpensive, which means that production should not be interrupted.

Controlling the quality of materials. GATF's Technical Services Report 7227, *Controlling the Quality of Pressroom Materials,* gives printers a variety of recommendations on how to reduce variation and defects in purchased materials by controlling plate, blankets, rollers, paper, ink, solvents, and lubricants. Control must be exercised in selection and purchase; receiving, handling, and inspection; proper storage; and proper use, including an accurate record of performance. The real differences between a testing laboratory and a production floor atmosphere must be recognized.

According to the Technical Services Report, there are five basics of quality control for management:

- **Standardization.** Management should standardize on a few suppliers and select materials on the basis of performance, delivery, and cost.
- **Specifications.** Specifications should be established for materials before an order is placed, and these specifications must be communicated to the supplier.
- **Inspection.** Inspection of incoming materials for verification of size, quantity, and/or weight and the detection of external damage is necessary. Some inspecting and testing are performed in the pressroom.

- **Proper handling and storage.** A first-in, first-out inventory system should be used to prevent newer materials from being used before older, dated material such as inks and plates. Remember also that careless handling ruins materials.
- **Recordkeeping.** Records should be kept on the conditions and performance of materials. This is essential in providing feedback to suppliers. Records not only help the printer confirm the existence of defects and deviations from specifications but also help the supplier resolve problems in the manufacture of the material.

Inking and Dampening System Washup

The washup belongs to and is charged to the job that the press was producing. But a *good* washup is considered a part of premakeready. A poor washup causes glazed rollers and other printing problems. A poor washup can mean that a makeready has to be stopped just to wash up a press unit again.

Rollers do not transfer ink properly if they are glazed. Controlling inking and dampening is troublesome. Obtaining a quality OK sheet is difficult—and maintaining the quality is even harder.

A good method of washup keeps rollers in a like new condition for a long time. A good washup is also a clean washup, so that fresh color will not be contaminated by old ink left on the rollers. Fortunately, on four-color presses, there is seldom a change in color on any one unit, but that is no reason to get careless with washups.

A good washup not only lessens the buildup of glaze on rollers but also prevents hickeys caused by dried ink particles. These particles come from the ink fountain, roller ends where dried ink has built up, and small cracks in a glazed roller's surface. Good washup techniques eliminate most hickey problems of this type.

The same general idea holds for the dampening system. It is easier, safer, and less time-consuming to keep the dampening system in good order than to wait until a problem occurs.

Teamwork

The operative word in the term "press crew" is "crew." Like the pit crew in racing, each member of a press crew should have certain clearly defined responsibilities and the necessary training to perform these responsibilities efficiently and effectively.

Downtime is reduced if each crew member is assigned specific duties. They must know exactly what to do, how to do it, and, just as importantly, when to do it. Any duties that can be performed during running time should be done then. These duties then become a part of premakeready.

Such duties as policing the workstation, getting supplies, and replenishing all receptacles are important but are not done during the time periods reserved for makeready or washup. Putting away makeready and washup equipment and supplies is most efficiently performed during running time. Preparing new blankets, checking stock, transporting stock to the pressroom, adjusting ink, mixing dampening solution, cleaning platforms, and reracking tools are only a few of the things that can be done while the press is running. The greater the number of duties that are performed while the press is running, the more systematic the washup and makeready are.

Training

Press crew training is a part of premakeready. Print quality is a function of the overall quality of the press crew; it is no better than that of the poorest trained crew member. Each crew member must become thoroughly familiar with his or her specific duties and the proper timing for these duties.

Any method of handling a press crew so that the crew works efficiently is a good method. The head press operator should assign specific duties and responsibilities to each crew member in writing. In addition, the head press operator specifies when to perform each duty. Thus, each press crew member is aware of the "what" and "when" of efficient press operation.

New crew members may have learned press operating in school or on a small offset press. However, they cannot be expected to function smoothly immediately upon becoming part of a crew for a large sheetfed offset press. Each crew member below the rating of first press operator can be considered as a person in training, with the head press operator functioning as an instructor. The head press operator does not have to be responsible for all instruction but must supervise. The second person in command learns from the head press operator and teaches the third in command. In turn, the third in command instructs the person in the fourth position, and so on until all crew members are trained in performing their duties. In other words, each crew member is coached by the person immediately superior. (As technology advances, crew size is becoming smaller. For example, on a high-tech 40-in. six-color sheetfed press, the crew size is only two people.)

New crew members are encouraged to read the press operating manual. It is also beneficial for new crew members to attend in-plant or school training courses. Reading articles in trade magazines and books on press operating helps to prepare the individual for the next job position. Learning about ink, paper, plates, and other materials makes the crew member a better problem-solver, if and when a problem occurs on press.

Scheduling

Proper scheduling of jobs is an important factor in plant efficiency. Without proper scheduling, time is lost all through the plant, but especially in the high hourly-rate pressroom.

The schedule should start in the control office and carry right through to shipping. Every department then knows what is coming, when it will arrive, and when it should be completed.

Most important of all, proper scheduling ensures the procurement of paper and ink for each job in time for the press to be made ready. It ensures ample time for paper inspection, cutting, and conditioning. It provides time for ink matching and testing and for arrival at the plant. It ensures that all plates will be ready when needed. Proper scheduling may even eliminate some press washups if the press operators know which ink is to be used on the next printing job.

The time to think about the next job is while the press is running for the current one. The head press operator or a designated crew member should check the next job and find out the following:

- What the job order says
- What the next job number is
- If the plates are ready
- If the paper has been conditioned and piled
- If the ink is ready to be used
- If there are any waste sheets that can be used to set up the press.
- If there is a spare blanket available and ready to use
- If the packing supply is sufficient to pack the press for the next job

Summary

Work smarter, not harder. Premakeready operations reduce downtime. Practically all preparatory steps taken in the pressroom help to reduce downtime if the press is running. These include getting all supplies from the storeroom and replenishing workstation cabinets, taking care of waste sheets that can be used on future jobs, and checking tools and equipment that will be used on the next washup and makeready.

With a little thought, the head press operator can make a list that includes many more things than those that have been mentioned here. Everything from the finishing of one job to obtaining an OK on the next job should be listed. The list can be enlarged to include all pressroom work. It may take a week or two and the cooperation of the press crew to get a complete list, but once the list is prepared, it is a great help in writing job descriptions, assigning duties to the crew, arranging a training program, and separating makeready steps from premakeready operations.

12 Makeready

Makeready is the series of operations that changes the press over from the end of one job to the start of the next one. Makeready ends when acceptable press sheets enter the delivery of the sheetfed press.

The press crew's responsibilities during makeready differ from plant to plant. Efficient makeready requires that materials for the next job are already on hand when the previous job ends. Following a premakeready program, as described in Chapter 11, is the only way this can occur.

Good preparation for makeready means having all necessary materials at the printing units at the time they are needed. Plates should be ready, blankets laid out and ready to go on the press (if needed), and packing cut and ready to go under the blankets. Paper, ink, and dampening solution should be ready. If a need for a color change arises, washup materials should be waiting at the press.

The key to efficient makeready is a press crew that knows its job and works together as a team. Each member of the crew should be fully occupied during makeready. Responsibility for this rests with the head press operator, who must know how to organize and supervise the crew. Each member of a well-organized crew should know what to do and when to do it. For example, two persons might work as a team in changing plates and blankets, a procedure made even more efficient if another crew member can hand the plates, blankets, and packing to the two persons working in the unit.

What Is Makeready?

Makeready is a term describing all of the operations necessary to get the press ready for the present job. Once acceptable printed sheets are being produced, makeready ends. During this period, paper is being "wasted" out of necessity. Therefore, waste can be minimized by completing the press makeready as quickly as possible. During makeready, the press is operated at a preset speed; for example, 6,000 iph. When the actual pressrun starts, the speed is increased to the press's maximum running speed.

Types of Makeready

Makeready can be divided into three categories: simple makeready, partial makeready, and full makeready.

Simple makeready occurs most often when printing books or forms on a single-color press. It consists of just a plate change. Other variables such as the ink, ink fountain settings, dampening system settings, and type and size of paper are unchanged.

Partial makeready occurs on single- and two-color presses that are printing four-color work. After the first two colors are printed, the press is stopped, and inking systems are cleaned. New plates are installed; blankets and packing may or may not be changed. The delivery is unloaded and the feeder is loaded, but feeder, guide, or delivery settings are not changed. The inking system is washed up, and the ink fountain is refilled and reset for the new color.

The most common type of makeready is the full makeready, which consists of all steps necessary to start an entirely new job. On single- and two-color presses, the entire press is washed up; a washup of the inking system on a four-color press is usually unnecessary if the same four inks will be used in the same color sequence. (A press/inking system washup is usually chargeable to the previous job.) Plates and packing are changed, and blankets are washed. Feeder, guide, and delivery settings are usually changed. The feeder is reloaded, and the delivery is emptied.

Makeready Procedures

The order in which a makeready progresses is largely dependent on the press crew's preferences. However, developing and following an established makeready procedure is strongly advised. In any analysis of pressrun time versus downtime (makeready, scheduled preventive maintenance, and unscheduled delays), the productivity of the press can be improved only if press downtimes are shortened; pressrun time cannot be shortened if the press is already operating at the maximum speed that produces prints of the desired quality. Therefore, better planning, improved preventive maintenance, precise control of all prepress operations, and coordinated use of the press crew reduce press downtime and improve productivity.

Of the four methods for reducing downtime, only better planning and coordinated use of the press crew are controlled by the press crew. This is where the "pit stop" concept of makeready comes into focus—like the pit crew for a racing car, the operating crew of a press must be prepared to service the machine as quickly and efficiently as possible. In the first case, the improved efficiency gets the racing car back on the track quicker; in the second case, it gets the press operating at full speed quicker. With the "pit stop" concept of press makeready, each crew member has specific, clearly identified responsibilities.

Makeready consists of the following steps:

1. Prepare the press for the new pressrun.
2. Check copy, plates, paper, and ink against instructions.
3. Set sheet-handling mechanisms.
4. Pack and mount the plates.
5. Check and prepare new blankets (if necessary).
6. Prepare the dampening system.
7. Prepare the inking system.
8. Prepare the makeready "books" for printing.
9. Make trial impressions.
10. Examine the trial impressions.
11. Make necessary adjustments to image position/register, impression quality, and color.
12. Obtain a color and position OK.

Steps 9–11 are repeated until a press sheet that is acceptable to the customer is produced. This press sheet is usually called the **okay,** or **OK, sheet.**

Many of the procedures followed during makeready are covered in detail in earlier chapters of this book.

Preparing the Press for the New Pressrun

Before makeready begins, the press is prepared for the new pressrun. The paper from the previous job is removed from the delivery, and plates are removed and stored for possible reuse. Damaged blankets are also removed. If there are any color changes, the inking system is also washed up. The dampening system may also have to be cleaned.

Inking system washup. The first step in cleaning the inking system is to remove all unused ink from the ink fountain. The press operator uses an ink knife to carefully remove the ink from the fountain. The unused ink is returned to the can. However, any ink that has been in the fountain for several hours should be discarded. **Note:** Use a *plastic* knife, instead

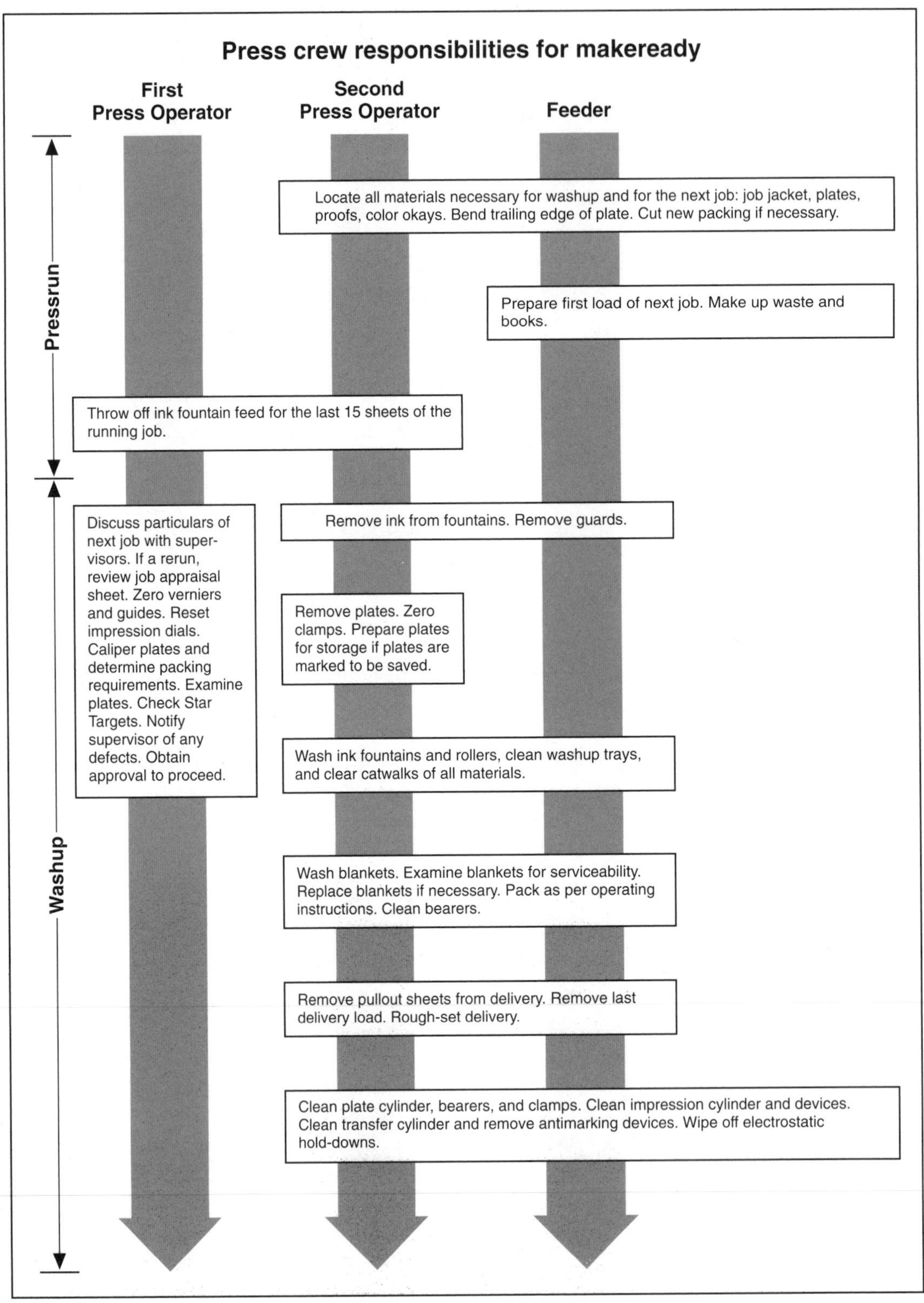
Press crew responsibilities for makeready
First Press Operator
Second Press Operator
Feeder
Pressrun
Washup
Locate all materials necessary for washup and for the next job: job jacket, plates, proofs, color okays. Bend trailing edge of plate. Cut new packing if necessary.
Prepare first load of next job. Make up waste and books.
Throw off ink fountain feed for the last 15 sheets of the running job.
Discuss particulars of next job with supervisors. If a rerun, review job appraisal sheet. Zero verniers and guides. Reset impression dials. Caliper plates and determine packing requirements. Examine plates. Check Star Targets. Notify supervisor of any defects. Obtain approval to proceed.
Remove ink from fountains. Remove guards.
Remove plates. Zero clamps. Prepare plates for storage if plates are marked to be saved.
Wash ink fountains and rollers, clean washup trays, and clear catwalks of all materials.
Wash blankets. Examine blankets for serviceability. Replace blankets if necessary. Pack as per operating instructions. Clean bearers.
Remove pullout sheets from delivery. Remove last delivery load. Rough-set delivery.
Clean plate cylinder, bearers, and clamps. Clean impression cylinder and devices. Clean transfer cylinder and remove antimarking devices. Wipe off electrostatic hold-downs.

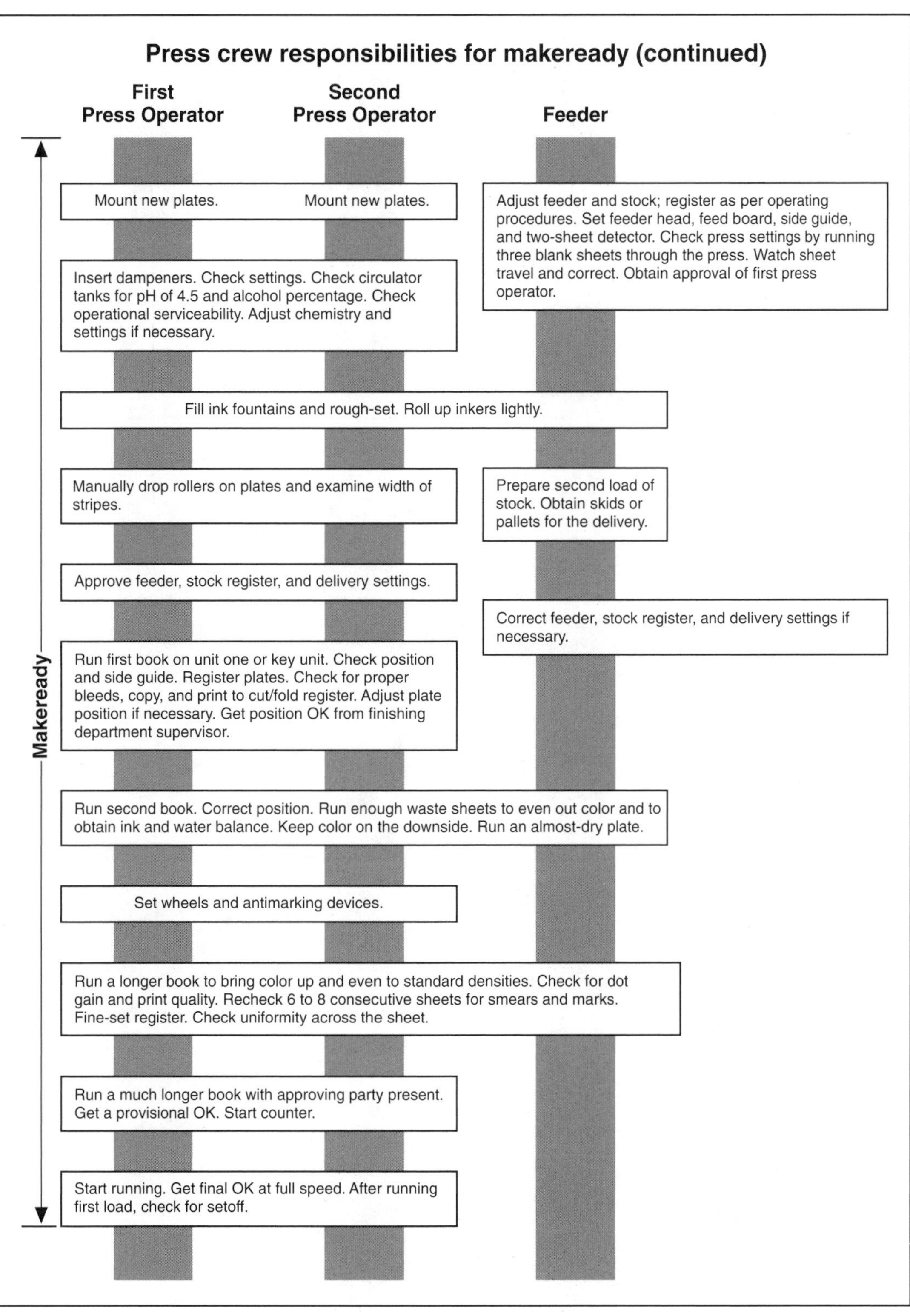
Press crew responsibilities for makeready (continued)
First Press Operator
Second Press Operator
Feeder
Makeready
Mount new plates.
Mount new plates.
Adjust feeder and stock; register as per operating procedures. Set feeder head, feed board, side guide, and two-sheet detector. Check press settings by running three blank sheets through the press. Watch sheet travel and correct. Obtain approval of first press operator.
Insert dampeners. Check settings. Check circulator tanks for pH of 4.5 and alcohol percentage. Check operational serviceability. Adjust chemistry and settings if necessary.
Fill ink fountains and rough-set. Roll up inkers lightly.
Manually drop rollers on plates and examine width of stripes.
Prepare second load of stock. Obtain skids or pallets for the delivery.
Approve feeder, stock register, and delivery settings.
Correct feeder, stock register, and delivery settings if necessary.
Run first book on unit one or key unit. Check position and side guide. Register plates. Check for proper bleeds, copy, and print to cut/fold register. Adjust plate position if necessary. Get position OK from finishing department supervisor.
Run second book. Correct position. Run enough waste sheets to even out color and to obtain ink and water balance. Keep color on the downside. Run an almost-dry plate.
Set wheels and antimarking devices.
Run a longer book to bring color up and even to standard densities. Check for dot gain and print quality. Recheck 6 to 8 consecutive sheets for smears and marks. Fine-set register. Check uniformity across the sheet.
Run a much longer book with approving party present. Get a provisional OK. Start counter.
Start running. Get final OK at full speed. After running first load, check for setoff.

Press operator using an ink knife to remove the ink from the ink fountain

Unused ink being returned to the ink can

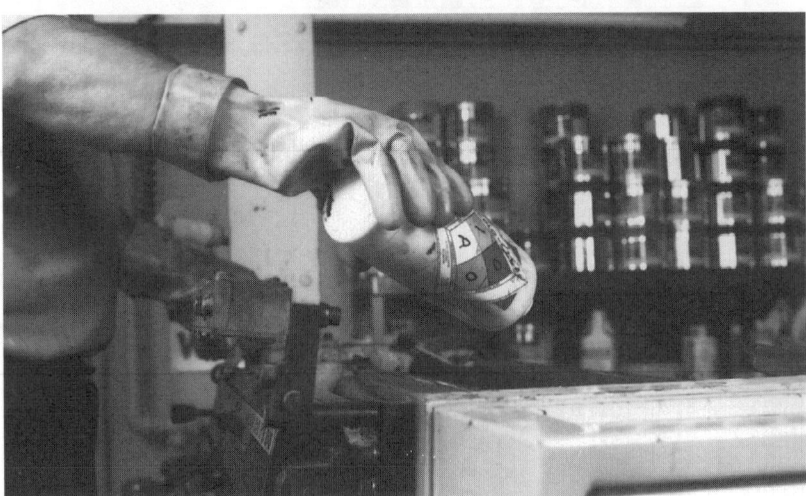

Press operator squirting washup solvent on the surface of the ink fountain roller

of a *metal* knife, when removing ink from the fountain of an automated inking system.

A washup machine is the quickest method of removing ink from the roller train. It consists of an adjustable scraper blade and a drip pan or trough, used in conjunction with approved commercial solvents. Read the manufacturer's guide carefully and follow cleanup and safety instructions in order to assure the best results when using a washup machine.

Routine washups usually involve a two-step solution. The first solvent is water-miscible and removes contaminants, gum, and alcohol substitutes; the second solvent flushes away the first solvent, leaving the rollers with no solvent residue. Special attention should be given to roller ends, where ink builds up and cakes during running. **Caution:** *Do not clean roller ends or any part of the inking system by hand while the press is running.* A good reconditioning washup will make it possible to change from black to yellow with no problem of residual color. The roller manufacturer can recommend suitable two-step washup solutions. Make sure the manufacturer supplies a Material Safety Data Sheet (MSDS) with each chemical solution purchased; an MSDS provides detailed information on use, handling, and storage of chemicals.

Although the actual solvents vary, two-step washup solutions perform the same functions. One solution cuts the dried ink and liquefies the wet ink, causing pigment particles to dissolve. These particles are carried down through the rollers to the washup machine. Water is then used to remove dried gum. Between each step, or in a separate final step, the inking system is rinsed to remove all traces of these solutions.

The solvents in a two-step washup solution must be used in their correct order because they are designed to work in a specific sequence. Never substitute solvents when using a two-step washup solution.

To remove ink, the press operator attaches a washup machine to the press. After use, the blade and pan of the washup machine are thoroughly cleaned. A washup machine does a thorough job of cleaning the rollers, but the press operator must learn the difference between rollers that look clean and rollers that are clean. The following is a basic procedure for using a press washup attachment:

1. Gum and dry the plate to protect it against stray drips.
2. Turn the press on and run it at medium speed, usually about 6,000–7,000 i.p.h. on newer presses.

3. Thoroughly wet the rollers away from the washup blade with solvent to soften the ink.
4. Allow the press to idle for a couple of minutes, and then gently engage the washup blade to the oscillator roller, increasing pressure until contact is achieved.
5. Add solvent to one side of the ink system at a time, being careful not to allow the washup blade on the other side to become too dry. In this way, roller skidding, drips, and excessive buildup of ink at roller ends are avoided.
6. Apply solvent with a squirt bottle to various points of the roller system away from the washup blade. To avoid waste and drips, do not apply more solvent than can be held at the nips of the rollers.
7. Continue applying solvent periodically until the fluid running into the drip tray appears clear, and the rollers are clean. **Note:** Never run a finger or a rag across the edge of the washup blade while it is working.
8. Apply a water-miscible solution to the rollers as a final flushing of the rollers.
9. When the rollers are satisfactorily clean, release the washup blade while the press is still operating. Occasionally, if the washup blade is released on the run, a buildup of ink behind the blade will run back into the rollers, meaning that they have to be washed again.
10. To evaluate the thoroughness of the washup, stop the press, put the safety on, and then rub cheesecloth across the rollers. Any residue remaining on the rollers will be easily seen on the cheesecloth.

On most presses, at one end of the ink fountain is a throw-off handle that raises the fountain roller away from the blade (or drops the fountain and blade away from the roller) and holds them apart for easy cleaning. A rag soaked with solvent is used to remove the remaining ink in the fountain. All parts of the fountain coming into contact with the ink should be thoroughly cleaned. A good washup routine includes cleaning the edge and as much of the underside of the blade as can be reached.

The copperizing of steel inking rollers on older presses is often made part of the reconditioning washup. Copperizing solutions deposit a thin layer of copper on the roller and make the roller more resistant to stripping. Copperizing requires that the roller be very clean, so the most appropriate time to do it is during the reconditioning washup. The surface of metal rollers on most new presses have a “Rilsan” (nylon 11) plastic coating that helps to reduce roller stripping and eliminates the need to copperize the rollers.

The durometer of rollers should be checked regularly (once a month). The information is used to determine whether the rollers need to be reconditioned or replaced. If the maximum recommended durometer has been exceeded (usually about 10 durometer points above the new roller durometer), the roller should be removed from the press and placed into a reconditioning wash. If the roller still exceeds the maximum, it should be reground or re-covered. A quick way to check the condition of a roller is to drag a finger across the surface of the roller (with the press stopped and on safe). If the nap of the roller moves (that is, the surface feels velvety), the roller should work satisfactorily in the press. If the nap no longer moves, due to a buildup of glaze, the roller should be removed and deglazed.

Cleaning the dampening system. Ordinarily, ink solvents are not used to clean the dampening system, though they can be used to clean some types of paper coverings. Cloth covers, which retain ink solvents, should only be cleaned with suitable detergents, then thoroughly rinsed.

Changing cloth covers is so time-consuming that the crew should have an extra set ready to go on the press at all times. The dirty rollers can be cleaned and changed during the pressrun. Cloth covers must be carefully mounted. The cover should be uniformly tight along the roller length, and there should be equal amounts of overhang at each end. When tied, the ends should be flat—not rounded off.

Whenever a roller is removed from the press, it should be reinstalled with the ends in the same direction. Reversing the ends of the roller causes a paper sleeve or cloth cover to creep.

Regardless of the type of cover used, changing dampener covers changes the running diameter of the rollers. Consequently, roller settings should be rechecked and adjustments made where necessary.

Preparing plates for storage. With some types of plates, any press shutdown longer than a few minutes requires that the plates be gummed. (In this section, the term "gum" refers to the finisher that is part of the plate chemistry, which may or may not be gum arabic.) The plate manufacturer can recommend suitable materials for cleaning and preserving the plate. Only use the finisher recommended by the plate manufacturer. Asphaltum-gum etch (AGE), for example, could cause gum blinding in the image areas of certain plates.

A thin coating of the finisher ("gum") designed for the printing plate being used prevents the surface of the plate from oxidizing, which can lead to scumming. A gummed plate generally starts up more rapidly than an untreated plate. Gumming a plate for storage while it is still mounted on the plate cylinder is difficult because of the restricted work space on most presses. By giving the mounted plate a quick gumming, the press crew can finish gumming the plate later (e.g., during the next pressrun) by placing the plate on a large worktable.

Usually, the press-mounted plate is first wiped with a sponge that has been dampened with gum in a water solution. The entire surface of the plate should then be rubbed down evenly with a soft, damp cloth. When the gum is applied in reasonable amounts, it does not cover the greasy image areas of the plate still carrying ink. When overapplied, the gum adheres to image areas in such a thick coating that it becomes impervious to solvent and causes gum blinding.

Once the gum has dried into a thin, even film, the plate is wiped with a solvent to remove ink from image areas and is covered with paper to protect it from scratches.

Checking Instructions

The copy, plates, paper, and ink are checked against the instructions written on the work order. Any differences must be immediately brought to the attention of the pressroom supervisor. Usually, the instructions should be checked before the previous pressrun ends as part of the premakeready procedure.

Setting Sheet-Handling Mechanisms

Setting the sheet-handling mechanisms is a time-consuming operation. If paper size and thickness have changed, practically all settings are adjusted. The nature of the work also influences the adjustments required. Chapter 5, "Sheet Control," discusses these adjustments in detail. Some newer presses have devices that automatically adjust the sheet-handling mechanisms when paper stock is changed.

The following sequence is representative of the steps involved in manually setting the sheet-handling mechanisms on a press when paper stock has changed:

1. Position the pile table and load paper stock onto the press.

2. Adjust the various components of the sheet-separation unit: pile height regulator, sheet steadiers, separator brushes and fingers, rear pickup suckers, forwarding suckers, and air-blast nozzles.
3. Adjust the various components of the feedboard: forwarding rollers, double-sheet detector, feedboard devices that transport the sheets to the front guides (e.g., hold-down rollers, feed tapes, and brushes), suction devices, and early and late sheet detectors.
4. Adjust front guides and side guides.
5. Set the infeed grippers and impression-cylinder stops. If necessary, compensate for fan-out of images on the press sheet by following the recommendations of the press manufacturer.
6. Set the impression cylinder pressure relative to the stock thickness.
7. Feed a sheet through the press and set the sheet joggers, delivery-assist devices (sheet slow-downs), and gripper release timing.

These steps are repeated until the sheet passes through the press smoothly. Additional minor adjustments to the side guide and feeder pile position are necessary to get image register, which occurs later.

Installing the Plate

Procedures used to mount the plates vary considerably, depending on the size of the press crew and whether the press is equipped with automatic or semiautomatic plate mounting attachments. In many cases, one crew member hands plates to another who is stationed between printing units mounting them. No matter which procedure is used, all members of the crew must know how to safely use the **inch** controls of the press.

The basic operations (most of which are discussed in detail in Chapter 8, "Plates") are as follows:

1. Check work order for the proper plates to be mounted.
2. Inspect the plate for quality and proper copy.
3. Measure the plate caliper (or thickness) with a micrometer, determine packing requirements, and prepare the packing. (If a print length adjustment is needed, make the required compensation in packing. Chapter 6, "Packing and Printing Pressures," discusses print length.)
4. Check that the plate cylinder and the back of the plate are clean. Adjust the plate cylinder and plate clamps to their starting or zero positions.

5. Mount plate and packing on the press, following the procedure in Chapter 8.

These three things must be remembered when mounting plates: (1) insert the correct packing, (2) make sure that the tension on all screws is set uniformly and that the plate conforms to the cylinder, and (3) align the plate with any preregister marks and gauges.

Occasionally, it is necessary to reposition a mounted plate to a predetermined position by twisting or cocking it. If the printed image is not exactly square in relation to the paper or previously printed colors, the plate must be repositioned. It is always better to reposition the plate than to adjust the front guides. The basic procedure of cocking a plate follows:

1. If the press does not have preregister marks and gauges, extend a pencil line from the plate to the cylinder body or gutter.
2. Determine how much the plate must be cocked to make the image square on the press sheet. Draw a new mark on the cylinder body or gutter. **Caution:** Cocking a plate excessively could damage the plate.
3. Release the trailing clamp tension bolts so that the plate can be pulled forward on the desired side.
4. Use the side bolts on the plate cylinder to push the trailing clamp sideways the same distance that the plate needs to be moved forward.
5. Tighten the leading clamp tension bolts to draw the positioning marks into alignment.
6. Tighten the trailing clamp tension bolts.

Automated plate mounting. In the last few years, several press manufacturers have added automatic or semiautomatic plate mounting devices to their presses. The exact procedure involved in using these devices varies with the level of the device's automation, as well as from manufacturer to manufacturer. Therefore, consult the operating manual for the specific procedure. The basic procedure with one automatic plate mounting system includes the following steps:

1. Press operator loads new plates into a plate cassette.
2. Press operator selects a unit that needs a new plate and depresses a pushbutton to start the mounting procedure.
3. Safety guard automatically opens, and rear of plate loader moves toward the plate cylinder.
4. Plate clamp opens, and old plate is discharged into the loader.

5. New plate leaves loader, is inserted into position, and is mounted on the plate cylinder.
6. Plate clamp closes, loader retracts to original position, and safety guard closes.

Preparing New Blankets

Changing blankets and packing is not required on all makereadies. But, on a long-run, four-color job or on any job that requires high quality, it can be a costly mistake to start up with damaged blankets on the press.

Blankets contaminated with ink must be scrubbed until they are immaculate. If any low spots have developed during the previous pressrun, the blanket should be replaced. A good time to determine if a blanket has any low spots is after the previous job is completed but before the inking system has been washed up. Simply gum and dry the plate, and then roll it up solid and print to the blanket. Depressions will be immediately noticeable.

Chapter 7, "Blankets," discusses blankets, blanket care, and mounting procedures in detail. Following is a summary of those procedures:

1. After removing the old blanket, clean the body of the cylinder and wipe off the bearers.
2. Lock the leading edge of the blanket into place, and insert the calculated amount of packing beneath the blanket. Work the packing slightly into the cylinder gap to prevent it from creeping while the press is running.
3. Slowly inch the press until the trailing edge can be locked in the trailing clamps. While the press is inching, maintain tension on the blanket. Lock the trailing edge into the trailing clamps, and use a torque wrench to tighten the reel mechanism to provide proper blanket tension.

Preparing the Dampening System

The following sequence is representative of the steps involved in preparing the conventional dampening system during makeready. The sequence varies somewhat with continuous-flow dampening systems.

1. Install clean roller covers where required.
2. Measure and adjust the dampener roller pressures, if necessary.
3. Prepare the dampening solution according to the manufacturer's directions.
4. Measure dampening solution pH, conductivity levels, and temperature; and adjust the dampening solution

until the proper operating levels are obtained. The proper pH and conductivity levels depend on plate, paper, and ink variables. The water used to prepare the dampening solution has a major impact on the solution's pH and conductivity.

5. Turn on the circulating pumps, and fill the fountain pan or circulating tanks with dampening solution.
6. Adjust the dwell of the ductor roller on the fountain roller to govern the amount of water transferred to the oscillator.
7. Set ductor and fountain roller controls for the pressrun. (These are only initial settings.)

With a continuous-flow dampening system, a typical procedure might include the following steps. However, since each manufacturer's dampening system starts up differently, refer to the manufacturer's instructions.

1. Add isopropyl alcohol or alcohol substitute in the minimum percentage necessary for the system to operate properly. Fill the circulating tanks with the solution, and turn on the circulating pumps to fill the fountain pan. Check pH, conductivity, and temperature.
2. Turn on the system's drive motors. Check that the metering roller is engaging with its drive gear. Adjust each printing unit's dampening control to the normal operating speed.
3. Make preliminary adjustments to the metering roller. Adjust the metering roller until it almost touches the chrome roller on each end. Tighten the adjustment screws on the gear and operator's sides until the heavy film of water disappears, and then tighten the screws an additional one-quarter or one-half turn. The metering roller must be parallel to adjust the overall feed evenly. Some metering rollers can be skewed to adjust dampening; therefore, refer to the press manual for initial setting of such a roller.
4. Adjust the speed of the chrome roller, which controls the amount of water delivered to the plate. The speed of this roller is adjusted during the pressrun to compensate for temperature changes, humidity variations, alcohol evaporation, and ink drying problems.

Preparing the Inking System

Chapter 3, "The Inking System," discusses the inking system, roller settings, inking problems, maintenance, and a basic operating procedure, which consists of the following steps:

1. Check the work order for the proper ink to be used. Mix ink to customer's specifications, if necessary.

2. Supply ink to ink fountain, and adjust ink flow from the fountain roller to the ductor roller. With the ductor roller and fountain roller contacting, rotate the fountain roller several times. Adjust the ink fountain keys to deposit a light, even film of ink on the ductor roller.

3. Ink the rollers in the ink train by starting the press and manually engaging the ductors. Use the image on the plate to determine how much ink should print across the press sheet, and adjust individual inking keys accordingly.

4. Set the swing (amount of rotation) to a 50% stroke, and set the speed of the fountain roller.

A large number of presses are now equipped with remote control consoles. If the press is also equipped with a plate scanner, the plate is scanned, and the readings obtained directly from the plate are used to automatically preset the inking fountain keys. If the press does not have a plate scanner, place the printing plate on the console, estimate the inking requirements at each point across the plate, and set the inking accordingly. Always keep the keys of a segmented blade open a little, even if the plate requires no inking in that area. A minimum ink flow is required to adequately lubricate the ink fountain roller.

The most common color sequence on a multicolor press, according to a survey by a major supplier, is black-cyan-magenta-yellow (KCMY), which is used over 80% of the time. CMYK is used 7% of the time, and YCMK is used 4% of the time.

Preparing the Makeready Book

The **makeready book** is a pile of press sheets consisting of both waste sheets (previously printed sheets) and clean, unprinted sheets. The ratio of clean sheets to waste sheets is typically 1:5. To make the book, cut the waste sheets to the same size as the clean, unprinted sheets. Insert 10 clean sheets between every 50 waste sheets. The completed book will have approximately 1,100 sheets; this number will vary depending on the complexity of the makeready. The makeready book is then placed on the feeder pile.

Making Trial Impressions

The press crew can now make the first trial impressions. The following is a general procedure:

1. Open the plate(s) with water to remove the gum, and turn on the press at a slow speed.

2. Turn on the dampening system, and check for even dampening on the printing plate.
3. Set the ink rollers to the automatic mode.
4. Start the feeder. Put the press on impression and continue printing until the first trial press sheet ("unprinted sheet") exits the delivery. Inspect for proper sheet feeding, forwarding, and delivery.
5. Stop feeder (the press will automatically come off impression), and disengage dampening system.

Sheets being removed from the delivery for inspection

Examining the Trial Impressions

The trial impressions are inspected on a slightly inclined, flat surface. According to ANSI standard PH2.30-1989, *Color Prints, Transparencies, and Photomechanical Reproductions—Viewing Conditions,* the lighting in this viewing booth must be 5,000 K, and any visible surfaces (the "surround") in the booth must be a neutral gray (Munsell N8/). GATF SecondSight 14, *Color Viewing Conditions for the Graphic Arts,* discusses this topic in detail.

The trial impressions are examined for the following points in sequence:

- Position and register of image
- Quality of print
- Ink/water balance
- Color of print

The major point to inspect with the first trial impression is the position of the image, because the inking and dampening systems are not yet balanced.

Image register and position. The first trial impression is checked for image position. If only one color appears on this press sheet, the image is registered to the paper. Make sure that the image is positioned properly and squarely on the page. If the image is not properly positioned sideways, adjust the side guide and the pile position. If the image must be moved toward or away from the gripper edge, adjust the plate cylinder accordingly. If all colors are printed on the first trial sheet, which is commonly done, the colors are registered to each other and to the paper.

When only one color is printed on the first trial impression, one or more additional colors are printed on the next trial impression. These are registered to the first color that was printed. The side guide can no longer be adjusted to get image register. Therefore, all position changes must be made by moving the printing cylinders or cocking the printing plate, if the images are not square with each other. Packing may have to be transferred from plate to blanket to get image fit if image length has changed.

Quality of print. The quality of the impression on the earlier trials is unlikely to be correct. The two principal quality defects that can be identified from these early trial impressions are an **overall weak print,** due to excessive dampening or insufficient ink, and a **heavy print,** due to excessive inking. Other problems include scumming and filling in of halftones, mottling, grainy prints, sheets that stick to the blanket, and excessive sheet curl in the delivery. Most of these problems have a common cause—incorrect inking and dampening. Therefore, the press operator must identify the proper cause and adjust the inking and dampening accordingly, while attempting to obtain ink/water balance at the lowest possible level. If the image is not transferring properly from the blanket, the squeeze pressures between blanket and impression cylinder must be rechecked and adjusted as necessary.

Color of print. Once the images are properly positioned and the impression quality is acceptable, the press operator then must adjust the inking system until the color of the print is acceptable.

The press sheet must be viewed under standard lighting conditions (5,000 K). The color proof supplied with the job guides the press operator in making adjustments to the inking system. The proof should have been prepared to match the hue and grayness of the printing inks. (An improperly prepared color proof will be impossible to match on the press.)

All multicolor jobs should have a color control bar, such as the GATF Six-Color Control Bar, printed in the trim area along the trailing edge of the press sheet. The press operator uses a hand-held densitometer or a scanning densitometer to measure the densities of the solid process-color patches. (The two- and three-color overprint solids can be used to check trapping of the last-down ink over the previous-down ink.) Many printing companies have established standard ink densities for the pressroom, such as yellow, 0.95±0.05, magenta, 1.30±0.05, cyan, 1.30±0.05, and black 1.60±0.10 for coated paper. (These densities, measured using a wide-band densitometer, are for example only; they should not be assumed to be applicable to all printing presses and all ink sets.) Setting ink fountains according to established reference values by means of a reflection densitometer enables achieving faster fine adjustment of ink using fewer sheets. When a computer-controlled scanning densitometer or plate scanner is used, the color OK can occur quicker because these devices indicate the relative amounts of inking required across the press sheet.

Since each horizontal position across the press sheet has different inking needs, the inking keys must be set according to those ink needs. In other words, the press operator must

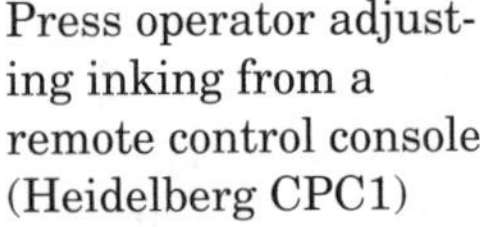

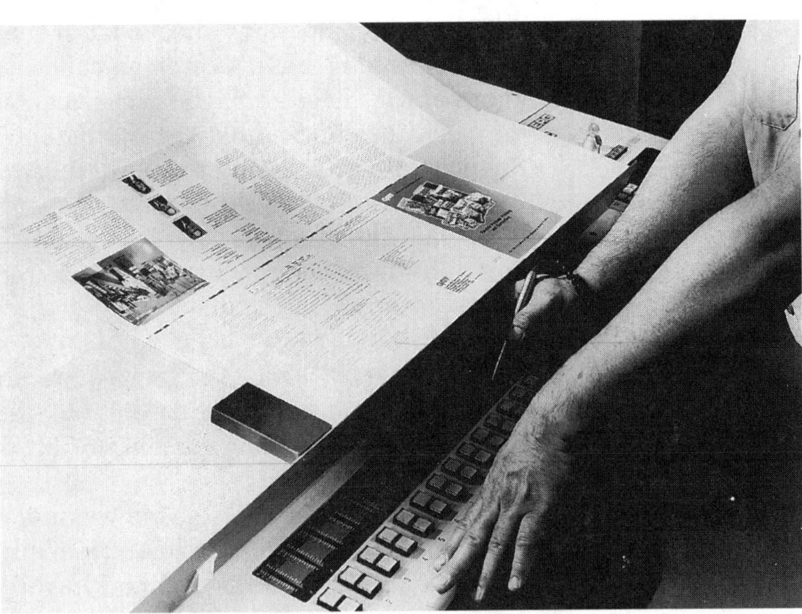

Press operator adjusting inking from a remote control console (Heidelberg CPC1)

open up the keys in areas requiring additional ink and close the keys in areas requiring less ink. A graph (or profile) of inking across a press sheet has high points (indicating areas of great ink demand) and low points (indicating areas of little or no ink demand, such as the unprinted trim areas of the press sheet).

Side-Guide Marks

A side-guide mark, a series of fine vertical and horizontal lines about 6 in. (150 mm) back from the paper's gripper edge, allows the press operator to fan a series of sheets to determine if the side guide is properly functioning, overpulling, or underpulling. If the vertical line is on the edge of the sheet, the guide is functioning properly. If the line is in slightly from the edge, the guide is overpulling the paper. If the line is missing completely, the guide is underpulling.

The horizontal line of the side-guide mark allows the press operator to check the consistency of circumferential (gripper-to-tail) register. A similar horizontal line should be positioned on the opposite side of the press sheet to monitor gripper-to-tail register on that side of the sheet. Any misregister, caused by sheets bouncing out of the front guides, will show as a jagged line.

Usually, the side-guide mark is added to the printing plate during platemaking. However, if necessary, the press operator can scribe a side-guide mark on the plate after the completion of makeready.

The GATF Side-Guide Mark, one of four image control marks marketed by GATF, is available as a film negative or

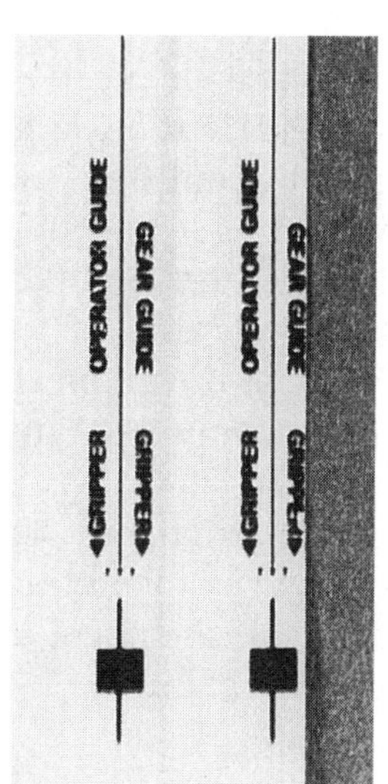

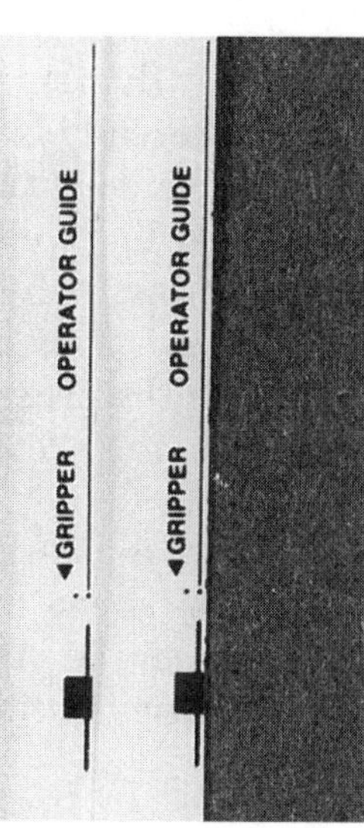

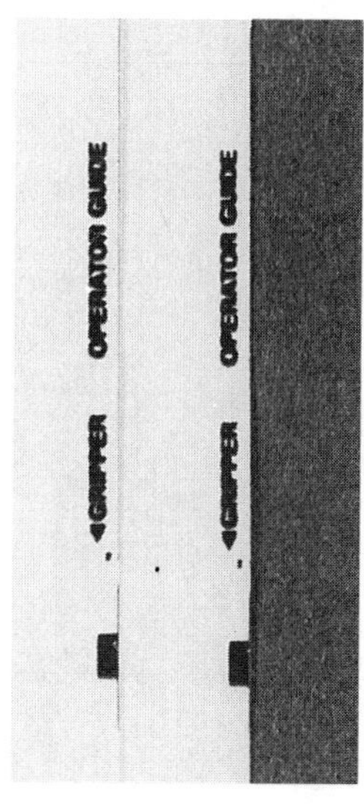

GATF Side-Guide Marks on a series of press sheets: excessive overpulling *(left),* slight overpulling and circumferential misregister *(middle),* and proper positioning on the edge of the sheet *(right)*

positive. The mark is a vertical line approximately ⅞ in. (22 mm) long with a 3/16-in. (5-mm) horizontal line. In film assembly, the side-guide mark is attached to the master marks flat (key sheet) so that it will print at the guide edge of the press sheet, and the plate is then exposed. During press makeready, the press operator adjusts the side guide until the vertical mark is positioned on the sheet edge so that half of the mark is bleeding off. By jogging several sheets on a square surface and then fanning them, the press operator can determine if the side guide is properly functioning.

If the printing plate does not have a side-guide mark, a mark can be scribed on the plate. The following method is one way of putting the mark on the plate:

1. After the image is in proper position on the sheet (i.e., makeready is complete), tap ink on the side edges of the paper about 6 in. away from the gripper edge. (This distance corresponds to the typical placement of the side guide in relation to the front guides.)
2. Place this inked sheet on the feeder pile and put six sheets of paper on top of it. Lock off the dampening and ink form rollers.
3. Run ten sheets of paper through the press under impression pressure. The ink marks will transfer from the paper to the blanket and then to the plate in exact register.
4. Align a plastic straightedge with the ink marks on the plate, and scribe a vertical line and a horizontal line on the guide side of the sheet and another horizontal line on the opposite side.

Another commonly used method for putting the mark on the plate follows:

1. After the image is in proper position on the sheet (i.e., makeready is complete), cut out a pie-shaped wedge on each side of the sheet about 6 in. away from the gripper edge. The wedge must be large enough to include at least an inch of image area to make it easier to register the press sheet to the plate.
2. Inch the press until the image on the plate is accessible. Tape the press sheet from step 1 in register over the plate.
3. Align a plastic straightedge with the edges of the taped press sheet, and scribe a vertical line and a horizontal line on the guide side of the sheet and another horizontal line on the opposite side.

13 The Pressrun

Once the pressrun starts, the press operator periodically removes press sheets from the press and compares them to the OK sheet and inspects them for various print defects, such as hickeys. In addition, the press operator double-checks the functioning of the press. For example, the press operator may have to make adjustments to the feeder during the pressrun. Perhaps, the pile is not rising fast enough, or the airflow that separates the top sheet from the rest of the pile is insufficient.

Inspection of Press Sheets

Periodically during the pressrun, the press operator will remove—**pull**—the most recently printed press sheets from the press delivery. Typically, one inspection sheet is pulled for each set of delivery grippers. For example, if the press has 10 sets of delivery grippers, 10 inspection sheets are pulled. Inspections are required every 10 min. or more frequently, depending on whether the printing is single-color or multicolor and the quality level.

In order to remove the set of inspection sheets, the press operator reaches into the delivery end of the operating press. Therefore, for obvious safety reasons, the press operator must be prohibited from wearing loose long hair, watches, rings, bracelets, or long-sleeved shirts. With most presses, whenever the front gate of the delivery is opened, a set of metal fingers extends into the delivery and catches the press sheet before it falls on the pile. This system allows the press operator to easily remove the required number of sheets from the top of the pile. When the front gate is closed, the fingers retract, allowing the printed sheets to drop on top of the paper pile again.

The set of pulled sheets are inspected either at the remote control console of the press or in a standard viewing booth where they are compared to the OK sheet and to each other.

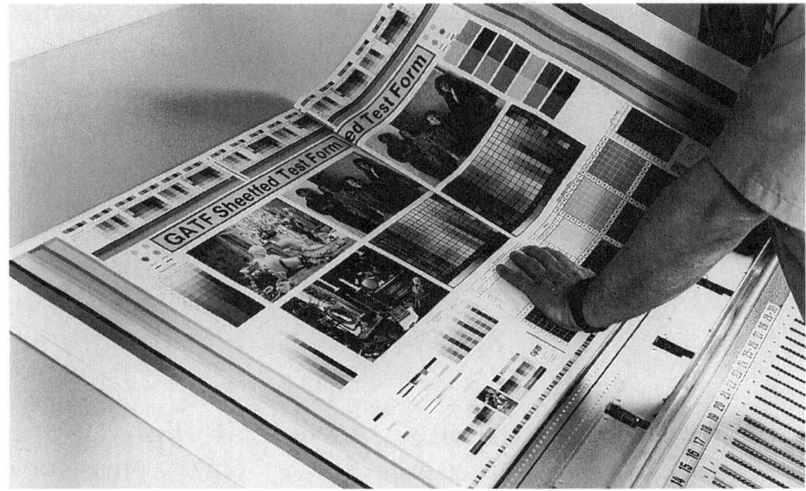

Press operator comparing an inspection sheet with the OK sheet

A reflection densitometer equipped with red, green, and blue filters; a 10×–20× magnifying glass for general work; and an illuminated 50× magnifier for critical inspection of halftone dots are the three principal tools used during inspection.

It is not necessary to use the densitometer to measure ink densities on every set of inspection sheets; using the densitometer once for every 1,000 sheets is a more common practice. A quality control color strip cut from an OK sheet is useful for visual comparison. Among the items checked during inspection are the following:

- **Positioning of side-guide marks** from one inspection sheet to the next. Fanning the sheets easily shows if the positioning is inconsistent. If the side guiding varies, the side guide mechanism and, perhaps, the paper pile may have to be adjusted.
- **Register and fit of the individual printed ink films.** If the problem is **misregister,** the side guide and plate cylinder may have to be adjusted. Most high-quality printers attempt to maintain register within one dot on a 150-line halftone. Even if the press is side-guiding properly, paper conditions such as tight or wavy edges, improper moisture balance, or poor paper trimming can cause misregister. A light table and a T square or a line-up table should be used to make sure that the images are straight. If the problem is **image fit,** packing must be transferred from the plate cylinder to the blanket cylinder, or vice versa, to compensate for dimensional changes in the paper. Unfortunately, fit problems can also be caused by platemaking and stripping errors, in which case the press

superintendent must be consulted to determine if a new plate must be made.

- **Plugging of halftones.** Inking must be reduced.
- **Dry-up of the plate in nonimage area.** Dry-up occurs more frequently on the gear side of the press because that side is warmer. Dampening must be increased.
- **Excessive inking.** The finger rub test is an easy way to determine if inking is excessive. Lightly draw a finger over the wet ink on the inspection sheet. The drag of the ink on the finger and the amount of smudging are compared to that experienced on the wet OK sheet.
- **Presence of printing defects.** The most common printing defect is the hickey. The press may have to be stopped in order to remove the hickey from the plate, blanket, or inking form rollers. Additional print quality problems include dot doubling, excessive dot gain, and slur. Several film quality control devices, discussed later in this chapter, are available to monitor for the presence of these factors. Unwanted images in the nonimage area of the printing plate can be corrected using a deletion pen; defects in the image area usually require a new printing plate. GATF's *Solving Sheetfed Offset Press Problems* and *Solving Offset Ink Problems* textbooks offer remedies for various printing problems occurring in sheetfed printing.
- **Consistency of color, compared to the OK sheet.** Visually compare the colors in the corresponding blocks of the color control bar and corresponding image areas. Remember, however, that adjacent colors can affect how a certain color is perceived. Periodically measure the densities of the inks printed in the cyan, magenta, and yellow solid patches of the color control guide. The densities should remain within the tolerance limits set for the inks being used. Inking can be adjusted either *locally,* by opening or closing individual ink fountain keys, or *overall,* by increasing or decreasing the rotation of the ink fountain roller or dwell of the ink ductor roller. Ink/water balance must be maintained at all times. Several times during the pressrun, check the trapping of secondary colors, hue error, and grayness, especially of the yellow ink.

Use of tags or tickets. Tickets or tags are inserted into the paper pile to indicate start of makeready, start of pressrun, and sheets that have defects. If the tag is not color-coded, a simple explanation of the problem is written on it.

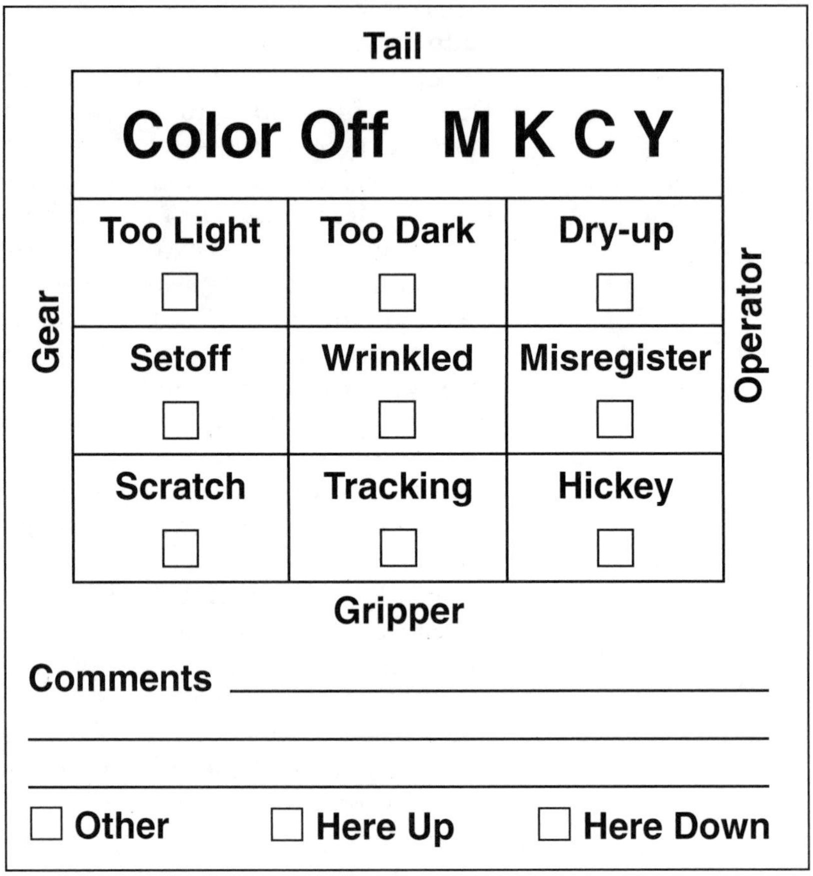

Tag inserted into pile to indicate start of makeready, start of pressrun, and sheets having detects

Tail

Color Off M K C Y

Too Light ☐	Too Dark ☐	Dry-up ☐
Setoff ☐	Wrinkled ☐	Misregister ☐
Scratch ☐	Tracking ☐	Hickey ☐

Gear

Operator

Gripper

Comments ______________________________

____

____

☐ Other ☐ Here Up ☐ Here Down

Control of Press Functions during Pressrun

Maintaining the Inking System

Consistent color is a primary objective during the pressrun. The ink fountain ratchet should be set halfway between the minimum and maximum strokes. Color will remain consistent only if the ink fountain is always at least half full. The ink in the fountain exerts pressure on the fountain blade. If the ink level is too low, the gap between fountain blade and fountain roller closes slightly, and less ink transfers to the ductor roller. As a result, the press operator increases the ink feed. Eventually, the press operator notices that the ink fountain level is too low and refills the fountain. When the fountain is refilled, the weight of the ink increases the gap between fountain roller and blade, resulting in a surplus of ink being fed to the ductor roller. The ink feed must now be reduced, and maintaining consistent color has become impossible.

Scratching a reference mark at the halfway point on the cheek or side of the ink fountain is one of the best ways to ensure that the ink level never drops below one-half.

The ink in the fountain must be periodically agitated. Agitation, either manual or automatic, prevents the ink from skinning (a major cause of hickeys). In addition, agitation lessens an ink's natural tendency to back away from the fountain blade. An automatic ink agitator is a recommended accessory for any press. However, if manual agitation is required, a good rule of thumb is to stir the ink once every 1,000 impressions.

Ink/water balance must be maintained during the pressrun. Inking is adjusted to obtain the proper densities on the printed sheet, and the dampening is adjusted according to the inking level. Press operators often use the glossiness of the plate surface as an indication of dampening and the thickness of the ink film as visual clues to ink/water balance. Additional clues are the dot quality and types of patterns or marks in the image and nonimage areas of the press sheet.

It is necessary in any given pressrun for the balance between ink and water to be achieved by trial-and-error adjustments of their feed rates. Enough water must be fed to keep nonimage areas clean and fine shadow dots open, but not so much that the water causes snowflake patterns in the ink film. The choice of initial settings for ink and water fountains are usually based on the press operator's experience with the type of press and its dampening system. After makeready, the ink film thickness and reflection density are generally close to the required standard and the water feed is near a satisfactory balance. Fine adjustments in either feed rate during the pressrun may require a corresponding adjustment in the other rate. After each adjustment, several inspection sheets should be pulled and checked after the press has reached a new equilibrium balance.

Among the problems encountered in controlling the balance point is differentiating normal sample-to-sample random print variations from those due to longer drifts that occur during the pressrun. Minor variations are inherent in press operation.

The press operator must make sure that all covered rollers remain clean and that the ink does not bleed into the dampening fountain.

Experienced press operators judge ink/water balance by inspecting the appearance of the *scum line* that occurs at the lead edge of the plate. A sharp, even line indicates perfect balance. If the line is indistinct and fuzzy, the plate is too dry. If the line is broken, the plate is too wet.

Maintaining the Dampening Solution

Like the inking level, maintaining a satisfactory level of dampening solution in the fountain is extremely important. Insufficient dampening leads to plate dry-up in the nonimage areas of the plate.

Periodically during the pressrun, the dampening solution's pH, conductivity, specific gravity, and temperature must be measured. Depending on the meters and hydrometers used, the measurements are made either in the dampening fountain (preferred) or in the supply tank. If a ball hydrometer is being used in the supply tank, wait until the air bubbles subside before reading it. If any measurement falls outside predetermined limits, immediate corrective action is required.

Operating the Feeder

Like all press subsystems, minor adjustments are necessary during the pressrun. Vacuum and air often have to be adjusted to separate more or fewer sheets from the paper pile, depending on what feeding problems are encountered. Wedges may be required if the paper develops a curl. Pile height, sheet separation, and sheet transfer mechanisms may also require minor adjustment during the pressrun.

One commonly overlooked cause of sheet transfer problems on the feedboard is glazed feedboard tapes and forwarding wheels. If they become glazed, they lose traction and send cocked sheets down the feedboard. They should be deglazed once every six months.

With a conventional feeder, the press must be stopped to change to a new paper pile. With a continuous feeder, the new pile is built below the expiring pile.

Operating the Delivery

If the press has a conventional delivery, it is stopped to unload the paper. If the press has a continuous delivery, some type of mechanism permits the press operator to unload the pile while a new one is building in the delivery. Recommended skid height in the delivery varies with ink coverage, spray powder usage, and the possibility of setoff.

If a paper jam occurs in the delivery (or feeder), the press is stopped immediately and the jammed sheets are manually removed. Once the press is restarted, monitor the first few sheets to make sure that the problem has been solved. Adjusting the delivery joggers is seldom necessary once makeready is finished. However, adjusting spray powder levels is extremely common. Spray powder, discussed extensively in GATF Technical Services Report 7220, *Cutting Down on Spray Powder,* is one means of reducing **setoff,** the transfer

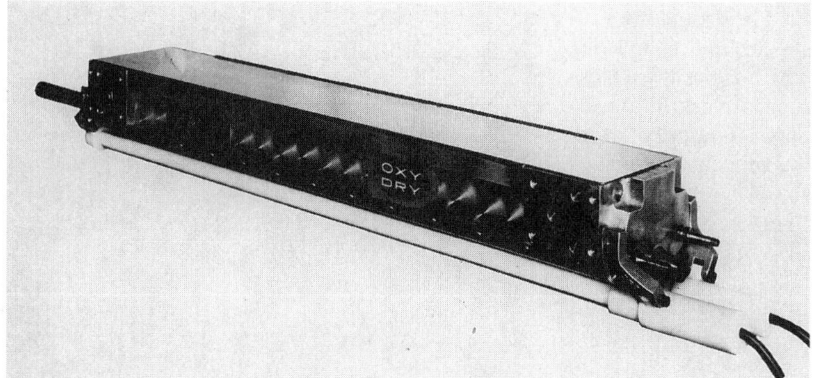

An electrostatic sprayer that dispenses antisetoff powder
Courtesy Oxy-Dry Corporation

of ink from the surface of the printed sheet to the back of the sheet on top of it. Excessive spray powder causes several problems:

- Quality problems, such as reduced gloss and scratches
- Maintenance problems, such as clogged filters in the ventilating system, worn bearings, and dust specks on plate and film in the stripping and camera areas
- Health problems, if the microscopic powder particles enter the worker's lungs
- Dust explosion potential in the pressroom if the concentration of spray powder in the atmosphere exceeds about 0.04 oz./cu.ft. (42 g/m^3)

Therefore, a minimum of spray powder should be run. The amount required is easily determined by conducting the following test:

1. At the start of the pressrun, reduce the spray powder discharge until it is just visible, and then reduce it slightly more. Spray levels will be enough for most jobs.
2. Near the start of the pressrun, reduce the spray powder discharge even more.
3. Print ten sheets at this reduced level, and tag them accordingly.
4. Inspect the sheets in the first skid for setoff. If setoff did not occur, the spray level can be reduced even more.

This step is repeated several times until the press operator determines the lowest level at which the spray powder still prevents setoff.

If the press operator has a choice of running excessive spray powder or racking the printed sheets in small lifts to lessen setoff, racking the sheets is preferred—although it causes the press operator additional work.

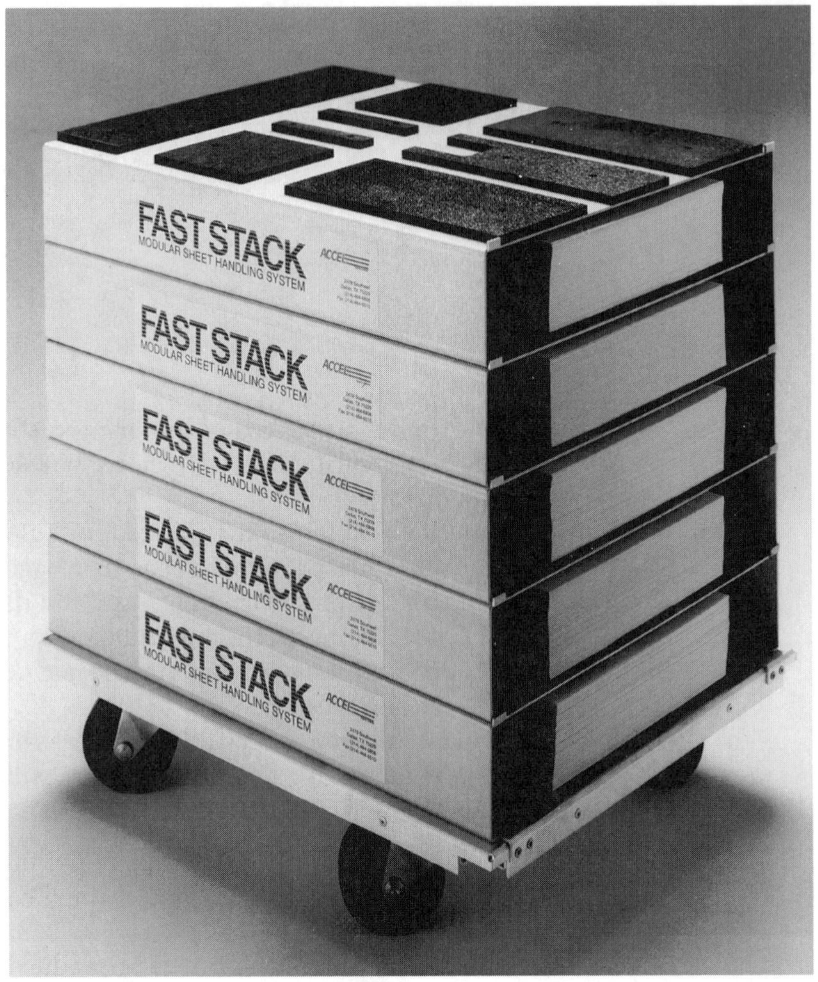

Fast Stack modular sheet handling system, which is designed to separate small lifts of paper to improve drying time and reduce setoff
Courtesy Accel Graphic Systems, Inc.

Racking can be used to stack several small lifts of paper. In racking, one lift of paper is placed on the delivery board, two L-shaped legs are placed at opposite corners of the paper pile, and a piece of plywood (cut to the same size as the delivery board) is placed on top of the legs. A second level is then built on top of the first piece of plywood, and a third level is then built on top of the second piece, and so on.

Quality Control during the Pressrun

Perception of color varies from person to person and from time to time by the same person. People cannot remember colors with any great degree of precision. Furthermore, control of production to reduce variation in color requires objective control that can be obtained only with instrumental measurement. On the other hand, the human eye is an excellent device for comparing two adjacent color samples and for

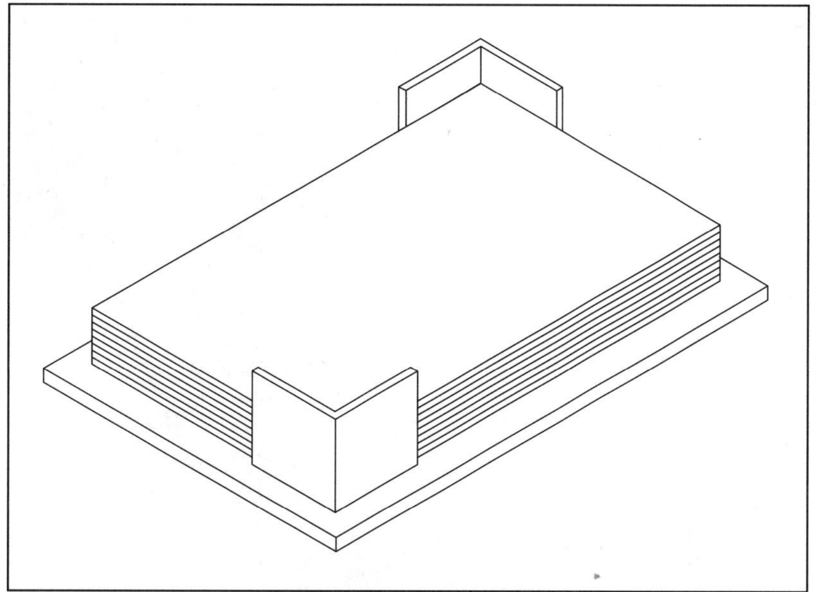

Use of L-shaped legs to stack small lifts of paper on multiple levels

detecting defects in print quality. Consequently, quality control has both visual and instrumental components.

Densitometry

The reflection densitometer is an indispensable quality control device. It can easily detect changes during a pressrun and indicate density variation between inspection press sheets and the OK sheet. Although some companies house the densitometer in quality control areas for periodic inspection at a central site, most densitometers are conveniently located at the press inspection area. Many modern presses have built-in densitometers. Stand-alone scanning densitometers, appropriate for any press, provide density readings on solid patches of color bars as well as critical halftone or solid image areas.

A program should be established to determine the optical density tolerances of each printing job. Density tolerances for each pressrun should be determined from density measurements taken on an approved press sheet *before* the pressrun begins. These measurements should be manually recorded or stored in computerized press densitometers or stand-alone densitometers.

If tolerances are established by a central quality control department, one of the approved sheets should be returned to the press on which printing will take place. It then becomes the press operator's responsibility to maintain color both numerically (using a densitometer) and visually (by comparing the inspection sheet with the OK sheet).

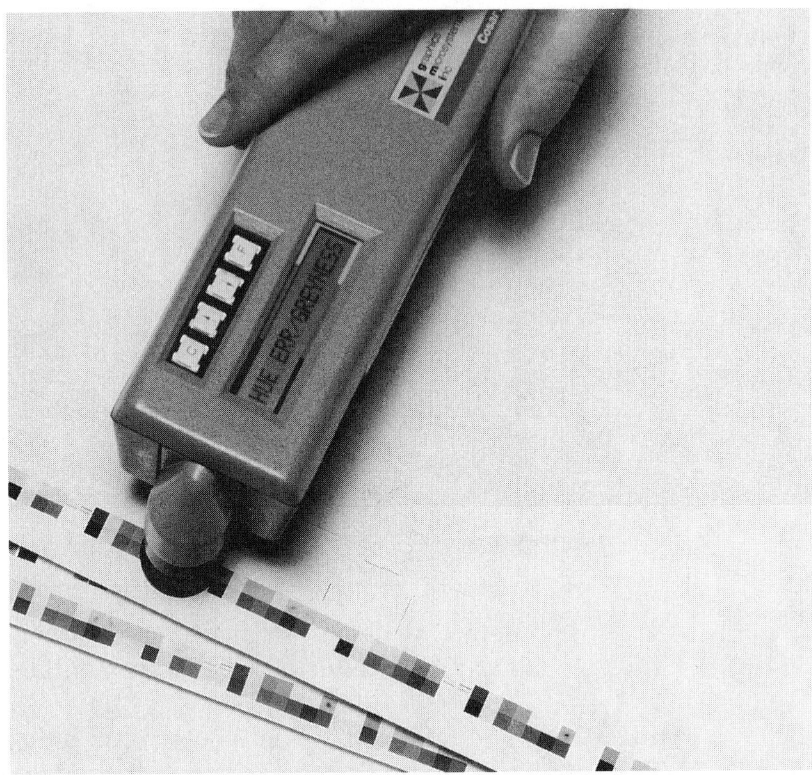

Cosar 200 series color reflection densitometer *Courtesy Graphics Microsystems, Inc.*

The X-Rite 418 computerized color reflection densitometer *Courtesy X-Rite, Inc.*

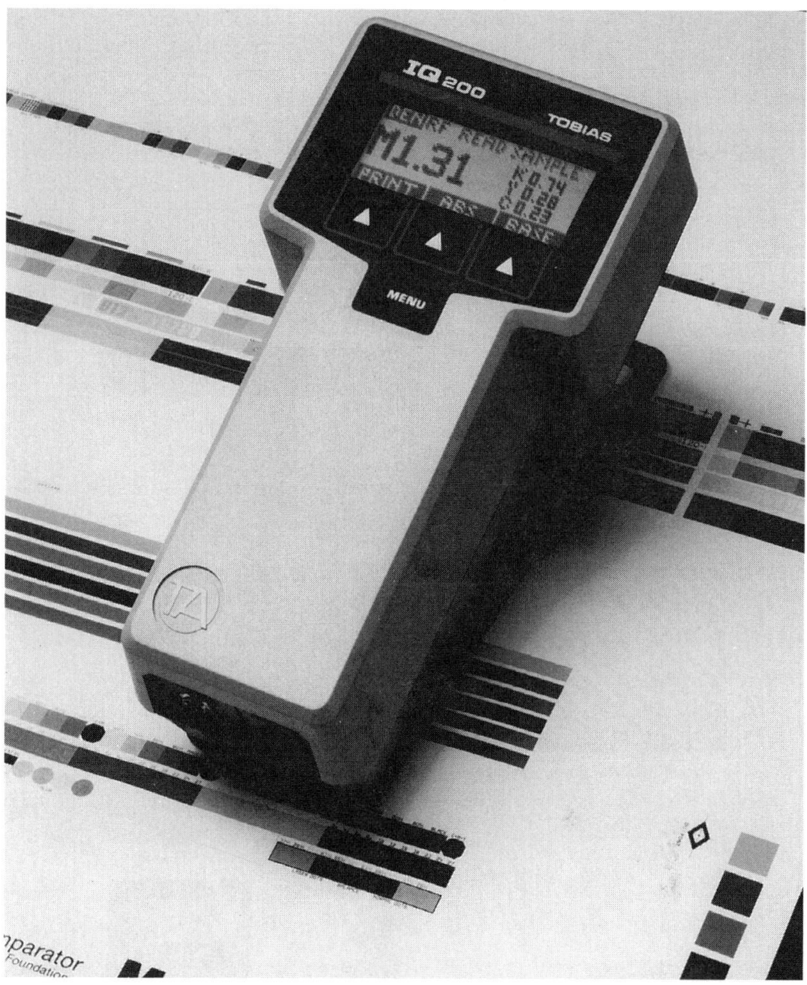

Tobias IQ 200 computing portable color reflection densitometer
Courtesy Tobias Associates, Inc.

Periodically measuring the densities of an inspection sheet indicates whether or not the press operator is maintaining the original numerical tolerances established on the OK sheet.

Color Control Bars

Density monitoring programs require the use of color control bars. The GATF 150-Line Color Control Bar is one example of such a bar. The strip not only supplies information on the consistency of ink density from sheet to sheet, but it also provides information on ink trapping, dot gain or sharpening, slurring or doubling tendencies, and gray balance of the inks being used.

Commercially available color bars, such as those produced by GATF, usually include overprints of two- and three-color solids and tints, in addition to solid and tint blocks for cyan,

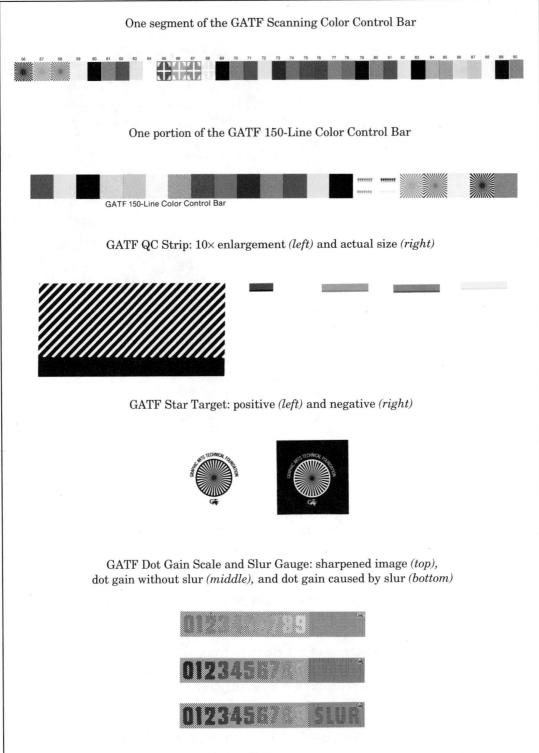

One segment of the GATF Scanning Color Control Bar

One portion of the GATF 150-Line Color Control Bar

GATF 150-Line Color Control Bar

GATF QC Strip: 10× enlargement *(left)* and actual size *(right)*

GATF Star Target: positive *(left)* and negative *(right)*

GATF Dot Gain Scale and Slur Gauge: sharpened image *(top),* dot gain without slur *(middle),* and dot gain caused by slur *(bottom)*

magenta, yellow, and black. Most also include additional aids to monitor other printing variables. The GATF 150-Line Color Control Bar, for example, also includes GATF Star Targets (also available separately), which visually indicate dot gain or sharpening, slur, and doubling.

Another GATF quality control device is the GATF Six-Color Control Bar, which is a 150-line/in. (5.9-line/mm) two-tiered press control bar for use on sheetfed presses. Designed for presses that are capable of printing up to six colors, the bar contains all of the elements from which ink densities, dot gain, trapping, and print contrast are measured. Elements are also included in the bar to allow the press operator to visually evaluate slur, doubling, and dot gain. The top tier of the bar contains twelve repeats of the six solid single colors and ten repeats of the green, blue, and red solid overprints. The lower tier contains four repeats of the GATF Star Targets for each of the six colors; four repeats of 25%, 50%, and 75% tint patches of the magenta, cyan, yellow, and black; four repeats of the GATF Dot Gain Scale-II© for each of the six colors; two sets of green, blue, and red 50% tint patches; and four repeats of three-color grays.

Color control bars are placed in the trim area across the tail end of the press sheet.

Other production QC devices from GATF. The GATF Dot Gain Scale-II© was designed to visually indicate dot gain in the middletone area of a halftone, which is the area most sensitive to dot gain and the area so critical to color balance and critical quality. The scale visually shows dot gain in seven increments (1%, 2%, 5%, 10%, 15%, 20%, and 30%).

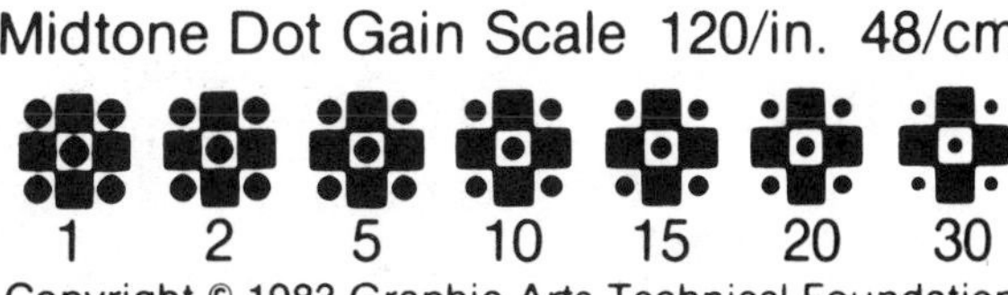

The GATF Dot Gain Scale-II© showing seven individual targets (approximately 11× enlargement)

The GATF Quality Control (QC) Strip was also designed to be a visual aid for the press operator. The strip on the OK sheet is placed alongside the strip on the inspection sheet, and the two strips are compared. Any difference between them alerts the press operator to look for the cause of the difference in press conditions. Ink film thickness, ink/water balance, and dot quality can be visually controlled with the Quality Control Strip.

The GATF Dot Gain and Slur Gauge visually indicates dot area changes and slurring or doubling on press. The dot gain portion of the device consists of a series of numbers created by finely spaced horizontal lines of differing thicknesses on a coarse-dot background. A change in the position of the number that blends into the background indicates that dot gain or sharpening has occurred. The slur portion of the device consists of the word "slur" created by finely spaced horizontal lines on a background of finely spaced vertical lines. The occurrence of slur or doubling causes either the word "slur" or the background to become predominant.

Controlling Color during the Pressrun

The problem of controlling and maintaining color during the pressrun involves controlling the thickness of the ink film, the ink trap in overprints, halftone tint values, and dot gain. Consequently, the ink film thickness is controlled by observing color changes and density differences that occur as the thickness varies.

A densitometer provides numerical feedback to changes in halftone tint values, and a dot gain scale visually indicates changes in dot gain and, usually, slurring and doubling. The color and reflection density of a halftone area is more sensitive to changes in dot size than to changes in ink film thickness. A densitometer equipped with red, green, and blue filters is necessary to measure the reflection densities of the magenta, cyan, and yellow inks and their overprints. The use of a densitometer allows trapping, hue error, grayness, and print contrast to be calculated. Many densitometers measure these directly.

Trapping. The reflection densities of magenta, cyan, yellow, and their two-color overprints are used in the following formula to determine percent trapping.

$$\text{Percent trap} = \frac{D_{OP} - D_1}{D_2} \times 100$$

In this equation, D_1 is the reflection density of the first-down ink, D_2 is the reflection density of the second-down ink, and D_{OP} is the reflection density of the overprint. These density readings are taken with the filter normally used for the second-down ink. This equation indicates *apparent trap,* because

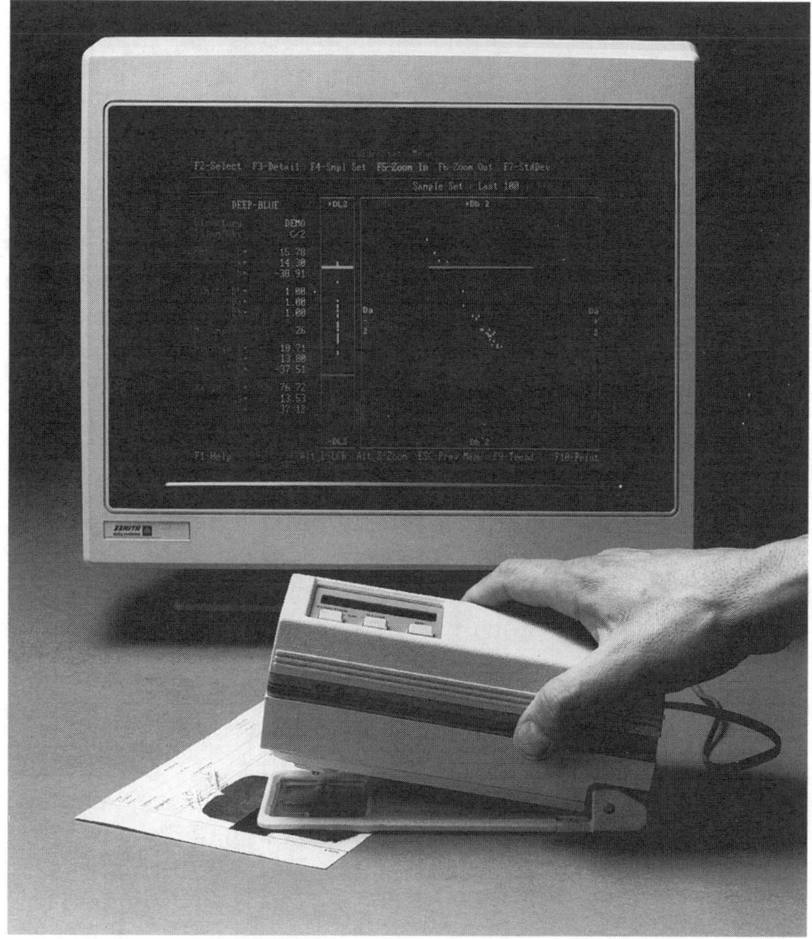

The X-Rite 938 SpectroDensitometer, which combines the capabilities of a spectrophotometer, a colorimeter, and a densitometer
Courtesy X-Rite, Inc.

effects such as changes in gloss between single- and two-layer ink films could influence the percentage.

In printing, the amount of ink film transferred to a previously printed ink film can be more than, equal to, or less than that transferred to paper. The amount of transfer is referred to as **trap.** In printing, wet trap seldom exceeds 90% in red and blue, although trap exceeding 90% occurs often with green; 80–90% trap values are most common. Wet trap values less than 75% on a sheetfed press are considered unacceptable. Although a high trap value is important, it is more important that the ink trap on production sheets match that of the OK sheet. Any change in ink trap causes changes in hue, saturation, and lightness of overprints. Such changes can be detected in the overprint portion of the color control bar when compared to those on the OK sheet. The following recommendations help to minimize trap problems:

- Use only inks that are balanced correctly for color strength. Trapping is improved if the ink film thickness increases slightly from one unit to the next. In order to increase ink film thicknesses in such a manner, the color strengths of the ink must be adjusted accordingly.
- Use tack-rated inks for wet-on-wet printing; that is, purchase a set of inks so that the highest tack-rated ink is printed on the first printing unit, the second highest tack-rated ink on the second unit, and so on. The difference in tack of consecutively printed inks should be only one or two tack units, as measured using an Inkometer.
- Make sure that the ink/water balance is correct and that the inking system is operating properly.

Hue error and grayness. Hue error is a term used to indicate the departure of a process ink from the ideal hue. To determine the hue error of an ink, density readings of the ink are taken through the red, green, and blue filters. The density readings are then used in the following formula to determine hue error:

$$\text{Hue error} = \frac{M - L}{H - L}$$

where M is the medium density reading, L is the lowest, and H is the highest.

Purity of a process color is judged by its freedom from gray. The following equation is used to calculate grayness:

$$\text{Grayness} = \frac{L}{H}$$

where L is the lowest density reading and H is the highest density reading. The lower the grayness of a process color, the higher its purity.

Print contrast ratio. Measurement of print contrast as a control parameter is increasing. High print contrast, an indication of good shadow contrast of a reproduction, yields better print quality. Printing conditions that cause print contrast to drop include excessive dot gain, low solid density, and fill-in due to insufficient water. Print contrast is calculated from a solid ink patch and a 75% tint patch, according to the following formula:

$$\text{Print contrast} = \frac{D_S - D_{75}}{D_S} \times 100$$

where D_S is the density of a solid (including paper) and D_{75} is the density of a 75% tint (including paper).

Pressroom Lighting and Standard Viewing Conditions

Proper lighting is important in the pressroom. Light levels must be sufficiently high around the press to permit the press crew to install plates, blankets, and packing easily and to make the necessary press adjustments without eye strain. Having a light shining between each pair of press units is recommended. However, the lights should not be placed directly above the press, but off to one side. Aisles around the press should also be illuminated for safety reasons.

In addition to lighting around the press, the booths or tables where press sheets are viewed must not only have sufficient lighting but must have lighting that conforms to recommended standard viewing conditions. To avoid misunderstandings, printer, supplier, and customer must agree on the illumination under which the print is to be viewed. Standard viewing conditions, consisting of standard lighting and surround conditions, are necessary to communicate the desired results and to ensure accuracy and consistency in color reproduction. Viewing conditions for the graphic arts industry are specified by the American National Standards Institute (ANSI) under ANSI PH2.30-1989, *Color Prints, Transparencies, and Photomechanical Reproductions—Viewing Conditions.*

The standard viewing conditions for photomechanical reproductions are as follows:

- Correlated color temperature of lighting—5,000 K (closely representing average white light)
- Spectral power distribution (the relative output of the light source across all the wavelengths of the visible spectrum)—D_{50}
- Color rendering index (how well a light source conforms to the color rendering of natural daylight)—at least 90
- Light intensity of print illumination—2,200 ± 470 lux (204 ± 44 footcandles)
- Uniformity of print illumination—the intensity at the edges of the viewing plane should be at least 60% of the intensity at the center
- Surround—matte, neutral gray of 60% reflectance, which is equivalent to Munsell N8/

Several companies manufacture viewing booths in which the lighting conforms to industry standards for illumination of the press sheet. For a detailed discussion of color viewing refer to GATF SecondSight 14, *Color Viewing Conditions for the Graphic Arts.*

Electronics in the Pressroom

In recent years, electronic devices have been added to most modern presses to make operation easier and to improve print quality. Although the types of devices available vary from press manufacturer to manufacturer, the following devices have become common in high-quality, high-productivity printing companies.

Remote Control Console

Most press manufacturers offer free-standing remote control consoles with their presses. A **remote control console** is a computerized device that enables the press operator to control a variety of press functions without leaving the press inspection table. Among the functions controlled are inking, dampening, and image register.

The console usually includes a remote set of fountain keys, usually a tumble switch or push-button array numbered to press position. The press operator determines which fountain position is to be altered and depresses the appropriate button to decrease or increase ink feed. The drive system that adjusts fountain key position is either continuous or modulated.

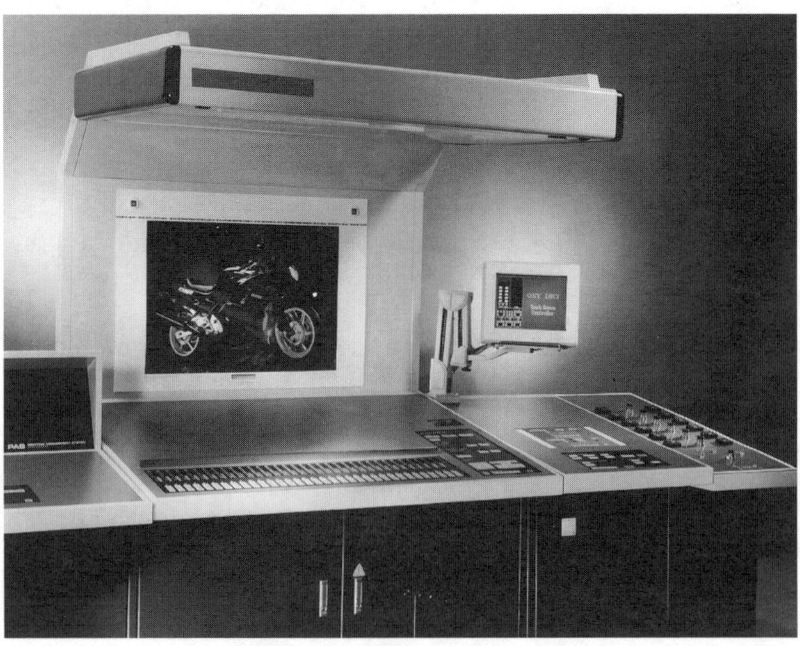

The Touch Screen Master Controller *(far right),* an interactive controller for Oxy-Dry's auxiliary equipment used on sheetfed presses, being used with a remote control console *(center)* for a Komori press
Courtesy Oxy-Dry Corporation

Usually, in case of electrical problems, the fountain keys on press can be manually adjusted. To take it a step further, some systems include an array of light-emitting diodes (LEDs) that shows the fountain blade profile. The details can be recorded on tape or other storage medium, allowing for automatic presetting of the fountain the next time the job is run.

Most remote control consoles allow the press operator to adjust the position of the plate cylinders.

Plate Scanner

Another auxiliary device is the plate scanner, which can be interfaced to an inking control console or record plate readings on tape or some other medium. A **plate scanner** is a device that measures the image area percentages at selected increments across the printing plate prior to mounting the plate on press. The information is recorded, often on a magnetic storage medium, so that it can be used to preset the ink fountain. Many plate scanners produce a printout that shows a graphic representation of the ink density of each individually controlled ink zone.

EPS plate scanner
Courtesy MAN Roland Inc., Sheetfed Press Division

Scanning Densitometer

A **scanning densitometer** is a computerized quality control table that measures and analyzes press-sheet color bars using a densitometer. The results are compared with a prerecorded tolerance program, and a printout indicates the degree of variation.

Ink fountain key adjustments and fountain roller adjustments can be made using the information provided by the scanning densitometer. The use of a hand-held densitometer

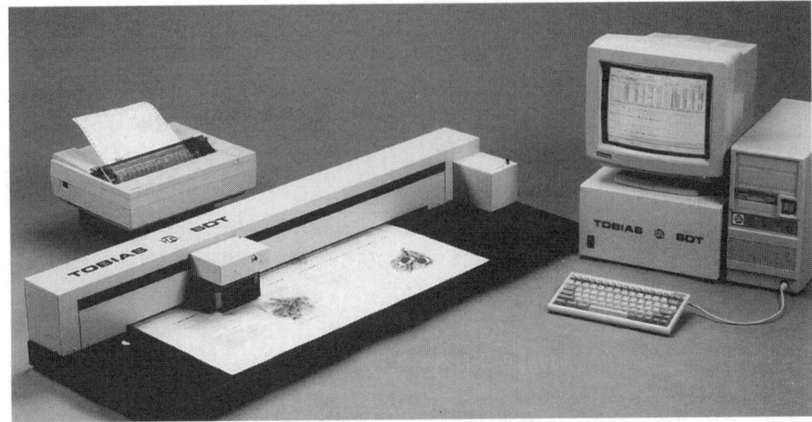

Tobias SDT scanning densitometer
Courtesy Tobias Associates, Inc.

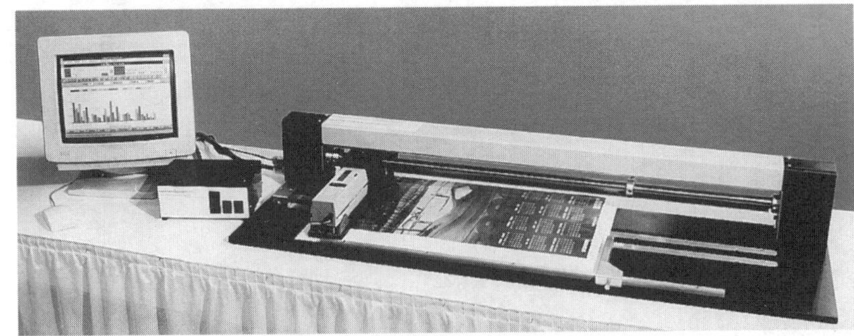

Macbeth® DataTrak scanning densitometer system
Courtesy Macbeth, a Division of Kollmorgen Instruments Corp.

Tobias SXY-40 scanning densitometry system
Courtesy Tobias Associates, Inc.

Autosmart x-y scanning densitometer
Courtesy Graphics Microsystems, Inc.

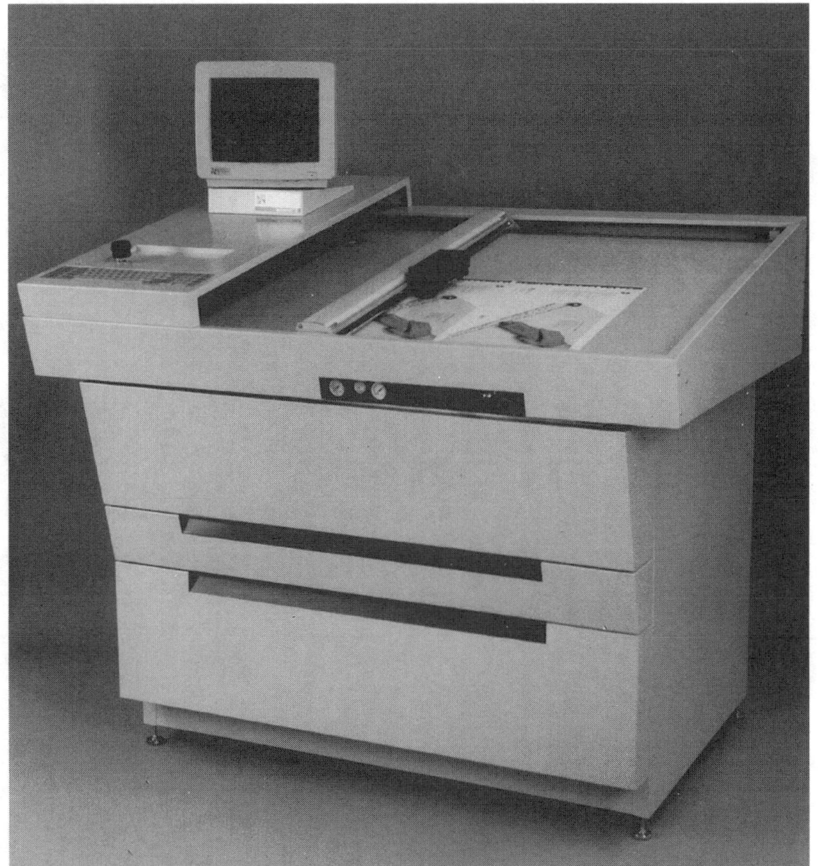

to individually measure each patch of a color bar is eliminated, and it is no longer necessary to make pen-and-paper calculations because the computerized equipment does that. Some scanning densitometers also provide information on dot gain, contrast, slurring, and doubling. Most systems also provide a data printout.

Closed-Loop Systems

A closed-loop system combines a remote control inking console, scanning densitometer, and computer together to automatically control and adjust inking. In addition to inking, many of the systems can monitor solid and halftone density, dot gain, print contrast, and ink trapping.

Unless the system has a press-mounted densitometer, the press operator still has to remove sheets from the press for measurement. Even with a closed-loop system, the ultimate control of the press remains with the press operator because a closed-loop system can not presently identify all process variables.

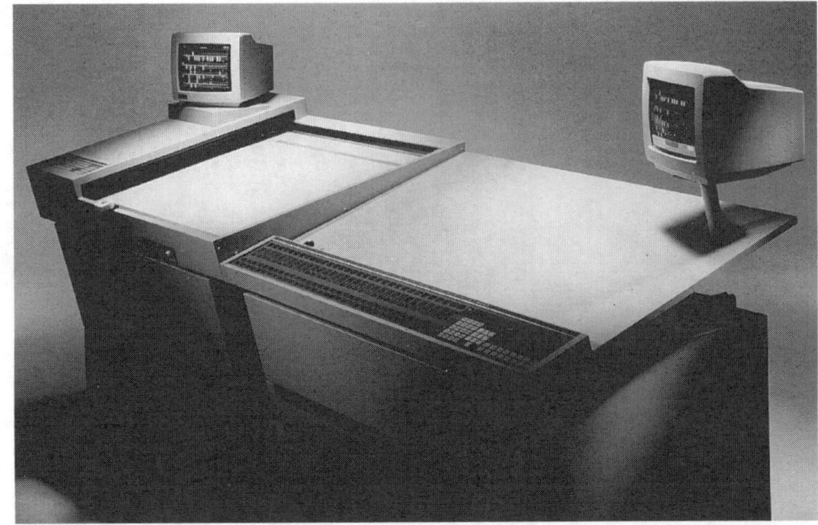

Autocolor closed-loop system
Courtesy Graphics Microsystems, Inc.

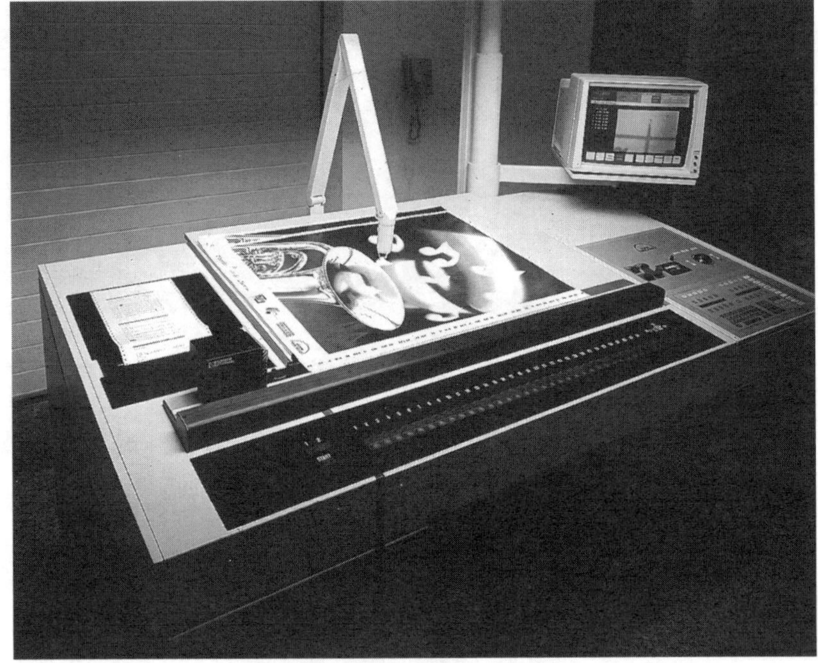

CCI computer console for a closed-loop inking system
Courtesy MAN Roland Inc., Sheetfed Press Division

14 Safety in the Pressroom

Press operators should work under the basic principle that all accidents in the pressroom can be prevented. Nearly 85% of all accidents are caused by unsafe acts, while the other 15% are caused by unsafe conditions. Chemicals, for example, that are not handled properly can present many hazards. To protect workers and the environment from chemical hazards, federal, state, and local agencies have established rules

Safety checklist, which covers some of the most important safety precautions in the pressroom

Safety must be stressed not only near the press but also in the pressroom as a whole. Following is a list of precautions that will make the pressroom a safer place to work:

- Never operate a press with cylinder guards removed.
- Do not override the interlocks that stop the press when the guards are raised.
- Use the inch/safe/service method.
- Inch the press carefully when working on a plate or blanket.
- Always lock the press on "safe" when working on a dangerous part of the press.
- Do not wear loose-fitting clothing, ties or necklaces, open-toe shoes, or shoes that will not offer adequate protection from dropped objects or chemical spills.
- Avoid the use of large, unfolded rags. Instead, use smaller rags or fold the larger rags into smaller sections.
- Remove finger rings to lessen the chance of having fingers crushed. Do not wear watches or bracelets.
- Wear safety goggles and gloves when handling hazardous chemicals.
- Understand and interpret the Material Safety Data Sheet that should accompany each chemical purchased.
- Understand the symbols/labels used with the Hazardous Materials Identification System (HMIS).
- Become familiar with emergency first-aid procedures for the chemicals used.

and regulations that help to assure safety, health, and a clean environment. This chapter highlights some of the major safety concerns in the pressroom.

To learn more about OSHA and the printing industry, obtain the latest copy of GATF's *Regulatory Concerns for the Printer: A Checklist* or contact the Foundation's Office of Environmental Information.

General Safety in the Printing Plant

To provide a safe workplace for employees and to meet OSHA requirements, a printing plant (regardless of size) should have a formal safety program, with responsibility formally assigned (even on a part-time basis) to one manager or department. This program includes all aspects of safety, including the safe operation of equipment.

Machine Guarding

Machine guards are used as barriers to protect workers from the dangers of pinch points and hazard points on industrial equipment. (A pinch point is where two rollers or cylinders first contact each other.) Manufacturers now enclose all moving parts so that workers cannot harm their fingers or hands. In addition to eliminating direct contact between workers and moving machine parts, guards prevent accidents caused by human error, prohibit worker contact with exposed electrical components, flying metal objects, and splashing machine oils, and permit safe maintenance practices. OSHA says that guards must be machine- and task-specific; prevent access to the safety hazard while the equipment is running; be impossible to remove during equipment operation; not

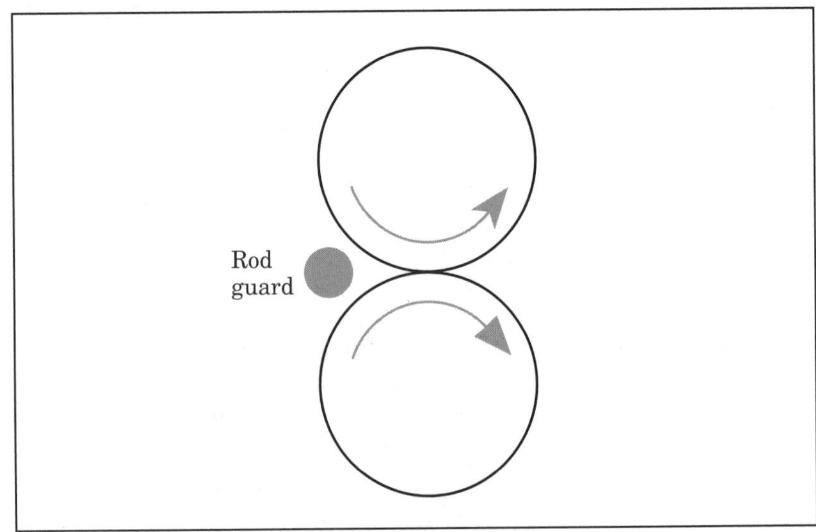

The use of guards to protect workers from pinch points

Such guards must be close enough to the rolling surface to prevent passage of a finger.

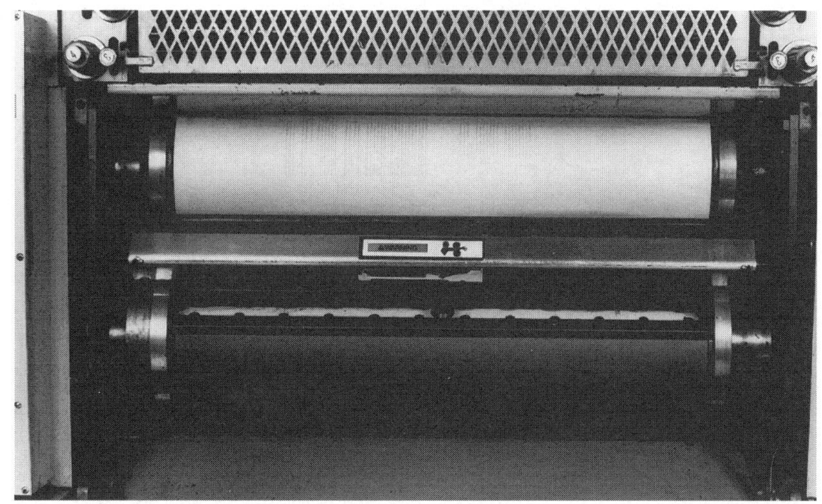

Nip guards between plate and blanket cylinders to prevent the operator's fingers from entering the in-running nip

constitute a hazard to the operator; and require a minimum of maintenance.

In the ideal situation then, a machine should not be able to run without its guard in place. Problems arise, however, when old equipment lacking guarding or equipment with damaged guarding is still in use. In either case, OSHA requires that working guards be installed. OSHA also states that employers should put in place an employee training program covering the proper placement of guards, the correct use of the "stop/safe/ready" button system, and safe cleaning procedures.

Press operator lifting press guard to gain access to the blanket for cleaning

Notice that the press operator is wearing protective gloves. The press should be in "safe" mode with the stop button depressed.

Lockout/Tagout Regulations

OSHA's Lockout/Tagout Standard went into effect on January 2, 1990. The standard requires that employees/operators place lockout/tagout devices on their machines whenever they are servicing them and there is a potential for a hazardous release of energy or accidental start-up. In other words, if the equipment is engaged in any activity other than its intended function, with the exception of minor servicing, maintenance, and setup activities that keep the employee's body out of the areas of potential contact with machine components, and/or do not expose the employee to unexpected energization, activation of the equipment, or release of stored energy, lockout/tagout requirements apply.

To comply with the Lockout/Tagout Standard, employers must complete the following:

1. Perform a job hazard analysis to identify activities and potential hazards associated with machinery or equipment.
2. Develop a detailed list of the specific lockout/tagout procedures and when they will be used for each appropriate piece of machinery with a potential energy hazard.
3. Develop a written program.
4. Develop and implement an employee training program.
5. Develop an outside contractor program.

Minor servicing, maintenance, and setup exceptions. Minor servicing and maintenance is defined by OSHA as "those tasks involving operations which can be safely accomplished by employees and where extensive disassembly of equipment is not required."* Minor servicing and maintenance activities include, but are not limited to the following:

- Clearing certain types of paper jams
- Minor cleaning (blanket washing, roller washing)
- Lubricating and adjusting operations
- Paper webbing and paper roll changing

Setup is defined as "any work performed to prepare a machine or equipment to perform its normal operation." Setup activities include the following:

- Mounting a plate
- Setting bearer pressures
- Setting folder adjustments
- Setting rollers

**OSHA's Lockout / Tagout Regulation and the Printing Industry.* GATF et al., pp. 23–29.

Printers have the option of using "alternative effective protection" for minor servicing and maintenance and setup procedures. OSHA defines an activity as meeting alternative effective protection requirements as they apply to the printing industry if the following conditions are met:

1. Servicing is conducted when the machine or equipment is stopped.
2. Each servicing employee has continuous, exclusive control of the means to start the machine or equipment.
3. Safeguarding is provided to each servicing employee to prevent exposure from the release of harmful, stored, or residual energy.

The inch-safe-service method used in conjunction with a safety system as described in the ANSI standard for printing presses (B65.1-1985) has been recognized by OSHA as one means of providing adequate alternative means of protection.

Servicing and/or maintenance activities that are not performed during normal production and require lockout/tagout procedures include, but are not limited to the following:

1. "Operations where auxiliary motors and pile motors are not disabled by the SAFE button and where the operator cannot maintain exclusive control of the machine or machine elements such as when:
   - Cleaning frames and braces
   - Cleaning the feeder and delivery on sheetfed presses
   - Cleaning the reel stand and other parts of the infeed on web presses
   - Cleaning or replacing air filters used to supply ventilation for toxic or flammable materials or heat generating electrical equipment."*
2. "Operations that require the machine operator to remove major parts of the equipment such as:
   - Panels or other barriers that restrict access to moving mechanical parts or energized electrical equipment
   - To perform extensive work without removal of such components
   - To perform work requiring the operator to leave the immediate area containing the operation controls where exclusive control by the operator is required."
3. "Roller removal would require Lockout/Tagout when two people are required and/or there are no quick release

*_OSHA's Lockout / Tagout Regulation and the Printing Industry._ GATF et al., pp. 23–29.

sockets which would permit safe roller removal by one person."*

4. Gripper bar repair/removal, gear replacement, and electrical work.

Circuit breaker lockout bracket with padlocks attached
Courtesy American Ed-Co, Inc.

Notice that the locks have identification tags attached.

Noise Exposure

OSHA requires hearing conservation programs, including annual training on the hazards of noise as well as baseline hearing tests within 30 days of employment and annual audiograms, for all employees exposed to noise levels at or above 85 decibels over an eight-hour time-weighted average. A **decibel** (dB) is a unit used to express relative intensities of sounds on a scale from zero for the average least-perceptible

**OSHA's Lockout/Tagout Regulation and the Printing Industry.* GATF et al., pp. 23–29.

Maximum exposure lengths per day at various sound levels

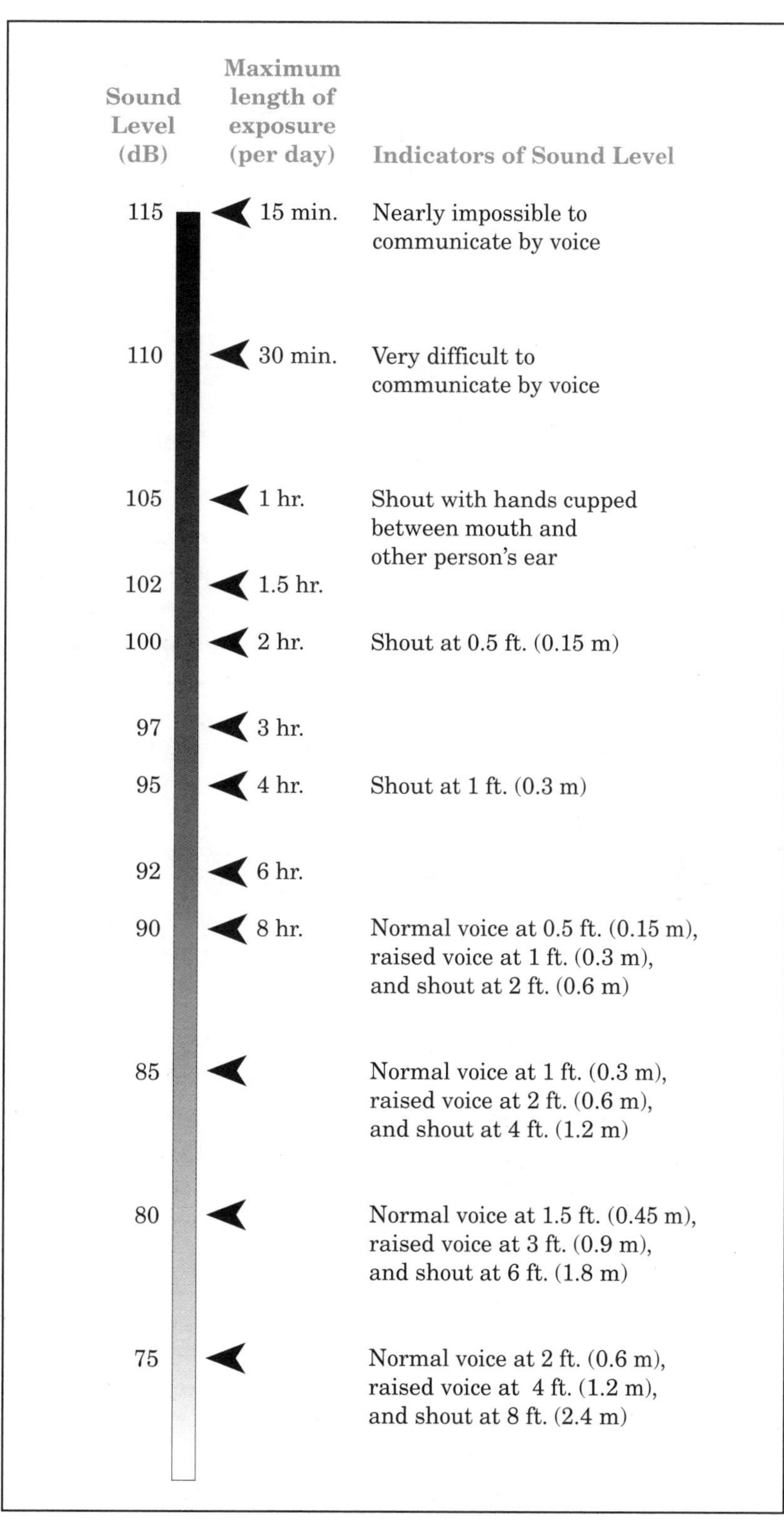
Sound Level (dB)
Maximum length of exposure (per day)
Indicators of Sound Level
115
15 min.
Nearly impossible to communicate by voice
110
30 min.
Very difficult to communicate by voice
105
1 hr.
Shout with hands cupped between mouth and other person's ear
102
1.5 hr.
100
2 hr.
Shout at 0.5 ft. (0.15 m)
97
3 hr.
95
4 hr.
Shout at 1 ft. (0.3 m)
92
6 hr.
90
8 hr.
Normal voice at 0.5 ft. (0.15 m), raised voice at 1 ft. (0.3 m), and shout at 2 ft. (0.6 m)
85
Normal voice at 1 ft. (0.3 m), raised voice at 2 ft. (0.6 m), and shout at 4 ft. (1.2 m)
80
Normal voice at 1.5 ft. (0.45 m), raised voice at 3 ft. (0.9 m), and shout at 6 ft. (1.8 m)
75
Normal voice at 2 ft. (0.6 m), raised voice at 4 ft. (1.2 m), and shout at 8 ft. (2.4 m)

sound to about 130 for the average level at which severe hearing damage can occur. Employers should monitor workplace noise exposure levels with calibrated meters that rate sound in decibels from 0 to 140 and post warnings in areas where the noise level exceeds 90 dB.

If noise levels exceed 90 dB over an eight-hour time-weighted average, workers must wear hearing protection. Personal hearing protection devices include earmuffs, rigid earplugs, and moldable inserts than can be shaped to fit the ear. Properly fitted and used commercial earplugs can reduce noise reaching the ear by 25–30 dB. Earmuffs or cups that cover the external ear provide the best acoustical barrier, reducing noise an additional 10–15 dB. Combining earplugs and earmuffs provides another 3–5 dB of protection.

There are several ways of reducing equipment noise levels. Acoustical ceiling tiles and sound-absorbing baffles and wall coatings, for example, assist in reducing pressroom noise levels. In addition, employees should be encouraged to wear shoes with rubber soles. Floor matting and thick-soled shoes absorb vibrations and reduce noise.

Repetitive Strain Injuries

Even though the pressroom has become increasingly automated, workers are still susceptible to injuries caused by repetitive motion. Each time a worker bends over, picks up a stack of press sheets, fans and jogs it, and places it on the pile table or a pallet, the chance of incurring a repetitive strain injury, also known as a cumulative trauma disorder, increases. Symptoms of repetitive strain injuries include swollen tendons, muscle spasms, numbness, and tingling.

Wrist strain. Carpal tunnel syndrome, the most well-known and debilitating of the repetitive strain injuries, occurs as a result of damage to, or pressure on, the medial nerve, which is located in the arm and travels through the wrist and into the palm of the hand. As the use of computers in the workplace increased throughout the 1980s, so did reported incidents of wrist strain, carpal tunnel syndrome in particular.

To date, most prevention and treatment efforts have concentrated on developing workstations that lessen the wrist and neck strain on office staff members. The specific concerns of pressroom or other printing industry personnel remain largely unaddressed. For the time being, it is helpful to instruct workers in minimizing wrist strain by observing some basic positioning and lifting requirements. Whenever possible, workers should lift with their elbows down. Elevating unsupported elbows or positioning them too far from the torso makes lifting much more difficult because it requires a physically demanding shoulder swing. Over several hours, the resulting fatigue will reduce efficiency.

Back strain. Back injuries are another common problem caused by repetitive strain. In fact, the National Safety Council reports that 31% of all workers' compensation cases are related to back injuries. At some firms, employees are required to wear back support belts that are advertised as offering enhanced lumbar and abdominal support while eliminating the need to overstretch muscles. Other companies require employees to wear audible-warning devices on the backs of their shirts. These devices emit 90-dB tones whenever workers bend or lift improperly.

Less controversial and more common are the exercise and training guidelines for avoiding back strain that, unlike the preventive measures for carpal tunnel syndrome, have been in place for sometime.

Employees should size up the weight of a load before lifting or lowering anything. Use two people to lift awkward loads or break the load into smaller groupings if help is not available. During a lift, bend the knees and place the feet close to the load to achieve better balance. Minimize movements of the spine, as even the smallest variations in posture can increase back strain. Keeping the load closer to the body's center of gravity also permits safer movement.

Do not overreach or lift with fast jerking motions, and make certain there are enough places to easily grip the load. Loads with hand grips are ideal. Be especially cautious when lowering a load because the spine is compressed at this time.

General Chemical Safety

All chemical substances can be dangerous if mishandled. Even common chemicals and formulations used in printing must be handled in a safe manner.

Every employer must comply with OSHA's Hazard Communication Standard. Employee training, container labeling, and MSDSs are cornerstones of this standard. The MSDS provides basic information to help employers and employees assess chemical hazards posed by materials they use.

To comply with the standard, printers must meet the following five requirements:

- Compile a list of all chemicals used in the plant.
- Obtain Material Safety Data Sheets (MSDSs) from the manufacturer or distributor for each chemical that appears on the list.
- Properly label each container that contains a hazardous chemical.
- Provide ongoing employee training, including the identification and proper use of all chemicals used in the plant.
- Develop a written hazard communication program.

Under certain conditions, inks, solvents, dampening solutions, and other chemicals used in printing can cause safety and health problems for the workers exposed to them. If any material contains chemical(s) that are defined as health hazards by the Occupational Safety and Health Administration (OSHA), its manufacturer or importer is required by law to provide a Material Safety Data Sheet (MSDS) for that material. An MSDS contains information on the chemical, physical characteristics, safe handling practices, and proper disposal procedures. Employers are required by OSHA regulations to make the MSDSs available to employees. MSDSs for materials no longer in use must be maintained for thirty years.

In order to help educate employees about the potential hazards associated with using chemicals, the printing industry has unofficially adopted the HMIS system. As part of fulfilling the requirements associated with the Hazard Communication Standard, HMIS labels should be affixed to all chemical containers. The label identifies the hazards associated with the chemical and lists the personal protection required when handling that chemical. Employees must be trained in how to read and interpret the HMIS labels.

Proper solvent handling is important. Ink solvents present fire, health, and environmental hazards. Training programs together with proper equipment are required to reduce accidents and injuries.

Before a new printing ink or any other new press chemical is used, the technical manager should review the MSDS and product label to evaluate any potential hazards. Some MSDSs contain warnings not present on a product label. The printer must have trained personnel and written emergency handling procedures to deal with accidental exposure and injury caused by hazardous chemicals. For personal injuries, the printer needs to file proper documentation as required by the Occupational Safety and Health Administration.

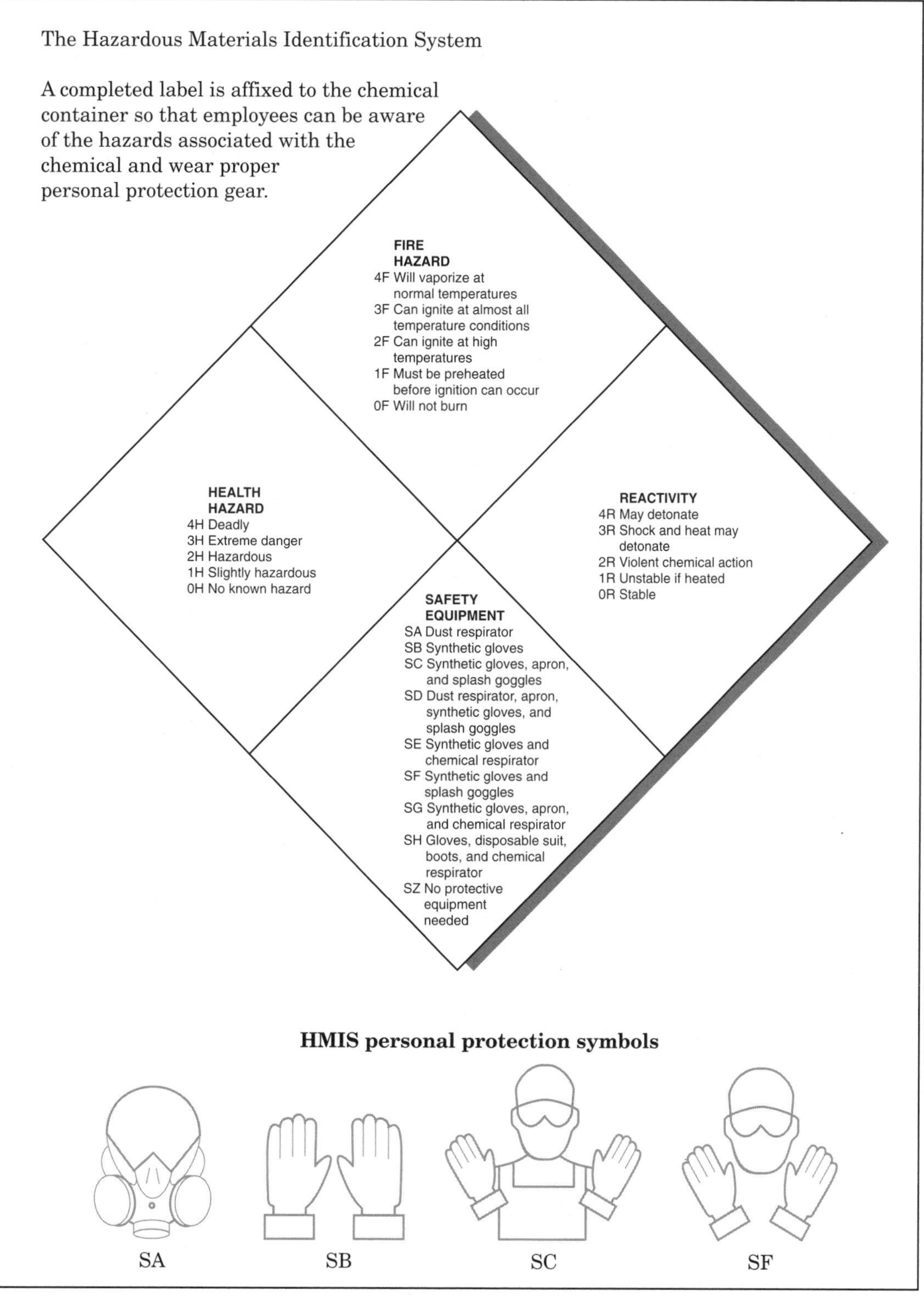
The Hazardous Materials Identification System
A completed label is affixed to the chemical container so that employees can be aware of the hazards associated with the chemical and wear proper personal protection gear.
FIRE HAZARD
4F Will vaporize at normal temperatures
3F Can ignite at almost all temperature conditions
2F Can ignite at high temperatures
1F Must be preheated before ignition can occur
0F Will not burn
HEALTH HAZARD
4H Deadly
3H Extreme danger
2H Hazardous
1H Slightly hazardous
0H No known hazard
REACTIVITY
4R May detonate
3R Shock and heat may detonate
2R Violent chemical action
1R Unstable if heated
0R Stable
SAFETY EQUIPMENT
SA Dust respirator
SB Synthetic gloves
SC Synthetic gloves, apron, and splash goggles
SD Dust respirator, apron, synthetic gloves, and splash goggles
SE Synthetic gloves and chemical respirator
SF Synthetic gloves and splash goggles
SG Synthetic gloves, apron, and chemical respirator
SH Gloves, disposable suit, boots, and chemical respirator
SZ No protective equipment needed
HMIS personal protection symbols
SA
SB
SC
SF

Glossary

air-blast nozzles Components of the sheet-separation unit that use forced air to separate the top sheets of the pile.

air-cushion drum A device that supports the sheet on a cushion of air to lessen the chance that ink will smear on the press sheet. *Alternative term:* air-transport drum.

alcohol, isopropyl An organic substance added to the dampening solution of a lithographic printing press to reduce the surface tension of water. *Alternative term:* isopropanol.

alcohol substitute A chemical used in a lithographic dampening solution in place of isopropyl alcohol (isopropanol).

antifoaming agent A substance that prevents the buildup of foam in a dampening solution.

antisetoff compound An ink additive that prevents the inked image on a press sheet from rubbing off on the sheet above it in the delivery pile by forming a protective layer on the ink surface or by shortening the ink (decreasing its gelling time).

antisetoff spray Ground starch particles sprayed onto sheets to keep the ink on each press sheet from direct contact with the ink on another sheet in the delivery. *Alternative term:* spray powder.

antiskinning agent A material added to ink to prevent a rubbery layer from forming on its surface when it is exposed to air.

back cylinder See *impression cylinder.*

back pressure The force between the blanket cylinder and the impression cylinder that facilitates the transfer of the image from the blanket to the printing substrate. *Alternative term:* impression pressure.

back-edge curl A curve that develops at the tail edge of a press sheet as a result of printing heavy solids close to this edge. Excessive dampening can also be a cause.

backing up Printing the reverse side of a sheet that has already been printed.

backlash gear A thin second gear bolted to the spur gear to reduce play between gears.

back-trap mottle Blotches and streaks in the solids and tones of an overprinted ink film on a press sheet due to the transfer of a printed ink film from the paper to the blanket of a subsequent printing unit. This trap problem occurs almost exclusively on sheetfed presses with four or more printing units.

bareback roller A form or ductor roller in a conventional dampening system that operates without cloth or paper covers.

basic size Sheet size in inches for a particular type of paper.

basis weight Weight, in pounds, of a ream of paper cut to its basic size, in inches.

bearer A hardened metal ring attached to the cylinder body or journal of the plate and blanket cylinders.

bearer pressure The force with which the bearers of opposed cylinders contact each other on a sheetfed offset press.

bearer-to-bearer The cylinder arrangement in which the bearers of the plate and blanket cylinders contact each other.

bladeless ink fountain A disposable sheet of polyester foil that is held in contact with the fountain roller by a series of small cylinders lying parallel to it.

blanket A fabric coated with synthetic or natural rubber that transfers the image from the printing plate to the substrate.

blanket, compressible A blanket with a specially manufactured layer designed to "give" or compress under pressure from the plate and impression cylinder.

blanket, conventional A hard, noncompressible blanket that bulges out on either or both sides of a nip under pressure.

blanket compressibility The extent to which blanket thickness reduces under pressure, such as during the printing impression.

blanket compression set The permanent reduction in thickness of a blanket or any of its component parts.

blanket creep The slight forward movement or slip of the part of the blanket surface that is in contact with the plate or paper.

blanket cylinder The cylinder that carries the printing blanket and has two primary functions: (1) to carry the offset rubber blanket into contact with the inked image on the plate cylinder and (2) to transfer, or offset, the ink film image to the paper (or other substrate) carried by the impression cylinder.

blow-downs A series of air holes, located near the top of the delivery, that assist in dropping the sheet onto the delivery table.

body The relative term describing the consistency of an ink, referring mainly to the stiffness or softness of an ink, but implying other things including length and thixotropy.

bonding The elimination of a difference in electrical potential between objects.

bridge roller A roller in a combination continuous-flow dampening system that contacts the dampening form roller and the first ink form roller and transports dampening solution from the dampening system into the inking system.

buffer A substance capable of neutralizing acids and bases in solutions and thereby maintaining the acidity or alkalinity level of the solution.

caliper The thickness of a sheet of paper or other material measured under specific conditions. Caliper is usually expressed in mils or points, both ways of expressing thousandths of an inch.

catch-up The condition that occurs when insufficient dampening causes the nonimage areas of the plate to become ink-receptive and print as scum or when excessive ink reaches the plate. *Alternative term:* dry-up.

chain transfer A principal method of sheet transfer where sets of grippers riding on a chain transport the sheet from one impression cylinder to the next.

chalking Poor adhesion of ink to the printing surface. This condition results when the substrate absorbs the ink vehicle too rapidly. The ink dries slowly and rubs off as a dusty powder.

color bar A device printed in a trim area of a press sheet to monitor printing variables such as trapping, ink density, dot gain, and print contrast. It usually consists of overprints of two- and three-color solids and tints; solid and tint blocks of cyan, magenta, yellow, and black; and additional aids such as resolution targets and dot gain scales. *Alternative terms:* color control strip; color control bar.

color match Condition resulting when no significant difference in hue, saturation, and lightness can be detected between two color samples viewed under standard illumination.

color sequence The order in which colors are printed on a substrate as indicated by the order that the inks are supplied to the printing units of the press. Color sequence determines how well inks trap on a substrate. *Alternative term:* color rotation.

color strength An ink's color power as determined by its pigment concentration.

color temperature The degree (expressed in Kelvins) to which a blackbody must be heated to produce a certain color radiation. For example, 5,000 Kelvin is the graphic arts viewing standard.

color variation Changes that occur in the density of a color during printing as a result of deviations in the amount of ink accepted by paper or the amount of ink fed to the paper.

common impression cylinder A drum-like cylinder that contacts several blanket cylinders, permitting multicolor printing on one side of the sheet.

corrosion inhibitor An additive to the dampening solution to prevent it from reacting with the plate.

crash bar A device that detects foreign objects on the feedboard and prevents their passage into the printing unit.

crystallization The drying of an ink to form a hard, impervious surface that interferes with dry trapping.

cylinder gap The opening in a press cylinder in which gripping mechanisms are placed.

cylinder undercut The difference between cylinder body radius and bearer radius.

dampener covers Molleton, paper, or fiber sleeves placed over dampening rollers in a conventional dampening system that aid in carrying the dampening solution.

dampening solution A mixture of water; gum arabic; an acid, neutral, or alkaline etch; and isopropyl alcohol or an alcohol substitute used to wet the nonimage areas of the lithographic printing plate before it is inked. *Alternative term:* fountain solution.

dampening system A group of rollers that moistens the nonimage areas of a printing plate with a water-based dampening solution that contains additives such as acid, gum arabic, and isopropyl alcohol or other wetting agents.

dampening system, continuous-feed A ductorless dampening system in which there is a continuous flow of dampening solution from the fountain roller to the form roller. *Alternative term:* continuous-flow dampening system.

dampening system, conventional A dampening system consisting of a fountain, fountain pan roller, ductor roller, oscillator roller, and one or more covered or uncovered form rollers. The ductor roller transfers dampening solution from the fountain roller to the oscillator roller. *Alternative term:* intermittent-flow dampening system.

dampening system, inker-feed An integrated, continuous-feed dampening system that delivers dampening solution to an ink form roller.

dampening system, plate-feed A continuous-feed dampening system that applies dampening solution directly to the plate using dampening form rollers, rather than indirectly using the first inking form roller.

deadweight micrometer A device that uses the deadweight of an anvil to obtain repeatable measurements on plate, blankets, and packing. *Alternative terms:* bench micrometer, blanket thickness gauge, Cady gauge.

delivery The section of a printing press that receives, jogs, and stacks the printed sheet.

delivery cylinder The cylinder after the last printing unit that powers the chain delivery and coordinates the transfer of the printed sheet from the last impression cylinder to the delivery gripper bars attached to the two delivery chains.

desensitization In platemaking, the making of an nonimage area less receptive to ink by the application of a gum solution.

dimensional stability How well an object maintains it size. The extent to which a sheet maintains its dimensions with changes in its moisture content or applied stressing.

dot gain The optical increase in the size of a halftone dot during prepress operations or the mechanical increase in halftone dot size that occurs as the image is transferred from plate to blanket to paper in lithography.

double-sheet detector A device that can be set to stop the feeding action of the sheet-separation unit if more than one sheet of paper is being forwarded. *Alternative terms:* two-sheet caliper, two-sheet detector.

drier An ink additive, such as a salt of cobalt or manganese, that acts as a catalyst to convert a wet ink film to a dry ink film.

drum (1) An oscillating metal ink distribution roller. (2) A synonym for “cylinder” in many press applications.

dry dusting A preliminary pass of the sheet under pressure through the press to remove excessive spray powder, surface material, or other debris.

dry offset Printing from relief plates by transferring the ink image from the plate to a rubber surface and then from the rubber surface to the paper. Printing with this process on an offset press eliminates the need to use water. *Alternative terms:* indirect letterpress, letterset, relief offset.

dry-back An optical loss of density and color strength that may occur while an ink is setting. To achieve the proper dry density, the ink is printed with a wet density slightly higher than the projected dry density.

drying agent An ink additive, such as a salt of cobalt or manganese, that acts as a catalyst to convert a wet ink film to a dry ink film.

drying section Section of a papermaking machine where water is removed by passing the web over hot drying cylinders.

drying stimulator A substance—e.g., cobalt chloride—that complements the drier in the ink.

dry-up The problem that occurs when ink appears in the nonimage area due to insufficient dampening of the plate. *Alternative term:* catch-up.

ductor (1) A small-diameter cylinder that alternately contacts the ink fountain roller and the first roller of the ink train. (2) In a conventional dampening system, a small-diameter cylinder that alternately contacts the dampening fountain roller and the oscillator. *Alternative term:* ductor roller.

ductor shock The vibration sent through the inking system when the ductor first contacts the oscillating roller.

duplicator Any press smaller than 11×17 in. (279×432 mm) without bearers (hardened metal disks attached to the ends of the cylinder or to the cylinder's journal).

durability The blanket's ability to withstand the pressure, tension, and physical abuse on the press.

durometer, type-A Instrument used in printing to measure the hardness of roller compounds.

dwell — The length of time that the ductor roller contacts the fountain roller.

emulsification — Condition that occurs when a lithographic ink picks up too much dampening solution and prints a weak, snowflaky pattern.

endplay — Undesirable lateral movement of a roller due to poor fit between roller shaft and roller bracket.

fan-out — An expansion of the sheet near the tail edge.

feedboard — A platform or ramp on which the sheet to be printed is transported to registering devices that properly position the sheet and time its entrance into the printing unit. *Alternative term:* feed table.

feeder — The paper-supply section of a sheetfed press where paper is lifted from the top of a pile table, forwarded on a feedboard to front stops, laterally positioned on the feedboard by a side guide, and fed into the first printing unit.

feeder, continuous — A feeder that can be reloaded without stopping the press.

feeder, single-sheet — A feeder where only one sheet of paper (traveling at press speed) is on the feedboard at any instant.

feeder, stream — A feeder where a number of sheets of paper (traveling slower than press speed) overlap on the feedboard.

feeder, successive-sheet — A feeder where only one sheet of paper (traveling at press speed) is on the feedboard at any instant.

feeder foot — A leveling device that can be adjusted up or down to control the height of the paper pile on a sheetfed press. It also blows a stream of air beneath the sheet lifted by the pickup suckers. *Alternative term:* pressure foot.

feeler gauge — A thin strip of steel ground to precise thickness and marked accordingly. It is used to adjust clearances between various press mechanisms.

fingers Devices that prevent the suckers in the sheet-separation unit from picking up more than one sheet at a time.

form roller A device, riding in contact with the printing plate, that transfers dampening solution or ink from an oscillator roller to the printing plate. Presses typically have one or two *dampening* form rollers and three to five *inking* form rollers.

form roller, oscillating A special roller substituted for the first and, sometimes, fourth (last) form rollers of a press to reduce ghosting on a job.

forwarding roller One of a series of rotating devices that transfer the sheet from the sheet-separation unit to the feedboard.

fountain A reservoir for the dampening solution or ink that is fed to the plate.

fountain blade A spring steel plate, steel segment, or plastic angled against the fountain roller and forming the bottom of the ink fountain. Moving the blade closer or farther from the fountain roller controls the thickness of the ink film across the roller.

fountain cheeks Vertical metal pieces contacting the edges of the fountain roller and blade to form an ink-tight trough.

fountain height monitor A sensing device, usually mechanical or ultrasonic, that checks the height of ink moving over the agitator.

fountain keys A series of thumb screws or motor-driven screws or cams behind the blade that provide for variable ink flow across the fountain.

fountain roller A metal roller that rotates intermittently or continuously in the ink or dampening fountain and carries the ink or dampening solution on its metal surface.

fountain solution See *dampening solution.*

fountain splitter A device that divides the ink fountain so that two or more inks can be used in the same ink fountain. Each ink will print a different section of the press sheet; e.g., red on the left side and blue on the right side.

front guide One of a series of stops that halt the forward movement of the sheet on the feedboard. The front guides square the sheet in relation to the printing cylinders and determine the front margin.

fungicide A substance that prevents the formation of mildew and the growth of fungus and bacteria in the dampening system.

furnish Mixture of fibrous and nonfibrous materials like colorants, fillers, and sizing in a water suspension from which paper or paperboard is made.

gear streaks Alternating light and dark marks that appear as bands in halftones and solids parallel to the gripper edge of the sheet. The distance between the marks is the same as the interval between the gear teeth on a cylinder.

ghosting The appearance of faint replicas of an image in undesirable places, caused by mechanical or chemical processes, other than setoff or show-through. *Mechanical ghosting* is caused by ink starvation. *Chemical ghosting* is the appearance of gloss or dull ghosts of images that are printed on the reverse side of the sheet and is caused by the chemical-activity influence that inks have on each other during their critical drying phases.

glaze A combination of oxidized roller surface, embedded ink pigment, dried ink vehicle, and gum from dampening solution on an inking roller.

gloss High reflectance of light from a smooth surface.

grain direction In papermaking, the alignment of fibers in the direction of web travel. In printing, paper is *grain-long* if the grain direction parallels the long dimension of the paper and *grain-short* if it parallels the short dimension.

grammage Weight in grams of a single sheet of paper having an area of one square meter (1 m^2).

gripper The metal clamps that grasp and hold a sheet in position as it travels through a sheetfed press.

gripper bite The amount of sheet—margin—under the paper gripper of the impression cylinder.

gripper-bowing device A device, usually part of an infeed drum, that compensates for the effects of fan-out by intentionally bowing the gripper bar as much as 0.008 in. (0.020 mm) at its center.

grounding The elimination of a difference in electrical potential between an object and the ground.

groundwood Mechanical pulp used in papermaking produced by forcing bark-free logs against a revolving, abrasive grinding stone in the presence of water.

helical gear A gear that has teeth cut at an angle.

hickey An imperfection in printing due to a particle on the blanket or, sometimes, the plate. A *doughnut hickey* consists of a small, solid printed area surrounded by a white halo, or unprinted area. A *void hickey* is a white, unprinted spot surrounded by printing.

hickey-picking roller A roller that has synthetic fibers embedded in its surface to help it remove hickeys from the surface of an offset printing plate or to fill in the white ring on the plate surface. This roller replaces one of the ink form rollers.

hold-down rods Rods that are positioned so that they hold down the back corners of the sheet as it enters the feedboard.

hot-weather scumming The tendency of ink to print in nonimage areas when the dampening feed rate is too low.

hydrophilic Water-receptive, as in the nonimage areas of the printing plate.

hydrophobic Water-repellent, as in the image areas of the printing plate.

image area On a printing plate, the area that has been specially treated to receive ink.

image fit The agreement in distance between the register marks on each color from the gripper to the tail edge of the press sheet.

impression (1) The printing pressure necessary to transfer an inked image from the blanket to the substrate. (2) A single print.

impression cylinder A large-diameter cylinder that transports the press sheet and forces the paper or other substrate against the inked blanket.

impression cylinder pressure The force of the impression (or back) cylinder against the blanket cylinder.

infeed The section of a sheetfed press where the sheet is transferred from the registering devices of the feedboard to the first impression cylinder of the printing press.

infeed, swing-arm A type of infeed in which front guides stop the sheet and move away at the proper time. Grippers on a swing-arm mechanism close on the sheet and transfer the sheet to the impression-cylinder grippers.

ink absorbency The extent that an ink penetrates the paper.

ink agitator A revolving cone-shaped device that moves from one end of the fountain to the other keeping the ink soft and flowing.

ink drying Process by which a sheetfed ink is transformed from an original semifluid or plastic state to a solid.

ink feed The amount of ink delivered to the ink form rollers.

ink holdout The extent to which paper resists or retards the penetration of the freshly printed ink film.

ink setting (1) The increase in viscosity or body (resistance to flow) that occurs immediately after the ink is printed. (2) An adjustment that the press operator makes to the inking system to control ink volume.

ink vehicle A complex liquid mixture in which pigment particles are dispersed.

inking control console A computerized device that enables the press operator to control inking and a variety of other functions without leaving the inspection table.

inking system A series of rollers that apply a metered film of ink to a printing plate.

ink/water balance In lithography, the appropriate amounts of ink and water required to ink the image areas of the plate and keep the nonimage areas clean.

isopropanol See *alcohol, isopropyl.*

joggers Two movable devices in the delivery of a sheetfed press that work along with the rear sheet guide and a front gate to align and stack printed press sheets.

kiss impression The minimum pressure at which proper ink transfer from the blanket to the substrate is possible.

knife rollers Small-diameter hard rollers that help to keep the ink system clean by picking up ink skin particles, lint, etc. *Alternative term:* lint roller.

lay Position of the printed image on the sheet.

lay sheet The first of several sheets run through the press to verify lineup, register, type, and nonimage areas.

lift A manageable amount of paper.

lint Loosely bonded paper surface fibers and dust that accumulates on an offset plate or blanket and interferes with print quality. *Alternative terms:* linting, fluffing.

liquid drier A drier in which metal salts are suspended in liquids such as a petroleum solvent.

lithography, offset A planographic printing process that requires an image carrier in the form of a plate on which photochemically produced image and nonimage areas are receptive to ink and water, respectively.

loupe An adjustable-focus magnifier incorporating a precise measuring scale, with or without a self-contained light source. It is used to inspect fine detail.

makeready All of the operations necessary to get the press ready to print the current job.

makeready book A pile of press sheets consisting of clean, unprinted sheets interspersed with waste sheets (previously printed sheets) and used during makeready.

masstone The color of ink in bulk, such as in a can, or a thick film of ink. It is the color of light reflected by the pigment and often differs from the printed color of the ink.

material safety data sheet A product specification form used to identify chemical substances and their physical properties and assess the potential hazards involved in their use.

metering nip The line of contact between the two rollers of an inker-feed dampening system.

milking A coating buildup on the nonimage areas of the offset blanket that usually occurs when the coating softens because it does not adequately resist water.

misregister Incorrectly positioned printed images, either in reference to each other or to the sheet's edges.

misregister, random Misregister that varies from sheet to sheet.

misting Flying ink that forms fine droplets or filaments that become diffused throughout the pressroom.

molleton A thick cotton fabric, similar to flannel, with a long nap and used to cover form rollers in conventional lithographic dampening systems.

mottle Irregular and unwanted variation in color or gloss caused by uneven absorbency of the paper.

multicolor printing The printing of two or more colors, often one over another.

nip The line of contact between two cylindrical objects, such as two rollers on an offset press.

nonimage area The portion of a lithographic printing plate that is treated to accept water and repel ink when the plate is on press. Only the ink-receptive areas will print an image.

offset blanket See *blanket.*

oleophilic Oil-receptive, as in the image areas of the printing plate.

oleophobic Oil-repellent, as in the dampened nonimage areas of the printing plate.

opacity (1) The ability of a printed ink film to hide what is underneath. (2) The extend to which light transmission is obstructed.

oscillator A driven inking or dampening roller that not only rotates but moves from side to side, distributing and smoothing out the ink film and erasing image patterns from the form roller. *Alternative terms:* oscillating drum, oscillating roller, or vibrator.

overfeed system A type of infeed in which front guides stop the sheet and move away at the proper time. Feed rolls or vacuum belts drive the sheet against stops (front guides) on the impression cylinder.

overpacking Packing the plate or blanket to a level that is excessively above the level of the cylinder bearer.

packing (1) The procedure for setting the pressure between the plate and blanket cylinders. (2) The paper or other material that is placed between the plate or blanket and its cylinder to raise the surface to printing height or to adjust cylinder diameter to obtain color register in multicolor printing.

packing gauge A device for measuring the height of the plate or blanket in relation to its cylinder bearers.

paste drier A highly viscous drier prepared by grinding the inorganic salts of manganese or other metals in linseed oil varnishes.

perfecting The printing of at least one color on both sides of a sheet in a single pass through a press.

perfector A sheetfed press that can print at least one color on both sides of a sheet in a single pass. *Alternative term:* perfecting sheetfed press.

perfector, convertible A perfecting press in which a special transfer cylinder tumbles the paper end for end between printing units so that the other side of the sheet is printed by the second unit. It has the capability, through transfer cylinder adjustment, to print either two colors on one side of the sheet or one color on each side in a single pass through the press.

pH A measure of a solution's acidity or alkalinity, specifically the negative logarithm of the concentration (in moles/liter) of the hydrogen ions in a solution. Measured on a scale of 0 to 14, with 7 as the neutral point.

pick resistance Ability of a paper to resist a force applied perpendicularly to its surface before picking or rupturing occurs.

picking The delamination, splitting, or tearing of the paper surface that occurs when the tack of the ink exceeds the surface strength of the paper.

pickup suckers Components of the sheet-separation unit that lift and forward the top sheet of the pile to forwarding rollers. The sheets are lifted by rear pickup suckers and are then transferred to the forwarding rollers by the forwarding pickup suckers.

pigment Finely divided solid material that gives an ink color.

pile height Maximum height of the paper pile in the feeder, usually $\frac{3}{16}$ in. (5 mm) below the forwarding flaps at the front of the pile.

pile table A raisable platform where the paper to be printed is loaded. *Alternative term:* pile board.

piling A buildup of paper, ink, or coating on the offset blanket, plate, or rollers in such quantity that it interferes with print quality.

pipe rollers Small-diameter hard rollers that help to keep the ink system clean by picking up ink skin particles, lint, etc.

pitch diameter The working diameter of the gear attached to the cylinder journal.

planography A printing process that uses a flat image carrier, such as the lithographic printing plate, which has no relief images and has image and nonimage areas on the same level (or plane).

plate A flexible image carrier with ink-receptive image areas and, when moistened with a water-based solution, ink-repellent nonimage areas. A thin metal, plastic, or paper sheet serves as the image carrier in many printing processes.

plate, bimetal A negative-working multimetal printing plate that usually consists of copper electroplated on a base metal such as aluminum or stainless steel.

plate, negative-working A printing plate that is exposed through a film negative. Plate areas exposed to light become the image areas.

plate, positive-working A printing plate that is exposed through a film positive. Plate areas exposed to light become the nonimage areas.

plate, presensitized A sheet of metal or paper supplied to the user with the light-sensitive material already coated on the surface and ready for exposure to a negative or positive.

plate, subtractive A printing plate in which the light-sensitive coating also contains an image-reinforcing material.

plate, surface A printing plate in which a light-sensitive coating applied to the plate surface is made ink-receptive in the image areas during exposure and processing, while in the nonimage areas it is removed or converted to a water-receptive layer.

plate, trimetal A positive-working multimetal printing plate consisting of a top layer of chromium (the nonimage metal) and a bottom layer of copper (the image metal) electroplated to a base metal.

plate, waterless A presensitized negative- or positive-working planographic image carrier that uses ink-repellent silicone rubber, instead of a water-based dampening solution, to keep ink from adhering to the nonimage areas of the plate.

plate blinding The loss of ink receptivity in the image area due to an excessively acidic fountain solution.

plate clamp A device that grips the lead and trailing edges of the plate and pulls it tight against the cylinder body.

plate cylinder A cylinder that carries the printing plate. It has four primary functions: (1) to hold the lithographic printing plate tightly and in register, (2) to carry the plate into contact with the dampening rollers that wet the nonimage area, (3) to bring the plate into contact with the inking rollers that ink the image area, and (4) to transfer the inked image to the blanket carried by the blanket cylinder.

plate scanner A device that measures all of the various densities in a plate's image area at selected increments across the printing plate before it is mounted on the press. The press operator then sets the ink fountain keys to match the ink densities indicated by the plate scanner's measurements before beginning to print the job.

plate scumming The pickup of ink in nonimage areas of the plate.

preloaded pressure The amount of force required to hold the plate and blanket cylinder in firm contact when the cylinders are overpacked to create the recommended squeeze pressure.

press, bearer-contact A press that runs with the bearers of the plate and blanket cylinders in contact.

press, blanket-to-blanket A perfecting press in which the blankets from two printing units are in contact, with the paper passing between the two blankets. Since each blanket acts as the impression cylinder for the other, no impression cylinder is needed.

press, multicolor A press consisting of two or more printing units (each with its own inking and dampening system), a feeder, a sheet transfer system, and a delivery. Two or more colors can be printed on one side of a sheet during a single pass through the press.

press, non–bearer-contact A press in which the bearers of the plate and blanket cylinders do not run in contact; i.e., there is a slight gap—clearance—between the bearers.

press, offset lithographic A mechanical device that dampens and inks a planographic printing plate and transfers the inked image to the blanket and then to the printing substrate.

press, perfecting A sheetfed press that can print at least one color on both sides of a sheet in a single pass. *Alternative term:* perfecting sheetfed press.

press, sheetfed offset An offset lithographic printing press that feeds and prints on individual sheets of paper (or other substrate) using the offset lithographic printing method.

press, single-color A press consisting of a single printing unit, with its integral inking and dampening systems, a feeder, a sheet transfer system, and a delivery. It can also be used for multicolor printing by changing the ink and plate and running the paper through the press again.

press, small offset Any press smaller than 11×17 in. (279×432 mm) without bearers (hardened metal disks attached to the ends of the cylinder or to the cylinder's journal).

press, web offset A offset lithographic press that prints on a continuous web, or ribbon, of paper fed from a roll and threaded through the press.

press section Section of papermaking machine where water is removed from the web by suction and applied pressure.

press sheet A single sheet of paper selected for the job to be printed on the press.

pressrun (1) The total of acceptable copies from a single printing. (2) Operating the press during an actual job.

presswork All operations performed on or by a printing press that lead to the transfer of inked images from the image carrier to the paper or other substrate. Presswork includes makeready.

printing pressure The force, in pounds per square inch, required to transfer the printed image to the substrate. In lithography, this includes the pressure between the plate and blanket, the blanket and the impression cylinder, and the impression cylinder and the substrate.

printing unit The section of the offset lithographic press that houses the components for reproducing an image on the substrate. With a sheetfed offset press, a printing unit includes the inking and dampening system and the plate, blanket, and impression cylinders.

proof A prototype of the printed job made photomechanically from plates (a press proof), photochemically from film, or digitally from electronic data (prepress proofs). Prepress proofs serve as samples for the customer and guides for the press operators. Press proofs are approved by the customer and/or plant supervisor before the actual pressrun.

proof, direct digital color A type of prepress proof in which digital information is used to directly image the color proofing material. Various technologies, such as ink jet and dye sublimation, are used to image the color proofing material. No film intermediates are required.

proof, overlay A type of photochemical prepress proof used in multicolor or process-color printing where pigmented or dyed sheets of plastic (for each process color and black) are exposed to a halftone negative or positive from a set of color separation films, processed, registered to each other, and taped or pin-registered to a base.

proof, prepress A simulation of the printed piece that is made digitally from electronic data or photochemically using light-sensitive papers (principally to proof single-color printing), colored films, or photopolymers. *Alternative term:* off-press proof.

proof, single-sheet A type of photochemical prepress proof used for multicolor or process-color proofing where the printing colors are built up on a base through lamination, exposure to a halftone negative or positive from a set of color separation films, and toning or other processing.

proof press A printing machine used to produce photomechanical proofs. It has most of the features of a true production machine but is not meant for long pressruns.

proofing Producing simulated versions of the final reproduction from films and dyes or digitized data (prepress proofing) or production trial images directly from the plate (press proofing).

pull A group of inspection sheets removed from the delivery of the press.

quality control Systematically planning, measuring, testing, and evaluating the combination of staff resources, materials, and machines during (and directly after) manufacture with the objective of producing a product that will satisfy established standards and profitability of an enterprise.

ream With a few exceptions, 500 sheets of paper.

reducer An ink additive that softens the ink and reduces its tack.

refiner mechanical pulp Papermaking pulp produced by passing wood chips through a disk refiner instead of pressing the wood against an abrasive grinding stone.

refractive index Measure of the ability of a material, such as a pigment particle, to bend or refract light rays. The result is expressed as the ratio of the speed of light in one medium to the speed of light in another medium (usually air or a vacuum).

register The accurate positioning of images—either in relation to images on other press sheets or in relation to an image already printed on that press sheet.

register plate A device that stops the lateral (sideways) movement of the sheet on the feedboard of a sheetfed press. *Alternative term:* register block.

release The readiness of the blanket to give up the paper after it leaves the nip.

remote control console A computerized device that enables the press operator to control a variety of functions without leaving the inspection table. Among the functions controlled are inking, dampening, and lateral and circumferential image register.

resilience The ability of a blanket to regain its thickness after pressure on its surface has been removed.

reverse slip nip The point of contact where two rollers are rotating in opposite directions in a dampening system.

roll sheeter A device that cuts paper on a roll into sheets and sends them to the press feeder.

roller, intermediate A friction- or gravity-driven roller between the ductor and form roller that transfers and conditions the ink. It is called a *distributor* if it contacts two rollers and a *rider* if it contacts a single oscillating drum.

roller cover Absorbent cloth or paper that covers the rollers and helps to provide more continuous dampening by increasing the solution-carrying and solution-storing capacity of the rollers.

roller stripping Condition that occurs in lithography when ink oscillators fail to accept ink because they have been desensitized by dampening solution.

roller-setting gauge A device that shows the amount of pressure exerted when the press operator pulls a metal feeler strip between the two rollers being set.

roller-stripe gauge A device that is marked with stripes of specified widths and used to visually determine the width of an ink stripe on a roller or plate.

rotary drum A type of infeed in which front guides stop the sheet and move out of the way at the proper time. The grippers on a rotating drum close on the sheet and transfer it to the impression-cylinder grippers.

safety bar A device that detects foreign objects on the feedboard and prevents their passage into the printing unit.

scanning densitometer A computerized quality control table that measures and analyzes press-sheet color bars using a densitometer.

scumming The problem that occurs when a permanent ink image—usually dots—appears in the nonimage area.

sensitization In platemaking, the making of an image area more ink-receptive.

separator brush One of a series of brushes that prevent the suckers from picking up more than one sheet at a time.

sequestering agent — A substance that prevents the calcium and magnesium compounds in the dampening solution from precipitating.

setoff — Condition that results when wet ink on the surface of the press sheets transfers or sticks to the backs of other sheets in the delivery pile. Sometimes referred to as "offset," a term that is reserved for the offset method of printing.

sheet decurler — A device that is designed to take troublesome curl out of press sheets.

sheet detector, early and late — A device that detects the early or late arrival of a sheet at the front guides.

sheet guide rods — Rods that are positioned so that they hold down the back corners of the sheet as it enters the feedboard.

sheet-separation unit — A device that uses both air and a vacuum to separate the top sheet from the feeder pile.

sheet steadiers — Weights positioned at the outside quarters of the feeder pile.

sheet transfer section — The portion of the press that transports the press sheet between the impression cylinders on a multicolor sheetfed press.

shortening compound — An ink additive that reduces ink flying, or misting.

side guide — The third point of the three-point sheet-registering system (also including the front guides) on the feedboard, responsible for moving the sheet in the sideways direction to facilitate register.

single-drum transfer — A principal method of sheet transfer where grippers on a large-diameter transfer cylinder transport the sheet from one impression cylinder to the next.

skeleton wheels — The series of movable disks that are mounted on a shaft of the delivery cylinder and positioned in nonprinting areas of the press sheet.

slip compound — An ink additive that improves scuff resistance of the printed ink film.

slip sheet A sheet of paper placed between freshly printed sheets to prevent setoff or blocking.

smash Undesirable localized compression of the blanket's surface.

smash-resistance The ability of a blanket to recover from being momentarily subjected to excessively high pressure.

smoother A device that helps to keep the sheet flat on the feedboard.

snowflaking The tiny, white, unprinted specks that appear in type and solids if the ink is excessively emulsified.

specific gravity Ratio of the weight of one material to the weight of an equal volume of water.

split fountain A divided ink fountain, or the use of dividers, to provide separate sections capable of holding two or more colors of ink, to permit the printing of two or more colors, side by side, in one pass through the press.

spray powder Ground starch particles sprayed onto sheets to keep the ink on each press sheet from direct contact with the ink on another sheet in the delivery. *Alternative term:* antisetoff spray.

spur gear A gear that has teeth cut straight across.

squeeze Printing pressure between the plate and blanket cylinders. It is expressed as the combined height of the plate and blanket over their respective bearers on a *bearer-contact press* and as the combined height of the plate and blanket over their respective bearers minus the distance between the bearers on a *non–bearer-contact press.*

start-of-print line A horizontal line that indicates the limit of the printing area. It is often engraved in the gutters about an inch behind the plate cylinder's leading edge.

static eliminator A printing press attachment that attempts to reduce the amount of static developing on a press because of low relative humidity and the movement of paper over metal surfaces. It can also be helpful in eliminating ink setoff or paper feeding problems. *Alternative term:* antistatic device.

substrate	Any base material with a surface that can be printed or coated.
suction plate	A device that holds the sheet by vacuum and then moves it against the register block.
suction rollers	Devices that slow down and steady the sheet as it enters the delivery.
supercalendering	Finishing operation in papermaking where the web of paper passes between a series of hard metal rollers and soft, resilient rollers that impart varying degrees of smoothness and gloss to the paper.
surface strength	Ability of a paper to resist a force applied perpendicularly to its surface before picking or rupturing occurs.
tack	Resistance of a liquid to splitting. It is measured by determining the force required to split an ink film between two surfaces.
tail-end hook	A curl in the paper that develops at the back edge of the sheet away from the printed side.
temperature conditioning	Process of allowing paper to reach pressroom temperature before unwrapping the paper.
texture	In inkmaking, the hardness or softness of a pigment in its dry form.
thermo-mechanical pulp	Papermaking pulp produced by preheating wood chips with steam prior to passing them through a disk refiner.
thixotropy	Characteristic of a material that causes it to change consistency on being worked.
three-drum transfer	A principal method of sheet transfer where three transfer cylinders are used to transport the sheet from one impression cylinder to the next.
through drier	A slow-acting drier that solidifies the ink film throughout and does not form a hard surface.

tight-edged paper A paper whose exposed edges have given up moisture to the atmosphere and shrunk.

tinting The bleeding of ink pigment particles into the dampening solution. *Alternative term:* toning.

top drier Drier that gives a very hard surface to the ink.

transfer cylinders The paper-transport cylinders that convey paper from one printing unit to another.

transfer devices Any of several devices (often auxiliary cylinders with sheet grippers) that facilitate sheet transport through the press.

trapping (1) Printing a wet ink over a previously printed dry or wet ink film. (2) How well one color overlaps another without leaving a white space between the two or generating a third color where they overprint.

trapping, dry (1) The ability of a dry, printed ink film to accept a wet ink film over it. The wet ink dries by oxidation polymerization. (2) Printing overprints, or one color on top of another, when the first color is already dry. Printing multicolor work on a single-color press is an example of dry trapping.

trapping, wet (1) The ability of a wet, printed ink film to accept another wet ink film printed over it. (2) Printing overprints, or one color on top of another, when the first color is not dry. Printing multicolor work on a multicolor press is an example of wet trapping.

true rolling A term often used to describe the condition when there is no slip in the printing nip.

undercut The difference between the radius of the cylinder body and the radius of the cylinder bearers.

undertone The color of a thin film of ink. It is the color of light reflected by the paper and transmitted through the ink film.

unitack A series of printing inks that have the same tack rating.

viscoelastic A material, like an offset ink, that behaves as both a fluid and an elastic solid.

warp The direction of maximum strength on a blanket.

washup The process of cleaning the inking systems and blankets of a press with specially formulated cleaning solutions to remove all ink as required at the end of the operating day or whenever an ink color change is necessary.

water pan A device that holds the dampening solution to be fed to the plate. *Alternative term:* water fountain.

water stop One of a series of devices that are set against the surface of the dampening fountain roller; commonly used to reduce the amount of solution reaching heavily inked areas of the printing plate.

waterless lithography A planographic printing process that does not require the use of a water-based dampening solution to prevent ink from adhering to nonimage areas of the printing plate. It requires special inks, presensitized waterless plates, and temperature-controlled inking systems.

wavy-edged paper A paper whose exposed edges have absorbed moisture and become wavy.

wedges Devices made out of wood or plastic that are used at startup to produce a neat pile in the feeder.

weft The direction of minimum strength on a blanket.

wet printing See *trapping, wet.*

wettability The ease with which a pigment can be completely wet by the ink vehicle.

wetting agent (1) In inkmaking, an additive that promotes the dispersion of pigments in the vehicle. (2) A substance, such as isopropanol or an alcohol substitute, found in a dampening solution, that decreases the surface tension of water and water-based solutions.

wire side Side of the paper that is in contact with the paper machine's wire during papermaking.

Index

About the Authors

Lloyd P. DeJidas is the director of GATF's Graphic Services and Facilities Group, a position he has held since 1989. Among his many responsibilities, he oversees GATF's in-plant printing operations. A contributor to numerous Foundation workshops, textbooks, and reports, DeJidas has worked at GATF since 1967. Starting as an apprentice and progressing through the ranks, he has held numerous press-related positions, including pressroom superintendent and production department director.

Thomas M. Destree is the editor in chief of the GATF*Press*. He supervises a staff of writer/editors in preparing textbooks, reference manuals, audiovisuals, technical and research reports, and promotional materials. Since joining GATF in 1977, he has contributed to numerous textbooks, including the ninth edition of the *Lithographers Manual, Web Offset Press Operating,* and *Solving Web Offset Press Problems*. Destree received a B.S. in industrial education from the University of Wisconsin—Stout and an M.B.A. from the University of Pittsburgh.

About GATF

The Graphic Arts Technical Foundation is a nonprofit, scientific, technical, and educational organization dedicated to the advancement of the graphic communications industries worldwide. Its mission is to serve the field as the leading resource for technical information and services through research and education.

For 74 years the Foundation has developed leading edge technologies and practices for printing. GATF's staff of researchers, educators, and technical specialists partner with nearly 2,000 corporate members in over 65 countries to help them maintain their competitive edge by increasing productivity, print quality, process control, and environmental compliance, and by implementing new techniques and technologies. Through conferences, satellite symposia, workshops, consulting, technical support, laboratory services, and publications, GATF strives to advance a global graphic communications community.

The GATF*Press* publishes books on nearly every aspect of the field: learning modules (step-by-step instruction booklets); audiovisuals (CD-ROMs, videocassettes, slides, and audiocassettes); and research and technology reports. It also publishes *GATFWorld,* a bimonthly magazine of technical articles, industry news, and reviews of specific products.

For more detailed information on GATF products and services, please visit our website *http://www.gatf.org* or write to us at 200 Deer Run Road, Sewickley, PA 15143-2600 (phone: 412/741-6860).

GATF*Press:* Selected Books

Careers in Graphic Communications: A Resource Book. Flecker, Sally Ann and Pamela J. Groff.

Computer-to-Plate: Automating the Printing Industry. Adams, Richard M. II, & Frank J. Romano.

Flexography Primer. Crouch, J. Page.

The GATF Encyclopedia of Graphic Communications. Romano, Frank J. and Richard M. Romano.

Glossary of Graphic Communications. Groff, Pamela J.

Gravure Primer. Kasunich, Cheryl L.

Handbook of Printing Processes. Stevenson, Deborah L.

Implementing Quality Management in the Graphic Arts. Apfelberg, Herschel L. & Michael J. Apfelberg.

The Lithographers Manual. Destree, Thomas M.

Lithography Primer. Wilson, Daniel G.

Materials Handling for the Printer. Geis, A. John and Paul L. Addy.

On-Demand Printing: The Revolution in Digital and Customized Printing. Fenton, Howard M. & Frank J. Romano.

The PDF Bible: The Complete Guide to Adobe Acrobat 3.0. Witkowski, Mark.

Printing Plant Layout and Facility Design. Geis, A. John.

Printing Production Management. Field, Gary G.

Screen Printing Primer. Ingram, Samuel T.

Sheetfed Offset Press Operating. DeJidas, Lloyd P. and Thomas M. Destree.

Solving Sheetfed Offset Press Problems. GATF Staff.

Solving Web Offset Press Problems. GATF Staff.

The Timetables of Communications. Romano, Frank

Total Production Maintenance: A Guide for the Printing Industry. Rizzo, Kenneth E.

Understanding Digital Color. Green, Phil.

Web Offset Press Operating. GATF Staff.

What the Printer Should Know about Ink. Eldred, Dr. Nelson R. and Terry Scarlett.

What the Printer Should Know about Paper. Wilson, Lawrence A.